DALE CARNEGIE

DALE CARNEGIE

HOW TO WIN FRIENDS
AND INFLUENCE PEOPLE

HOW TO STOP WORRYING
AND START LIVING

CHANCELLOR
PRESS

How to Win Friends and Influence People
first published in Great Britain in 1953 by Cedar

How to Stop Worrying and Start Living
first published in Great Britain in 1952 by Cedar

This collected edition first published in Great Britain in 1994
by Chancellor Press
an imprint of Reed International Books Ltd
Michelin House, 81 Fulham Road, London SW3 6RB
and Auckland, Melbourne, Singapore and Toronto

A CIP catalogue for this book is available from
the British Library

ISBN 1 85152 576 9

Printed and bound in Great Britain by The Bath Press

CONTENTS

HOW TO WIN FRIENDS
AND INFLUENCE PEOPLE

This book is dedicated to a man who doesn't need to read it

My cherished friend

HOMER CROY

Contents

4

Preface to revised edition

How to Win Friends and Influence People was first published in 1937 in an edition of only five thousand copies. Neither Dale Carnegie nor the publishers, Simon and Schuster, anticipated more than this modest sale. To their amazement, the book became an overnight sensation, and edition after edition rolled off the presses to keep up with the increasing public demand. *How to Win Friends and Influence People* took its place in publishing history as one of the all-time international best-sellers. It touched a nerve and filled a human need that was more than a faddish phenomenon of post-Depression days, as evidenced by its continued and uninterrupted sales into the eighties, almost half a century later.

Dale Carnegie used to say that it was easier to make a million dollars than to put a phrase into the English language. *How to Win Friends and Influence People* became such a phrase, quoted, paraphrased, parodied, used in innumerable contexts from political cartoon to novels. The book itself was translated into almost every known written language. Each generation has discovered it anew and has found it relevant.

Which brings us to the logical question: Why revise a book that has proven and continues to prove its vigorous and universal appeal? Why tamper with success?

To answer that, we must realize that Dale Carnegie himself was a tireless reviser of his own work during his lifetime. *How to Win Friends and Influence People* was written to be used as a textbook for his courses in Effective Speaking and Human Relations and is still used in those courses today. Until his death in 1955 he constantly improved and revised the course itself to make it applicable to the evolving needs of an ever-growing public. No one was more sensitive to the changing currents of present-day life than Dale Carnegie. He constantly improved and refined his methods of teaching; he updated his book on Effective Speaking several times. He had lived longer, he himself would have revised *How to Win Friends and Influence People* to better reflect the changes that have taken place in the world since the thirties.

Many of the names of prominent people in the book, well known at the time of first publication, are no longer recognized by many of today's readers. Certain examples and phrases seem as quaint and dated in our social climate as those in a Victorian novel. The important message and overall impact of the book is weakened to that extent.

Our purpose, therefore, in this revision is to clarify and strengthen the book for a modern reader without tampering with the content. We have not 'changed' *How to Win Friends and Influence People* except to make a few excisions and add a few more contemporary examples. The brash, breezy Carnegie style is intact – even the thirties slang is still there. Dale Carnegie wrote as he spoke, in an intensively exuberant colloquial, conversational manner.

So his voice speaks as forcefully as ever, in the book and in his work. Thousands of people all over the world are being trained in Carnegie courses in increasing numbers each year. And other thousands are reading and studying *How to Win Friends and Influence People* and being inspired to use its principles to better their lives. To all of them, we offer this revision in the spirit of the honing and polishing of a finely made tool.

Dorothy Carnegie
(Mrs. Dale Carnegie)

How this book was written – and why

by Dale Carnegie

During the first thirty-five years of the twentieth century, the publishing houses of America printed more than a fifth of a million different books. Most of them were deadly dull, and many were financial failures. 'Many,' did I say? The president of one of the largest publishing houses in the world confessed to me that his company, after seventy-five years of publishing experience, still lost money on seven out of every eight books it published.

Why, then, did I have the temerity to write another book? And, after I had written it, why should you bother to read it?

Fair questions, both; and I'll try to answer them.

I have, since 1912, been conducting educational courses for business and professional men and women in New York. At first, I conducted courses in public speaking only – courses designed to train adults, by actual experience, to think on their feet and express their ideas with more clarity, more effectiveness and more poise, both in business interviews and before groups.

But gradually, as the seasons passed, I realized that as sorely as these adults needed training in effective speaking, they needed still more training in the fine art of getting along with people in everyday business and social contacts.

I also gradually realized that I was sorely in need of such training myself. As I look back across the years, I am appalled at my own frequent lack of finesse and understanding. How I wish a book such as this had been placed in my hands twenty years ago! What a priceless boon it would have been.

Dealing with people is probably the biggest problem you face, especially if you are in business. Yes, and that is also true if you are a housewife, architect or engineer. Research done a few years ago under the auspices of the Carnegie Foundation for the Advancement of Teaching uncovered a most important and significant fact – a fact later confirmed by additional studies made at the Carnegie Institute of Technology. These investigations revealed that even in such technical lines as engineering, about 15 percent of one's financial success is due to one's technical knowledge and about 85 percent is due to skill in human engineering – to personality and the ability to lead people.

For many years, I conducted courses each season at the Engineers' Club of

Philadelphia, and also courses for the New York Chapter of the American Institute of Electrical Engineers. A total of probably more than fifteen hundred engineers have passed through my classes. They came to me because they had finally realized, after years of observation and experience, that the highest-paid personnel in engineering are frequently not those who know the most about engineering. One can, for example, hire mere technical ability in engineering, accountancy, architecture or any other profession at nominal salaries. But the person who has technical knowledge *plus* the ability to express ideas, to assume leadership, and to arouse enthusiasm among people – that person is headed for higher earning power.

In the heyday of his activity, John D. Rockefeller said that 'the ability to deal with people is as purchasable a commodity as sugar or coffee.' 'And I will pay more for that ability,' said John D., 'than for any other under the sun.'

Wouldn't you suppose that every college in the land would conduct courses to develop the highest-priced ability under the sun? But if there is just one practical, common-sense course of that kind given for adults in even one college in the land, it had escaped my attention up to the present writing.

The University of Chicago and the United Y.M.C.A. Schools conducted a survey to determine what adults want to study.

That survey cost $25,000 and took two years. The last part of the survey was made in Meriden, Connecticut. It had been chosen as a typical American town. Every adult in Meriden was interviewed and requested to answer 156 questions – questions such as 'What is your business or profession? Your education? How do you spend your spare time? What is your income? Your hobbies? Your ambitions? Your problems? What subjects are you most interested in studying?' And so on. That survey revealed that health is the prime interest of adults – and that their second interest is people; how to understand and get along with people; how to make people like you; and how to win others to your way of thinking.

So the committee conducting this survey resolved to conduct such a course for adults in Meriden. They searched diligently for a practical textbook on the subject and found – not one. Finally they approached one of the world's outstanding authorities on adult education and asked him if he knew of any book that met the needs of this group. 'No,' he replied, 'I know what those adults want. But the book they need has never been written.'

I knew from experience that this statement was true, for I myself had been searching for years to discover a practical, working handbook on human relations.

Since no such book existed, I have tried to write one for use in my own courses. And here it is. I hope you like it.

In preparation for this book, I read everything that I could find on the subject – everything from newspaper columns, magazine articles, records of the family courts, the writings of the old philosophers and the new psychologists. In addition, I hired a trained researcher to spend one and a half years in various libraries reading everything I had missed, ploughing through erudite tomes on psychology, poring over hundreds of magazine articles, searching through countless biographies, trying to ascertain how the great leaders of all ages had dealt with people. We read their biographies. We read the life stories of all great leaders from Julius Caesar to Thomas Edison. I recall that we read over one hundred biographies of Theodore Roosevelt alone. We were determined to spare no time, no expense, to discover every practical idea that anyone had ever used throughout the ages for winning friends and influencing people.

I personally interviewed scores of successful people, some of them world-famous – inventors like Marconi and Edison; political leaders like Franklin D. Roosevelt and James Farley; business leaders like Owen D. Young; movie stars like Clark Gable and Mary Pickford; and explorers like Martin Johnson – and tried to discover the techniques they used in human relations.

From all this material, I prepared a short talk. I called it 'How to Win Friends and Influence People.' I say 'short.' It was short in the beginning, but it soon expanded to a lecture that consumed one hour and thirty minutes. For years, I gave this talk each season to the adults in the Carnegie Institute courses in New York.

I gave the talk and urged the listeners to go out and test it in their business and social contacts, and then come back to class and speak about their experiences and the results they had achieved. What an interesting assignment! These men and women, hungry for self-improvement, were fascinated by the idea of working in a new kind of laboratory – the first and only laboratory of human relationships for adults that had ever existed.

This book wasn't written in the usual sense of the word. It grew as a child grows. It grew and developed out of that laboratory, out of the experiences of thousands of adults.

Years ago, we started with a set of rules printed on a card no larger than a postcard. The next season we printed a larger card, then a leaflet, then a series of booklets, each one expanding in size and scope. After fifteen years of experiment and research came this book.

The rules we have set down here are not mere theories or guesswork. They work like magic. Incredible as it sounds, I have seen the application of these principles literally revolutionize the lives of many people.

To illustrate: A man with 314 employees joined one of these courses. For years, he had driven and criticized and condemned his employees without stint or discretion. Kindness, words of appreciation and encouragement were alien to his lips. After studying the principles discussed in this book, this employer sharply altered his philosophy of life. His organization is now inspired with a new loyalty, a new enthusiasm, a new spirit of teamwork. Three hundred and fourteen enemies have been turned into 314 friends. As he proudly said in a speech before the class: 'When I used to walk through my establishment, no one greeted me. My employees actually looked the other way when they saw me approaching. But now they are all my friends and even the janitor calls me by my first name.'

This employer gained more profit, more leisure and – what is infinitely more important – he found far more happiness in his business and in his home.

Countless numbers of salespeople have sharply increased their sales by the use of these principles. Many have opened up new accounts – accounts that they had formerly solicited in vain. Executives have been given increased authority, increased pay. One executive reported a large increase in salary because he applied these truths. Another, an executive in the Philadelphia Gas Works Company, was slated for demotion when he was sixty-five because of his belligerence, because of his inability to lead people skilfully. This training not only saved him from the demotion but brought him a promotion with increased pay.

On innumerable occasions, spouses attending the banquet given at the end of the course have told me that their homes have been much happier since their husbands or wives started this training.

People are frequently astonished at the new results they achieve. It all seems like magic. In some cases, in their enthusiasm, they have telephoned my at my home on Sundays because they couldn't wait forty-eight hours to report on their achievements at the regular session of the course.

One man was so stirred by a talk on these principles that he sat far into the night discussing them with other members of the class. At three o'clock in the morning, the others went home. But he was so shaken by a realization of his own mistakes, so inspired by the vista of a new and richer world opening before him, that he was unable to sleep. He didn't sleep that night or the next day or the next night.

Who was he? A naïve, untrained individual ready to gush over any new theory that came along? No. Far from it. He was a sophisticated, blasé dealer in art, very much the man about town, who spoke three languages fluently and was a graduate of two European universities.

While writing this chapter, I received a letter from a German of the old school, an aristocrat whose forebears had served for generations as professional army officers under the Hohenzollerns. His letter, written from a transatlantic steamer, telling about the application of these principles, rose almost to a religious fervour.

Another man, an old New Yorker, a Harvard graduate, a wealthy man, the owner of a large carpet factory, declared he had learned more in fourteen weeks through this system of training about the fine art of influencing people than he had learned about the same subject during his four years in college. Absurd? Laughable? Fantastic? Of course, you are privileged to dismiss this statement with whatever adjective you wish. I am merely reporting, without comment, a declaration made by a conservative and eminently successful

Harvard graduate in a public address to approximately six hundred people at the Yale Club in New York on the evening of Thursday, February 23, 1933.

'Compared to what we ought to be,' said the famous Professor William James of Harvard, 'compared to what we ought to be, we are only half awake. We are making use of only a small part of our physical and mental resources. Stating the thing broadly, the human individual thus lives far within its limits. He possesses powers of various sorts which he habitually fails to use.'

These powers which you 'habitually fail to use'! The sole purpose of this book is to help you discover, develop and profit by those dormant and unused assets.

'Education,' said Dr. John G. Hibben, former president of Princeton University, 'is the ability to meet life's situations.'

If by the time you have finished reading the first three chapters of this book – if you aren't then a little better equipped to meet life's situations, then I shall consider this book to be a total failure so far as you are concerned. For 'the great aim of education,' said Herbert Spencer, 'is not knowledge but action.'

And this is an action book.

Dale Carnegie 1936

Nine suggestions on how to get the most out of this book

1 If you wish to get the most out of this book, there is one indispensable requirement, one essential infinitely more important than any rule or technique. Unless you have this one fundamental requisite, a thousand rules on how to study will avail little. And if you do have this cardinal endowment, then you can achieve wonders without reading any suggestions for getting the most out of a book.

What is this magic requirement? Just this: a deep, driving desire to learn, a vigorous determination to increase your ability to deal with people.

How can you develop such an urge? By constantly reminding yourself how important these principles are to you. Picture to yourself how their mastery will aid you in leading a richer, fuller, happier and more fulfilling life. Say to yourself over and over: 'My popularity, my happiness and sense of worth depend to no small extent upon my skill in dealing with people.'

2 Read each chapter rapidly at first to get a bird's-eye view of it. You will probably be tempted then to rush on to the next one. But don't – unless you are reading merely for entertainment. But if you are reading because you want to increase your skill in human relations, then go back and reread each chapter thoroughly. In the long run, this will mean saving time and getting results.

3 Stop frequently in your reading to think over what you are reading. Ask yourself just how and when you can apply each suggestion.

4 Read with a crayon, pencil, pen, magic marker or highlighter in your hand. When you come across a suggestion that you feel you can use, draw a line beside it. If it is a four-star suggestion, then underscore any sentence or highlight it, or mark it with '****.' Marking and underscoring a book makes it more interesting, and far easier to review rapidly.

5 I knew a woman who had been office manager for a large insurance concern for fifteen years. Every month, she read all the insurance contracts her company had issued that month. Yes, she read many of the same contracts over month after month, year after year. Why? Because experience had taught her that that was the only way she could keep their provisions clearly in mind.

I once spent almost two years writing a book on public speaking and yet I found I had to keep going back over it from time to time in order to remember what I had written in my own book. The rapidity with which we forget is astonishing.

So, if you want to get a real, lasting benefit out of this book, don't imagine that skimming through it once will suffice. After reading it thoroughly, you ought to spend a few hours reviewing it every month. Keep it on your desk in front of you every day. Glance through it often. Keep constantly impressing yourself with the rich possibilities for improvement that still lie in the offing. Remember that the use of these principles can be made habitual only by a constant and vigorous campaign of review and application. There is no other way.

6 Bernard Shaw once remarked: 'If you teach a man anything, he will never learn.' Shaw was right. Learning is an active process. We learn by doing. So, if you desire to master the principles you are studying in this book, do something about them. Apply these rules at every opportunity. If you don't you will forget them quickly. Only knowledge that is used sticks in your mind.

You will probably find it difficult to apply these suggestions all the time. I know because I wrote the book, and yet frequently I found it difficult to apply everything I advocated. For example, when you are displeased, it is much easier to criticize and condemn than it is to try to understand the other person's viewpoint. It is frequently easier to find fault than to find praise. It is more natural to talk about what you want than to talk about what the other person wants. And so on. So, as you read this book, remember that you are not merely trying to acquire information. You are attempting to form new habits. Ah yes, you are attempting a new way of life. That will require time and persistence and daily application.

So refer to these pages often. Regard this as a working handbook on human relations; and whenever you are confronted with some specific problem – such as handling a child, winning your spouse to your way of thinking, or satisfying an irritated customer – hesitate about doing the natural thing, the impulsive thing. This is usually wrong. Instead, turn to these pages and review the paragraphs you have underscored. Then try these new ways and watch them achieve magic for you.

7 Offer your spouse, your child or some business associate a dime or a dollar every time he or she catches you violating a certain principle. Make a lively game out of mastering these rules.

8 The president of an important Wall Street bank once described, in a talk before one of my classes, a highly efficient system he used for self-improvement. This man had little formal schooling; yet he had become one of the most important financiers in America, and he confessed that he owed most of his success to the constant application of his homemade system. This is what he does. I'll put it in his own words as accurately as I can remember.

'For years I have kept an engagement book showing all the appointments I had during the day. My family never made any plans for me on Saturday night, for the family knew that I devoted a part of each Saturday evening to the illuminating process of self-examination and review and appraisal. After dinner I went off by myself, opened my engagement book, and thought over all the interviews, discussions and meetings that had taken place during the week. I asked myself:

'What mistakes did I make that time?'

'What did I do that was right – and in what way could I have improved my performance?'

'What lessons can I learn from that experience?'

'I often found that this weekly review made me very unhappy. I was frequently astonished at my own blunders. Of course, as the years passed, these blunders became less frequent. Sometimes I was inclined to pat myself on the back a little after one of these sessions. This system of self-analysis, self-education, continued year after year, did more for me than any other thing I have ever attempted.

'It helped me improve my ability to make decisions – and it aided me enormously in all my contacts with people. I cannot recommend it too highly.'

Why not use a similar system to check up on your application of the principles discussed in this book? If you do, two things will result.

First, you will find yourself engaged in an educational process that is both intriguing and priceless.

Second, you will find that your ability to meet and deal with people will grow enormously.

9 You will find at the end of this book several blank pages on which you should record your triumphs in the application of these principles. Be specific. Give names, dates, results. Keeping such a record will inspire you to greater efforts; and how fascinating these entries will be when you chance upon them some evening years from now!

In order to get the most out of this book:

a Develop a deep desire to master the principles of human relations.

b Read each chapter twice before going on to the next one.

c As you read, stop frequently to ask yourself how you can apply each suggestion.

d Underscore each important idea.

e Review this book each month.

f Apply these principles at every opportunity. Use this volume as a working handbook to help you solve your daily problems.

g Make a lively game out of your learning by offering some friend a dime or a dollar for every time he or she catches you violating one of these principles.

h Check up each week on the progress you are making. Ask yourself what mistakes you have made, what improvement, what lessons you have learned for the future.

i Keep notes in the back of this book showing how and when you have applied these principles.

Part One

FUNDAMENTAL TECHNIQUES

IN HANDLING PEOPLE

□ 1 □

'If you want to gather honey, don't kick over the beehive'

On May 7, 1931, the most sensational manhunt New York City had ever known had come to its climax. After weeks of search, 'Two Gun' Crowley – the killer, the gunman who didn't smoke or drink – was at bay, trapped in his sweetheart's apartment on West End Avenue.

One hundred and fifty policemen and detectives laid siege to his top-floor hideaway. They chopped holes in the roof; they tried to smoke out Crowley, the 'cop killer', with teargas. Then they mounted their machine guns on surrounding buildings, and for more than an hour one of New York's fine residential areas reverberated with the crack of pistol fire and the *rat-tat-tat* of machine guns. Crowley, crouching behind an overstuffed chair, fired incessantly at the police. Ten thousand excited people watched the battle. Nothing like it had ever been seen before on the sidewalks of New York.

When Crowley was captured, Police Commissioner, E. P. Mulrooney declared that the two-gun desperado was one of the most dangerous criminals ever encountered in the history of New York. 'He will kill,' said the Commissioner, 'at the drop of a feather.'

But how did 'Two Gun' Crowley regard himself? We know, because while the police were firing into his apartment, he wrote a letter addressed 'To whom it may concern.' And, as he wrote, the blood flowing from his wounds left a crimson trail on the paper. In this letter Crowley said: 'Under my coat is a weary heart, but a kind one – one that would do nobody any harm.'

A short time before this, Crowley had been having a necking party with his girl friend on a country road out on Long Island. Suddenly a policeman walked up to the car and said: 'Let me see your licence.'

Without saying a word, Crowley drew his gun and cut the policeman down with a shower of lead. As the dying officer fell, Crowley leaped out of the car, grabbed the officer's revolver, and fired another bullet into the prostrate body. And that was the killer who said: 'Under my coat is a weary heart, but a kind one – one that would do nobody any harm.'

Crowley was sentenced to the electric chair. When he arrived at the death house in Sing Sing, did he say, 'This is what I get for killing people'? No, he said: 'This is what I get for defending myself.'

The point of the story is this: 'Two Gun' Crowley didn't blame himself for anything.

Is that an unusual attitude among criminals? If you think so, listen to this:

'I have spent the best years of my life giving people the lighter pleasures, helping them have a good time, and all I get is abuse, the existence of a hunted man.'

That's Al Capone speaking. Yes, America's most notorious Public Enemy – the most sinister gang leader who ever shot up Chicago. Capone didn't condemn himself. He actually regarded himself as a public benefactor – an unappreciated and misunderstood public benefactor.

And so did Dutch Schultz before he crumpled up under gangster bullets in Newark. Dutch Schultz, one of New York's most notorious rats, said in a newspaper interview that he was a public benefactor. And he believed it.

I have had some interesting correspondence with Lewis Lawes, who was warden of New York's infamous Sing Sing prison for many years, on this subject, and he declared that 'few of the criminals in Sing Sing regard themselves as bad men. They are just as human as you and I. So they rationalize, they explain. They can tell you why they had to crack a safe or be quick on the trigger finger. Most of them attempt by a form of reasoning, fallacious or logical, to justify their antisocial acts even to themselves, consequently stoutly maintaining that they should never have been imprisoned at all.'

If Al Capone, 'Two Gun' Crowley, Dutch Schultz, and the desperate men and women behind prison walls don't blame themselves for anything – what about the people with whom you and I come in contact?

John Wanamaker, founder of the American stories that bear his name, once confessed: 'I learned thirty years ago that it is foolish to scold. I have enough trouble overcoming my own limitations without fretting over the fact that God has not seen fit to distribute evenly the gift of intelligence.'

Wanamaker learned this lesson early, but I personally had to blunder through this old world for a third of a century before it even began to dawn upon me that ninety-nine times out of a hundred, people don't criticize themselves for anything no matter how wrong it may be.

Criticism is futile because it puts a person on the defensive and usually makes him strive to justify himself. Criticism is dangerous, because it wounds a person's precious pride, hurts his sense of importance, and arouses resentment.

B. F. Skinner, the world-famous psychologist, proved through his experiments that an animal rewarded for good behaviour will learn much more rapidly and retain what it learns far more effectively than an animal punished for bad behaviour. Later studies have shown that the same applies to humans. By criticizing, we do not make lasting changes and often incur resentment.

Hans Selye, another great psychologist, said, 'As much as we thirst for approval, we dread condemnation.'

The resentment that criticism engenders can demoralize employees, family members and friends, and still not correct the situation that has been condemned.

George B. Johnston of Enid, Oklahoma, is the safety coordinator for an engineering company. One of his responsibilities is to see that employees wear their hard hats whenever they are on the job in the field. He reported that whenever he came across workers who were not wearing hard hats, he would tell them with a lot of authority of the regulation and that they must comply. As a result he would get sullen acceptance, and often after he left, the workers would remove the hats.

He decided to try a different approach. The next time he found some of the workers not wearing their hard hat, he asked if the hats were uncomfortable or did not fit properly. Then he reminded the men in a pleasant tone of voice that the hat was designed to protect them from injury and suggested that it always be worn on the job. The result was increased compliance with the regulation with no resentment or emotional upset.

You will find examples of the futility of criticism bristling on a thousand pages of history. Take, for example, the famous quarrel between Theodore Roosevelt and President Taft – a quarrel that split the Republican party, put Woodrow Wilson in the White House, and wrote bold, luminous lines across the First World War and altered the flow of history. Let's review the facts quickly. When Theodore Roosevelt stepped out of the White House in 1908, he supported Taft, who was elected President. Then Theodore Roosevelt went off to Africa to shoot lions. When he returned, he exploded. He denounced Taft for his conservatism, tried to secure the nomination for a third term himself, formed the Bull Moose party, and all but demolished the G.O.P. In the election that followed, William Howard Taft and the Republican party carried only two states – Vermont and Utah. The most disastrous defeat the party had ever known.

Theodore Roosevelt blamed Taft, but did President Taft blame himself? Of course not. With tears in his eyes, Taft said: 'I don't see how I could have done any differently from what I have.'

Who was to blame? Roosevelt or Taft? Frankly, I don't know, and I don't care. The point I am trying to make is that all of Theodore Roosevelt's criticism didn't persuade Taft that he was wrong. It merely made Taft strive to justify himself and to reiterate with tears in his eyes: 'I don't see how I could have done any differently from what I have.'

Or, take the Teapot Dome oil scandal. It kept the newspapers ringing with indignation in the early 1920s. It rocked the nation! Within the memory of living men, nothing like it had ever happened before in American public life. Here are the bare facts of the scandal: Albert B. Fall, secretary of the interior in Harding's cabinet, was entrusted with the leasing of government oil reserves at Elk Hill and Teapot Dome – oil reserves that had been set aside for the future use of the Navy. Did Secretary Fall permit competitive bidding? No sir.

He handed the fat, juicy contract outright to his friend Edward L. Doheny. And what did Doheny do? He gave Secretary Fall what he was pleased to call a 'loan' of one hundred thousand dollars. Then, in a high-handed manner, Secretary Fall ordered United States Marines into the district to drive off competitors whose adjacent wells were sapping oil out of the Elk Hill reserves. These competitors, driven off their ground at the ends of guns and bayonets, rushed into court – and blew the lid off the Teapot Dome scandal. A stench arose so vile that it ruined the Harding Administration, nauseated an entire nation, threatened to wreck the Republican party, and put Albert B. Fall behind prison bars.

Fall was condemned viciously – condemned as few men in public life have ever been. Did he repent? Never! Years later Herbert Hoover intimated in a public speech that President Harding's death had been due to mental anxiety and worry because a friend had betrayed him. When Mrs. Fall heard that, she sprang from her chair, she wept, she shook her fists at fate and screamed: 'What! Harding betrayed by Fall? No! My husband never betrayed anyone. This whole house full of gold would not tempt my husband to do wrong. He is the one who has been betrayed and led to the slaughter and crucified.'

There you are; human nature in action, wrongdoers, blaming everybody but themselves. We are all like that. So when you and I are tempted to criticize someone tomorrow, let's remember Al Capone, 'Two Guns' Crowley and Albert Fall. Let's realize that criticisms are like homing pigeons. They always return home. Let's realize that the person we are going to correct and condemn will probably justify himself or herself, and condemn us in return; or, like the gentle Taft, will say: 'I don't see how I could have done any differently from what I have.'

On the morning of April 15, 1865, Abraham Lincoln lay dying in a hall bedroom of a cheap lodging house directly across the street from Ford's Theatre, where John Wilkes Booth had shot him. Lincoln's big body lay stretched diagonally across a sagging bed that was too short for him. A cheap reproduction of Rosa Bonheur's famous painting *The Horse Fair* hung above the bed, and a dismal gas jet flickered yellow light.

As Lincoln lay dying. Secretary of War Stanton said, 'There lies the most perfect ruler of men that the world has ever seen.'

What was the secret of Lincoln's success in dealing with people? I studied the life of Abraham Lincoln for ten years and devoted all of three years to writing and rewriting a book entitled *Lincoln the Unknown*. I believe I have made as detailed and exhaustive a study of Lincoln's personality and home life as it is possible for any being to make. I made a special study of Lincoln's method of dealing with people. Did he indulge in criticism? Oh, yes. As a young man in the Pigeon Creek Valley of Indiana, he not only criticized but he wrote letters and poems ridiculing people and dropped these letters on the country roads where they were sure to be found. One of these letters aroused resentments that burned for a lifetime.

Even after Lincoln had become a practising lawyer in Springfield, Illinois, he attacked his opponents openly in letters published in the newspapers. But he did this just once too often.

In the autumn of 1842 he ridiculed a vain, pugnacious politician by the name of James Shields. Lincoln lampooned him through an anonymous letter published in the Springfield *Journal*. The town roared with laughter. Shields, sensitive and proud, boiled with indignation. He found out who wrote the letter, leaped on his horse, started after Lincoln, and challenged him to fight a duel. Lincoln didn't want to fight. He was opposed to duelling, but he couldn't get out of it and save his honour. He was given the choice of weapons. Since he had very long arms, he chose cavalry broadswords and took lessons in sword fighting from a West Point graduate; and, on the appointed day, he and Shields met on a sandbar in the Mississippi River, prepared to fight to the death; but, at the last minute, their seconds interrupted and stopped the duel.

That was the most lurid personal incident in Lincoln's life. It taught him an invaluable lesson in the art of dealing with people. Never again did he write an insulting letter. Never again did he ridicule anyone. And from that time on, he almost never criticized anybody for anything.

Time after time, during the Civil War, Lincoln put a new general at the head of the Army of the Potomac, and each one in turn – McClellan, Pope, Burnside, Hooker, Meade – blundered tragically and drove Lincoln to pacing the floor in despair. Half the nation savagely condemned these incompetent generals, but Lincoln, 'with malice toward none, with charity for all,' held his peace. One of his favourite quotations was 'Judge not, that ye be not judged.'

And when Mrs Lincoln and others spoke harshly of the southern people, Lincoln replied: 'Don't criticize them; they are just what we would be under similar circumstances.'

Yet if any man ever had occasion to criticize, surely it was Lincoln. Let's take just one illustration.

The Battle of Gettysburg was fought during the first three days of July 1863. During the night of July 4, Lee began to retreat southward while storm clouds deluged the country with rain. When Lee reached the Potomac with his defeated army, he found a swollen, impassable river in front of him, and a victorious Union Army behind him. Lee was in a trap. He couldn't escape. Lincoln saw that. Here was a golden heaven-sent opportunity – the opportunity to capture Lee's army and end the war immediately. So, with a surge of hope, Lincoln ordered Meade not to call a council of war but to attack Lee immediately. Lincoln telegraphed his orders and then sent a special messenger to Meade demanding immediate action.

And what did General Meade do? He did the very opposite of what he was told to do. He called a council of war in direct violation of Lincoln's orders. He hesitated. He procrastinated. He telegraphed all manner of excuses. He refused point-blank to attack Lee. Finally the waters receded and Lee escaped over the Potomac with his forces.

Lincoln was furious. 'What does this mean?' Lincoln cried to his son Robert. 'Great God! What does this mean? We had them within our grasp, and had only to stretch forth our hands and they were ours; yet nothing that I could say or do could make the army move. Under the circumstances, almost any general could have defeated Lee. If I had gone up there, I could have whipped him myself.'

In bitter disappointment, Lincoln sat down and wrote Meade this letter. And remember, at this period of his life Lincoln was extremely conservative and restrained in his phraseology. So this letter coming from Lincoln in 1863 was tantamount to the severest rebuke.

> *My dear General,*
>   *I do not believe you appreciate the magnitude of the misfortune involved in Lee's escape. He was within our easy grasp, and to have closed upon him would, in connection with our other late successes, have ended the war. As it is, the war will be prolonged indefinitely. If you could not safely attack Lee last Monday, how can you possibly do so south of the river, when you can take with you very few – no more than two-thirds of the force you then had in hand? It would be unreasonable to expect and I do not expect that you can now effect much. Your golden opportunity is gone, and I am distressed immeasurably because of it.*

What do you suppose Meade did when he read the letter?

Meade never saw that letter. Lincoln never mailed it. It was found among his papers after his death.

My guess is – and this is only a guess – that after writing that letter, Lincoln looked out of the window and said to himself, 'Just a minute. Maybe I ought not to be so hasty. It is easy enough for me to sit here in the quiet of the White House and order Meade to attack; but if I had been up at Gettysburg, and if I had seen as much blood as Meade has seen during the last week, and if my ears had been pierced with the screams and shrieks of the wounded and dying, maybe I wouldn't be so anxious to attack either. If I had Meade's timid temperament, perhaps I would have done just what he had done. Anyhow, it is water under the bridge now. If I send this letter, it will relieve my feelings, but it will make Meade try to justify himself. It will make him condemn me. It will arouse hard feelings, impair all his further usefulness as a commander, and perhaps force him to resign from the army.'

So, as I have already said, Lincoln put the letter aside, for he had learned by bitter experience that sharp criticisms and rebukes almost invariably end in futility.

Theodore Roosevelt said that when he, as President, was confronted with a perplexing problem, he used to lean back and look up at a large painting of Lincoln which hung above his desk in the White House and ask himself,

'What would Lincoln do if he were in my shoes? How would he solve this problem?'

Mark Twain lost his temper occasionally and wrote letters that turned the paper brown. For example, he once wrote to a man who had aroused his ire: 'The thing for you is a burial permit. You have only to speak and I will see that you get it.' On another occasion he wrote to an editor about a proof-reader's attempts to 'improve my spelling and punctuation.' He ordered: 'Set the matter according to my copy hereafter and see that the proofreader retains his suggestions in the mush of his decayed brain.'

The writing of these stinging letters made Mark Twain feel better. They allowed him to blow off steam, and the letters didn't do any real harm, because Mark's wife secretly lifted them out of the mail. They were never sent.

Do you know someone you would like to change and regulate and improve? Good! That's fine. I am all in favour of it. But why not begin on yourself? From a purely selfish standpoint, that is a lot more profitable than trying to improve others – yes, and a lot less dangerous. 'Don't complain about the snow on your neighbour's roof,' said Confucious, 'when your own doorstep is unclean.'

When I was still young and trying to impress people, I wrote a foolish letter to Richard Harding Davis, an author who once loomed large on the literary horizon of America. I was preparing a magazine article about authors, and I asked Davis to tell me about his method of work. A few weeks earlier, I had received a letter from someone with this notation at the bottom: 'Dictated but not read.' I was quite impressed. I felt that the writer must be very big and busy and important. I wasn't the slightest bit busy, but I was eager to make an impression on Richard Harding Davis, so I ended my short note with the words: 'Dictated but not read.'

He never troubled to answer the letter. He simply returned it to me with this scribbled across the bottom: 'Your bad manners are exceeded only by your bad manners.' True, I had blundered, and perhaps I deserved this rebuke. But, being human, I resented it. I resented it so sharply that when I read of the death of Richard Harding Davis ten years later, the one thought that still persisted in my mind – I am ashamed to admit – was the hurt he had given me.

If you and I want to stir up a resentment tomorrow that may rankle across the decades and endure until death, just let us indulge in a little stinging criticism – no matter how certain we are that it is justified.

When dealing with people, let us remember we are not dealing with crea-tures of logic. We are dealing with creatures of emotion, creatures bristling with prejudices and motivated by pride and vanity.

Bitter criticism caused the sensitive Thomas Hardy, one of the finest novelists ever to enrich English literature, to give up forever the writing of fiction. Criticism drove Thomas Chatterton, the English poet, to suicide.

Benjamin Franklin, tactless in his youth, became so diplomatic, so adroit at handling people, that he was made American Ambassador to France. The secret of his success? 'I will speak ill of no man,' he said, '. . . and speak all the good I know of everybody.'

Any fool can criticize, condemn and complain – and most fools do.

But it takes character and self-control to be understanding and forgiving.

'A great man shows his greatness,' said Carlyle, 'by the way he treats little men.'

Bob Hoover, a famous test pilot and frequent performer at air shows, was returning to his home in Los Angeles from an air show in San Diego. As described in the magazine *Flight Operations*, at three hundred feet in the air, both engines suddenly stopped. By deft manoeuvring he managed to land the plane, but it was badly damaged although nobody was hurt.

Hoover's first act after the emergency landing was to inspect the aeroplane's fuel. Just as he suspected, the World War II propeller plane he had been flying had been fuelled with jet fuel rather than gasoline.

Upon returning to the airport, he asked to see the mechanic who had serviced his aeroplane. The young man was sick with the agony of his mistake. Tears streamed down his face as Hoover approached. He had just caused the loss of a very expensive plane and could have caused the loss of three lives as well.

You can imagine Hoover's anger. One could anticipate the tongue-lashing that this proud and precise pilot would unleash for that carelessness. But Hoover didn't scold the mechanic; he didn't even criticize him. Instead, he put his big arm around the man's shoulder and said, 'To show you I'm sure that you'll never do this again, I want you to service my F–51 tomorrow.'

Often parents are tempted to criticize their children. You would expect me to say 'don't.' But I will not. I am merely going to say, '*Before* you criticize them, read one of the classics of American journalism, "Father Forgets." ' It originally appeared as an editorial in the *People's Home Journal*. We are reprinting it here with the author's permission, as condensed in the *Reader's Digest*:

'Father Forgets' is one of those little pieces which – dashed off in a moment of sincere feeling – strikes an echoing chord in so many readers as to become a perennial reprint favourite. Since its first appearance, 'Father Forgets' has been reproduced, writes the author, W. Livingstone Larned, 'in hundreds of magazines and house organs, and in newspapers the country over. It has been reprinted almost as extensively in many foreign languages. I have given personal permission to thousands who wished to read it from school, church, and lecture platforms. It has been "on the air" on countless occasions and programmes. Oddly enough, college periodicals have used it, and high-school magazines. Sometimes a little piece seems mysteriously to "click." This one certainly did.'

FATHER FORGETS

W. Livingston Larned

Listen, son: I am saying this as you lie asleep, one little paw crumpled under your cheek and the blond curls stickily wet on your damp forehead. I have stolen into your room alone. Just a few minutes ago, as I sat reading my paper in the library, a stifling wave of remorse swept over me. Guiltily I came to your bedside.

There are the things I was thinking, son: I had been cross to you. I scolded you as you were dressing for school because you gave your face merely a dab with a towel. I took you to task for not cleaning your shoes. I called out angrily when you threw some of your things on the floor.

At breakfast I found fault, too. You spilled things. You gulped down your food. You put your elbows on the table. You spread butter too thick on your bread. And as you started off to play and I made for my train, you turned and waved a hand and called, 'Goodbye, Daddy!' and I frowned, and said in reply, 'Hold your shoulders back!'

Then it began all over again in the late afternoon. As I came up the road I spied you, down on your knees, playing marbles. There were holes in your stockings. I humiliated you before your boyfriends by marching you ahead of me to the house. Stockings were expensive – and if you had to buy them you would be more careful! Imagine that, son, from a father!

Do you remember, later, when I was reading in the library, how you came in timidly, with a sort of hurt look in your eyes? When I glanced up over my paper, impatient at the interruption, you hesitated at the door. 'What is it you want?' I snapped.

You said nothing, but ran across in one tempestuous plunge, and threw your arms around my neck and kissed me, and your small arms tightened with an affection that God had set blooming in your heart and which even neglect could not wither. And then you were gone, pattering up the stairs.

Well, son, it was shortly afterwards that my paper slipped from my hands and a terrible sickening fear came over me. What has habit been doing to me? The habit of finding fault, of reprimanding – this was my reward to you for being a boy. It was not that I did not love you; it was that I expected too much of youth. I was measuring you by the yardstick of my own years.

And there was so much that was good and fine and true in your character. The little heart of you was as big as the dawn itself over the wide hills. This was shown by your spontaneous impulse to rush in and kiss me good night. Nothing else matters tonight, son. I have come to your bedside in the darkness, and I have knelt there, ashamed!

It is a feeble atonement: I know you would not understand these things if I told them to you during your waking hours. But tomorrow I will be a real daddy! I will chum with you, and suffer when you suffer, and laugh when you laugh. I will bite my tongue when impatient words come. I will keep saying as if it were a ritual: 'He is nothing but a boy – a little boy!'

I am afraid I have visualized you as a man. Yet as I see you now, son, crumpled and weary in your cot, I see that you are still a baby. Yesterday you were in your mother's arms, your head on her shoulder. I have asked too much, too much.

Instead of condemning people, let's try to understand them. Let's try to figure out why they do what they do. That's a lot more profitable and intriguing than criticism; and it breeds sympathy, tolerance and kindness. 'To know all is to forgive all.'

As Dr. Johnson said: 'God himself, sir, does not propose to judge man until the end of his days.'

Why should you and I?

PRINCIPLE 1

Don't criticize, condemn or complain.

□ **2** □

The big secret of dealing with people

There is only one way under high heaven to get anybody to do anything. Did you ever stop to think of that? Yes, just one way. And that is by making the other person want to do it.

Remember, there is no other way.

Of course, you can make someone want to give you his watch by sticking a revolver in his ribs. You can make your employees give you cooperation – until your back is turned – by threatening to fire them. You can make a child do what you want it to do by a whip or a threat. But these crude methods have sharply undesirable repercussions.

The only way I can get you to do anything is by giving you what you want.

What do you want?

Sigmund Freud said that everything you and I do springs from two motives: the sex urge and the desire to be great.

John Dewey, one of America's most profound philosophers, phrased it a bit differently. Dr. Dewey said that the deepest urge in human nature is 'the desire to be important.' Remember that phrase: 'the desire to be important.' It is significant. You are going to hear a lot about it in this book.

What do you want? Not many things, but the few things that you do wish, you crave with an insistence that will not be denied. Some of the things most people want include:

1 Health and the preservation of life.
2 Food.
3 Sleep.
4 Money and the things money will buy.
5 Life in the hereafter.
6 Sexual gratification.
7 The well-being of our children.
8 A feeling of importance.

Almost all these wants are usually gratified – all except one. But there is one longing – almost as deep, almost as imperious, as the desire for food or sleep – which is seldom gratified. It is what Freud calls 'the desire to be great.' It is what Dewey calls the 'desire to be important.'

Lincoln once began a letter saying: 'Everybody likes a compliment.' William James said: 'That deepest principle in human nature is the craving to be appreciated.' He didn't speak, mind you, of the 'wish' or the 'desire' or the 'longing' to be appreciated. He said the 'craving' to be appreciated.

Here is a gnawing and unfaltering human hunger, and the rare individual who honestly satisfies this heart hunger will hold people in the palm of his or her hand and 'even the undertaker will be sorry when he dies.'

The desire for a feeling of importance is one of the chief distinguishing differences between mankind and the animals. To illustrate: When I was a farm boy out in Missouri, my father bred fine Duroc-Jersey hogs and pedigreed white-faced cattle. We used to exhibit our hogs and white-faced cattle at the country fairs and livestock shows throughout the Middle West. We won first prizes by the score. My father pinned his blue ribbons on a sheet of white muslin, and when friends or visitors came to the house, he would get out the long sheet of muslin. He would hold one end and I would hold the other while he exhibited the blue ribbons.

The hogs didn't care about the ribbons they had won. But Father did. These prizes gave him a feeling of importance.

If our ancestors hadn't had this flaming urge for a feeling of importance, civilization would have been impossible. Without it, we should have been just about like animals.

It was this desire for a feeling of importance that led an uneducated, poverty-stricken grocery clerk to study some law book he found in the bottom of a barrel of household plunder that he had bought for fifty cents. You have probably heard of this grocery clerk. His name was Lincoln.

It was this desire for a feeling of importance that inspired Dickens to write his immortal novels. This desire inspired Sir Christopher Wren to design his symphonies in stone. This desire made Rockefeller amass millions that he never spent! And this same desire made the richest family in your town build a house far too large for its requirements.

This desire makes you want to wear the latest styles, drive the latest cars, and talk about your brilliant children.

It is this desire that lures many boys and girls into joining gangs and engaging in criminal activities. The average young criminal, according to E. P. Mulrooney, onetime police commissioner of New York, is filled with ego, and his first request after arrest is for those lurid newspapers that make him out a hero. The disagreeable prospect of serving time seems remote so long as he can gloat over his likeness sharing space with pictures of sports figures, movie and TV stars and politicians.

If you tell me how you get your feeling of importance, I'll tell you what you are. That determines your character. That is the most significant thing about you. For example, John D. Rockefeller got his feeling of importance by giving money to erect a modern hospital in Peking, China, to care for millions of poor people whom he had never seen and never would see. Dillinger, on the other hand, got his feeling of importance by being a bandit, a bank robber and killer. When the FBI agents were hunting him, he dashed into a farmhouse up in Minnesota and said, 'I'm Dillinger!' He was proud of the fact that he was Public Enemy Number One. 'I'm not going to hurt you, but I'm Dillinger!' he said.

Yes, the one significant difference between Dillinger and Rockefeller is how they got their feeling of importance.

History sparkles with amusing examples of famous people struggling for a feeling of importance. Even George Washington wanted to be called 'His Mightiness, the President of the United States'; and Columbus pleaded for the title 'Admiral of the Ocean and Viceroy of India.' Catherine the Great refused to open letters that were not addressed to 'Her Imperial Majesty'; and Mrs. Lincoln, in the White House, turned upon Mrs. Grant like a tigress and shouted, 'How dare you be seated in my presence until I invite you!'

Our millionaires helped finance Admiral Byrd's expedition to the Antarctic in 1928 with the understanding that ranges of icy mountains would be named after them; and Victor Hugo aspired to have nothing less than the city of Paris renamed in his honour. Even Shakespeare, mightiest of the might, tried to add lustre to his name by procuring a coat of arms for his family.

People sometimes became invalids in order to win sympathy and attention, and get a feeling of importance. For example, take Mrs. McKinley. She got a feeling of importance by forcing her husband, the President of the United States, to neglect important affairs of state while he reclined on the bed beside her for hours at a time, his arm about her, soothing her to sleep. She fed her gnawing desire for attention by insisting that he remain with her while she was having her teeth fixed, and once created a stormy scene when he had to leave her alone with the dentist while he kept an appointment with John Hay, his secretary of state.

The writer Mary Roberts Rinehart once told me of a bright, vigorous young woman who became an invalid in order to get a feeling of importance. 'One day,' said Mrs. Rinehart, 'this woman had been obliged to face something, her age perhaps. The lonely years were stretching ahead and there was little left for her to anticipate.

'She took to her bed; and for ten years her old mother travelled to the third floor and back, carrying trays, nursing her. Then one day the old mother, weary with service, lay down and died. For some weeks, the invalid languished; then she got up, put on her clothing, and resumed living again.'

Some authorities declare that people may actually go insane in order to find, in the dreamland of insanity, the feeling of importance that has been denied them in the harsh world of reality. There are more patients suffering from mental diseases in the United States than from all other diseases combined.

What is the cause of insanity?

Nobody can answer such a sweeping question, but we know that certain diseases, such as syphilis, break down and destroy the brain cells and result in insanity. In fact, about one-half of all mental diseases can be attributed to such physical causes as brain lesions, alcohol, toxins and injuries. But the other half – and this is the appalling part of the story – the other half of the people who go insane apparently have nothing organically wrong with their brain cells. In post-mortem examinations, when their brain tissues are studied under the highest-powered microscopes, these tissues are found to be apparently just as healthy as yours and mine.

Why do these people go insane?

I put that question to the head physician of one of our most important psychiatric hospitals. This doctor, who has received the highest honours and the most coveted awards for his knowledge of this subject, told me frankly that he didn't know why people went insane. Nobody knows for sure. But he did say that many people who go insane find in insanity a feeling of importance that they were unable to achieve in the world of reality. Then he told me this story:

'I have a patient right now whose marriage proved to be a tragedy. She wanted love, sexual gratification, children and social prestige, but life blasted all her hopes. Her husband didn't love her. He refused even to eat with her and forced her to serve his meals in his room upstairs. She had no children, no social standing. She went insane; and, in her imagination, she divorced her husband and resumed her maiden name. She now believes she has married into English aristocracy, and she insists on being called Lady Smith.

'And as for children, she imagines now that she has had a new child every night. Each time I call on her she says: "Doctor, I had a baby last night." '

Life once wrecked all her dream ships on the sharp rocks of reality; but in the sunny, fantasy isles of insanity, all her barkentines race into port with canvas billowing and winds winging through the masts.

Tragic? Oh, I don't know. Her physician said to me: 'If I could stretch out my hand and restore her sanity, I wouldn't do it. She's much happier as she is.'

If some people are so hungry for a feeling of importance that they actually go insane to get it, imagine what miracle you and I can achieve by giving people honest appreciation this side of insanity.

One of the first people in American business to be paid a salary of over a million dollars a year (when there was no income tax and a person earning fifty dollars a week was considered well off) was Charles Schwab. He had been picked by Andrew Carnegie to become the first president of the newly formed United States Steel Company in 1921, when Schwab was only thirty-eight years old. (Schwab later left U.S. Steel to take over the then-troubled Bethlehem Steel Company, and he rebuilt it into one of the most profitable companies in America.)

Why did Andrew Carnegie pay a million dollars a year, or more than three thousand dollars a day, to Charles Schwab? Why? Because Schwab was a genius? No. Because he knew more about the manufacture of steel than other people? Nonsense. Charles Schwab told me himself that he had many men working for him who knew more about the manufacture of steel than he did.

Schwab says that he was paid this salary largely because of his ability to deal with people. I asked him how he did it. Here is his secret set down in his own words – words that ought to be cast in eternal bronze and hung in every home and school, every shop and office in the land – words that children ought to memorize instead of wasting their time memorizing the conjugation of Latin verbs or the amount of the annual rainfall in Brazil – words that will all but transform your life and mine if we will only live them:

'I consider my ability to arouse enthusiasm among my people,' said Schwab, 'the greatest asset I possess, and the way to develop the best that is in a person is by appreciation and encouragement.

'There is nothing else that so kills the ambitions of a person as criticisms from superiors. I never criticize anyone. I believe in giving a person incentive to work. So I am anxious to praise but loath to find fault. If I like anything, *I am hearty in my approbation and lavish in my praise.*'

That is what Schwab did. But what do average people do? The exact opposite. If they don't like a thing, they bawl out their subordinates; if they do like it, they say nothing. As the old couplet says: 'Once I did bad and that I heard ever/Twice I did good, but that I heard never.'

'In my wide association in life, meeting with many and great people in various parts of the world,' Schwab declared, 'I have yet to find the person, however great or exalted his station, who did not do better work and put forth greater effort under a spirit of approval than he would ever do under a spirit of criticism.'

That he said, frankly, was one of the outstanding reasons for the phenomenal success of Andrew Carnegie. Carnegie praised his associates publicly as well as privately.

Carnegie wanted to praise his assistants even on his tombstone. He wrote an epitaph for himself which read: 'Here lies one who knew how to get around him men who were cleverer than himself.'

Sincere appreciation was one of the secrets of the first John D. Rockefeller's success in handling men. For example, when one of his partners, Edward T. Bedford, lost a million dollars for the firm by a bad buy in South America, John D. might have criticized; but he knew Bedford had done his best – and the incident was closed. So Rockefeller found something to praise; he congratulated Bedford because he had been able to save 60 percent of the money he had invested. 'That's splendid,' said Rockefeller. 'We don't always do as well as that upstairs.'

I have among my clippings a story that I know never happened, but it illustrates a truth, so I'll repeat it:

According to this silly story, a farm woman, at the end of a heavy day's work, set before her menfolks a heaping pile of hay. And when they indignantly demanded whether she had gone crazy, she replied: 'Why, how did I know you'd notice? I've been cooking for you men for the last twenty years and in all that time I ain't heard no word to let me know you wasn't just eating hay.'

When a study was made a few years ago on runaway wives, what do you think was discovered to be the main reason wives ran away? It was 'lack of appreciation.' And I'd bet that a similar study made of runaway husbands would come out the same way. We often take our spouses so much for granted that we never let them know we appreciate them.

A member of one of our classes told of a request made by his wife. She and a group of other women in her church were involved in a self-improvement programme. She asked her husband to help her by listing six things he believed she could do to help her become a better wife. He reported to the class: 'I was surprised by such a request. Frankly, it would have been easy for me to list six things I would like to change about her – my heavens, she could have listed a thousand things she would like to change about me – but I didn't. I said to her, "Let me think about it and give you an answer in the morning."

'The next morning I got up very early and called the florist and had them send six red roses to my wife with a note saying: "I can't think of six things I would like to change about you. I love you the way you are."

'When I arrived home that evening, who do you think greeted me at the door. That's right. My wife! She was almost in tears. Needless to say, I was extremely glad I had not criticized her as she had requested.

'The following Sunday at church, after she had reported the results of her assignment, several women with whom she had been studying came up to me and said, "That was the most considerate thing I have ever heard." It was then I realized the power of appreciation.'

Florenz Ziegfeld, the most spectacular producer who ever dazzled Broadway, gained his reputation by his subtle ability to 'glorify the American girl'. Time after time, he took drab little creatures that no one ever looked at twice and transformed them on the stage into glamorous visions of mystery and seduction. Knowing the value of appreciation and confidence, he made women feel beautiful by the sheer power of his gallantry and consideration. He was practical: he raised the salary of chorus girls from thirty dollars a week to as high as one hundred and seventy-five. And he was also chivalrous; on opening night at the Follies, he sent telegrams to the stars in the cast, and he deluged every chorus girl in the show with American Beauty roses.

I once succumbed to the fad of fasting and went for six days and nights without eating. It wasn't difficult. I was less hungry at the end of the sixth day than I was at the end of the second. Yet I know, as you know, people would think they had committed a crime if they let their families or employees go for six days without food; but they will let them go six days, and six weeks, and sometimes sixty years without giving them the hearty appreciation that they crave almost as much as they crave food.

When Alfred Lunt, one of the great actors of his time, played the leading role in *Reunion in Vienna*, he said, 'There is nothing I need so much as nourishment for my self-esteem.'

We nourish the bodies of our children and friends and employees, but how seldom do we nourish their self-esteem? We provide them with roast beef and potatoes to build energy, but we neglect to give them kind words of appreciation that would sing in their memories for years like the music of the morning stars.

Paul Harvey, in one of his radio broadcasts, 'The Rest of the Story,' told how showing sincere appreciation can change a person's life. He reported that years ago a teacher in Detroit asked Stevie Morris to help her find a mouse that was lost in the classroom. You see, she appreciated the fact that nature had given Stevie something no one else in the room had. Nature had given Stevie a remarkable pair of ears to compensate for his blind eyes. But this was really the first time Stevie had been shown appreciation for those talented ears. Now, years later, he says that this act of appreciation was the beginning of a new life. You see, from that time on he developed his gift of hearing and went on to become, under the stage name of Stevie Wonder, one of *the* great pop singers and songwriters of the seventies.*

Some readers are saying right now as they read these lines: 'Oh, phooey! *Flattery! Bear oil!* I've tried that stuff. It doesn't work – not with intelligent people.'

* Paul Aurandt, *Paul Harvey's The Rest of the Story* (New York: Doubleday, 1977). Edited and compiled by Lynne Harvey. Copyright © by Paulynne, Inc.

Of course flattery seldom works with discerning people. It is shallow, selfish and insincere. It ought to fail and it usually does. True, some people are so hungry, so thirsty, for appreciation that they will swallow anything, just as a starving man will eat grass and fishworms.

Even Queen Victoria was susceptible to flattery. Prime Minister Benjamin Disraeli confessed that he put it on thick in dealing with the Queen. To use his exact words, he said he 'spread it on with a trowel'. But Disraeli was one of the most polished, deft and adroit men who ever ruled the far-flung British Empire. He was a genius in his line. What would work for him wouldn't necessarily work for you and me. In the long run, flattery will do you more harm than good. Flattery is counterfeit, and like counterfeit money, it will eventually get you into trouble if you pass it to someone else.

The difference between appreciation and flattery? That is simple. One is sincere and the other insincere. One comes from the heart out; the other from the teeth out. One is unselfish; the other selfish. One is universally admired; the other universally condemned.

I recently saw a bust of Mexican hero General Alvaro Obregon in the Chapultepec palace in Mexico City. Below the bust are carved these wise words from General Obregon's philosophy: 'Don't be afraid of enemies who attack you. Be afraid of the friends who flatter you.'

No! No! No! I am not suggesting flattery! Far from it. I'm talking about a new way of life. Let me repeat. *I am talking about a new way of life.*

King George V had a set of six maxims displayed on the walls of his study at Buckingham Palace. One of these maxims said: 'Teach me neither to proffer nor receive cheap praise.' That's all flattery is – cheap praise. I once read a definition of flattery that may be worth repeating: 'Flattery is telling the other person precisely what he thinks about himself.'

'Use what language you will,' said Ralph Waldo Emerson, 'you can never say anything but what you are.'

If all we had to do was flatter, everybody would catch one and we should all be experts in human relations.

When we are not engaged in thinking about some definite problem, we usually spend about 95 percent of our time thinking about ourselves. Now, if we stop thinking about ourselves for a while and begin to think of the other person's good points, we won't have to resort to flattery so cheap and false that it can be spotted almost before it is out of the mouth.

One of the most neglected virtues of our daily existence is appreciation. Somehow, we neglect to praise our son or daughter when he or she brings home a good report card, and we fail to encourage our children when they first succeed in baking a cake or building a birdhouse. Nothing pleases children more than this kind of parental interest and approval.

The next time you enjoy filet mignon at the club, send word to the chef that it was excellently prepared, and when a tired salesman shows you unusual courtesy, please mention it.

Every minister, lecturer and public speaker knows the discouragement of pouring himself or herself out to an audience and not receiving a single ripple of appreciative comment. What applies to professionals applies doubly to workers in offices, shops and factories and our families and friends. In our interpersonal relations we should never forget that all our associates are human beings and hunger for appreciation. It is the legal tender that all souls enjoy.

Try leaving a friendly trail of little sparks of gratitude on your daily trips. You will be surprised how they will set small flames of friendship that will be rose beacons on your next visit.

Pamela Dunham of New Fairfield, Connecticut, had among her responsibilities on her job the supervision of a janitor who was doing a very poor job. The other employees would jeer at him and litter the hallways to show him what a bad job he was doing. It was so bad, productive time was being lost in the shop.

Without success, Pam tried various ways to motivate this person. She noticed that occasionally he did a particularly good piece of work. She made a point to praise him for it in front of other people. Each day the job he did all around got better, and pretty soon he started doing all his work efficiently. Now he does an excellent job and other people give him appreciation and recognition. Honest appreciation got results where criticism and ridicule failed.

Hurting people not only does not change them, it is never called for. There is an old saying that I have cut out and pasted on my mirror where I cannot help but see it every day:

I shall pass this way but once; any good, therefore, that I can do or any kindness that I can show to any human being, let me do it now. Let me not defer nor neglect it, for I shall not pass this way again.

Emerson said: 'Every man I meet is my superior in some way. In that, I learn of him.'

If that was true of Emerson, isn't it likely to be a thousand times more true of you and me? Let's cease thinking of our accomplishments, our wants. Let's try to figure out the other person's good points. Then forget flattery. Give honest sincere appreciation. Be 'hearty in your approbation and lavish in your praise,' and people will cherish your words and treasure them and repeat them over a lifetime – repeat them years after you have forgotten them.

PRINCIPLE 2

Give honest and sincere appreciation.

'He who can do this has the whole world with him. He who cannot walks a lonely way'

I often went fishing up in Maine during the summer. Personally I am very fond of strawberries and cream, but I have found that for some strange reason, fish prefer worms. So when I went fishing, I didn't think about what I wanted. I didn't bait the hook with strawberries and cream. Rather, I dangled a worm or a grasshopper in front of the fish and said: 'Wouldn't you like to have that?'

Why not use the same common sense when fishing for people?

That is what Lloyd George, Great Britain's Prime Minister during World War I, did. When someone asked him how he managed to stay in power after the other wartime leaders – Wilson, Orlando and Clemenceau – had been forgotten, he replied that if his staying on top might be attributed to any one thing, it would be to his having learned that it was necessary to bait the hook to suit the fish.

Why talk about what we want? That is childish. Absurd. Of course, you are interested in what you want. You are eternally interested in it. But no one else is. The rest of us are just like you: we are interested in what we want.

So the only way on earth to influence other people is to talk about what *they* want and show them how to get it.

Remember that tomorrow when you are trying to get somebody to do something. If, for example, you don't want your children to smoke, don't preach at them, and don't talk about what you want; but show them that cigarettes may keep them from making the basketball team or winning the hundred-yard dash.

This is a good thing to remember regardless of whether you are dealing with children or calves or chimpanzees. For example: one day Ralph Waldo Emerson and his son tried to get a calf into the barn. But they made the common mistake of thinking only of what they wanted: Emerson pushed and his son pulled. But the calf was doing just what they were doing: he was thinking only of what he wanted; so he stiffened his legs and stubbornly refused to leave the pasture. The Irish housemaid saw their predicament. She couldn't write essays and books; but, on this occasion at least, she had more horse sense, or calf sense, than Emerson had. She thought of what the calf wanted; so she put her maternal finger in the calf's mouth and let the calf suck her finger as she gently led him into the barn.

Every act you have ever performed since the day you were born was performed because you wanted something. How about the time you gave a large contribution to the Red Cross? Yes, that is no exception to the rule. You gave the Red Cross the donation because you wanted to lend a helping hand; you wanted to do a beautiful, unselfish, divine act. 'Inasmuch as ye have done it unto one of the least of these my brethren, ye have done it unto me.'

If you hadn't wanted that feeling more than you wanted your money, you would not have made the contribution. Of course, you might have made the contribution because you were ashamed to refuse or because a customer asked you to do it. But one thing is certain. You made the contribution because you wanted something.

Harry A. Overstreet in his illuminating book *Influencing Human Behaviour* said: 'Action springs out of what we fundamentally desire . . . and the best piece of advice which can be given to would-be persuaders, whether in business, in the home, in the school, in politics, is: First, arouse in the other person an eager want. He who can do this has the whole world with him. He who cannot walks a lonely way.'

Andrew Carnegie, a poverty-stricken Scotch lad who started to work at two cents an hour and finally gave away $365 million, learned early in life that the only way to influence people is to talk in terms of what the other person wants. He attended school only four years; yet he learned how to handle people.

To illustrate: His sister-in-law was worried sick over her two boys. They were at Yale, and they were so busy with their own affairs that they neglected to write home and paid no attention whatever to their mother's frantic letters.

Then Carnegie offered to wager a hundred dollars that he could get an answer by return mail, without even asking for it. Someone called his bet; so he wrote his nephews a chatty letter, mentioning casually in a postscript that he was sending each one a five-dollar bill.

He neglected, however, to enclose the money.

Back came replies by return mail thanking 'Dear Uncle Andrew' for his kind note and – you can finish the sentence yourself.

Another example of persuading comes from Stan Novak of Cleveland, Ohio, a participant in our course. Stan came home from work one evening to find his youngest son, Tim, kicking and screaming on the living-room floor. He was to start kindergarten the next day and was protesting that he would not go. Stan's normal reaction would have been to banish the child to his room and tell him he'd better make up his mind to go. He had no choice. But tonight, recognizing that this would not really help Tim start kindergarten in the best frame of mind, Stan sat down and thought, 'If I were Tim, why would I be excited about going to kindergarten?' He and his wife made a list of all the fun things Tim would do such as finger-painting, singing songs, making new friends. Then they put them into action. 'We all started finger-painting on the kitchen table – my wife, Lil, my other son Bob, and myself, all having fun. Soon Tim was peeping around the corner. Next he was begging to participate. 'Oh, no! You have to go to kindergarten first to learn how to finger-paint.' With all the enthusiasm I could muster I went through the list talking in terms he could understand – telling him all the fun he would have in kindergarten. The next morning, I thought I was the first one up. I went downstairs and found Tim sitting sound asleep in the living-room chair. 'What are you doing here?' I asked. 'I'm waiting to go to kindergarten. I don't want to be late.' The enthusiasm of our entire family had aroused in Tim an eager want that no amount of discussion or threat could have possibly accomplished.'

Tomorrow you may want to persuade somebody to do something. Before you speak, pause and ask yourself: 'How can I make this person want to do it?'

That question will stop us from rushing into a situation heedlessly, with futile chatter about our desires.

At one time I rented the grand ballroom of a certain New York hotel for twenty nights in each season in order to hold a series of lectures.

At the beginning of one season, I was suddenly informed that I should have to pay almost three times as much rent as formerly. This news reached me after the tickets had been printed and distributed and all the announcements had been made.

Naturally, I didn't want to pay the increase, but what was the use of talking to the hotel about what I wanted? They were only interested in what they wanted. So a couple of days later I went to see the manager.

'I was a bit shocked when I got your letter,' I said, 'but I don't blame you at all. If I had been in your position, I should probably have written a similar letter myself. Your duty as the manager of the hotel is to make all the profit possible. If you don't do that you will be fired and you ought to be fired. Now, let's take a piece of paper and write down the advantages and the disadvantages that will accrue to you, if you insist on this increase in rent.'

Then I took a letterhead and ran a line through the centre and headed one column 'Advantages' and the other column 'Disadvantages.'

I wrote down under the head 'Advantages' these words: 'Ballroom free.' Then I went on to say: 'You will have the advantages of having the ballroom, free to rent for dances and conventions. That is a big advantage, for affairs like that will pay you much more than you can get for a series of lectures. If I tie your ballroom up for twenty nights during the course of the season, it is sure to mean a loss of some very profitable business to you.

'Now, let's consider the disadvantages. First, instead of increasing your income from me, you are going to decrease it. In fact, you are going to wipe it out because I cannot pay the rent you are asking. I shall be forced to hold these lectures at some other place.

'There's another disadvantage to you also. These lectures attract crowds of educated and cultured people to your hotel. That is good advertising for you, isn't it? In fact, if you spent five thousand dollars advertising in the news-papers, you couldn't bring as many people to look at your hotel as I can bring by these lectures. That is worth a lot to a hotel, isn't it?'

As I talked, I wrote these two 'disadvantages' under the proper heading, and handed the sheet of paper to the manager saying: 'I wish you would carefully consider both the advantages and disadvantages that are going to accrue to you and then give me your final decision.'

I received a letter the next day, informing me that my rent would be increased only 50 percent instead of 300 percent.

Mind you, I got this reduction without saying a word about what I wanted. I talked all the time about what the other person wanted and how he could get it.

Suppose I had done the human, natural thing; suppose I had stormed into his office and said, 'What do you mean by raising my rent three hundred percent when you know the tickets have been printed and the announcements made? Three hundred percent! Ridiculous! Absurd! I won't pay it!'

What would have happened then? An argument would have begun to steam and boil and sputter – and you know how arguments end. Even if I had convinced him that he was wrong, his pride would have made it difficult for him to back down and give in.

Here is one of the best bits of advice ever given about the fine art of human relationships. 'If there is any one secret of success,' said Henry Ford, 'it lies in the ability to get the other person's point of view and see things from that person's angle as well as from your own.'

That is so good, I want to repeat it: *'If there is any one secret of success, it lies in the ability to get the other person's point of view and see things from that person's angle as well as from your own.'*

That is so simple, so obvious, that anyone ought to see the truth of it at a glance; yet 90 percent of the people on this earth ignore it 90 percent of the time.

An example? Look at the letters that come across your desk tomorrow morning, and you will find that most of them violate this important canon of common sense. Take this one, a letter written by the head of the radio department of an advertising agency with offices scattered across the conti-nent. This letter was sent to the managers of local radio stations throughout the country. (I have set down, in brackets, my reactions to each paragraph.)

Mr. John Blank,
Blankville,
Indiana

Dear Mr. Blank:

The ____ company desires to retain its position in advertising agency leadership in the radio field.

[Who cares about your company's desires? I am worried about my own problems. The bank is foreclosing the mortgage on my house, the bugs are destroying the hollyhocks, the stock market tumbled yesterday. I missed the eight-fifteen this morning. I wasn't invited to the Jones's dance last night, the doctor tells me I have high blood pressure and neuritis and dandruff. And then what happens? I come down to the office this morning worried, open my mail and here is some little whippersnapper off in New York yapping about what his company wants. Bah! If he only realized what sort of impression his letter makes, he would get out of the advertising business and start manufacturing sheep dip.]

This agency's national advertising accounts were the bulwark of the network. Our subsequent clearances of station time have kept us at the top of agencies year after year.

[You are big and rich and right at the top, are you? So what? I don't give two whoops in Hades if you are as big as General Motors and General Electric and the General Staff of the U.S. Army all combined. If you had as much sense as a half-witted hummingbird, you would realize that I am interested in how big I am – not how big you are. All this talk about your enormous success makes me feel small and unimportant.]

We desire to service our accounts with the last word on radio station information.

[You desire! You desire. You unmitigated ass. I'm not interested in what you desire or what the President of the United States desires. Let me tell you once and for all that I am interested in what I desire – and you haven't said a word about that yet in this absurd letter of yours.]

Will you, therefore, put the ____ company on your preferred list for weekly station information ____ every single detail that will be useful to an agency in intelligently booking time.

['Preferred list.' You have your nerve! You make me feel insignificant by your big talk about your company – and then you ask me to put you on a 'preferred' list, and you don't even say 'please' when you ask it.]

41

A prompt acknowledgement of this letter, giving us your latest 'doings' will be mutually helpful.

[You fool! you mail me a cheap form letter – a letter scattered far and wide like the autumn leaves – and you have the gall to ask me, when I am worried about the mortgage and the hollyhocks and my blood pressure, to sit down and dictate a personal note acknowledging your form letter – and you ask me to do it 'promptly'. What do you mean, 'promptly'? Don't you know I am just as busy as you are – or, at least, I like to think I am. And while we are on the subject, who gave you the lordly right to order me around? . . . You say it will be 'mutually helpful'. At last, at last, you have begun to see my viewpoint. But you are vague about how it will be to my advantage.]

> Very truly yours,
> John Doe
> Manager Radio Department

P.S. The enclosed reprint from the Bankville Journal *will be of interest to you, and you may want to broadcast it over your station.*

[Finally, down here in the postscript, you mention something that may help me solve one of my problems. Why didn't you begin your letter with – but what's the use? Any advertising man who is guilty of perpetrating such drivel as you have sent me has something wrong with his medulla oblongata. You don't need a letter giving our latest doings. What you need is a quart of iodine in your thyroid gland.]

Now, if people who devote their lives to advertising and who pose as experts in the art of influencing people to buy – if they write a letter like that, what can we expect from the butcher and baker or the auto mechanic?

Here is another letter, written by the superintendent of a large freight terminal to a student of this course, Edward Vermylen. What effect did this letter have on the man to whom it was addressed? Read it and then I'll tell you.

A. Zerega's Sons,Inc
28 Front St.
Brooklyn, N.Y. 11201
Attention: Mr. Edward Vermylen

Gentlemen:

The operations at our outbound-rail-receiving station are handicapped because a material percentage of the total business is delivered us in the late afternoon. This condition results in congestion, overtime on the part of our forces, delays to trucks, and in some cases delays to freight. On

November 10, we received from your company a lot of 510 pieces, which reached here at 4.20. p.m.

We solicit your cooperation toward overcoming the undesirable effects arising from late receipt of freight. May we ask that, on days on which you ship the volume which was received on the above date, effort be made either to get the truck here earlier or to deliver us part of the freight during the morning?

The advantage that would accrue to you under such an arrangement would be that of more expeditious discharge of your trucks and the assurance that your business would go forward on the date of its receipt.

Very truly yours,

J ___ B ___, Supt.

After reading this letter, Mr. Vermylen, sales manager for A. Zerega's Sons, Inc., sent it to me with the following comment:

This letter had the reverse effect from that which was intended. The letter begins by describing the Terminal's difficulties, in which we are not interested, generally speaking. Our cooperation is then requested without any thought as to whether it would inconvenience us, and then finally, in the last paragraph, the fact is mentioned that if we do cooperate it will mean more expeditious discharge of our trucks with the assurance that our freight will go forward on the date of its receipt.

In other words, that in which we are most interested is mentioned last, and the whole effect is one of raising a spirit of antagonism rather than of cooperation.

Let's see if we can't rewrite and improve this letter. Let's not waste any time talking about our problems. As Henry Ford admonishes, let's 'get the other person's point of view and see things from his or her angle, as well as from our own.'

Here is one way of revising the letter. It may not be the best way, but isn't it an improvement?

Mr. Edward Vermylen
c/o A Zerega's Sons, Inc.
28 Front St.
Brooklyn, N.Y. 11201

Dear Mr. Vermylen:

Your company has been one of our good customers for fourteen years. Naturally, we are very grateful for your patronage and are eager to give you the speedy, efficient service you deserve. However, we regret to say that it isn't possible for us to do that when your trucks bring us a large shipment late in the afternoon, as they did on November 10. Why? Because many other customers make late afternoon deliveries also. Naturally, that causes congestion. That means your trucks are held up unavoidably at the pier and sometimes even your freight is delayed.

That's bad, but it can be avoided. If you make your deliveries at the pier in the morning when possible, your trucks will be able to keep moving, your freight will get immediate attention, and our workers will get home early at night to enjoy a dinner of the delicious macaroni noodles that you manufacture.

Regardless of when your shipments arrive, we shall always cheerfully do all in our power to serve you promptly.

You are busy. Please don't trouble to answer this note.

> Yours truly,
> J ____ B ____, Supt.

Barbara Anderson, who worked in a bank in New York, desired to move to Phoenix, Arizona, because of the health of her son. Using the principles she had learned in our course, she wrote the following letter to twelve banks in Phoenix:

Dear Sir:

My ten years of bank experience should be of interest to a rapidly growing bank like yours.

In various capacities in bank operations with the Bankers Trust Company in New York, leading to my present assignment as Branch Manager, I have acquired skills in all phases of banking including depositor relations, credits, loans and administration.

I will be relocating to Phoenix in May and I am sure I can contribute to your growth and profit. I will be in Phoenix the week of April 3 and would appreciate the opportunity to show you how I can help your bank meet its goals.

> Sincerely,
> Barbara L. Anderson

Do you think Mrs. Anderson received any response from that letter? Eleven out of the twelve banks invited her to be interviewed, and she had a choice of which bank's offer to accept. Why? Mrs. Anderson did not state what *she* wanted, but wrote in the letter how she could help them, and focused on *their* wants, not her own.

Thousands of salespeople are pounding the pavements today, tired, discouraged and underpaid. Why? Because they are always thinking only of what they want. They don't realize that neither you nor I want to buy anything. If we did, we would go out and buy it. But both of us are eternally interested in solving our problems. And if salespeople can show us how their services or merchandise will help us solve our problems, they won't need to sell us. We'll buy. And customers like to feel that they are buying – not being sold.

Yet many salespeople spend a lifetime in selling without seeing things from the customer's angle. For example, for many years I lived in Forest Hills, a little community of private homes in the centre of Greater New York. One day as I was rushing to the station, I chanced to meet a real-estate operator who had bought and sold property in that area for many years. He knew Forest Hills well, so I hurriedly asked him whether or not my stucco house was built with metal lath or hollow tile. He said he didn't know and told me what I already knew – that I could find out by calling the Forest Hills Garden Association. The following morning, I received a letter from him. Did he give me the information I wanted? He could have gotten it in sixty seconds by a telephone call. But he didn't. He told me again that I could get it by telephoning, and then asked me to let him handle my insurance.

He was not interested in helping me. He was interested only in helping himself.

J. Howard Lucas of Birmingham, Alabama, tells how two salespeople from the same company handled the same type of situation. He reported:

'Several years ago I was on the management team of a small company. Headquartered near us was the district office of a large insurance company. Their agents were assigned territories, and our company was assigned to two agents, whom I shall refer to as Carl and John.

'One morning, Carl dropped by our office and casually mentioned that his company had just introduced a new life insurance policy for executives and thought we might be interested later on and he would get back to us when he had more information on it.

'The same day, John saw us on the sidewalk while returning from a coffee break, and he shouted: "Hey, Luke, hold up, I have some great news for you fellows." He hurried over and very excitedly told us about an executive life insurance policy his company had introduced that very day. (It was the same policy that Carl had casually mentioned.) He wanted us to have one of the first issued. He gave us a few important facts about the coverage and ended saying: "The policy is so new, I'm going to have someone from the home office come out tomorrow and explain it. Now, in the meantime, let's get the applications signed and on the way so he can have more information to work with." His enthusiasm aroused in us an eager want for this policy even though we still did not have details. When they were made available to us, they confirmed John's initial understanding of the policy, and he had not only sold each of us a policy but later doubled our coverage.

'Carl could have had those sales, but he made no effort to arouse in us any desire for those policies.'

The world is full of people who are grabbing and self-seeking. So the rare individual who unselfishly tries to serve others has an enormous advantage. He has little competition. Owen D. Young, a noted lawyer and one of America's great business leaders, once said: 'People who can put themselves in the place of other people, who can understand the workings of their minds, need never worry about what the future has in store for them.'

If out of reading this book you get just one thing – an increased tendency to think always in terms of other people's point of view, and see things from their angle – if you get that one thing out of this book, it may easily prove to be one of the building blocks of your career.

Looking at the other person's point of view and arousing in him an eager want for something is not to be construed as manipulating that person so that he will do something that is only for your benefit and his detriment. Each party should gain from the negotiation. In the letters to Mr. Vermylen, both the sender and the receiver of the correspondence gained by implementing what was suggested. Both the bank and Mrs. Anderson won by her letter in that the bank obtained a valuable employee and Mrs. Anderson a suitable job. And in the example of John's sale of insurance to Mr. Lucas, both gained through this transaction.

Another example in which everybody gains through this principle of arousing an eager want comes from Michael E. Whidden of Warwick, Rhode Island, who is a territory salesman for the Shell Oil Company. Mike wanted to become the Number One salesperson in his district, but one service station was holding him back. It was run by an older man who could not be motivated to clean up his station. It was in such poor shape that sales were declining significantly.

This manager would not listen to any of Mike's pleas to upgrade the station. After many exhortations and heart-to-heart talks – all of which had no impact – Mike decided to invite the manager to visit the newest Shell station in his territory.

The manager was so impressed by the facilities at the new station that when Mike visited him the next time, his station was cleaned up and had recorded a sales increase. This enabled Mike to reach the Number One spot in his district. All his talking and discussion hadn't helped, but by arousing an eager want in the manager, by showing him the modern station, he had accomplished his goal, and both the manager and Mike benefited.

Most people go through college and learn to read Virgil and master the mysteries of calculus without ever discovering how their own minds function. For instance: I once gave a course in Effective Speaking for the young college graduates who were entering the employ of the Carrier Corporation, the large air-conditioning manufacturer. One of the participants wanted to persuade the others to play basketball in their free time, and this is about what he said: 'I want you to come out and play basketball. I like to play basketball, but the last few times I've been to the gymnasium there haven't been enough people to get up a game. Two or three of us got by throwing the ball around the other night – and I got a black eye. I wish all of you would come down tomorrow night. I want to play basketball.'

Did he talk about anything you want? You don't want to go to a gymnasium that no one else goes to, do you? You don't care about what he wants. You don't want to get a black eye.

Could he have shown you how to get the things you want by using the gymnasium? Surely. More pep. Keener edge to the appetite. Clearer brain. Fun. Games. Basketball.

To repeat Professor Overstreet's wise advice: *First, arouse in the other person an eager want. He who can do this has the whole world with him. He who cannot walks a lonely way.*

One of the students in the author's training course was worried about his little boy. The child was underweight and refused to eat properly. His parents used the usual method. They scolded and nagged. 'Mother wants you to eat this and that.' 'Father wants you to grow up to be a big man.'

Did the boy pay any attention to these pleas? Just about as much as you pay to one fleck of sand on a sandy beach.

No one with a trace of horse sense would expect a child three years old to react to the viewpoint of a father thirty years old. Yet that was precisely what the father had expected. It was absurd. He finally saw that. So he said to himself? 'What does that boy want? How can I tie up what I want to what he wants?'

It was easy for the father when he started thinking about it. His boy had a tricycle that he loved to ride up and down the sidewalk in front of the house in Brooklyn. A few doors down the street lived a bully – a bigger boy who would pull the little boy off his tricycle and ride it himself.

Naturally, the little boy would run screaming to his mother, and she would have to come out and take the bully off the tricycle and put her little boy on again. This happened almost every day.

What did the little boy want? It didn't take a Sherlock Holmes to answer that one. His pride, his anger, his desire for a feeling of importance – all the strongest emotions in his makeup – goaded him to get revenge, to smash the bully in the nose. And when his father explained that the boy would be able to wallop the daylights out of the bigger kid someday if he would only eat the things his mother wanted him to eat – when his father promised him that – there was no longer any problem of dietetics. That boy would have eaten spinach, sauerkraut, salt mackerel – anything in order to be big enough to whip the bully who had humiliated him so often.

After solving that problem, the parents tackled another: the little boy had the unholy habit of wetting his bed.

He slept with his grandmother. In the morning, his grandmother would wake up and feel the sheet and say: 'Look, Johnny, what you did again last night.'

He would say: 'No, I didn't do it. You did it.'

Scolding, spanking, shaming him, reiterating that the parents didn't want him to do it – none of these things kept the bed dry. So the parents asked: 'How can we make this boy want to stop wetting his bed?'

What were his wants? First, he wanted to wear pyjamas like Daddy instead of wearing a nightgown like Grandmother. Grandmother was getting fed up with his nocturnal iniquities, so she gladly offered to buy him a pair of pyjamas if he would reform. Second, he wanted a bed of his own. Grandmother didn't object.

His mother took him to a department store in Brooklyn, winked at the salesgirl, and said: 'Here is a little gentleman who would like to do some shopping.'

The salesgirl made him feel important by saying: 'Young man, what can I show you?'

He stood a couple of inches taller and said: 'I want to buy a bed for myself.'

When he was shown the one his mother wanted him to buy, she winked at the salesgirl and the boy was persuaded to buy it.

The bed was delivered the next day; and that night, when Father came home, the little boy ran to the door shouting: 'Daddy! Daddy! Come upstairs and see my bed that I bought!'

The father looking at the bed, obeyed Charles Schwab's injunction: he was 'hearty in his approbation and lavish in his praise.'

'You are not going to wet this bed, are you?' the father said.

'Oh no, no! I am not going to wet this bed.' The boy kept his promise, for his pride was involved. That was his bed. He and he alone had bought it. And he was wearing pyjamas now like a little man. He wanted to act like a man. And he did.

Another father, K. T. Dutschmann, a telephone engineer, a student of this course, couldn't get his three-year-old daughter to eat breakfast food. The usual scolding, pleading, coaxing methods had all ended in futility. So the parents asked themselves: 'How can we make her want to do it?'

The little girl loved to imitate her mother, to feel big and grown up; so one morning they put her on her chair and let her make the breakfast food. At just the psychological moment, Father drifted into the kitchen while she was stirring the breakfast cereal and she said: 'Oh, look, Daddy, I am making the cereal this morning.'

She ate two helpings of the cereal without any coaxing, because she was interested in it. She had achieved a feeling of importance; she had found in making the cereal an avenue of self-expression.

William Winter once remarked that 'self-expression is the dominant necessity of human nature.' Why can't we adapt this same psychology to business dealings? When we have a brilliant idea, instead of making others think it is ours, why not let them cook and stir the idea themselves. They will then regard it as their own; they will like it and maybe eat a couple of helpings of it.

Remember: 'First, arouse in the other person an eager want. He who can do this has the whole world with him. He who cannot walks a lonely way.'

PRINCIPLE 3

Arouse in the other person an eager want.

_____

☐ IN A NUTSHELL ☐

FUNDAMENTAL TECHNIQUES IN HANDLING PEOPLE

PRINCIPLE 1

Don't criticize, condemn or complain.

PRINCIPLE 2

Give honest and sincere appreciation.

PRINCIPLE 3

Arouse in the other person an eager want.

Part Two

SIX WAYS TO MAKE PEOPLE LIKE YOU

□ 1 □

Do this and you'll be welcome anywhere

Why read this book to find out how to win friends? Why not study the technique of the greatest winner of friends the world has ever known? Who is he? You may meet him tomorrow coming down the street. When you get within ten feet of him, he will begin to wag his tail. If you stop and pat him he will almost jump out of his skin to show you how much he likes you. And you know that behind this show of affection on his part, there are no ulterior motives: he doesn't want to sell you any real estate, and he doesn't want to marry you.

Did you ever stop to think that a dog is the only animal that doesn't have to work for a living? A hen has to lay eggs, a cow has to give milk, and a canary has to sing. But a dog makes his living by giving you nothing but love.

When I was five years old, my father bought a little yellow-haired pup for fifty cents. He was the light and joy of my childhood. Every afternoon about four-thirty, he would sit in the front yard with his beautiful eyes staring steadfastly at the path, and as soon as he heard my voice or saw me swinging my dinner pail through the buck brush, he was off like a shot, racing breathlessly up the hill to greet me with leaps of joy and barks of sheer ecstasy.

Tippy was my constant companion for five years. Then one tragic night – I shall never forget it – he was killed within ten feet of my head, killed by lightning. Tippy's death was the tragedy of my boyhood.

You never read a book on psychology, Tippy. You didn't need to. You knew by some divine instinct that you can make more friends in two months by becoming genuinely interested in other people than you can in two years by trying to get other people interested in you. Let me repeat that. You can make more friends in two months by becoming interested in other people than you can in two years by trying to get other people interested in you.

Yet I know and you know people who blunder through life trying to wigwag other people into becoming interested in them.

Of course, it doesn't work. People are not interested in you. They are not interested in me. They are interested in themselves – morning, noon and after dinner.

The New York Telephone Company made a detailed study of telephone conversations to find out which word is the most frequently used. You have guessed it: it is the personal pronoun 'I'. 'I'. 'I'. It was used 3,900 times in 500 telephone conversations. 'I'. 'I'. 'I'. 'I'.

When you see a group photograph that you are in, whose picture do you look for first?

If we merely try to impress people and get people interested in us, we will never have many true, sincere friends. Friends, real friends, are not made that way.

Napoleon tried it, and in his last meeting with Josephine he said: 'Josephine, I have been as fortunate as any man ever was on this earth; and yet, at this hour, you are the only person in the world on whom I can rely.' And historians doubt whether he could rely even on her.

Alfred Adler, the famous Viennese psychologist, wrote a book entitled *What Life Should Mean to You*. In that book he says: 'It is the individual who is not interested in his fellow men who has the greatest difficulties in life and provides the greatest injury to others. It is from among such individuals that all human failures spring.'

You may read scores of erudite tomes on psychology without coming across a statement more significant for you and me. Adler's statement is so rich with meaning that I am going to repeat it in italics:

It is the individual who is not interested in his fellow men who has the greatest difficulties in life and provides the greatest injury to others. It is from among such individuals that all human failures spring.

I once took a course in short-story writing at New York University, and during that course the editor of a leading magazine talked to our class. He said he could pick up any one of the dozens of stories that drifted across his desk every day and after reading a few paragraphs he could feel whether or not the author liked people. 'If the author doesn't like people,' he said, 'people won't like his or her stories.'

This hard-boiled editor stopped twice in the course of his talk on fiction writing and apologized for preaching a sermon. 'I am telling you,' he said, 'the same things your preacher would tell you, but remember, you have to be interested in people if you want to be a successful writer of stories.'

If that is true of writing fiction, you can be sure it is true of dealing with people face-to-face.

I spent an evening in the dressing room of Howard Thurston the last time he appeared on Broadway – Thurston was the acknowledged dean of magicians. For forty years he had travelled all over the world, time and again, creating illusions, mystifying audiences, and making people gasp with astonishment. More than 60 million people had paid admission to his show, and he had made almost $2 million in profit.

I asked Mr. Thurston to tell me the secret of his success. His schooling certainly had nothing to do with it, for he ran away from home as a small boy, became a hobo, rode in boxcars, slept in haystacks, begged his food from door to door, and learned to read by looking out of boxcars at signs along the railway.

Did he have a superior knowledge of magic? No, he told me hundreds of books had been written about legerdemain and scores of people knew as much about it as he did. But he had two things that the others didn't have. First, he had the ability to put his personality across the footlights. He was a master showman. He knew human nature. Everything he did, every gesture, every intonation of his voice, every lifting of an eyebrow had been carefully rehearsed in advance, and his actions were timed to split seconds. But, in addition to that, Thurston had a genuine interest in people. He told me that many magicians would look at the audience and say to themselves, 'Well, there is a bunch of suckers out there, a bunch of hicks; I'll fool them all right.' But Thurston's method was totally different. He told me that every time he went on stage he said to himself: 'I am grateful because these people came to see me. They make it possible for me to make my living in a very agreeable way. I'm going to give them the very best I possibly can.'

He declared he never stepped in front of the footlights without first saying to himself over and over: 'I love my audience. I love my audience.' Ridiculous? Absurd? You are privileged to think anything you like. I am merely passing it on to you without comment as a recipe used by one of the most famous magicians of all time.

George Dyke of North Warren, Pennsylvania, was forced to retire from his service station business after thirty years when a new highway was constructed over the site of his station. It wasn't long before the idle days of retirement began to bore him, so he started filling in his time trying to play music and talk with many of the accomplished fiddlers. In his humble and friendly way he became generally interested in learning the background and interests of every musician he met. Although he was not a great fiddler himself, he made many friends in this pursuit. He attended competitions and soon became known to the country music fans in the eastern part of the United States as 'Uncle George, the Fiddle Scraper from Kinzua County.' When we heard Uncle George, he was seventy-two and enjoying every minute of his life. By having a sustained interest in other people, he created a new life for himself at a time when most people consider their productive years over.

That, too, was one of the secrets of Theodore Roosevelt's astonishing popularity. Even his servants loved him. His valet, James E. Amos, wrote a book about him entitled *Theodore Roosevelt, Hero to His Valet*. In that book Amos relates this illuminating incident:

My wife one time asked the President about a bobwhite. She had never seen one and he described it to her fully. Sometime later, the telephone at our cottage rang. [Amos and his wife lived in a little cottage on the

Roosevelt estate at Oyster Bay.] My wife answered it and it was Mr. Roosevelt himself. He had called her, he said, to tell her that there was a bobwhite outside her window and that if she would look out she might see it. Little things like that were so characteristic of him. Whenever he went by our cottage even though we were out of sight, we would hear him call out: 'Oo-oo-oo, Annie?' or 'Oo-oo-oo, James!' It was just a friendly greeting as he went by.

How could employees keep from liking a man like that? How could anyone keep from liking him?

Roosevelt called at the White House one day when the President and Mrs Taft were away. His honest liking for humble people was shown by the fact that he greeted all the old White House servants by name, even the scullery maids.

'But when he saw Alice, the kitchen maid,' writes Archie Butt, 'he asked her if she still made corn bread. Alice told him that she sometimes made it for the servants, but no one ate it upstairs.

' "They show bad taste," Roosevelt boomed, "and I'll tell the President so when I see him."

'Alice brought a piece to him on a plate, and he went over to the office eating it as he went and greeting gardeners and labourers as he passed . . .

'He addressed each person just as he had addressed them in the past. Ike Hoover, who had been head usher at the White House for forty years, said with tears in his eyes: "It is the only happy day we had in nearly two years, and not one of us would exchange it for a hundred-dollar bill." '

The same concern for the seemingly unimportant people helped sales representative Edward M. Sykes, Jr., of Chatham, New Jersey, retain an account. 'Many years ago,' he reported, 'I called on customers for Johnson and Johnson in the Massachusetts area. One account was a drug store in Hingham. Whenever I went into this store I would always talk to the soda clerk and sales clerk for a few minutes before talking to the owner of the store to obtain his order. One day I went up to the owner of the store, and he told me to leave as he was not interested in buying J & J products anymore because he felt they were concentrating their activities on food and discount stores to the detriment of the small drugstore. I left with my tail between my legs and drove around the town for several hours. Finally, I decided to go back and try at least to explain our position to the owner.

'When I returned I walked in and as usual said hello to the soda clerk and sales clerk. When I walked up to the owner, he smiled at me and welcomed me back. He then gave me double the usual order. I looked at him with surprise and asked him what had happened since my visit only a few hours earlier. He pointed to the young man at the soda fountain and said that after I had left, the boy had come over and said that I was one of the few salespeople that called on the store that even bothered to say hello to him and to the others in the store. He told the owner that if any salesperson deserved his business, it was I. The owner agreed and remained a loyal customer. I never forgot that to be genuinely interested in other people is a most important quality for a salesperson to possess – for any person, for that matter.'

I have discovered from personal experience that one can win the attention and time and cooperation of even the most sought-after people by becoming genuinely interested in them. Let me illustrate.

Years ago I conducted a course in fiction writing at the Brooklyn Institute of Arts and Sciences, and we wanted such distinguished and busy authors as Kathleen Norris, Fannie Hurst, Ida Tarbell, Albert Payson Terhune and Rupert Hughes to come to Brooklyn and give us the benefit of their experiences. So we wrote them, saying we admired their work and were deeply interested in getting their advice and learning the secrets of their success.

Each of these letters was signed by about a hundred and fifty students. We said we realized that these authors were busy – too busy to prepare a lecture. So we enclosed a list of questions for them to answer about themselves and their methods of work. They liked that. Who wouldn't like it? So they left their homes and travelled to Brooklyn to give us a helping hand.

By using the same method, I persuaded Leslie M. Shaw, secretary of the treasury in Theodore Roosevelt's cabinet; George W. Wickersham, attorney general in Taft's cabinet; William Jennings Bryan; Franklin D. Roosevelt and many other prominent men to come to talk to the students of my courses in public speaking.

All of us, be we workers in a factory, clerks in an office or even a king upon his throne – all of us like people who admire us. Take the German Kaiser, for example. At the close of World War I he was probably the most savagely and universally despised man on this earth. Even his own nation turned against him when he fled over into Holland to save his neck. The hatred against him was so intense that millions of people would have loved to tear him limb from limb or burn him at the stake. In the midst of all this forest fire of fury, one little boy wrote the Kaiser a simple, sincere letter glowing with kindliness and admiration. This little boy said that no matter what the others thought, he would always love Wilhelm as his Emperor. The Kaiser was deeply touched by this letter and invited the little boy to come to see him. The boy came, so did his mother – and the Kaiser married her. That little boy didn't need to read a book on how to win friends and influence people. He knew how instinctively.

If we want to make friends, let's put ourselves out to do things for other people – things that require time, energy, unselfishness and thoughtfulness. When the Duke of Windsor was Prince of Wales, he was scheduled to tour South America, and before he started out on that tour he spent months studying Spanish so that he could make public talks in the language of the country; and the South Americans loved him for it.

For years I made it a point to find out the birthdays of my friends. How?

Although I haven't the foggiest bit of faith in astrology, I began by asking the other party whether he believed the date of one's birth has anything to do with character and disposition. I then asked him or her to tell me the month and day of birth. If he or she said November 24, for example, I kept repeating to myself, 'November 24, November 24.' The minute my friend's back was turned I wrote down the name and birthday and later would transfer it to a birthday book. At the beginning of each year, I had these birthday dates scheduled in my calendar pad so that they came to my attention automatically. When the natal day arrived, there was my letter or telegram. What a hit it made! I was frequently the only person on earth who remembered.

If we want to make friends, let's greet people with animation and enthusiasm. When somebody calls you on the telephone use the same psychology. Say 'Hello' in tones that bespeak how pleased you are to have the person call. Many companies train their telephone operators to greet all callers in a tone of voice that radiates interest and enthusiasm. The caller feels the company is concerned about them. Let's remember that when we answer the telephone tomorrow.

Showing a genuine interest in others not only wins friends for you, but may develop in its customers a loyalty to your company. In an issue of the publication of the National Bank of North America of New York, the following letter from Madeline Rosedale, a depositor, was published:*

'I would like you to know how much I appreciate your staff. Everyone is so courteous, polite and helpful. What a pleasure it is, after waiting on a long line, to have the teller greet you pleasantly.

'Last year my mother was hospitalized for five months. Frequently I went to Marie Petrucello, a teller. She was concerned about my mother and inquired about her progress.'

Is there any doubt that Mrs Rosedale will continue to use this bank?

Charles R. Walters, of one of the large banks in New York City, was assigned to prepare a confidential report on a certain corporation. He knew of only one person who possessed the facts he needed so urgently. As Mr. Walters was ushered into the president's office, a young woman stuck her head through the door and told the president that she didn't have any stamps for him that day.

'I am collecting stamps for my twelve-year-old son,' the president explained to Mr. Walters.

Mr. Walters stated his mission and began asking questions. The president was vague, general, nebulous. He didn't want to talk, and apparently nothing could persuade him to talk. The interview was brief and barren.

'Frankly, I didn't know what to do,' Mr. Walters said as he related the story to the class. 'Then I remembered what his secretary had said to him – stamps, twelve-year-old son . . . And I also recalled that the foreign department of our

---

* *Eagle*, publication of the National Bank of North America, New York, March 31, 1978.

bank collected stamps – stamps taken from letters pouring in from every continent washed by the seven seas.

'The next afternoon I called on this man and sent in word that I had some stamps for his boy. Was I ushered in with enthusiasm? Yes sir. He couldn't have shaken my hand with more enthusiasm if he had been running for Congress. He radiated smiles and good will. "My George will love this one," he kept saying as he fondled the stamps. "And look at this! This is a treasure."

'We spent half an hour talking stamps and looking at a picture of his boy, and then he devoted more than an hour of his time to giving me every bit of information I wanted – without my even suggesting that he do it. He told me all he knew, and then called in his subordinates and questioned them. He telephoned some of his associates. He loaded me down with facts, figures, reports and correspondence. In the parlance of newspaper reporters, I had a scoop.'

Here is another illustration:

C. M. Knaphle, Jr., of Philadelphia had tried for years to sell fuel to a large chain-store organization. But the chain-store company continued to purchase its fuel from an out-of-town dealer and haul it right past the door of Knaphle's office. Mr. Knaphle made a speech one night before one of my classes, pouring out his hot wrath upon chain stores, branding them as a curse to the nation.

And still he wondered why he couldn't sell them.

I suggested that he try different tactics. To put it briefly, this is what happened. We staged a debate between members of the course on whether the spread of the chain store is doing the country more harm than good.

Knaphle, at my suggestion, took the negative side; he agreed to defend the chain stores, and then went straight to an executive of the chain-store organization that he despised and said: 'I am not here to try to sell fuel. I have come to ask you to do me a favour.' He then told about his debate and said: 'I have come to you for help because I can't think of anyone else who would be more capable of giving me the facts I want. I'm anxious to win this debate, and I'll deeply appreciate whatever help you can give me.'

Here is the rest of the story in Mr. Knaphle's own words:

I had asked this man for precisely one minute of his time. It was with that understanding that he consented to see me. After I had stated my case, he motioned me to a chair and talked to me for exactly one hour and forty-seven minutes. He called in another executive who had written a book on chain stores. He wrote to the National Chain Store Association and secured me a copy of a debate on the subject. He feels that the chain store is rendering a real service to humanity. He is proud of what he is doing for hundreds of communities. His eyes fairly glowed as he talked, and I must confess that he opened my eyes to things I had never dreamed of. He changed my whole mental attitude.

As I was leaving, he walked with me to the door, put his arm around my shoulder, wished me well in my debate, and asked me to stop in and see him again and let him know how I made out. The last words he said to me were: 'Please see me again later in the spring. I should like to place an order with you for fuel.'

To me that was almost a miracle. Here he was offering to buy fuel without my even suggesting it. I had made more headway in two hours by becoming genuinely interested in him and his problems than I could have made in ten years trying to get him interested in me and my product.

You didn't discover a new truth, Mr. Knaphle, for a long time ago, a hundred years before Christ was born, a famous old Roman poet, Publilius Syrus remarked: 'We are interested in others when they are interested in us.'

A show of interest, as with every other principle of human relations, must be sincere. It must pay off not only for the person showing the interest, but for the person receiving the attention. It is a two-way street – both parties benefit.

Martin Ginsberg, who took our course in Long Island, New York, reported how the special interest a nurse took in him profoundly affected his life:

'It was Thanksgiving Day and I was ten years old. I was in a welfare ward of a city hospital and was scheduled to undergo major orthopaedic surgery the next day. I knew that I could only look forward to months of confinement, convalescence and pain. My father was dead; my mother and I lived alone in a small apartment and we were on welfare. My mother was unable to visit me that day.

'As the day went on, I became overwhelmed with the feeling of loneliness, despair and fear. I knew my mother was at home alone worrying about me, not having anyone to be with, not having anyone to eat with and not even having enough money to afford a Thanksgiving Day dinner.

'The tears welled up in my eyes, and I stuck my head under the pillow and pulled the covers over it. I cried silently, but oh so bitterly, so much that my body racked with pain.

'A young student nurse heard my sobbing and came over to me. She took the covers off my face and started wiping my tears. She told me how lonely she was, having to work that day and not being able to be with her family. She asked me whether I would have dinner with her. She brought two trays of food: sliced turkey, mashed potatoes, cranberry sauce and ice cream for dessert. She talked to me and tried to calm my fears. Even though she was scheduled to go off duty at 4 p.m., she stayed on her own time until almost 11 p.m. She played games with me, talked to me and stayed with me until I finally fell asleep.

'Many Thanksgivings have come and gone since I was ten, but one never passes without me remembering that particular one and my feelings of frustration, fear, loneliness and the warmth and tenderness of the stranger that somehow made it all bearable.'

If you want others to like you, if you want to develop real friendships, if you want to help others at the same time as you help yourself, keep this principle in mind;

PRINCIPLE 1

Become genuinely interested in other people.

☐ 2 ☐

A simple way to make a good first impression

At a dinner party in New York, one of the guests, a woman who had inherited money, was eager to make a pleasing impression on everyone. She had squandered a modest fortune on sables, diamonds and pearls. But she hadn't done anything whatever about her face. It radiated sourness and selfishness. She didn't realize what everyone knows: namely, that the expression one wears on one's face is far more important than the clothes one wears on one's back.

Charles Schwab told me his smile had been worth a million dollars. And he was probably understating the truth. For Schwab's personality, his charm, his ability to make people like him, were almost wholly responsible for his extraordinary success; and one of the most delightful factors in his personality was his captivating smile.

Actions speak louder than words, and a smile says, 'I like you. You make me happy. I am glad to see you.'

That is why dogs make such a hit. They are so glad to see us that they almost jump out of their skins. So, naturally, we are glad to see them.

A baby's smile has the same effect.

Have you ever been in a doctor's waiting room and looked around at all the glum faces waiting impatiently to be seen? Dr. Stephen K. Sproul, a veterinarian in Raytown, Missouri, told of a typical spring day when his waiting room was full of clients waiting to have their pets inoculated. No one was talking to anyone else, and all were probably thinking of a dozen other things they would rather be doing than 'wasting time' sitting in that office. He told one of our classes: 'There were six or seven clients waiting when a young woman came in with a nine-month-old baby and a kitten. As luck would have it, she sat down next to a gentleman who was more than a little distraught about the long wait for service. The next thing he knew, the baby just looked up at him with that great big smile that is so characteristic of babies. What did that gentleman do? Just what you and I would do, of course; he smiled back at the baby. Soon he struck up a conversation with the woman about her baby and his grandchildren, and soon the entire reception room joined in, and the boredom and tension were converted into a pleasant and enjoyable experience.'

An insincere grin? No. That doesn't fool anybody. We know it is mechanical and we resent it. I am talking about a real smile, a heartwarming smile, a smile that comes from within, the kind of smile that will bring a good price in the marketplace.

Professor James V. McConnell, a psychologist at the University of Michigan, expressed his feelings about a smile. 'People who smile,' he said, 'tend to manage, teach and sell more effectively, and to raise happier children. There's far more information in a smile than a frown. That's why encouragement is a much more effective teaching device than punishment.'

The employment manager of a large New York department store told me she would rather hire a sales clerk who hadn't finished grade school, if he or she has a pleasant smile, than to hire a doctor of philosophy with a sombre face.

The effect of a smile is powerful – even when it is unseen. Telephone companies throughout the United States have a programme called 'phone power' which is offered to employers who use the telephone for selling their services or products. In this programme they suggest that you smile when talking on the phone. Your 'smile' comes through in your voice.

Robert Cryer, manager of a computer department for a Cincinnati, Ohio, company, told how he had successfully found the right applicant for a hard-to-fill position:

'I was desperately trying to recruit a Ph.D. in computer science for my department. I finally located a young man with ideal qualifications who was about to be graduated from Purdue University. After several phone conversations I learned that he had several offers from other companies, many of them larger and better known than mine. I was delighted when he accepted my offer. After he started on the job, I asked him why he had chosen us over the others. He paused for a moment and then he said: "I think it was because managers in the other companies spoke on the phone in a cold, businesslike manner, which made me feel like just another business transaction. Your voice sounded as if you were glad to hear from me . . . that you really wanted me to be part of your organization." You can be assured, I am still answering my phone with a smile.'

The chairman of the board of directors of one of the largest rubber companies in the United States told me that, according to his observations, people rarely succeed at anything unless they have fun doing it. This industrial leader doesn't put much faith in the old adage that hard work alone is the magic key that will unlock the door to our desires. 'I have known people,' he said, 'who succeeded because they had a rip-roaring good time conducting their business. Later, I saw those people change as the fun became work. The business had grown dull. They lost all joy in it, and they failed.'

You must have a good time meeting people if you expect them to have a good time meeting you.

I have asked thousands of business people to smile at someone every hour of the day for a week and then come to class and talk about the results. How did it work? Let's see . . . Here is a letter from William B. Steinhardt, a New York stockbroker. His case isn't isolated. In fact, it is typical of hundreds of cases.

'I have been married for over eighteen years,' wrote Mr. Steinhardt, 'and in all that time I seldom smiled at my wife or spoke two dozen words to her from the time I got up until I was ready to leave for business. I was one of the worst grouches who ever walked down Broadway.

'When you asked me to make a talk about my experience with smiles, I thought I would try it for a week. So the next morning, while combing my hair, I looked at my glum mug in the mirror and said to myself, "Bill, you are going to wipe the scowl off that sour puss of yours today. You are going to smile. And you are going to begin right now." As I sat down to breakfast, I greeted my wife with a "Good morning, my dear," and smiled as I said it.

'You warned me that she might be surprised. Well, you underestimated her reaction. She was bewildered. She was shocked. I told her that in the future she could expect this as a regular occurrence, and I kept it up every morning.

'This changed attitude of mine brought more happiness into our home in the two months since I started than there was during the last year.

'As I leave for my office, I greet the elevator operator in the apartment house with a "Good morning" and a smile. I greet the doorman with a smile. I smile at the cashier in the subway booth when I ask for change. As I stand on the floor of the Stock Exchange, I smile at people who until recently never saw me smile.

'I soon found that everybody was smiling back at me. I treat those who come to me with complaints or grievances in a cheerful manner. I smile as I listen to them and I find that adjustments are accomplished much easier. I find that smiles are bringing me dollars, many dollars every day.

'I share my office with another broker. One of his clerks is a likeable young chap, and I was so elated about the results I was getting that I told him recently about my new philosophy of human relations. He then confessed that when I first came to share my office with his firm he thought me a terrible grouch – and only recently changed his mind. He said I was really human when I smiled.

'I have also eliminated criticism from my system. I give appreciation and praise now instead of condemnation. I have stopped talking about what I want. I am now trying to see the other person's viewpoint. And these things have literally revolutionized my life. I am a totally different man, a happier man, a richer man, richer in friendships and happiness – the only things that matter much after all.'

You don't feel like smiling? Then what? Two things. First, force yourself to smile. If you are alone, force yourself to whistle or hum a tune or sing. Act as if you were already happy, and that will tend to make you happy. Here is the way the psychologist and philosopher William James put it:

'Action seems to follow feeling, but really action and feeling go together, and by regulating the action, which is under the more direct control of the will, we can directly regulate the feeling, which is not.

'Thus the sovereign voluntary path to cheerfulness, if our cheerfulness be lost, is to sit up cheerfully and to act and speak as if cheerfulness were already there . . .'

Everybody in the world is seeking happiness – and there is one sure way to find it. That is by controlling your thoughts. Happiness doesn't depend on outward conditions. It depends on inner conditions.

It isn't what you have or who you are or where you are or what you are doing that makes you happy or unhappy. It is what you think about it. For example, two people may be in the same place, doing the same thing; both may have about an equal amount of money and prestige – and yet one may be miserable and the other happy. Why? Because of a different mental attitude. I have seen just as many happy faces among the poor peasants toiling with their primitive tools in the devastating heat of the tropics as I have seen in air-conditioned offices in New York, Chicago or Los Angeles.

'There is nothing either good or bad,' said Shakespeare, 'but thinking makes it so.'

Abe Lincoln once remarked that 'most folks are about as happy as they make up their minds to be.' He was right. I saw a vivid illustration of that truth as I was walking up the stairs of the Long Island Railroad station in New York. Directly in front of me thirty or forty crippled boys on canes and crutches were struggling up the stairs. One boy had to be carried up. I was astonished at their laughter and gaiety. I spoke about it to one of the men in charge of the boys. 'Oh, yes,' he said, 'when a boy realizes that he is going to be a cripple for life, he is shocked at first; but after he gets over the shock, he usually resigns himself to his fate and then becomes as happy as normal boys.'

I felt like taking my hat off to those boys. They taught me a lesson I hope I shall never forget.

Working all by oneself in a closed-off room in an office not only is lonely, but it denies one the opportunity of making friends with other employees in the company. Señora Maria Gonzalez of Guadalajara, Mexico, had such a job. She envied the shared comradeship of other people in the company as she heard their chatter and laughter. As she passed them in the hall during the first weeks of her employment, she shyly looked the other way.

After a few weeks, she said to herself, 'Maria, you can't expect those women to come to you. You have to go out and meet them.' The next time she walked to the water cooler, she put on her brightest smile and said, 'Hi, how are you today' to each of the people she met. The effect was immediate. Smiles and hellos were returned, the hallway seemed brighter, the job friendlier. Acquaintanceships developed and some ripened into friendships. Her job and her life became more pleasant and interesting.

Peruse this bit of sage advice from the essayist and publisher Elbert Hubbard – but remember, perusing it won't do you any good unless you apply it:

Whenever you go out-of-doors, draw the chin in, carry the crown of the head high, and fill the lungs to the utmost; drink in the sunshine; greet your friends with a smile, and put soul into every handclasp. Do not fear being misunderstood and do not waste a minute thinking about your enemies. Try to fix firmly in your mind what you would like to do; and then, without veering off direction, you will move straight to the goal. Keep your mind on the great and splendid things you would like to do, and then, as the days go gliding away, you will find yourself unconsciously seizing upon the opportunities that are required for the fulfillment of your desire, just as the coral insect takes from the running tide the element it needs. Picture in your mind the able, earnest, useful person you desire to be, and the thought you hold is hourly transforming you into that particular individual . . . Thought is supreme. Preserve a right mental attitude – the attitude of courage, frankness, and good cheer. To think rightly is to create. All things come through desire and every sincere prayer is answered. We become like that on which our hearts are fixed. Carry your chin in and the crown of your head high. We are gods in the chrysalis.

The ancient Chinese were a wise lot – wise in the ways of the world; and they had a proverb that you and I ought to cut out and paste inside our hats. It goes like this: 'A man without a smiling face must not open a shop.'

Your smile is a messenger of your good will. Your smile brightens the lives of all who see it. To someone who has seen a dozen people frown, scowl or turn their faces away, your smile is like the sun breaking through the clouds. Especially when that someone is under pressure from his bosses, his customers, his teachers or parents or children, a smile can help him realize that all is not hopeless – that there is joy in the world.

Some years ago, a department store in New York City, in recognition of the pressures its sales clerks were under during the Christmas rush, presented the readers of its advertisements with the following homely philosophy:

THE VALUE OF A SMILE AT CHRISTMAS

It costs nothing, but creates much.

It enriches those who receive, without impoverishing those who give.

It happens in a flash and the memory of its sometimes lasts forever.

None are so rich they can get along without it, and none so poor but are richer for its benefits.

It creates happiness in the home, fosters good will in a business, and is the countersign of friends.

It is rest to the weary, daylight to the discouraged, sunshine to the sad, and Nature's best antidote for trouble.

Yet it cannot be bought, begged, borrowed, or stolen, for it is something that is no earthly good to anybody till it is given away.

And if in the last-minute rush of Christmas buying some of our salespeople should be too tired to give you a smile, may we ask you to leave one of yours?

For nobody needs a smile so much as those who have none left to give!

PRINCIPLE 2

Smile.

□ **3** □

If you don't do this, you are headed for trouble

Back in 1898, a tragic thing happened in Rockland County, New York. A child had died, and on this particular day the neighbours were preparing to go to the funeral. Jim Farley went out to the barn to hitch up his horse. The ground was covered with snow, the air was cold and snappy; the horse hadn't been exercised for days, and as he was led out to the watering trough, he wheeled playfully, kicked both his heels high in the air, and killed Jim Farley. So the little village of Stony Point had two funerals that week instead of one.

Jim Farley left behind him a widow and three boys, and a few hundred dollars in insurance.

His oldest boy, Jim, was ten, and he went to work in a brickyard, wheeling sand and pouring it into the moulds and turning the brick on edge to be dried by the sun. This boy Jim never had a chance to get much education. But with his natural geniality, he had a flair for making people like him, so he went into politics, and as the years went by, he developed an uncanny ability for remembering people's names.

He never saw the inside of a high school; but before he was forty-six years of age, four colleges had honoured him with degrees and he had become chairman of the Democratic National Committee and Postmaster General of the United States.

I once interviewed Jim Farley and asked him the secret of his success. He said, 'Hard work,' and I said, 'Don't be funny.'

He then asked me what I thought was the reason for his success. I replied: 'I understand you can call ten thousand people by their first names.'

'No. You are wrong,' he said. 'I can call fifty thousand people by their first names.'

Make no mistake about it. That ability helped Mr. Farley put Franklin D. Roosevelt in the White House when he managed Roosevelt's campaign in 1932.

During the years that Jim Farley travelled as a salesman for a gypsum concern, and during the years that he held office as town clerk in Stony Point, he built up a system for remembering names.

In the beginning, it was a very simple one. Whenever he met a new acquaintance, he found out his or her complete name and some facts about his or her family, business and political opinions. He fixed all these facts well in mind as part of the picture, and the next time he met that person, even if it was a year later, he was able to shake hands, inquire after the family, and ask about the hollyhocks in the backyard. No wonder he developed a following!

For months before Roosevelt's campaign for President began, Jim Farley wrote hundreds of letters a day to people all over the western and northwestern states. Then he hopped onto a train and in nineteen days covered twenty states and twelve thousand miles, travelling by buggy, train, automobile and boat. He would drop into town, meet his people at lunch or breakfast, tea or dinner, and give them a 'heart-to-heart talk'. Then he'd dash off again on another leg of his journey.

As soon as he arrived back East, he wrote to one person in each town he had visited, asking for a list of all the guests to whom he had talked. The final list contained thousands and thousands of names: yet each person on that list was paid the subtle flattery of getting a personal letter from James Farley. These letters began 'Dear Bill' or 'Dear Jane', and they were always signed 'Jim'.

Jim Farley discovered early in life that the average person is more interested in his or her own name than in all the other names on earth put together. Remember that name and call it easily, and you have paid a subtle and very effective compliment. But forget it or misspell it – and you have placed yourself at a sharp disadvantage. For example, I once organized a public-speaking course in Paris and sent form letters to all the American residents in the city. French typists with apparently little knowledge of English filled in the names and naturally they made blunders. One man, the manager of a large American bank in Paris, wrote me a scathing rebuke because his name had been misspelled.

Sometimes it is difficult to remember a name, particularly if it is hard to pronounce. Rather than even try to learn it, many people ignore it or call the person by an easy nickname. Sid Levy called on a customer for some time whose name was Nicodemus Papadoulos. Most people just called him 'Nick'. Levy told us: 'I made a special effort to say his name over several times to myself before I made my call. When I greeted him by his full name: "Good afternoon, Mr. Nicodemus Papadoulos," he was shocked. For what seemed like several minutes there was no reply from him at all. Finally, he said with tears rolling down his cheeks, "Mr Levy, in all the fifteen years I have been in this country, nobody has ever made the effort to call me by my right name." '

What was the reason for Andrew Carnegie's success?

He was called the Steel King; yet he himself knew little about the manufacture of steel. He had hundreds of people working for him who knew far more about steel than he did.

But he knew how to handle people, and that is what made him rich. Early in life, he showed a flair for organization, a genius for leadership. By the time he was ten, he too had discovered the astounding importance people place on their own name. And he used that discovery to win cooperation. To illustrate: when he was a boy back in Scotland, he got hold of a rabbit, a mother rabbit. Presto! He soon had a whole nest of little rabbits – and nothing to feed them. But he had a brilliant idea. He told the boys and girls in the neighbourhood that if they would go out and pull enough clover and dandelions to feed the rabbits, he would name the bunnies in their honour.

The plan worked like magic, and Carnegie never forgot it.

Years later, he made millions by using the same psychology in business. For example, he wanted to sell steel rails to the Pennsylvania Railroad. J. Edgar Thomson was the president of the Pennsylvania Railroad then. So Andrew Carnegie built a huge steel mill in Pittsburgh and called it the 'Edgar Thomson Steel Works.'

Here is a riddle. See if you can guess it. When the Pennsylvania Railroad needed steel rails, where do you suppose J. Edgar Thomson bought them? . . . From Sears, Roebuck? No. No. You're wrong. Guess again.

When Carnegie and George Pullman were battling each other for supremacy in the railroad sleeping-car business, the Steel King again remembered the lesson of the rabbits.

The Central Transportation Company, which Andrew Carnegie controlled, was fighting with the company that Pullman owned. Both were struggling to get the sleeping-car business of the Union Pacific Railroad, bucking each other, slashing prices, and destroying all chance of profit. Both Carnegie and Pullman had gone to New York to see the board of directors of the Union Pacific. Meeting one evening in the St. Nicholas Hotel, Carnegie said: 'Good evening, Mr. Pullman, aren't we making a couple of fools of ourselves?'

'What do you mean?' Pullman demanded.

Then Carnegie expressed what he had on his mind – a merger of their two interests. He pictured in glowing terms the mutual advantages of working with, instead of against, each other. Pullman listened attentively, but he was not wholly convinced. Finally he asked, 'What would you call the new company?' and Carnegie replied promptly: 'Why, the Pullman Palace Car Company, of course.'

Pullman's face brightened. 'Come into my room,' he said. 'Let's talk it over.' That talk made industrial history.

This policy of remembering and honouring the names of his friends and business associates was one of the secrets of Andrew Carnegie's leadership. He was proud of the fact that he could call many of his factory workers by their first names, and he boasted that while he was personally in charge, no strike ever disturbed his flaming steel mills.

Benton Love, chairman of Texas Commerce Bancshares, believes that the bigger a corporation gets, the colder it becomes. 'One way to warm it up,' he said, 'is to remember people's names. The executive who tells me he can't remember names is at the same time telling me he can't remember a significant part of his business and is operating on quicksand.'

Karen Kirsch of Rancho Palos Verdes, California, a flight attendant for TWA, made it a practice to learn the names of as many passengers in her cabin as possible and use the name when serving them. This resulted in many compliments on her service expressed both to her directly and to the airline. One passenger wrote: 'I haven't flown TWA for some time, but I'm going to start flying nothing but TWA from now on. You make me feel that your airline has become a very personalized airline and that is important to me.'

People are so proud of their names that they strive to perpetuate them at any cost. Even blustering, hard-boiled old P. T. Barnum, the greatest showman of his time, disappointed because he had no sons to carry on his name, offered his grandson, C. H. Seeley, $25,000 dollars if he would call himself 'Barnum' Seeley.

For many centuries, nobles and magnates supported artists, musicians and authors so that their creative works would be dedicated to them.

Libraries and museums owe their richest collections to people who cannot bear to think that their names might perish from the memory of the race. The

New York Public Library has its Astor and Lenox collections. The Metropolitan Museum perpetuates the names of Benjamin Altman and J. P. Morgan. And nearly every church is beautified by stained-glass windows commemorating the names of their donors. Many of the buildings on the campus of most universities bear the names of donors who contributed large sums of money for this honour.

Most people don't remember names, for the simple reason that they don't take the time and energy necessary to concentrate and repeat and fix names indelibly in their minds. They make excuses for themselves; they are too busy.

But they were probably no busier than Franklin D. Roosevelt, and he took time to remember and recall even the names of mechanics with whom he came into contact.

To illustrate: The Chrysler organization built a special car for Mr. Roosevelt, who could not use a standard car because his legs were paralyzed. W. F. Chamberlain and a mechanic delivered it to the White House. I have in front of me a letter from Mr. Chamberlain relating his experiences. 'I taught President Roosevelt how to handle a car with a lot of unusual gadgets, but he taught me a lot about the fine art of handling people.

'When I called at the White House,' Mr. Chamberlain writes, 'the President was extremely pleasant and cheerful. He called me by name, made me feel very comfortable, and particularly impressed me with the fact that he was vitally interested in things I had to show him and tell him. The car was so designed that it could be operated entirely by hand. A crowd gathered around to look at the car; and he remarked: "I think it is marvellous. All you have to do is to touch a button and it moves away and you can drive it without effort. I think it is grand – I don't know what makes it go. I'd love to have the time to tear it down and see how it works."

'When Roosevelt's friends and associates admired the machine, he said in their presence: "Mr. Chamberlain, I certainly appreciate all the time and effort you have spent in developing this car. It is a mighty fine job.' He admired the radiator, the special rear-vision mirror and clock, the special spotlight, the kind of upholstery, the sitting position of the driver's seat, the special suitcases in the trunk with his monogram on each suitcase. In other words, he took notice of every detail to which he knew I had given considerable thought. He made a point of bringing these various pieces of equipment to the attention of Mrs. Roosevelt, Miss Perkins, the Secretary of Labour, and his secretary. He even brought the old White House porter into the picture by saying, "George, you want to take particularly good care of the suitcases."

'When the driving lesson was finished, the President turned to me and said: "Well, Mr. Chamberlain, I have been keeping the Federal Reserve Board waiting thirty minutes. I guess I had better get back to work."

'I took a mechanic with me to the White House. He was introduced to Roosevelt when he arrived. He didn't talk to the President, and Roosevelt heard his name only once. He was a shy chap, and he kept in the background.

But before leaving us, the President looked for the mechanic, shook his hand, called him by name, and thanked him for coming to Washington. And there was nothing perfunctory about his thanks. He meant what he said. I could feel that.

'A few days after returning to New York, I got an autographed photograph of President Roosevelt and a little note of thanks again expressing his appreciation for my assistance. How he found time to do it is a mystery to me.'

Franklin D. Roosevelt knew that one of the simplest, most obvious and most important ways of gaining good will was by remembering names and making people feel important – yet how many of us do it?

Half the time we are introduced to a stranger, we chat a few minutes and can't even remember his or her name by the time we say goodbye.

One of the first lessons a politician learns is this: 'To recall a voter's name is statesmanship. To forget it is oblivion.'

And the ability to remember names is almost as important in business and social contacts as it is in politics.

Napoleon the Third, Emperor of France and nephew of the great Napoleon, boasted that in spite of all his royal duties he could remember the name of every person he met.

His technique? Simple. If he didn't hear the name distinctly, he said, 'So sorry. I didn't get the name clearly.' Then, if it was an unusual name, he would say, 'How is it spelled?'

During the conversation, he took the trouble to repeat the name several times, and tired to associate it in his mind with the person's features, expression and general appearance.

If the person was someone of importance, Napoleon went to even further pains. As soon as His Royal Highness was alone, he wrote the name down on a piece of paper, looked at it, concentrated on it, fixed it securely in his mind, and then tore up the paper. In this way, he gained an eye impression of the name as well as an ear impression.

All this takes time, but 'Good manners,' said Emerson, 'are made up of petty sacrifices.'

The importance of remembering and using names is not just the prerogative of kings and corporate executives. It works for all of us. Ken Nottingham, an employee of General Motors in Indiana, usually had lunch at the company cafeteria. He noticed that the woman who worked behind the counter always had a scowl on her face. 'She had been making sandwiches for about two hours and I was just another sandwich to her. I told her what I wanted. She weighed out the ham on a little scale, then she gave me one leaf of lettuce, a few potato chips and handed them to me.

'The next day I went through the same line. Same woman, same scowl. I smiled and said, "Hello, Eunice," and then told her what I wanted. Well, she forgot the scale, piled on the ham, gave me three leaves of lettuce and heaped on the potato chips until they fell of the plate.'

We should be aware of the *magic* contained in a name and realize that this single item is wholly and completely owned by the person with whom we are dealing ... and nobody else. The name sets the individual apart; it makes him or her unique among all others. The information we are imparting or the request we are making takes on a special importance when we approach the situation with the name of the individual. From the waitress to the senior executive, the name will work magic as we deal with others.

PRINCIPLE 3

Remember that a person's name is to that person the sweetest and most important sound in any language.

☐ 4 ☐

An easy way to become a good conversationalist

Some time ago, I attended a bridge party. I don't play bridge – and there was a woman there who didn't play bridge either. She had discovered that I had once been Lowell Thomas' manager before he went on the radio and that I had travelled in Europe a great deal while helping him prepare the illustrated travel talks he was then delivering. So she said: 'Oh, Mr. Carnegie, I do want you to tell me about all the wonderful places you have visited and the sights you have seen.'

As we sat down on the sofa, she remarked that she and her husband had recently returned from a trip to Africa. 'Africa!' I exclaimed. 'How interesting! I've always wanted to see Africa, but I never got there except for a twenty-four-hour stay once in Algiers. Tell me, did you visit the big-game country? Yes? How fortunate. I envy you. Do tell me about Africa.'

That kept her talking for forty-five minutes. She never again asked me where I had been or what I had seen. She didn't want to hear me talk about my travels. All she wanted was an interested listener, so she could expand her ego and tell about where she had been.

Was she unusual? No. Many people are like that.

For example, I met a distinguished botanist at a dinner party given by a New York book publisher. I had never talked with a botanist before, and I found him fascinating. I literally sat on the edge of my chair and listened while he spoke of exotic plants and experiments in developing new forms of plant life and indoor gardens (and even told me astonishing facts about the humble potato). I had a small indoor garden of my own – and he was good enough to tell me how to solve some of my problems.

As I said, we were at a dinner party. There must have been a dozen other guests, but I violated all the canons of courtesy, ignored everyone else, and talked for hours to the botanist.

Midnight came. I said good night to everyone and departed. The botanist then turned to our host and paid me several flattering compliments. I was 'most stimulating'. I was this and I was that, and he ended by saying I was a 'most interesting conversationalist'.

An interesting conversationalist? Why, I had said hardly anything at all. I couldn't have said anything if I had wanted to without changing the subject, for I didn't know any more about botany than I knew about the anatomy of a penguin. But I had done this: I had listened intently. I had listened because I was genuinely interested. And he felt it. Naturally that pleased him. That kind of listening is one of the highest compliments we can pay anyone. 'Few human begins,' wrote Jack Woodford in *Strangers in Love*, 'few human beings are proof against the implied flattery of rapt attention.' I went even further than giving him rapt attention. I was 'hearty in my approbation and lavish in my praise.'

I told him that I had been immensely entertained and instructed – and I had. I told him I wished I had his knowledge – and I did. I told him that I should love to wander the fields with him – and I have. I told him I must see him again – and I did.

And so I had him thinking of me as a good conversationalist when, in reality, I had been merely a good listener and had encouraged him to talk.

What is the secret, the mystery, of a successful business interview? Well, according to former Harvard president Charles W. Eliot, 'There is no mystery about successful business intercourse . . . Exclusive attention to the person who is speaking to you is very important. Nothing else is so flattering as that.'

Eliot himself was a past master of the art of listening. Henry James, one of America's first great novelists, recalled: 'Dr. Eliot's listening was not mere silence, but a form of activity. Sitting very erect on the end of his spine with hands joined in his lap, making no movement except that he revolved his thumbs around each other faster or slower, he faced his interlocutor and seemed to be hearing with his eyes as well as his ears. He listened with his mind and attentively considered what you had to say while you said it . . . At the end of an interview the person who had talked to him felt that he had had his say.'

Self-evident, isn't it? You don't have to study for four years in Harvard to discover that. Yet I know and you know department store owners who will rent expensive space, buy their goods economically, dress their windows appealingly, spend thousands of dollars in advertising and then hire clerks who haven't the sense to be good listeners – clerks who interrupt customers, contradict them, irritate them, and all but drive them from the store.

A department store in Chicago almost lost a regular customer who spent several thousand dollars each year in that store because a sales clerk wouldn't listen. Mrs Henrietta Douglas, who took our course in Chicago, had purchased a coat at a special sale. After she had brought it home she noticed that there was a tear in the lining. She came back the next day and asked the sales clerk to exchange it. The clerk refused even to listen to her complaint. 'You bought this at a special sale,' she said. She pointed to a sign on the wall. 'Read that,' she exclaimed. ' "*All sales are final.*" Once you bought it, you have to keep it. Sew up the lining yourself.'

'But this was damaged merchandise,' Mrs Douglas complained.

'Makes no difference,' the clerk interrupted. 'Final's final.'

Mrs Douglas was about to walk out indignantly, swearing never to return to that store ever, when she was greeted by the department manager, who knew her from her many years of patronage. Mrs Douglas told her what had happened.

The manager listened attentively to the whole story, examined the coat and then said: 'Special sales are "final" so we can dispose of merchandise at the end of the season. But this "no return" policy does not apply to damaged goods. We will certainly repair or replace the lining, or if you prefer, give you your money back.'

What a difference in treatment! If that manager had not come along and listened to the customer, a long-term patron of that store could have been lost forever.

Listening is just as important in one's home life as in the world of business. Millie Esposito of Croton-on-Hudson, New York, made it her business to listen carefully when one of her children wanted to speak with her. One evening she was sitting in the kitchen with her son, Robert, and after a brief discussion of something that was on his mind, Robert said: 'Mom, I know that you love me very much.'

Mrs. Esposito was touched and said: 'Of course I love you very much. Did you doubt it?'

Robert responded: 'No, but I really know you love me because whenever I want to talk to you about something you stop whatever you are doing and listen to me.'

The chronic kicker, even the most violent critic, will frequently soften and be subdued in the presence of a patient, sympathetic listener – a listener who will be silent while the irate fault-finder dilates like a king cobra and spews the poison out of his system. To illustrate: The New York Telephone Company discovered a few years ago that it had to deal with one of the most vicious customers who ever cursed a customer service representative. And he did curse. He raved. He threatened to tear the phone out by its roots. He refused to pay certain charges that he declared were false. He wrote letters to the newspapers. He filed innumerable complaints with the Public Service Commission, and he started several suits against the telephone company.

At last, one of the company's most skilful 'troubleshooters' was sent to interview this stormy petrel. This 'troubleshooter' listened and let the cantankerous customer enjoy himself pouring out his tirade. The telephone representative listened and said 'yes' and sympathized with his grievance.

'He raved on and I listened for nearly three hours,' the 'troubleshooter' said as he related his experiences before one of the author's classes. 'Then I went back and listened some more. I interviewed him four times, and before the fourth visit was over I had become a charter member of an organization he was starting. He called it the "Telephone Subscribers' Protective Association". I am still a member of this organization, and, so far as I know, I'm the only member in the world today besides Mr. —.

'I listened and sympathized with him on every point that he had made during these interviews. He had never had a telephone representative talk with him that way before, and he became almost friendly. The point on which I went to see him was not even mentioned on the first visit, nor was it mentioned on the second or third, but upon the fourth interview, I closed the case completely, he paid all his bills in full, and for the first time in the history of his difficulties with the telephone company he voluntarily withdrew his complaints from the Public Service Commission.'

Doubtless Mr. — had considered himself a holy crusader, defending the public rights against callous exploitation. But in reality what he had really wanted was a feeling of importance. He got this feeling of importance at first by kicking and complaining. But as soon as he got his feeling of importance from a representative of the company, his imagined grievances vanished into thin air.

One morning years ago, an angry customer stormed into the office of Julian F. Detmer, founder of the Detmer Woollen Company, which later became the world's largest distributor of woollens to the tailoring trade.

'This man owed us a small sum of money,' Mr. Detmer explained to me. 'The customer denied it, but we knew he was wrong. So our credit department had insisted that he pay. After getting a number of letters from our credit department, he packed his grip, made a trip to Chicago, and hurried into my office to inform me not only that he was not going to pay that bill, but that he was never going to buy another dollar's worth of goods from the Detmer Woollen Company.

'I listened patiently to all he had to say. I was tempted to interrupt, but I realized that would be bad policy. So I let him talk himself out. When he finally simmered down and got in a receptive mood, I said quietly: "I want to thank you for coming to Chicago to tell me about this. You have done me a great favour, for if our credit department has annoyed you, it may annoy other good customers, and that would be just too bad. Believe me, I am far more eager to hear this than you are to tell it."

'That was the last thing in the world he expected me to say. I think he was a trifle disappointed, because he had come to Chicago to tell me a thing or two, but here I was thanking him instead of scrapping with him. I assured him we would wipe the charge off the books and forget it, because he was a very careful man with only one account to look after, while our clerks had to look after thousands. Therefore, he was less likely to be wrong than we were.

'I told him that I understood exactly how he felt and that, if I were in his shoes, I should undoubtedly feel precisely as he did. Since he wasn't going to buy from us anymore, I recommended some other woollen houses.

'In the past, we had usually lunched together when he came to Chicago, so I invited him to have lunch with me this day. He accepted reluctantly, but when we came back to the office he placed a larger order than ever before. He returned home in a softened mood and, wanting to be just as fair with us as we had been with him, looked over his bills, found one had been mislaid, and sent us a cheque with his apologies.

'Later, when his wife presented him with a baby boy, he gave his son the middle name of Detmer, and he remained a friend and customer of the house until his death twenty-two years afterwards.'

Years ago, a poor Dutch immigrant boy washed the windows of a bakery shop after school to help support his family. His people were so poor that in addition he used to go out in the street with a basket every day and collect stray bits of coal that had fallen in the gutter where the coal wagons had delivered fuel. That boy, Edward Bok, never got more than six years of schooling in his life; yet eventually he made himself one of the most successful magazine editors in the history of American journalism. How did he do it? That is a long story, but how he got his start can be told briefly. He got his start by using the principles in this chapter.

He left school when he was thirteen, and became an office boy for Western Union, but he didn't for one moment give up the idea of an education. Instead, he started to educate himself. He saved his car fares and went without lunch until he had enough money to buy an encyclopaedia of American biography – and then he did an unheard-of thing. He read the lives of famous people and wrote them asking for additional information about their childhoods. He was a good listener. He asked famous people to tell him more about themselves. He wrote General James A. Garfield, who was then running for President, and asked if it was true that he was once a tow boy on a canal; and Garfield replied. He wrote General Grant asking about a certain battle, and Grant drew a map for him and invited this fourteen-year-old boy to dinner and spent the evening talking to him.

Soon our Western Union messenger boy was corresponding with many of the most famous people in the nation: Ralph Waldo Emerson, Oliver Wendell Holmes, Longfellow, Mrs. Abraham Lincoln, Louisa May Alcott, General Sherman and Jefferson Davis. Not only did he correspond with these distinguished people, but as soon as he got a vacation, he visited many of them as a welcome guest in their homes. This experience imbued him with a confidence that was invaluable. These men and women fired him with a vision and ambition that shaped his life. And all this, let me repeat, was made possible solely by the application of the principles we are discussing here.

Isaac F. Marcosson, a journalist who interviewed hundreds of celebrities, declared that many people fail to make a favourable impression because they don't listen attentively. 'They have been so much concerned with what they are going to say next that they do not keep their ears open . . . Very important people have told me that they prefer good listeners to good talkers, but the ability to listen seems rarer than almost any other good trait.'

And not only important personages crave a good listener, but ordinary folk do too. As the *Reader's Digest* once said: 'Many persons call a doctor when all they want is an audience.'

During the darkest hours of the Civil War, Lincoln wrote to an old friend in Springfield, Illinois, asking him to come to Washington. Lincoln said he had some problems he wanted to discuss with him. The old neighbour called at the White House, and Lincoln talked to him for hours about the advisability of issuing a proclamation freeing the slaves. Lincoln went over all the arguments for and against such a move, and then read letters and newspaper articles, some denouncing him for not freeing the slaves and others denouncing him for fear he was going to free them. After talking for hours, Lincoln shook hands with his old neighbour, said good night, and sent him back to Illinois without even asking for his opinion. Lincoln had done all the talking himself. That seemed to clarify his mind. 'He seemed to feel easier after that talk,' the old friend said. Lincoln hadn't wanted advice. He had wanted merely a friendly, sympathetic listener to whom he could unburden himself. That's what we all want when we are in trouble. That is frequently all the irritated customer wants, and the dissatisfied employee or the hurt friend.

One of the great listeners of modern times was Sigmund Freud. A man who met Freud described his manner of listening. 'It struck me so forcibly that I shall never forget him. He had qualities which I had never seen in any other man. Never had I seen such concentrated attention. There was none of the piercing 'soul penetrating gaze' business. His eyes were mild and genial. His voice was low and kind. His gestures were few. But the attention he gave me, his appreciation of what I said, even when I said it badly, was extraordinary. *You've no idea what it meant to be listened to like that.'*

If you want to know how to make people shun you and laugh at you behind your back and even despise you, here is the recipe: Never listen to anyone for long. Talk incessantly about yourself. If you have an idea while the other person is talking, don't wait for him or her to finish: bust right in and interrupt in the middle of a sentence.

Do you know people like that? I do, unfortunately; and the astonishing part of it is that some of them are prominent.

Bores, that is all they are – bores intoxicated with their own egos, drunk with a sense of their own importance.

People who talk only of themselves think only of themselves. And 'those people who think only of themselves,' Dr. Nicholas Murray Butler, longtime president of Columbia University, said, 'are hopelessly uneducated. They are not educated,' said Dr. Butler, 'no matter how instructed they may be.'

So if you aspire to be a good conversationalist, be an attentive listener. To be interesting, be interested. Ask questions that other persons will enjoy answering. Encourage them to talk about themselves and their accomplishments.

Remember that the people you are talking to are a hundred times more interested in themselves and their wants and problems than they are in you and your problems. A person's toothache means more to that person than a famine in China which kills a million people. A boil on one's neck interests one more than forty earthquakes in Africa. Think of that the next time you start a conversation.

PRINCIPLE 4

Be a good listener. Encourage others to talk about themselves.

□ **5** □

How to interest people

Everyone who was ever a guest of Theodore Roosevelt was astonished at the range and diversity of his knowledge. Whether his visitor was a cowboy or a Rough Rider, a New York politician or a diplomat, Roosevelt knew what to say. And how was it done? The answer was simple. Whenever Roosevelt expected a visitor, he sat up late the night before, reading up on the subject in which he knew his guest was particularly interested.

For Roosevelt knew, as all leaders know, that the royal road to a person's heart is to talk about the things he or she treasures most.

The genial William Lyon Phelps, essayist and professor of literature at Yale, learned this lesson early in life.

'When I was eight years old and was spending a weekend visiting my Aunt Libby Linsley at her home in Stratford on the Housatonic,' he wrote in his essay on *Human Nature*, 'a middle-aged man called one evening, and after a polite skirmish with my aunt, he devoted his attention to me. At that time, I happened to be excited about boats, and the visitor discussed the subject in a way that seemed particularly interesting. After he left, I spoke of him with enthusiasm. What a man! My aunt informed me he was a New York lawyer, that he cared nothing whatever about boats – that he took not the slightest interest in the subject. 'But why then did he talk all the time about boats?'

' "Because he is a gentleman. He saw you were interested in boats, and he talked about the things he knew would interest and please you. He made himself agreeable." '

And William Lyon Phelps added: 'I never forgot my aunt's remark.'

As I write this chapter, I have before me a letter from Edward L. Chalif, who was active in Boy Scout work.

'One day I found I needed a favor,' wrote Mr. Chalif. 'A big Scout jamboree was coming off in Europe, and I wanted the president of one of the largest corporations in America to pay the expenses of one of my boys for the trip.

'Fortunately, just before I went to see this man, I heard that he had drawn a cheque for a million dollars, and that after it was cancelled, he had it framed.

'So the first thing I did when I entered his office was to ask to see the cheque. A cheque for a million dollars! I told him I never knew that anybody had ever written such a cheque, and that I wanted to tell my boys that I had actually seen a cheque for a million dollars. He gladly showed it to me; I admired it and asked him to tell me all about how it happened to be drawn.'

You notice, don't you, that Mr. Chalif didn't begin by talking about the Boy Scouts, or the jamboree in Europe, or what it was he wanted? He talked in terms of what interested the other man. Here's the result:

'Presently, the man I was interviewing said: "Oh, by the way, what was it you wanted to see me about?" So I told him.

'To my vast surprise,' Mr. Chalif continues, 'he not only granted immediately what I asked for, but much more. I had asked him to send only one boy to Europe, but he sent five boys and myself, gave me a letter of credit for a thousand dollars and told us to stay in Europe for seven weeks. He also gave me letters of introduction to his branch presidents, putting them at our service, and he himself met us in Paris and showed us the town. Since then, he has given jobs to some of the boys whose parents were in want, and he is still active in our group.

'Yet I know if I hadn't found out what he was interested in, and got him warmed up first, I wouldn't have found him one-tenth as easy to approach.'

Is this a valuable technique to use in business? Is it? Let's see. Take Henry G. Duvernoy of Duvernoy and Sons, a wholesale baking firm in New York.

Mr. Duvernoy had been trying to sell bread to a certain New York hotel. He had called on the manager every week for four years. He went to the same social affairs the manager attended. He even took rooms in the hotel and lived there in order to get the business. But he failed.

'Then,' said Mr. Duvernoy, 'after studying human relations, I resolved to change my tactics. I decided to find out what interested this man – what caught his enthusiasm.

'I discovered he belonged to a society of hotel executives called the Hotel Greeters of America. He not only belonged, but his bubbling enthusiasm had made him president of the organization, and the president of the International Greeters. No matter where its conventions were held, he would be there.

'So when I saw him the next day, I began talking about the Greeters. What a response I got. What a response! he talked to me for half an hour about the Greeters, his tones vibrant with enthusiasm. I could plainly see that this society was not only his hobby, it was the passion of his life. Before I left his office, he had "sold" me a membership in his organization.

'In the meantime, I had said nothing about bread. But a few days later, the steward of his hotel phoned me to come over with samples and prices.

' "I don't know what you did to the old boy," the steward greeted me, "but he sure is sold on you!"

'Think of it! I had been drumming at that man for four years – trying to get his business – and I'd still be drumming at him if I hadn't finally taken the trouble to find out what he was interested in, and what he enjoyed talking about.'

Edward E. Harriman of Hagerstown, Maryland, chose to live in the beautiful Cumberland valley of Maryland after he completed his military service. Unfortunately, at that time there were few jobs available in the area. A little research uncovered the fact that a number of companies in the area were either owned or controlled by an unusual business maverick, R. J. Funkhouser, whose rise from poverty to riches intrigued Mr. Harriman. However, he was known for being inaccessible to job seekers. Mr. Harriman wrote:

'I interviewed a number of people and found that his major interest was anchored in his drive for power and money. Since he protected himself from people like me by use of a dedicated and stern secretary, I studied her interests and goals and only then I paid an unannounced visit at her office. She had been Mr. Funkhouser's orbiting satellite for about fifteen years. When I told her I had a proposition for him which might translate itself into financial and political success for him, she became enthused. I also conversed with her about her constructive participation in his success. After this conversation she arranged for me to meet Mr. Funkhouser.

'I entered his huge and impressive office determined not to ask directly for a job. He was seated behind a large carved desk and thundered at me, "How about it, young man?" I said, "Mr. Funkhouser, I believe I can make money for you." He immediately rose and invited me to sit in one of the large upholstered chairs. I enumerated my ideas and the qualifications I had to realize these ideas, as well as how they would contribute to his personal success and that of his businesses.

' "R. J.", as he became known to me, hired me at once and for over twenty years I have grown in his enterprises and we both have prospered.'

Talking in terms of the other person's interests pays off for both parties. Howard Z. Herzig, a leader in the field of employee communications, has always followed this principle. When asked what reward he got from it, Mr. Herzig responded that he not only received a different reward from each person but that in general the reward had been an enlargement of his life each time he spoke to someone.

PRINCIPLE 5

Talk in terms of the other person's interests.

☐ 6 ☐

How to make people like you instantly

I was waiting in line to register a letter in the post office at Thirty-third Street and Eighth Avenue in New York. I noticed that the clerk appeared to be bored with the job – weighing envelopes, handing out stamps, making change, issuing receipts – the same monotonous grind year after year. So I said to myself: 'I am going to try to make that clerk like me. Obviously to make him like me, I must say something nice, not about myself, but about him. So I asked myself, "What is there about him that I can honestly admire?" ' That is sometimes a hard question to answer, especially with strangers; but, in this case, it happened to be easy. I instantly saw something I admired no end.

So while he was weighing my envelope, I remarked with enthusiasm: 'I wish I had your head of hair.'

He looked up, half-startled, his face beaming with smiles. 'Well, it isn't as good as it used to be,' he said modestly. I assured him that although it might have lost some of its pristine glory, nevertheless it was still magnificent. He was immensely pleased. We carried on a pleasant little conversation and the last thing he said to me was: 'Many people have admired my hair.'

I'll bet that person went to lunch that day walking on air. I'll bet he went home that night and told his wife about it. I'll bet he looked in the mirror and said: 'It is a beautiful head of hair.'

I told this story once in public and a man asked me afterwards: 'What did you want to get out of him?'

What was I trying to get out of him!!! What was I trying to get out of him!!!

If we are so contemptibly selfish that we can't radiate a little happiness and pass on a bit of honest appreciation without trying to get something out of the other person in return – if our souls are no bigger than sour crab apples, we shall meet with the failure we so richly deserve.

Oh yes, I did want something out of that chap. I wanted something priceless. And I got it. I got the feeling that I had done something for him without his being able to do anything whatever in return for me. That is a feeling that flows and sings in your memory long after the incident is past.

There is one all-important law of human conduct. If we obey that law, we shall almost never get into trouble. In fact, that law, if obeyed, will bring us countless friends and constant happiness. But the very instant we break the law, we shall get into endless trouble. The law is this: *Always make the other person feel important.* John Dewey, as we have already noted, said that the desire to be important is the deepest urge in human nature; and William James said: 'The deepest principle in human nature is the craving to be appreciated.' As I have already pointed out, it is this urge that differentiates us from the animals. It is this urge that has been responsible for civilization itself.

Philosophers have been speculating on the rules of human relationships for thousands of years, and out of all that speculation, there has evolved only one important precept. It is not new. It is as old as history. Zoroaster taught it to his followers in Persia twenty-five hundred years ago. Confucius preached it in China twenty-four centuries ago. Lao-tse, the founder of Taoism, taught it to his disciples in the Valley of the Han. Buddha preached it on the bank of the Holy Ganges five hundred years before Christ. The sacred books of Hinduism taught it among the stony hills of Judea nineteen centuries ago. Jesus summed it up in one thought – probably the most important rule in the world: 'Do unto others as you would have others do unto you.'

You want the approval of those with whom you come in contact. You want recognition of your true worth. You want a feeling that you are important in your little world. You don't want to listen to cheap, insincere flattery, but you do crave sincere appreciation. you want your friends and associates to be, as Charles Schwab put it, 'hearty in their approbation and lavish in their praise.' All of us want that.

So let's obey the Golden Rule, and give unto others what we would have others give unto us.

How? When? Where? The answer is: All the time, everywhere.

David G. Smith of Eau Claire, Wisconsin, told one of our classes how he handled a delicate situation where he was asked to take charge of the refreshment booth at a charity concert.

'The night of the concert I arrived at the park and found two elderly ladies in a very bad humour standing next to the refreshment stand. Apparently each thought that she was in charge of this project. As I stood there pondering what to do, one of the members of the sponsoring committee appeared and handed me a cash box and thanked me for taking over the project. She introduced Rose and Jane as my helpers and then ran off.

'A great silence ensued. Realizing that the cash box was a symbol of authority (of sorts), I gave the box to Rose and explained that I might not be able to keep the money straight and that if she took care of it I would feel better. I then suggested to Jane that she show two teenagers who had been assigned to refreshments how to operate the soda machine, and asked her to be responsible for that part of the project.

'The whole evening was very enjoyable with Rose happily counting the money, Jane supervising the teenagers, and me enjoying the concert.'

You don't have to wait until you are ambassador to France or chairman of the Clambake Committee of your lodge before you use this philosophy of appreciation. You can work magic with it almost every day.

If, for example, the waitress brings us mashed potatoes when we have ordered French fried, let's say, 'I'm sorry to trouble you, but I prefer the French fried.' She'll probably reply, 'No trouble at all' and will be glad to change the potatoes, because we have shown respect for her.

Little phrases such as 'I'm sorry to trouble you,' 'Would you be so kind as to—?' 'Won't you please?' 'Would you mind?' 'Thank you' – little courtesies like these oil the cogs of the monotonous grind of everyday life – and incidentally, they are the hallmark of good breeding.

Let's take another illustration. Hall Caine's novels – *The Christian, The Deemster, The Manxman*, among them – were all best-sellers in the early part of this century. Millions of people read his novels, countless millions. He was the son of a blacksmith. He never had more than eight years' schooling in his life; yet when he died he was the richest literary man of his time.

The story goes like this: Hall Caine loved sonnets and ballads; so he devoured all of Dante Gabriel Rossetti's poetry. He even wrote a lecture chanting the praises of Rossetti's artistic achievement – and sent a copy to Rossetti himself. Rossetti was delighted. 'Any young man who has such an exalted opinion of my ability,' Rossetti probably said to himself, 'must be brilliant.' So Rossetti invited this blacksmith's son to come to London and act as his secretary. That was the turning point in Hall Caine's life; for, in his new position, he met the literary artists of the day. Profiting by their advice and inspired by their encouragement, he launched upon a career that emblazoned his name across the sky.

His home, Greeba Castle, on the Isle of Man, became a Mecca for tourists from the far corners of the world, and he left a multimillion dollar estate. Yet – who knows – he might have died poor and unknown had he not written an essay expressing his admiration for a famous man.

Such is the power, the stupendous power, of sincere heartfelt appreciation.

Rossetti considered himself important. That is not strange. Almost everyone considers himself important, very important.

The life of many a person could probably be changed if only someone would make him feel important. Ronald J. Rowland, who is one of the instructors of our course in California, is also a teacher of arts and crafts. He wrote to us about a student named Chris in his beginning-crafts class:

> Chris was a very quiet, shy boy lacking in self-confidence, the kind of student that often does not receive the attention he deserves. I also teach an advanced class that had grown to be somewhat of a status symbol and a privilege for a student to have earned the right to be in it.
>
> On Wednesday, Chris was diligently working at his desk. I really felt there was a hidden fire deep inside him. I asked Chris if he would like to be in the advanced class. How I wish I could express the look in Chris's face, the emotions in that shy fourteen-year-old boy, trying to hold back his tears.
>
> 'Who me, Mr. Rowland? Am I good enough?'
>
> 'Yes, Chris, you are good enough.'
>
> I had to leave at that point because tears were coming to my eyes. As Chris walked out of class that day, seemingly two inches taller, he looked at me with bright blue eyes and said in a positive voice, 'Thank you, Mr. Rowland.'
>
> Chris taught me a lesson I will never forget – our deep desire to feel important. To help me never forget this rule, I made a sign which reads 'YOU ARE IMPORTANT.' This sign hangs in the front of the classroom for all to see and to remind me that each student I face is equally important.

The unvarnished truth is that almost all the people you meet feel themselves superior to you in some way, and a sure way to their hearts is to let them realize in some subtle way that you realize their importance, and recognize it sincerely.

Remember what Emerson said: 'Every man I meet is my superior in some way. In that, I learn of him.'

And the pathetic part of it is that frequently those who have the least justification for a feeling of achievement bolster up their egos by a show of tumult and conceit which is truly nauseating. As Shakespeare put it:

'. . . man, proud man, /Drest in a little brief authority,/ . . . Plays such fantastic tricks before high heaven/As make the angels weep.'

I am going to tell you how business people in my own courses have applied these principles with remarkable results. Let's take the case of a Connecticut attorney (because of his relatives he prefers not to have his name mentioned).

Shortly after joining the course, Mr. R — drove to Long Island with his wife to visit some of her relatives. She left him to chat with an old aunt of hers and then rushed off by herself to visit some of the younger relatives. Since he soon had to give a speech professionally on how he applied the principles of appreciation, he thought he would gain some worthwhile experience talking with the elderly lady. So he looked around the house to see what he could honestly admire.

'This house was built about 1890, wasn't it?' he inquired.

'Yes,' she replied, 'that is precisely the year it was built.'

'It reminds me of the house I was born in,' he said. 'It's beautiful. Well built. Roomy. You know, they don't build houses like this anymore.'

'You're right,' the old lady agreed. 'The young folks nowadays don't care for beautiful homes. All they want is a small apartment, and then they go gadding about in their automobiles.

'This is a dream house,' she said in a voice vibrating with tender memories. 'This house was built with love. My husband and I dreamed about it for years before we built it. We didn't have an architect. We planned it all ourselves.;

She showed Mr. R. — about the house, and he expressed his hearty admiration for the beautiful treasures she had picked up in her travels and cherished over a lifetime – paisley shawls, an old English tea set, Wedgwood china, French beds and chairs, Italian paintings, and silk draperies that had once hung in a French château.

After showing Mr. R. — through the house, she took him out to the garage. There, jacked up on blocks, was a Packard car – in mint condition.

'My husband bought that car for me shortly before he passed on,' she said softly. 'I have never ridden in it since his death . . . You appreciate nice things, and I'm going to give this car to you.'

'Why, aunty,' he said, 'you overwhelm me. I appreciate your generosity, of course; but I couldn't possibly accept it. I'm not even a relative of yours. I have a new car, and you have many relatives that would like to have that Packard.'

'Relatives!' she exclaimed. 'Yes, I have relatives who are just waiting till I die so they can get that car. But they are not going to get it.'

'If you don't want to give it to them, you can very easily sell it to a secondhand dealer,' he told her.

'Sell it!' she cried. 'Do you think I would sell this car? Do you think I could stand to see strangers riding up and down the street in that car – that car that my husband bought for me? I wouldn't dream of selling it. I'm going to give it to you. You appreciate beautiful things.'

He tried to get out of accepting the car, but he couldn't without hurting her feelings.

This lady, left all alone in a big house with her paisley shawls, her French antiques, and her memories, was starving for a little recognition. She had once been young and beautiful and sought after. She had once built a house warm with love and had collected things from all over Europe to make it beautiful. Now, in the isolated loneliness of old age, she craved a little human warmth, a little genuine appreciation – and no one gave it to her. And when she found it, like a spring in the desert, her gratitude couldn't adequately express itself with anything less than the gift of her cherished Packard.

Let's take another case: Donald M. McMahon, who was superintendent of Lewis and Valentine, nurserymen and landscape architects in Rye, New York, related this incident:

'Shortly after I attended the talk on "How to Win Friends and Influence People", I was landscaping the estate of a famous attorney. The owner came out to give me a few instructions about where he wished to plant a mass of rhododendrons and azaleas.

'I said, "Judge, you have a lovely hobby. I've been admiring your beautiful dogs. I understand you win a lot of blue ribbons every year at the show in Madison Square Garden."

'The effect of this little expression of appreciation was striking.

' "Yes," the judge replied, "I do have a lot of fun with my dogs. Would you like to see my kennel?"

'He spent almost an hour showing me his dogs and the prizes they had won. He even brought out their pedigrees and explained about the bloodlines responsible for such beauty and intelligence.

'Finally, turning to me, he asked: "Do you have any small children?"

' "Yes, I do," I replied, "I have a son."

' "Well, wouldn't he like a puppy?" the judge inquired.

' "Oh, yes, he'd be tickled pink."

' "All right, I'm going to give him one," the judge announced.

'He started to tell me how to feed the puppy. Then he paused. "You'll forget it if I tell you. I'll write it out." So the judge went in the house, typed out the pedigree and feeding instructions, and gave me a puppy worth several hundred dollars and one hour and fifteen minutes of his valuable time largely because I had expressed my honest admiration for his hobby and achievements.'

George Eastman, of Kodak fame, invented the transparent film that made motion pictures possible, amassed a fortune of a hundred million dollars, and made himself ōne of the most famous businessmen on earth. Yet in spite of all these tremendous accomplishments, he craved little recognitions even as you and I.

To illustrate: When Eastman was building the Eastman School of Music and also Kilbourn Hall in Rochester, James Adamson, then president of the Superior Seating Company of New York, wanted to get the order to supply the theatre chairs for these buildings. Phoning the architect, Mr. Adamson made an appointment to see Mr. Eastman in Rochester.

When Adamson arrived, the architect said: 'I know you want to get this order, but I can tell you right now that you won't stand a ghost of a show if you take more than five minutes of George Eastman's time. He is a strict disciplinarian. He is very busy. So tell your story quickly and get out.'

Adamson was prepared to do just that.

When he was ushered into the room he saw Mr. Eastman bending over a pile of papers at his desk. Presently, Mr. Eastman looked up, removed his glasses, and walked toward the architect and Mr. Adamson, saying: 'Good morning gentlemen, what can I do for you?'

The architect introduced them, and then Mr. Adamson said: 'While we've been waiting for you, Mr. Eastman, I've been admiring your office. I wouldn't mind working in a room like this myself. I'm in the interior-woodworking-business, and I never saw a more beautiful office in all my life.'

George Eastman replied: 'You remind me of something I had almost forgotten. It is beautiful, isn't it? I enjoyed it a great deal when it was first built. But I come down here now with a lot of other things on my mind and sometimes don't even see the room for weeks at a time.'

Adamson walked over and rubbed his hand across a panel. 'This is English oak, isn't it? A little different texture from the Italian oak.'

'Yes,' Eastman replied. 'Imported English oak. It was selected for me by a friend who specializes in fine woods.'

Then Eastman showed him about the room, commenting on the proportions, the colouring, the hand carving and other effects he had helped to plan and execute.

While drifting about the room, admiring the woodwork, they paused before a window, and George Eastman, in his modest, soft-spoken way, pointed out some of the institutions through which he was trying to help humanity: the University of Rochester, the General Hospital, the Homoeopathic Hospital, the Friendly Home, the Children's Hospital. Mr. Adamson congratulated him warmly on the idealistic way he was using his wealth to alleviate the sufferings of humanity. Presently, George Eastman unlocked a glass case and pulled out the first camera he had ever owned – an invention he had bought from an Englishman.

Adamson questioned him at length about his early struggles to get started in business, and Mr. Eastman spoke with real feeling about the poverty of his childhood, telling how his widowed mother had kept a boarding house while he clerked in an insurance office. The terror of poverty haunted him day and night, and he resolved to make enough money so that his mother wouldn't have to work. Mr. Adamson drew him out with further questions and listened, absorbed, while he related the story of his experiments with dry photographic plates. He told how he had worked in an office all day, and sometimes experimented all night, taking only brief naps while the chemicals were working, sometimes working and sleeping in his clothes for seventy-two hours at a stretch.

James Adamson had been ushered into Eastman's office at ten-fifteen and had been warned that he must not take more than five minutes; but an hour had passed, then two hours passed. And they were still talking.

Finally, George Eastman turned to Adamson and said, 'The last time I was in Japan I bought some chairs, brought them home, and put them in my sun porch. But the sun peeled the paint, so I went downtown the other day and bought some paint and painted the chairs myself. Would you like to see what sort of job I can do painting chairs? All right. Come up to my home and have lunch with me and I'll show you.'

After lunch, Mr. Eastman showed Adamson the chairs he had brought from Japan. They weren't worth more than a few dollars, but George Eastman, now a multimillionaire, was proud of them because he himself had painted them.

The order for the seats amounted to $90,000. Who do you suppose got the order – James Adamson or one of his competitors?

From the time of this story until Mr. Eastman's death, he and James Adamson were close friends.

Claude Marais, a restaurant owner in Rouen, France, used this principle and saved his restaurant the loss of a key employee. This woman had been in his employ for five years and was a vital link between M. Marais and his staff of twenty-one people. He was shocked to receive a registered letter from her advising him of her resignation.

M. Marais reported: 'I was very surprised and, even more, disappointed, because I was under the impression that I had been fair to her and receptive to her needs. Inasmuch as she was a friend as well as an employee, I probably had taken her too much for granted and maybe was even more demanding of her than of other employees.

'I could not, of course, accept this resignation without some explanation. I took her aside and said, "Paulette, you must understand that I cannot accept your resignation. You mean a great deal to me and to this company, and you are as important to the success of this restaurant as I am." I repeated this in front of the entire staff, and I invited her to my home and reiterated my confidence in her with my family present.

'Paulette withdrew her resignation, and today I can rely on her as never before. I frequently reinforce this by expressing my appreciation for what she does and showing her how important she is to me and to the restaurant.'

'Talk to people about themselves,' said Disraeli, one of the shrewdest men who ever ruled the British Empire. 'Talk to people about themselves and they will listen for hours.'

Make the other person feel important – and do it sincerely.

PART TWO

☐ **IN A NUTSHELL** ☐

SIX WAYS TO MAKE PEOPLE LIKE YOU

PRINCIPLE 1

Become genuinely interested in other people.

PRINCIPLE 2

Smile.

PRINCIPLE 3

Remember that a person's name is to that person the sweetest
and most important sound in any language.

PRINCIPLE 4

Be a good listener. Encourage others to talk about themselves.

PRINCIPLE 5

Talk in terms of the other person's interests.

PRINCIPLE 6

Make the other person feel important – and do it sincerely.

Part Three

HOW TO WIN PEOPLE TO YOUR WAY

OF THINKING

□ 1 □

You can't win an argument

Shortly after the close of World War I, I learned an invaluable lesson one night in London. I was manager at the time for Sir Ross Smith. During the war, Sir Ross had been the Australian ace out in Palestine; and shortly after peace was declared, he astonished the world by flying halfway around it in thirty days. No such feat had ever been attempted before. It created a tremendous sensation. The Australian government awarded him fifty thousand dollars; the King of England knighted him; and, for a while, he was the most talked-about man under the Union Jack. I was attending a banquet one night given in Sir Ross's honour; and during the dinner, the man sitting next to me told a humorous story which hinged on the quotation 'There's a divinity that shapes our ends, rough-hew them how we will.'

The raconteur mentioned that the quotation was from the Bible. He was wrong. I knew that. I knew it positively. There couldn't be the slightest doubt about it. And so, to get a feeling of importance and display my superiority, I appointed myself as an unsolicited and unwelcome committee of one to correct him. He stuck to his guns. What? From Shakespeare? Impossible! Absurd! That quotation was from the Bible. And he knew it.

The storyteller was sitting on my right; and Frank Gammond, an old friend of mine, was seated at my left. Mr. Gammond had devoted years to the study of Shakespeare. So the storyteller and I agreed to submit the question to Mr. Gammond. Mr. Gammond listened, kicked me under the table, and then said: 'Dale, you are wrong. The gentleman is right. It *is* from the Bible.'

On our way home that night, I said to Mr. Gammond: 'Frank, you knew that quotation was from Shakespeare.'

'Yes, of course,' he replied, '*Hamlet*, Act Five, Scene Two. But we were guests at a festive occasion, my dear Dale. Why prove to a man he is wrong? Is that going to make him like you? Why not let him save his face? He didn't ask for your opinion. He didn't want it. Why argue with him? Always avoid the acute angle.' The man who said that taught me a lesson I'll never forget. I not only had made the storyteller uncomfortable, but had put my friend in an embarrassing situation. How much better it would have been had I not become argumentative.

It was a sorely needed lesson because I had been an inveterate arguer.

During my youth, I had argued with my brother about everything under the Milky Way. When I went to college, I studied logic and argumentation and went in for debating contests. Talk about being from Missouri, I was born there. I had to be shown. Later, I taught debating and argumentation in New York; and once, I am ashamed to admit, I planned to write a book on the subject. Since then, I have listened to, engaged in, and watched the effect of thousands of arguments. As a result of all this, I have come to the conclusion that there is only one way under high heaven to get the best of an argument – and that is to avoid it. Avoid it as you would avoid rattlesnakes and earthquakes.

Nine times out of ten, an argument ends with each of the contestants more firmly convinced than ever that he is absolutely right.

You can't win an argument. You can't because if you lose it, you lose it; and if you win it, you lose it. Why? Well, suppose you triumph over the other man and shoot his argument full of holes and prove that he is *non compos mentis*. Then what? You will feel fine. But what about him? You have made him feel inferior. You have hurt his pride. He will resent your triumph. And –

A man convinced against his will
Is of the same opinion still.

Years ago Patrick J. O'Haire joined one of my classes. He had had little education, and how he loved a scrap! He had once been a chauffeur, and he came to me because he had been trying, without much success, to sell trucks. A little questioning brought out the fact that he was continually scrapping with and antagonizing the very people he was trying to do business with. If a prospect said anything derogatory about the trucks he was selling, Pat saw red and was right at the customer's throat. Pat won a lot of arguments in those days. As he said to me afterward, 'I often walked out of an office saying: "I told that bird something." Sure I had told him something, but I hadn't sold him anything.'

My first problem was not to teach Patrick J. O'Haire to talk. My immediate task was to train him to refrain from talking and to avoid verbal fights.

Mr. O'Haire became one of the star salesmen for the White Motor Company in New York. How did he do it? Here is his story in his own words: 'If I walk into a buyer's office now and he says: "What? A White truck? They're no good! I wouldn't take one if you gave it to me. I'm going to buy the Whose-It truck," I say, "The Whose-It is a good truck. If you buy the Whose-It, you'll never make a mistake. The Whose-Its are made by a fine company and sold by good people."

'He is speechless then. There is no room for an argument. If he says the Whose-It is best and I say sure it is, he has to stop. He can't keep on all afternoon saying, "It's the best" when I'm agreeing with him. We then get off the subject of Whose-It and I begin to talk about the good points of the White truck.

'There was a time when a remark like his first one would have made me see scarlet and red and orange. I would start arguing against the Whose-It; and the more I argued against it, the more my prospect argued in favour of it; and the more he argued, the more he sold himself on my competitor's product.

'As I look back now I wonder how I was ever able to sell anything. I lost years of my life in scrapping and arguing. I keep my mouth shut now. It pays.'

As wise old Ben Franklin used to say:

If you argue and rankle and contradict, you may achieve a victory sometimes; but it will be an empty victory because you will never get your opponent's good will.

So figure it out for yourself. Which would you rather have, an academic, theatrical victory or a person's good will? You can seldom have both.

The Boston *Transcript* once printed this bit of significant doggerel:

Here lies the body of William Jay,
Who died maintaining his right of way –
He was right, dead right, as he sped along,
But he's just as dead as if he were wrong.

You may be right, dead right, as you speed along in your argument; but as far as changing another's mind is concerned, you will probably be just as futile as if you were wrong.

Frederick S. Parsons, an income tax consultant, had been disputing and wrangling for an hour with a government tax inspector. An item of nine thousand dollars was at stake. Mr. Parsons claimed that this nine thousand dollars was in reality a bad debt, that it would never be collected, that it ought not to be taxed. 'Bad debt, my eye!' retorted the inspector. 'It must be taxed.'

'This inspector was cold, arrogant and stubborn,' Mr. Parsons said as he told the story to the class. 'Reason was wasted and so were facts . . . The longer we argued, the more stubborn he became. So I decided to avoid argument, change the subject, and give him appreciation.

'I said, "I suppose this is a very petty matter in comparison with the really important and difficult decisions you're required to make. I've made a study of taxation myself. But I've had to get my knowledge from books. You are getting yours from the firing line of experience. I sometimes wish I had a job like yours. It would teach me a lot." I meant every word I said.

' "Well," The inspector straightened up in his chair, leaned back, and talked for a long time about his work, telling me of the clever frauds he had uncovered. His tone gradually became friendly, and presently he was telling me about his children. As he left, he advised me that he would consider my problem further and give me his decision in a few days.

'He called at my office three days later and informed me that he had decided to leave the tax return exactly as it was filed.'

This tax inspector was demonstrating one of the most common of human frailties. He wanted a feeling of importance; and as long as Mr. Parsons argued with him, he got his feeling of importance by loudly asserting his authority. But as soon as his importance was admitted and the argument stopped and he was permitted to expand his ego, he became a sympathetic and kindly human being.

Buddha said: 'Hatred is never ended by hatred but by love,' and a misunderstanding is never ended by an argument but by tact, diplomacy, conciliation and a sympathetic desire to see the other person's viewpoint.

Lincoln once reprimanded a young army officer for indulging in a violent controversy with an associate. 'No man who is resolved to make the most of himself,' said Lincoln, 'can spare time for personal contention. Still less can he afford to take the consequences, including the vitiation of his temper and the loss of self-control. Yield larger things to which you show no more than equal rights; and yield lesser ones though clearly your own. Better give your path to a dog than be bitten by him in contesting for the right. Even killing the dog would not cure the bite.'

In an article in *Bits and Pieces*,* some suggestions are made on how to keep a disagreement from becoming an argument:

> **Welcome the disagreement.** Remember the slogan, 'When two partners always agree, one of them is not necessary.' If there is some point you haven't thought about, be thankful if it is brought to your attention. Perhaps this disagreement is your opportunity to be corrected before you make a serious mistake.
>
> **Distrust your first instinctive impression.** Our first natural reaction in a disagreeable situation is to be defensive. Be careful. Keep calm and watch out for your first reaction. It may be you at your worst, not your best.
>
> **Control your temper.** Remember, you can measure the size of a person by what makes him or her angry.
>
> **Listen first.** Give your opponents a chance to talk. Let them finish. Do not resist, defend or debate. This only raises barriers. Try to build bridges of understanding. Don't build higher barriers of misunderstanding.
>
> **Look for areas of agreement.** When you have heard your opponents out, dwell first on the points and areas on which you agree.

---

* *Bits and Pieces*, published by The Economics Press, Fairfield, N.J.

Be honest. Look for areas where you can admit error and say so. Apologize for your mistakes. It will help disarm your opponents and reduce defensiveness.

Promise to think over your opponents' ideas and study them carefully. And mean it. Your opponents may be right. It is a lot easier at this stage to agree to think about their points than to move rapidly ahead and find yourself in a position where your opponents can say: 'We tried to tell you, but you wouldn't listen.'

Thank your opponents sincerely for their interest. Anyone who takes the time to disagree with you is interested in the same things you are. Think of them as people who really want to help you, and you may turn your opponents into friends.

Postpone action to give both sides time to think through the problem. Suggest that a new meeting be held later that day or the next day, when all the facts may be brought to bear. In preparation for this meeting, ask yourself some hard questions:

Could my opponents be right? Partly right? Is there truth or merit in their position or argument? Is my reaction one that will relieve the problem, or will it just relieve any frustration? Will my reaction drive my opponents further away or draw them closer to me? Will my reaction elevate the estimation good people have of me? Will I win or lose? What price will I have to pay if I win? If I am quiet about it, will the disagreement blow over? Is this difficult situation an opportunity for me?

Opera tenor Jan Peerce, after he was married nearly fifty years, once said: 'My wife and I made a pact a long time ago, and we've kept it no matter how angry we've grown with each other. When one yells, the other should listen – because when two people yell, there is no communication, just noise and bad vibrations.'

PRINCIPLE 1

The only way to get the best of an argument is to avoid it.

□ **2** □

A sure way of making enemies – and how
to avoid it

When Theodore Roosevelt was in the White House, he confessed that if he could be right 75 percent of the time, he would reach the highest measure of his expectation.

If that was the highest rating that one of the most distinguished men of the twentieth century could hope to obtain, what about you and me?

If you can be sure of being right only 55 percent of the time, you can go down to Wall Street and make a million dollars a day. If you can't be sure of being right even 55 percent of the time, why should you tell other people they are wrong?

You can tell people they are wrong by a look or an intonation or a gesture just as eloquently as you can in words – and if you tell them they are wrong, do you make them want to agree with you? Never! For you have struck a direct blow at their intelligence, judgement, pride and self-respect. That will make them want to strike back. But it will never make them want to change their minds. You may then hurl at them all the logic of a Plato or an Immanuel Kant, but you will not alter their opinions, for you have hurt their feelings.

Never begin by announcing 'I am going to prove so-and-so to you.' That's bad. That's tantamount to saying: 'I'm smarter than you are. I'm going to tell you a thing or two and make you change your mind.'

That is a challenge. It arouses opposition and makes the listener want to battle with you before you even start.

It is difficult, under even the most benign conditions, to change people's minds. So why make it harder? Why handicap yourself?

If you are going to prove anything, don't let anybody know it. Do it so subtly, so adroitly, that no one will feel that you are doing it. This was expressed succinctly by Alexander Pope:

> Men must be taught as if you taught them not
> And things unknown proposed as things forgot.

Over three hundred years ago Galileo said:

You cannot teach a man anything; you can only help him to find it within himself.

As Lord Chesterfield said to his son:

Be wiser than other people if you can; but do not tell them so.

Socrates said repeatedly to his followers in Athens:

One thing only I know, and that is that I know nothing.

Well, I can't hope to be any smarter than Socrates, so I have quit telling people they are wrong. And I find that it pays.

If a person makes a statement that you think is wrong – yes, even that you know is wrong – isn't it better to begin by saying: 'Well, now, look. I thought otherwise but I may be wrong. I frequently am. And if I am wrong, I want to be put right. Let's examine the facts.'

There's magic, positive magic, in such phrases as: 'I may be wrong, I frequently am. Let's examine the facts.'

Nobody in the heavens above or on the earth beneath or in the waters under the earth will ever object to your saying: 'I may be wrong. Let's examine the facts.'

One of our class members who used this approach in dealing with customers was Harold Reinke, a Dodge dealer in Billings, Montana. He reported that because of the pressures of the automobile business, he was often hardboiled and callous when dealing with customers' complaints. This caused flared tempers, loss of business and general unpleasantness.

He told his class: 'Recognizing that this was getting me nowhere fast, I tried a new tack. I would say something like this: "Our dealership has made so many mistakes that I am frequently ashamed. We may have erred in your case. Tell me about it."

'This approach becomes quite disarming, and by the time the customer releases his feelings, he is usually much more reasonable when it comes to settling the matter. In fact, several customers have thanked me for having such an understanding attitude. And two of them have even brought in friends to buy new cars. In this highly competitive market, we need more of this type of customer, and I believe that showing respect for all customers' opinions and treating them diplomatically and courteously will help beat the competition.'

You will never get into trouble by admitting that you may be wrong. That will stop all argument and inspire your opponent to be just as fair and open and broad-minded as you are. It will make him want to admit that he, too, may be wrong.

If you know positively that a person is wrong, and you bluntly tell him or her so, what happens? Let me illustrate. Mr. S —, a young New York attorney, once argued a rather important case before the United States Supreme Court (*Lustgarten v. Fleet Corporation* 280 U.S. 320). The case involved a considerable sum of money and an important question of law. During the argument, one of the Supreme Court justices said to him: 'The statute of limitations in admiralty law is six years, is it not?'

Mr. S — stopped, stared at the Justice for a moment, and then said bluntly: 'Your Honour, there is no statute of limitations in admiralty.'

'A hush fell on the court,' said Mr. S — as he related his experience to one of the author's classes, 'and the temperature in the room seemed to drop to zero. I was right. Justice — was wrong. And I had told him so. But did that make him friendly? No. I still believe that I had the law on my side. And I know that I spoke better than I ever spoke before. But I didn't persuade. I made the enormous blunder of telling a very learned and famous man that he was wrong.'

Few people are logical. Most of us are prejudiced and biased. Most of us are blighted with preconceived notions, with jealousy, suspicion, fear, envy and pride. And most citizens don't want to change their minds about their religion or their haircut or communism or their favourite movie star. So, if you are inclined to tell people they are wrong, please read the following paragraph every morning before breakfast. It is from James Harvey Robinson's enlightening book *The Mind in the Making*.

We sometimes find ourselves changing our minds without any resistance or heavy emotion, but if we are told we are wrong, we resent the imputation and harden our hearts. We are incredibly heedless in the formation of our beliefs, but find ourselves filled with an illicit passion for them when anyone proposes to rob us of their companionship. It is obviously not the ideas themselves that are dear to us, but our self-esteem which is threatened ... The little word 'my' is the most important one in human affairs, and properly to reckon with it is the beginning of wisdom. It has the same force whether it is 'my' dinner, 'my' dog, and 'my' house, or 'my' father, 'my' country, and 'my' God. We not only resent the imputation that our watch is wrong, or our car shabby, but that our conception of the canals of Mars, of the pronunciations of 'Epictetus,' of the medicinal value of salicin, or of the date of Sargon I is subject to revision. We like to continue to believe what we have been accustomed to accept as true, and the resentment aroused when doubt is cast upon any of our assumptions leads us to seek every manner of excuse for clinging to it. The result is that most of our so-called reasoning consists in finding arguments for going on believing as we already do.

Carl Rogers, the eminent psychologist, wrote in his book *On Becoming a Person*:

I have found it of enormous value when I can permit myself to understand the other person. The way in which I have worded this statement may seem strange to you. Is it necessary to permit oneself to understand another? I think it is. Our first reaction to most of the statements (which we hear from other people) is an evaluation or judgment, rather than an understanding of it. When someone expresses some feeling, attitude or belief, our tendency is almost immediately to feel 'that's right,' or 'that's stupid,' 'that's abnormal,' 'that's unreasonable,' 'that's incorrect,' 'that's not nice.' Very rarely do we permit ourselves to *understand* precisely what the meaning of the statement is to the other person.*

I once employed an interior decorator to make some draperies for my home. When the bill arrived, I was dismayed.

A few days later, a friend dropped in and looked at the draperies. The price was mentioned, and she exclaimed with a note of triumph: 'What? That's awful. I am afraid he put one over on you.'

True? Yes, she had told the truth, but few people like to listen to truths that reflect on their judgement. So, being human, I tried to defend myself. I pointed out that the best is eventually the cheapest, that one can't expect to get quality and artistic taste at bargain-basement prices, and so on and on.

The next day another friend dropped in, admired the draperies, bubbled over with enthusiasm, and expressed a wish that she could afford such exquisite creations for her home. My reaction was totally different. 'Well, to tell the truth,' I said, 'I can't afford them myself. I paid too much. I'm sorry I ordered them.'

When we are wrong, we may admit it to ourselves. And if we are handled gently and tactfully, we may admit it to others and even take pride in our frankness and broadmindedness. But not if someone else is trying to ram the unpalatable fact down our oesophagus.

Horace Greeley, the most famous editor in America during the time of the Civil War, disagreed violently with Lincoln's policies. He believed that he could drive Lincoln into agreeing with him by a campaign of argument, ridicule and abuse. He waged this bitter campaign month after month, year after year. In fact, he wrote a brutal, bitter, sarcastic and personal attack on President Lincoln the night Booth shot him.

But did all this bitterness make Lincoln agree with Greeley? Not at all. Ridicule and abuse never do.

If you want some excellent suggestions about dealing with people and managing yourself and improving your personality, read Benjamin Franklin's autobiography – one of the most fascinating life stories ever written, one of the classics of American literature. Ben Franklin tells how he conquered the

---

* Adapted from Carl R. Rogers, *On Becoming a Person* (Boston: Houghton Mifflin, 1961), pp. 18ff.

iniquitous habit of argument and transformed himself into one of the most able, suave and diplomatic men in American history.

One day, when Ben Franklin was a blundering youth, an old Quaker friend took him aside and lashed him with a few stinging truths, something like this:

Ben, you are impossible. Your opinions have a slap in them for everyone who differs with you. They have become so offensive that nobody cares for them. Your friends find they enjoy themselves better when you are not around. You know so much that no man can tell you anything. Indeed, no man is going to try, for the effort would lead only to discomfort and hard work. So you are not likely ever to know any more than you do now, which is very little.

One of the finest things I know about Ben Franklin is the way he accepted that smarting rebuke. He was big enough and wise enough to realize that it was true, to sense that he was headed for failure and social disaster. So he made a right-about-face. He began immediately to change his insolent, opinionated ways.

'I made it a rule,' said Franklin, 'to forbear all direct contradiction to the sentiment of others, and all positive assertion of my own. I even forbade myself the use of every word or expression in the language that imported a fix'd opinion, such as "certainly," "undoubtedly," etc., and I adopted, instead of them, "I conceive," "I apprehend," or "I imagine" a thing to be so or so, or "it so appears to me at present." When another asserted something that I thought an error, I deny'd myself the pleasure of contradicting him abruptly, and of showing immediately some absurdity in his proposition: and in answering I began by observing that in certain cases or circumstances his opinion would be right, but in the present case there appear'd or seem'd to me some difference, etc. I soon found the advantage of this change in my manner; the conversations I engag'd in went on more pleasantly. The modest way in which I propos'd my opinions procur'd them a readier reception and less contradiction; I had less mortification when I was found to be in the wrong, and I more easily prevail'd with others to give up their mistakes and join with me when I happened to be in the right.

"And this mode, which I at first put on with some violence to natural inclination, became at length so easy, and so habitual to me, that perhaps for these fifty years past no one has ever heard a dogmatical expression escape me. And to this habit (after my character of integrity) I think it principally owing that I had earned so much weight with my fellow citizens when I proposed new institutions, or alterations in the old, and so much influence in public councils when I became a member; for I was but a bad speaker, never eloquent, subject to much hesitation in my choice of words, hardly correct in language, and yet I generally carried my points.'

How do Ben Franklin's methods work in business? Let's take two examples.

Katherine A. Allred of Kings Mountain, North Carolina, is an industrial engineering supervisor for a yarn-processing plant. She told one of our classes how she handled a sensitive problem before and after taking our training:

'Part of my responsibility,' she reported, 'deals with setting up and maintaining incentive systems and standards for our operators so they can make more money by producing more yarn. The system we were using had worked fine when we had only two or three different types of yarn, but recently we had expanded our inventory and capabilities to enable us to run more than twelve different varieties. The present system was no longer adequate to pay the operators fairly for the work being performed and give them an incentive to increase production. I had worked up a new system which would enable us to pay the operator by the class of yarn she was running at any one particular time. With my new system in hand, I entered the meeting determined to prove to the management that my system was the right approach. I told them in detail how they were wrong and showed where they were being unfair and how I had all the answers they needed. To say the least, I failed miserably! I had become so busy defending my position on the new system that I had left them no opening to graciously admit their problems on the old one. The issue was dead.

'After several sessions of this course, I realized all too well where I had made my mistakes. I called another meeting and this time I asked where they felt their problems were. We discussed each point, and I asked them their opinions on which was the best way to proceed. With a few low-keyed suggestions, at proper intervals, I let them develop my system themselves. At the end of the meeting when I actually presented my system, they enthusiastically accepted it.

'I am convinced now that nothing good is accomplished and a lot of damage can be done if you tell a person straight out that he or she is wrong. You only succeed in stripping that person of self-dignity and making yourself an unwelcome part of any discussion.

Let's take another example – and remember these cases I am citing are typical of the experiences of thousands of other people. R. V. Crowley was a salesman for a lumber company in New York. Crowley admitted that he had been telling hard-boiled lumber inspectors for years that they were wrong. And he had won the arguments too. But it hadn't done any good. 'For these lumber inspectors,' said Mr. Crowley, 'are like baseball umpires. Once they make a decision, they never change it.'

Mr. Crowley saw that his firm was losing thousands of dollars through the arguments he won. So while taking my course, he resolved to change tactics and abandon arguments. With what results? Here is the story as he told it to the fellow members of his class:

'One morning the phone rang in my office. A hot and bothered person at the other end proceeded to inform me that a car of lumber we had shipped into his plant was entirely unsatisfactory. His firm had stopped unloading and requested that we make immediate arrangements to remove the stock from their yard. After about one-fourth of the car had been unloaded, their lumber inspector reported that the lumber was running 55 percent below grade. Under the circumstances, they refused to accept it.

'I immediately started for his plant and on the way turned over in my mind the best way to handle the situation. Ordinarily, under such circumstances, I should have quoted grading rules and tried, as a result of my own experience and knowledge as a lumber inspector, to convince the other inspector that the lumber was actually up to grade, and that he was misinterpreting the rules in his inspection. However, I thought I would apply the principles learned in this training.

'When I arrived at the plant, I found the purchasing agent and the lumber inspector in a wicked humour, both set for an argument and a fight. We walked out to the car that was being unloaded, and I requested that they continue to unload so that I could see how things were going. I asked the inspector to go right ahead and lay out the rejects, as he had been doing, and to put the good pieces in another pile.

'After watching him for a while it began to dawn on me that his inspection actually was much too strict and that he was misinterpreting the rules. This particular lumber was white pine, and I knew the inspector was thoroughly schooled in hard woods but not a competent, experienced inspector on white pine. White pine happened to be my own strong suit, but did I offer any objection to the way he was grading the lumber? None whatever. I kept on watching and gradually began to ask questions as to why certain pieces were not satisfactory. I didn't for one instant insinuate that the inspector was wrong. I emphasized that my only reason for asking was in order that we could give his firm exactly what they wanted in future shipments.

'By asking questions in a very friendly, cooperative spirit, and insisting continually that they were right in laying out boards not satisfactory to their purpose, I got him warmed up, and the strained relations between us began to thaw and melt away. An occasional carefully put remark on my part gave birth to the idea in his mind that possibly some of these rejected pieces were actually within the grade that they had bought, and that their requirements demanded a more expensive grade. I was very careful, however, not to let him think I was making an issue of this point.

'Gradually his whole attitude changed. He finally admitted to me that he was not experienced on white pine and began to ask me questions about each piece as it came out of the car. I would explain why such a piece came within the grade specified, but kept on insisting that we did not want him to take it if it was unsuitable for their purpose. He finally got to the point where he felt guilty every time he put a piece in the rejected pile. And at last he saw that the mistake was on their part for not having specified as good a grade as they needed.

'The ultimate outcome was that he went through the entire carload again after I left, accepted the whole lot, and we received a check in full.

'In that one instance alone, a little tact, and the determination to refrain from telling the other man he was wrong, saved my company a substantial amount of cash, and it would be hard to place a money value on the good will that was saved.'

Martin Luther King was asked how, as a pacifist, he could be an admirer of Air Force General Daniel 'Chappie' James, then the nation's highest-ranking black officer. Dr. King replied, 'I judge people by their own principles – not by my own.'

In a similar way, General Robert E. Lee once spoke to the president of the Confederacy, Jefferson Davis, in the most glowing terms about a certain officer under his command. Another officer in attendance was astonished. 'General,' he said, 'do you not know that the man of whom you speak so highly is one of your bitterest enemies who misses no opportunity to malign you?' 'Yes,' replied General Lee, 'but the president asked my opinion of him; he did not ask for his opinion of me.'

By the way, I am not revealing anything new in this chapter. Two thousand years ago, Jesus said: 'Agree with thine adversary quickly.'

And 2,200 years before Christ was born, King Akhtoi of Egypt gave his son some shrewd advice – advice that is sorely needed today. 'Be diplomatic,' counselled the King. 'It will help you gain your point.'

In other words, don't argue with your customer or your spouse or your adversary. Don't tell them they are wrong, don't get them stirred up. Use a little diplomacy.

PRINCIPLE 2

Show respect for the other person's opinions. Never say, 'You're wrong.'

□ **3** □

If you're wrong, admit it

Within a minute's walk of my house there was a wild stretch of virgin timber, where the blackberry thickets foamed white in the springtime, where the squirrels nested and reared their young, and the horseweeds grew as tall as a horse's head. This unspoiled woodland was called Forest Park – and it was a forest, probably not much different in appearance from what it was when Columbus discovered America. I frequently walked in this park with Rex, my little Boston bulldog. He was a friendly, harmless little hound; and since we rarely met anyone in the park, I took Rex along without a leash or a muzzle.

One day we encountered a mounted policeman in the park, a policeman itching to show his authority.

'What do you mean by letting that dog run loose in the park without a muzzle and leash?' he reprimanded me. 'Don't you know it's against the law?'

'Yes, I know it is,' I replied softly, 'but I didn't think he would do any harm out here.'

'You didn't think! You didn't think! The law doesn't give a tinker's damn about what you think. That dog might kill a squirrel or bite a child. Now, I'm going to let you off this time; but if I catch this dog out here again without a muzzle and a leash, you'll have to tell it to the judge.'

I meekly promised to obey.

And I did obey – for a few times. But Rex didn't like the muzzle, and neither did I; so we decided to take a chance. Everything was lovely for a while, and then we struck a snag. Rex and I raced over the brow of a hill one afternoon and there, suddenly – to my dismay – I saw the majesty of the law, astride a bay horse. Rex was out in front, heading straight for the officer.

I was in for it. I knew it. So I didn't wait until the policeman started talking. I beat him to it. I said: 'Officer, you've caught me red-handed. I'm guilty. I have no alibis, no excuses. You warned me last week that if I brought the dog out here again without a muzzle you would fine me.'

'Well, now,' the policeman responded in a soft tone. 'I know it's a temptation to let a little dog like that have a run out here when nobody is around.'

'Sure it's a temptation,' I replied, 'but it is against the law.'

'Well, a little dog like that isn't going to harm anybody,' the policeman remonstrated.

'No, but he may kill squirrels,' I said.

'Well now, I think you are taking this a bit too seriously,' he told me. 'I'll tell you what you do. You just let him run over the hill there where I can't see him – and we'll forget all about it.'

That policeman, being human, wanted a feeling of importance; so when I began to condemn myself, the only way he could nourish his self-esteem was to take the magnanimous attitude of showing mercy.

But suppose I had tried to defend myself – well, did you ever argue with a policeman?

But instead of breaking lances with him, I admitted that he was absolutely right and I was absolutely wrong; I admitted it quickly, openly, and with enthusiasm. The affair terminated graciously in my taking his side and his taking my side. Lord Chesterfield himself could hardly have been more gracious than this mounted policeman, who, only a week previously, had threatened to have the law on me.

If we know we are going to be rebuked anyhow, isn't it far better to beat the other person to it and do it ourselves? Isn't it much easier to listen to self-criticism than to bear condemnation from alien lips?

Say about yourself all the derogatory things you know the other person is thinking or wants to say or intends to say – and say them before that person has a chance to say them. The chances are a hundred to one that a generous, forgiving attitude will be taken and your mistakes will be minimized just as the mounted policeman did with me and Rex.

Ferdinand E. Warren, a commercial artist, used this technique to win the good will of a petulant, scolding buyer of art.

'It is important, in making drawings for advertising and publishing purposes, to be precise and very exact,' Mr. Warren said as he told the story.

'Some art editors demand that their commissions be executed immediately; and in these cases, some slight error is liable to occur. I knew one art director in particular who was always delighted to find fault with some little thing. I have often left his office in disgust, not because of the criticism, but because of his method of attack. Recently I delivered a rush job to this editor, and he phoned me to call at his office immediately. He said something was wrong. When I arrived, I found just what I had anticipated – and dreaded. He was hostile, gloating over his chance to criticize. He demanded with heat why I had done so and so. My opportunity had come to apply the self-criticism I had been studying about. So I said: "Mr. So-and-so, if what you say is true, I am at fault and there is absolutely no excuse for my blunder. I have been doing drawings for you long enough to know better. I'm ashamed of myself."

'Immediately he started to defend me. "Yes, you're right, but after all, this isn't a serious mistake. It is only – '

'I interrupted him. "Any mistake," I said, "may be costly and they are all irritating."

'He started to break in, but I wouldn't let him. I was having a grand time. For the first time in my life, I was criticizing myself – and I loved it.

' "I should have been more careful," I continued. "You give me a lot of work, and you deserve the best; so I'm going to do this drawing all over."

' "No! No!" he protested. "I wouldn't think of putting you to all that trouble." He praised my work, assured me that he wanted only a minor change and that my slight error hadn't cost his firm any money; and, after all, it was a mere detail – not worth worrying about.

'My eagerness to criticize myself took all the fight out of him. He ended up by taking me to lunch; and before we parted, he gave me a cheque and another commission.'

There is a certain degree of satisfaction in having the courage to admit one's errors. It not only clears the air of guilt and defensiveness, but often helps solve the problem created by the error.

Bruce Harvey of Albuquerque, New Mexico, had incorrectly authorized payment of full wages to an employee on sick leave. When he discovered his error, he brought it to the attention of the employee and explained that to correct the mistake he would have to reduce his next paycheque by the entire amount of the overpayment. The employee pleaded that as that would cause him a serious financial problem, could the money be repaid over a period of time? In order to do this, Harvey explained, he would have to obtain his supervisor's approval. 'And this I knew,' reported Harvey, 'would result in a boss-type explosion. While trying to decide how to handle this situation better, I realized that the whole mess was my fault and I would have to admit it to my boss.

'I walked into his office, told him that I had made a mistake and then informed him of the complete facts. He replied in an explosive manner that it was the fault of the personnel department. I repeated that it was my fault. He exploded again about carelessness in the accounting department. Again I explained it was my fault. He blamed two other people in the office. But each time I reiterated it was my fault. Finally, he looked at me and said, "Okay, it was your fault. Now straighten it out." The error was corrected and nobody got into trouble. I felt great because I was able to handle a tense situation and had the courage not to seek alibis. My boss has had more respect for me ever since.'

Any fool can try to defend his or her mistakes – and most fools do – but it raises one above the herd and gives one a feeling of nobility and exultation to admit one's mistakes. For example, one of the most beautiful things that history records about Robert E. Lee is the way he blamed himself and only himself for the failure of Pickett's charge at Gettysburg.

Pickett's charge was undoubtedly the most brilliant and picturesque attack that ever occurred in the Western world. General George E. Pickett himself was picturesque. He wore his hair so long that his auburn locks almost touched his shoulders; and, like Napoleon in his Italian campaigns, he wrote ardent love-letters almost daily while on the battlefield. His devoted troops cheered him that tragic July afternoon as he rode off jauntily toward the Union lines, his cap set at a rakish angle over his right ear. They cheered and they followed him, man touching man, rank pressing rank, with banners flying and bayonets gleaming in the sun. It was a gallant sight. Daring. Magnificent. A murmur of admiration ran through the Union lines as they beheld it.

Pickett's troops swept forward at an easy trot, through orchard and cornfield, across a meadow and over a ravine. All the time, the enemy's cannon was tearing ghastly holes in their ranks. But on they pressed, grim, irresistible.

Suddenly the Union infantry rose from behind the stone wall on Cemetery Ridge where they had been hiding and fired volley after volley into Pickett's onrushing troops. The crest of the hill was a sheet of flame, a slaughterhouse, a blazing volcano. In a few minutes, all of Pickett's brigade commanders except one were down, and four-fifths of his five thousand men had fallen.

General Lewis A. Armistead, leading the troops in the final plunge, ran forward, vaulted over the stone wall, and, waving his cap on the top of his sword, shouted:

'Give 'em the steel, boys!'

They did. They leaped over the wall, bayoneted their enemies, smashed skulls with clubbed muskets, and planted the battleflags of the South on Cemetery Ridge.

The banners waved there only for a moment. But that moment, brief as it was, recorded the high-water mark of the Confederacy.

Pickett's charge – brilliant, heroic – was nevertheless the beginning of the end. Lee had failed. He could not penetrate the North. And he knew it.

The South was doomed.

Lee was so saddened, so shocked, that he sent in his resignation and asked Jefferson Davis, the president of the Confederacy, to appoint 'a younger and abler man'. If Lee had wanted to blame the disastrous failure of Pickett's charge on someone else, he could have found a score of alibis. Some of his division commanders had failed him. The cavalry hadn't arrived in time to support the infantry attack. This had gone wrong and that had gone awry.

But Lee was far too noble to blame others. As Pickett's beaten and bloody troops struggled back to the Confederate lines, Robert E. Lee rode out to meet them all alone and greeted them with a self-condemnation that was little short of sublime. 'All this has been my fault,' he confessed. 'I and I alone have lost this battle.'

Few generals in all history have had the courage and character to admit that.

Michael Cheung, who teaches our course in Hong Kong, told of how the Chinese culture presents some special problems and how sometimes it is necessary to recognize that the benefit of applying a principle may be more advantageous than maintaining an old tradition. He had one middle-aged class member who had been estranged from his son for many years. The father had been an opium addict, but was now cured. In Chinese tradition an older person cannot take the first step. The father felt that it was up to his son to take the initiative toward a reconciliation. In an early session, he told the class about the grandchildren he had never seen and how much he desired to be reunited with his son. His classmates, all Chinese, understood his conflict between his desire and long-established tradition. The father felt that young people should have respect for their elders and that he was right in not giving in to his desire, but to wait for his son to come to him.

Toward the end of the course the father again addressed his class. 'I have pondered this problem,' he said. 'Dale Carnegie says, "If you are wrong, admit it quickly and emphatically." It is too late for me to admit it quickly, but I can admit it emphatically. I wronged my son. He was right in not wanting to see me and to expel me from his life. I may lose face by asking a younger person's forgiveness, but I was at fault and it is my responsibility to admit this.' The class applauded and gave him their full support. At the next class he told how he went to his son's house, asked for and received forgiveness and was now embarked on a new relationship with his son, his daughter-in-law and the grandchildren he had at last met.

Elbert Hubbard was one of the most original authors who ever stirred up a nation, and his stinging sentences often aroused fierce resentment. But Hubbard with his rare skill for handling people frequently turned his enemies into friends.

For example, when some irritated reader wrote in to say that he didn't agree with such and such an article and ended by calling Hubbard this and that, Elbert Hubbard would answer like this:

> Come to think it over, I don't entirely agree with it myself. Not everything I wrote yesterday appeals to me today. I am glad to learn what you think on the subject. The next time you are in the neighbourhood you must visit us and we'll get this subject threshed out for all time. So here is a handclasp over the miles, and I am,
>
> Yours sincerely,

What could you say to a man who treated you like that?

When we are right, let's try to win people gently and tactfully to our way of thinking, and when we are wrong – and that will be surprisingly often, if we are honest with ourselves – let's admit our mistakes quickly and with enthusiasm. Not only will that technique produce astonishing results; but, believe it or not, it is a lot more fun, under the circumstances, than trying to defend oneself.

Remember the old proverb: 'By fighting you never get enough, but by yielding you get more than you expected.'

PRINCIPLE 3

If you are wrong, admit it quickly and emphatically.

□ 4 □

A drop of honey

If your temper is aroused and you tell 'em a thing or two, you will have a fine time unloading your feelings. But what about the other person? Will he share your pleasure? Will your belligerent tones, your hostile attitude, make it easy for him to agree with you?

'If you come at me with your fists doubled,' said Woodrow Wilson, 'I think I can promise you that mine will double as fast as yours; but if you come to me and say, "Let us sit down and take counsel together, and, if we differ from each other, understand why it is that we differ, just what the points at issue are," we will presently find that we are not so far apart after all, that the points on which we differ are few and the points on which we agree are many, and that if we only have the patience and the candour and the desire to get together, we will get together.'

Nobody appreciated the truth of Woodrow Wilson's statement more than John D. Rockefeller, Jr. Back in 1915, Rockefeller was the most fiercely despised man in Colorado. One of the bloodiest strikes in the history of American industry had been shocking the state for two terrible years. Irate, belligerent miners were demanding higher wages from the Colorado Fuel and Iron Company; Rockefeller controlled that company. Property had been destroyed, troops had been called out. Blood had been shed. Strikers had been shot, their bodies riddled with bullets.

At a time like that, with the air seething with hatred, Rockefeller wanted to win the strikers to his way of thinking. And he did it. How? Here's the story. After weeks spent in making friends, Rockefeller addressed the representatives of the strikers. This speech, in its entirety, is a masterpiece. It produced astonishing results. It calmed the tempestuous waves of hate that threatened to engulf Rockefeller. It won him a host of admirers. It presented facts in such a friendly manner that the strikers went back to work without saying another word about the increase in wages for which they had fought so violently.

The opening of that remarkable speech follows. Note how it fairly glows with friendliness. Rockefeller, remember, was talking to men who, a few days previously, had wanted to hang him by the neck to a sour apple tree; yet he couldn't have been more gracious, more friendly if he had addressed a group of medical missionaries. His speech was radiant with such phrases as: I am *proud* to be here, having *visited* in *your homes*, met many of your wives and children, we meet here not as strangers, but as *friends . . .* spirit of *mutual friendship*, our *common interests*, it is only by *your courtesy* that I am here.

'This is a red-letter day in my life,' Rockefeller began. 'It is the first time I have ever had the good fortune to meet the representatives of the employees of this great company, its officers and superintendents, together, and I can assure you that I am proud to be here, and that I shall remember this gathering as long as I live. Had this meeting been held two weeks ago, I should have stood here a stranger to most of you, recognizing a few faces. Having had the opportunity last week of visiting all the camps in the southern coal field and of talking individually with practically all of the representatives, except those who were away; having visited in your homes, met many of your wives and children, we meet here not as strangers, but as friends, and it is in that spirit of mutual friendship that I am glad to have this opportunity to discuss with you our common interests.

'Since this is a meeting of the officers of the company and the representatives of the employees, it is only by your courtesy that I am here, for I am not so fortunate as to be either one or the other; and yet I feel that I am intimately associated with you men, for, in a sense, I represent both the stockholders and the directors.'

Isn't that a superb example of the fine art of making friends out of enemies?

Suppose Rockefeller had taken a different tack. Suppose he had argued with those miners and hurled devastating facts in their faces. Suppose he had told them by his tones and insinuations that they were wrong. Suppose that, by all the rules of logic, he had proved that they were wrong. What would have happened? More anger would have been stirred up, more hatred, more revolt.

If a man's heart is rankling with discord and ill feeling toward you, you can't win him to your way of thinking with all the logic in Christendom. Scolding parents and domineering bosses and husbands and nagging wives ought to realize that people don't want to change their minds. They can't be forced or driven to agree with you or me. But they may possibly be led to, if we are gentle and friendly, ever so gentle and ever so friendly.

Lincoln said that, in effect, over a hundred years ago. Here are his words:

It is an old and true maxim that 'a drop of honey catches more flies than a gallon of gall.' So with men, if you would win a man to your cause, first convince him that you are his sincere friend. Therein is a drop of honey that catches his heart; which, say what you will, is the great high road to his reason.

Business executives have learned that it pays to be friendly to strikers. For

How to Win Friends and Influence People

example, when 2,500 employees in the White Motor Company's plant struck for higher wages and a union shop, Robert F. Black, then president of the company, didn't lose his temper and condemn and threaten and talk of tyranny and Communists. He actually praised the strikers. He published an advertisement in the Cleveland papers, complimenting them on 'the peaceful way in which they laid down their tools.' Finding the strike pickets idle, he bought them a couple of dozen baseball bats and gloves and invited them to play ball on vacant lots. For those who preferred bowling, he rented a bowling alley.

This friendliness on Mr. Black's part did what friendliness always does: it begot friendliness. So the strikers borrowed brooms, shovels, and rubbish carts, and began picking up matches, papers, cigarette stubs, and cigar butts around the factory. Imagine it! Imagine strikers tidying up the factory grounds while battling for higher wages and recognition of the union. Such an event had never been heard of before in the long, tempestuous history of American labour wars. That strike ended with a compromise settlement within a week – ended without any ill feeling or rancour.

Daniel Webster, who looked like a god and talked like Jehovah, was one of the most successful advocates who ever pleaded a case; yet he ushered in his most powerful arguments with such friendly remarks as: 'It will be for the jury to consider,' 'This may, perhaps, be worth thinking of,' 'Here are some facts that I trust you will not lose sight of,' or 'You, with your knowledge of human nature, will easily see the significance of these facts.' No bulldozing. No high-pressure methods. No attempt to force his opinions on others. Webster used the soft-spoken, quiet, friendly approach, and it helped to make him famous.

You may never be called upon to settle a strike or address a jury, but you may want to get your rent reduced. Will the friendly approach help you then? Let's see.

O. L. Straub, an engineer, wanted to get his rent reduced. And he knew his landlord was hard-boiled. 'I wrote him,' Mr. Straub said in a speech before the class, 'notifying him that I was vacating my apartment as soon as my lease expired. The truth was, I didn't want to move. I wanted to stay if I could get my rent reduced. But the situation seemed hopeless. Other tenants had tried – and failed. Everyone told me that the landlord was extremely difficult to deal with. But I said to myself, "I am studying a course in how to deal with people, so I'll try it on him – and see how it works."

'He and his secretary came to see me as soon as he got my letter. I met him at the door with a friendly greeting. I fairly bubbled with good will and enthusiasm. I didn't begin talking about how high the rent was. I began talking about how much I liked the apartment house. Believe me, I was "hearty in my approbation and lavish in my praise." I complimented him on the way he ran the building and told him I should like so much to stay for another year but I couldn't afford it.

'He had evidently never had such a reception from a tenant. He hardly knew what to make of it.

113

'Then he started to tell me his troubles. Complaining tenants. One had written him fourteen letters, some of them positively insulting. Another threatened to break his lease unless the landlord kept the man on the floor above from snoring. "What a relief it is," he said, "to have a satisfied tenant like you." And then, without my even asking him to do it, he offered to reduce my rent a little. 1 wanted more, so I named the figure I could afford to pay, and he accepted without a word.

'As he was leaving, he turned to me and asked, "What decorating can I do for you?"

'If I had tried to get the rent reduced by the methods the other tenants were using, I am positive I should have met with the same failure they encountered. It was the friendly, sympathetic, appreciative approach that won.'

Dean Woodcock of Pittsburgh, Pennsylvania, is the superintendent of a department of the local electric company. His staff was called upon to repair some equipment on top of a pole. This type of work had formerly been performed by a different department and had only recently been transferred to Woodcock's section. Although his people had been trained in the work, this was the first time they had ever actually been called upon to do it. Everybody in the organization was interested in seeing if and how they could handle it. Mr. Woodcock, several of his subordinate managers, and members of other departments of the utility went to see the operation. Many cars and trucks were there, and a number of people were standing around watching the two lone men on top of the pole.

Glancing around, Woodcock noticed a man up the street getting out of his car with a camera. He began taking pictures of the scene. Utility people are extremely conscious of public relations, and suddenly Woodcock realized what this setup looked like to the man with the camera – overkill, dozens of people being called out to do a two-person job. He strolled up the street to the photographer.

'I see you're interested in our operation.'

'Yes, and my mother will be more than interested. She owns stock in your company. This will be an eye-opener for her. She may even decide her investment was unwise. I've been telling her for years there's a lot of waste motion in companies like yours. This proves it. The newspapers might like these pictures, too.'

'It does look like it, doesn't it? I'd think the same thing in your position. But this is a unique situation, . . .' and Dean Woodcock went on to explain how this was the first job of this type for his department and how everybody from executives down was interested. He assured the man that under normal conditions two people could handle the job. The photographer put away his camera, shook Woodcock's hand, and thanked him for taking the time to explain the situation to him.

Dean Woodcock's friendly approach saved his company much embarrassment and bad publicity.

Another member of one of our classes, Gerald H. Winn of Littleton, New Hampshire, reported how by using a friendly approach, he obtained a very satisfactory settlement on a damage claim.

'Early in the spring,' he reported, 'before the ground had thawed from the winter freezing, there was an unusually heavy rainstorm and the water, which normally would have run off to nearby ditches and storm drains along the road, took a new course onto a building lot where I had just built a new home.

'Not being able to run off, the water pressure built up around the foundation of the house. The water forced itself under the concrete basement floor, causing it to explode, and the basement filled with water. This ruined the furnace and the hot-water heater. The cost to repair this damage was in excess of two thousand dollars. I had no insurance to cover this type of damage.

'However, I soon found out that the owner of the subdivision had neglected to put in a storm drain near the house which could have prevented this problem. I made an appointment to see him. During the twenty-five-mile trip to his office, I carefully reviewed the situation and, remembering the principles I learned in this course, I decided that showing my anger would not serve any worthwhile purpose. When I arrived, I kept very calm and started by talking about his recent vacation to the West Indies; then, when I felt the timing was right, I mentioned the "little" problem of water damage. He quickly agreed to do his share in helping to correct the problem.

'A few days later he called and said he would pay for the damage and also put in a storm drain to prevent the same thing from happening in the future.

'Even though it was the fault of the owner of the subdivision, if I had not begun in a friendly way, there would have been a great deal of difficulty in getting him to agree to the total liability.'

Years ago, when I was a barefoot boy walking through the woods to a country school out in northwest Missouri, I read a fable about the sun and the wind. They quarrelled about which was the stronger, and the wind said, 'I'll prove I am. See the old man down there with a coat? I bet I can get his coat off him quicker than you can.'

So the sun went behind a cloud, and the wind blew until it was almost a tornado, but the harder it blew, the tighter the old man clutched his coat to him.

Finally, the wind calmed down and gave up, and then the sun came out from behind the clouds and smiled kindly on the old man. Presently, he mopped his brow and pulled off his coat. The sun then told the wind that gentleness and friendliness were always stronger than fury and force.

The use of gentleness and friendliness is demonstrated day after day by people who have learned that a drop of honey catches more flies than a gallon of gall. F. Gale Connor of Lutherville, Maryland, proved this when he had to take his four-month-old car to the service department of the car dealer for the third time. He told our class: 'It was apparent that talking to, reasoning with or shouting at the service manager was not going to lead to a satisfactory resolution of my problems.

'I walked over to the showroom and asked to see the agency owner, Mr. White. After a short wait, I was ushered into Mr. White's office. I introduced myself and explained to him that I had bought my car from his dealership because of the recommendations of friends who had had previous dealings with him. I was told that his prices were very competitive and his service was outstanding. He smiled with satisfaction as he listened to me. I then explained the problem I was having with the service department. "I thought you might want to be aware of any situation that might tarnish your fine reputation," I added. He thanked me for calling this to his attention and assured me that my problem would be taken care of. Not only did he personally get involved, but he also lent me his car to use while mine was being repaired.'

Aesop was a Greek slave who lived at the court of Croesus and spun immortal fables six hundred years before Christ. Yet the truths he taught about human nature are just as true in Boston and Birmingham now as they were twenty-six centuries ago in Athens. The sun can make you take off your coat more quickly than the wind; and kindliness, the friendly approach and appreciation can make people change their minds more readily than all the bluster and storming in the world.

Remember what Lincoln said: 'A drop of honey catches more flies than a gallon of gall.'

PRINCIPLE 4

Begin in a friendly way.

□ 5 □

The secret of Socrates

In talking with people, don't begin by discussing the things on which you differ. Begin by emphasizing – and keep on emphasizing – the things on which you agree. Keep emphasizing, if possible, that you are both striving for the same end and that your only difference is one of method and not of purpose.

Get the other person saying 'Yes, yes' at the outset. Keep your opponent, if possible, from saying 'No.'

A 'No' response, according to Professor Overstreet,* is a most difficult handicap to overcome. When you have said 'No,' all your pride of personality demands that you remain consistent with yourself. You may later feel that the 'No' was ill-advised; nevertheless, there is your precious pride to consider! Once having said a thing, you feel you must stick to it. Hence it is of the very greatest importance that a person be started in the affirmative direction.

The skilful speaker gets, at the outset, a number of 'Yes' responses. This sets the psychological process of the listeners moving in the affirmative direction. It is like the movement of a billiard ball. Propel in one direction, and it takes some force to deflect it; far more force to send it back in the opposite direction.

The psychological patterns here are quite clear. When a person says 'No' and really means it, he or she is doing far more than saying a word of two letters. The entire organism – glandular, nervous, muscular – gathers itself together into a condition of rejection. There is, usually in minute but sometimes in observable degree, a physical withdrawal or readiness for withdrawal. The whole neuromuscular system, in short, sets itself on guard against acceptance. When, to the contrary, a person says 'Yes', none of the withdrawal activities takes place. The organism is in a forward-moving, accepting, open attitude. Hence the more 'Yeses' we can, at the very outset, induce, the more likely we are to succeed in capturing the attention for our ultimate proposal.

It is a very simple technique – this yes response. And yet, how much it is neglected! It often seems as if people get a sense of their own importance by antagonizing others at the outset.

Get a student to say 'No' at the beginning, or a customer, child, husband, or wife, and it takes the wisdom and the patience of angels to transform that bristling negative into an affirmative.

The use of this 'yes, yes' technique enabled James Eberson, who was a teller in the Greenwich Savings Bank, in New York City, to secure a prospective customer who might otherwise have been lost.

'This man came in to open an account,' said Mr. Eberson, 'and I gave him our usual form to fill out. Some of the questions he answered willingly, but there were others he flatly refused to answer.

'Before I began the study of human relations, I would have told this prospective depositor that if he refused to give the bank this information, we should have to refuse to accept this account. I am ashamed that I have been guilty of doing that very thing in the past. Naturally, an ultimatum like that made me feel good. I had shown who was boss, that the bank's rules and regulations couldn't be flouted. But that sort of attitude certainly didn't give a feeling of welcome and importance to the man who had walked in to give us his patronage.

* Harry A. Overstreet, *Influencing Human Behavior* (New York: Norton, 1925).

'I resolved this morning to use a little horse sense. I resolved not to talk about what the bank wanted but about what the customer wanted. And above all else, I was determined to get him saying "yes, yes" from the very start. So I agreed with him. I told him the information he refused to give was not absolutely necessary.

' "However," I said, "suppose you have money in this bank at your death. Wouldn't you like to have the bank transfer it to your next of kin, who is entitled to it according to law?'

' "Yes, of course," he replied.

' "Don't you think," I continued, "that it would be a good idea to give us the name of your next of kin so that, in the event of your death, we could carry out your wishes without error or delay?"

'Again he said, "Yes."

'The young man's attitude softened and changed when he realized that we weren't asking for this information for our sake but for his sake. Before leaving the bank, this young man not only gave me complete information about himself but he opened, at my suggestion, a trust account, naming his mother as the beneficiary for his account, and he had gladly answered all the questions concerning his mother also.

'I found that by getting him to say "yes, yes" from the outset, he forgot the issue at stake and was happy to do all the things I suggested."

Joseph Allison, a sales representative for Westinghouse Electric Company, had this story to tell: 'There was a man in my territory that our company was most eager to sell to. My predecessor had called on him for ten years without selling anything. When I took over the territory, I called steadily for three years without getting an order. Finally, after thirteen years of calls and sales talk, we sold him a few motors. If these proved to be all right, an order for several hundred more would follow. Such was my expectation.

'Right? I knew they would be all right. So when I called three weeks later, I was in high spirits.

'The chief engineer greeted me with this shocking announcement: "Allison, I can't buy the remainder of the motors from you."

' "Why?" I asked in amazement. "Why?"

' "Because your motors are too hot. I can't put my hand on them."

'I knew it wouldn't do any good to argue. I had tried that sort of thing too long. So I thought of getting the "yes, yes" response.

' "Well, now look, Mr. Smith," I said. "I agree with you a hundred percent; if those motors are running too hot, you ought not to buy any more of them. You must have motors that won't run any hotter than standards set by the National Electrical Manufacturers Association. Isn't that so?"

'He agreed it was. I had gotten my first "yes".

' "The Electrical Manufacturers Association regulations say that a properly designed motor may have a temperature of 72 degrees Fahrenheit above room temperature. Is that correct?"

' "Yes," he agreed. "That's quite correct. But your motors are much hotter."
'I didn't argue with him. I merely asked: "How hot is the mill room?"
' "Oh," he said, "about 75 degrees Fahrenheit."
' "Well," I replied, "if the mill room is 75 degrees and you add 72 to that, that makes a total of 147 degrees Fahrenheit. Wouldn't you scald your hand if you held it under a spigot of hot water at a temperature of 147 degrees Fahrenheit?"
'Again he had to say "yes".
' "Well," I suggested, "wouldn't it be a good idea to keep your hands off those motors?"
' "Well, I guess you're right," he admitted. We continued to chat for a while. Then he called his secretary and lined up approximately $35,000 worth of business for the ensuing month.
'It took me years and cost me countless thousands of dollars in lost business before I finally learned that it doesn't pay to argue, that it is much more profitable and much more interesting to look at things from the other person's viewpoint and try to get that person saying "yes, yes".'

Eddie Snow, who sponsors our courses in Oakland, California, tells how he became a good customer of a shop because the proprietor got him to say 'yes, yes'. Eddie had become interested in bow hunting and had spent considerable money in purchasing equipment and supplies from a local bow store. When his brother was visiting him he wanted to rent a bow for him from this store. The sales clerk told him they didn't rent bows, so Eddie phoned another bow store. Eddie described what happened:

'A very pleasant gentleman answered the phone. His response to my question for a rental was completely different from the other place. He said he was sorry but they no longer rented bows because they couldn't afford to do so. He then asked me if I had rented before. I replied, "Yes, several years ago." He reminded me that I probably paid $25 to $30 for the rental. I said "yes" again. He then asked if I was the kind of person who liked to save money. Naturally, I answered "yes". he went on to explain that they had bow sets with all the necessary equipment on sale for $34.95. I could buy a complete set for only $4.95 more than I could rent one. He explained that is why they had discontinued renting them. Did I think that was reasonable? My "yes" response led to a purchase of the set, and when I picked it up I purchased several more items at this shop and have since become a regular customer.'

Socrates, 'the gadfly of Athens', was one of the greatest philosophers the world has ever known. He did something that only a handful of men in all history have been able to do: he sharply changed the whole course of human thought; and now, twenty-four centuries after his death, he is honoured as one of the wisest persuaders who ever influenced this wrangling world.

His method? Did he tell people they were wrong? Oh, no, not Socrates. He was far too adroit for that. His whole technique, now called the 'Socratic method', was based upon getting a 'yes, yes' response. He asked questions with which his opponent would have to agree. He kept on winning one admission after another until he had an armful of yeses. He kept on asking questions until finally, almost without realizing it, his opponents found themselves embracing a conclusion they would have bitterly denied a few minutes previously.

The next time we are tempted to tell someone he or she is wrong, let's remember old Socrates and ask a gentle question – a question that will get the 'yes, yes' response.

The Chinese have a proverb pregnant with the age-old wisdom of the Orient: 'He who treads softly goes far.'

They have spent five thousand years studying human nature, those cultured Chinese, and they have garnered a lot of perspicacity: *'He who treads softly goes far.'*

PRINCIPLE 5

Get the other person saying 'yes, yes' immediately.

□ **6** □

The safety valve in handling complaints

Most people trying to win others to their way of thinking do too much talking themselves. Let the other people talk themselves out. They know more about their business and problems than you do. So ask them questions. Let them tell you a few things.

If you disagree with them you may be tempted to interrupt. But don't. It is dangerous. They won't pay attention to you while they still have a lot of ideas of their own crying for expression. So listen patiently and with an open mind. Be sincere about it. Encourage them to express their ideas fully.

Does this policy pay in business? Let's see. Here is the story of a sales representative who was *forced* to try it.

One of the largest automobile manufacturers in the United States was negotiating for a year's requirements of upholstery fabrics. Three important manufacturers had worked up fabrics in sample bodies. These had all been inspected by the executives of the motor company, and notice had been sent to each manufacturer saying that, on a certain day, a representative from each supplier would be given an opportunity to make a final plea for the contract.

G.B.R., a representative of one manufacturer, arrived in town with a severe attack of laryngitis. 'When it came my turn to meet the executives in conference,' Mr. R — said as he related the story before one of my classes, 'I had lost my voice. I could hardly whisper. I was ushered into a room and found myself face to face with the textile engineer, the purchasing agent, the director of sales and the president of the company. I stood up and made a valiant effort to speak, but I couldn't do anything more than squeak.

'They were all seated around a table, so I wrote on a pad of paper: "Gentlemen, I have lost my voice. I am speechless."

' "I'll do the talking for you," the president said. He did. He exhibited my samples and praised their good points. A lively discussion arose about the merits of my goods. And the president, since he was talking for me, took the position I would have had during the discussion. My sole participation consisted of smiles, nods and a few gestures.

'As a result of this unique conference, I was awarded the contract, which called for over half a million yards of upholstery fabrics at an aggregate value of $1,600,000 – the biggest order I had ever received.

'I know I would have lost the contract if I hadn't lost my voice, because I had the wrong idea about the whole proposition. I discovered, quite by accident, how richly it sometimes pays to let the other person do the talking.'

Letting the other person do the talking helps in family situations as well as in business. Barbara Wilson's relationship with her daughter, Laurie, was deteriorating rapidly. Laurie, who had been a quiet, complacent child, had grown into an uncooperative, sometimes belligerent teenager. Mrs. Wilson lectured her, threatened her and punished her, but all to no avail.

'One day,' Mrs. Wilson told one of our classes, 'I just gave up. Laurie had disobeyed me and had left the house to visit her girl friend before she had completed her chores. When she returned I was about to scream at her for the ten thousandth time, but I just didn't have the strength to do it. I just looked at her and said sadly, "Why, Laurie, Why?"

'Laurie noted my condition and in a calm voice asked, "Do you really want to know?" I nodded and Laurie told me, first hesitantly, and then it all flowed out. I had never listened to her. I was always telling her to do this or that. When she wanted to tell me her thoughts, feelings, ideas, I interrupted with more orders. I began to realize that she needed me – not as a bossy mother, but as a confidante, an outlet for all her confusion about growing up. And all I had been doing was talking when I should have been listening. I never heard her.

'From that time on I let her do all the talking she wanted. She tells me what is on her mind, and our relationship has improved immeasurably. She is again a cooperative person.'

A large advertisement appeared on the financial page of a New York newspaper calling for a person with unusual ability and experience. Charles T. Cubellis answered the advertisement, sending his reply to a box number. A few days later, he was invited by letter to call for an interview. Before he called, he spent hours in Wall Street finding out everything possible about the person who had founded the business. During the interview, he remarked: 'I should be mighty proud to be associated with an organization with a record like yours. I understand you started twenty-eight years ago with nothing but desk room and one stenographer. Is that true?'

Almost every successful person likes to reminisce about his early struggles. This man was no exception. He talked for a long time about how he had started with $450 in cash and an original idea. He told how he had fought against discouragement and battled against ridicule, working Sundays and holidays, twelve to sixteen hours a day; how he had finally won against all odds until now the most important executives on Wall Street were coming to him for information and guidance. He was proud of such a record. He had a right to be, and he had a splendid time telling about it. Finally, he questioned Mr. Cubellis briefly about his experience, then called in one of his vice presidents and said: 'I think this is the person we are looking for.'

Mr. Cubellis had taken the trouble to find out about the accomplishments of his prospective employer. He showed an interest in the other person and his problems. He encouraged the other person to do most of the talking – and made a favourable impression.

Roy G. Bradley of Sacramento, California, had the opposite problem. He listened as a good prospect for a sales position talked himself into a job with Bradley's firm. Roy reported:

'Being a small brokerage firm, we had no fringe benefits, such as hospitalization, medical insurance and pensions. Every representative is an independent agent. We don't even provide leads for prospects, as we cannot advertise for them as our larger competitors do.

'Richard Pryor had the type of experience we wanted for this position, and he was interviewed first by my assistant, who told him about all the negatives related to this job. He seemed slightly discouraged when he came into my office. I mentioned the one benefit of being associated with my firm, that of being an independent contractor and therefore virtually being self-employed.

'As he talked about these advantages to me, he talked himself out of each negative thought he had when he came in for the interview. Several times it seemed as though he was half talking to himself as he was thinking through each thought. At times I was tempted to add to his thoughts; however, as the interview came to a close I felt he had convinced himself very much on his own that he would like to work for my firm.

'Because I had been a good listener and let Dick do most of the talking, he was able to weigh both sides fairly in his mind, and he came to the positive conclusion, which was a challenge he created for himself. We hired him and he has been an outstanding representative for our firm.'

Even our friends would much rather talk to us about their achievements than listen to us boast about ours.

La Rochefoucauld, the French philosopher said: 'If you want enemies, excel your friends; but if you want friends, let your friends excel you.'

Why is that true? Because when our friends excel us, they feel important; but when we excel them, they – or at least some of them – will feel inferior and envious.

By far the best-liked placement counsellor in the Midtown Personnel Agency in New York City was Henrietta G —. It hadn't always been that way. During the first few months of her association with the agency, Henrietta didn't have a single friend among her colleagues. Why? Because every day she would brag about the placements she had made, the new accounts she had opened, and anything else she had accomplished.

'I was good at my work and proud of it,' Henrietta told one of our classes. 'But instead of my colleagues sharing my triumphs, they seemed to resent them. I wanted to be liked by these people. I really wanted them to be my friends. After listening to some of the suggestions made in this course, I started to talk about myself less and listen more to my associates. They also had things to boast about and were more excited about telling me about their accomplishments than about listening to my boasting. Now, when we have some time to chat, I ask them to share their joys with me, and I only mention my achievements when they ask.'

PRINCIPLE 6

Let the other person do a great deal of the talking.

☐ **7** ☐

How to get cooperation

Don't you have much more faith in ideas that you discover for yourself than in ideas that are handed to you on a silver platter? If so, isn't it bad judgement to try to ram your opinions down the throats of other people? Isn't it wiser to make suggestions – and let the other person think out the conclusion?

Adolph Seltz of Philadelphia, sales manager in an automobile showroom and a student in one of my courses, suddenly found himself confronted with the necessity of injecting enthusiasm into a discouraged and disorganized group of automobile salespeople. Calling a sales meeting, he urged his people to tell him exactly what they expected from him. As they talked, he wrote their ideas on the blackboard. He then said: 'I'll give you all these qualities you expect from me. Now I want you to tell me what I have a right to expect from you.' The replies came quick and fast: loyalty, honesty, initiative, optimism, teamwork, eight hours a day of enthusiastic work. The meeting ended with a new courage, a new inspiration – one salesperson volunteered to work fourteen hours a day – and Mr. Seltz reported to me that the increase of sales was phenomenal.

'The people had made a sort of moral bargain with me,' said Mr. Seltz, 'and as long as I lived up to my part in it, they were determined to live up to theirs. Consulting them about their wishes and desires was just the shot in the arm they needed.'

No one likes to feel that he or she is being sold something or told to do a thing. We much prefer to feel that we are buying of our own accord or acting on our own ideas. We like to be consulted about our wishes, our wants, our thoughts.

Take the case of Eugene Wesson. He lost countless thousands of dollars in commissions before he learned this truth. Mr. Wesson sold sketches for a studio that created designs for stylists and textile manufacturers. Mr. Wesson had called on one of the leading stylists in New York once a week, every week for three years. 'He never refused to see me,' said Mr. Wesson, 'but he never bought. He always looked over my sketches very carefully and then said: "No, Wesson, I guess we don't get together today." '

After 150 failures, Wesson realized he must be in a mental rut, so he resolved to devote one evening a week to the study of influencing human behaviour, to help him develop new ideas and generate new enthusiasm.

He decided on this new approach. With half a dozen unfinished artists' sketches under his arm, he rushed over to the buyer's office. 'I want you to do me a little favour, if you will,' he said. 'Here are some uncompleted sketches. Won't you please tell me how we could finish them up in such a way that you could use them?'

The buyer looked at the sketches for a while without uttering a word. Finally he said: 'Leave these with me for a few days, Wesson, and then come back and see me.'

Wesson returned three days later, got his suggestions, took the sketches back to the studio and had them finished according to the buyer's ideas. The result? All accepted.

After that, this buyer ordered scores of other sketches from Wesson, all drawn according to the buyer's ideas. 'I realized why I had failed for years to sell him,' said Mr. Wesson. 'I had urged him to buy what I thought he ought to have. Then I changed my approach completely. I urged him to give me his ideas. This made him feel that he was creating the designs. And he was. I didn't have to sell him. He bought.'

Letting the other person feel that the idea is his or hers not only works in business and politics, it works in family life as well. Paul M. Davis of Tulsa, Oklahoma, told his class how he applied this principle:

'My family and I enjoyed one of the most interesting sightseeing vacation trips we have ever taken. I had long dreamed of visiting such historic sites as the Civil War battlefield in Gettysburg, Independence Hall in Philadelphia, and our nation's capital. Valley Forge, Jamestown and the restored colonial village of Williamsburg were high on the list of things I wanted to see.

'In March my wife, Nancy, mentioned that she had ideas for our summer vacation which included a tour of the western states, visiting points of interest in New Mexico, Arizona, California and Nevada. She had wanted to make this trip for several years. But we couldn't obviously make both trips.

'Our daughter, Anne, had just completed a course in U.S. history in junior high school and had become very interested in the events that had shaped our country's growth. I asked her how she would like to visit the places she had learned about on our next vacation. She said she would love to.

'Two evenings later as we sat around the dinner table, Nancy announced that if we all agreed, the summer's vacation would be to the eastern states, that it would be a great trip for Anne and thrilling for all of us. We all concurred.'

This same psychology was used by an X-ray manufacturer to sell his equipment to one of the largest hospitals in Brooklyn. This hospital was building an addition and preparing to equip it with the finest X-ray department in America. Dr. L —, who was in charge of the X-ray department, was overwhelmed with sales representatives, each caroling the praises of his own company's equipment.

One manufacturer, however, was more skilful. He knew far more about handling human nature than the others did. He wrote a letter something like this:

Our factory has recently completed a new line of X-ray equipment. The first shipment of these machines has just arrived at our office. They are not perfect. We know that, and we want to improve them. So we should be deeply obligated to you if you could find time to look them over and give us your ideas about how they can be made more serviceable to your profession. Knowing how occupied you are, I shall be glad to send my car for you at any hour you specify.

'I was surprised to get that letter,' Dr. L — said as he related the incident before the class. 'I was both surprised and complimented. I had never had an X-ray manufacturer seeking my advice before. It made me feel important. I was busy every night that week, but I cancelled a dinner appointment in order to look over the equipment. The more I studied it, the more I discovered for myself how much I liked it.

'Nobody had tried to sell it to me. I felt that the idea of buying that equipment for the hospital was my own. I sold myself on its superior qualities and ordered it installed.'

Ralph Waldo Emerson in his essay 'Self-Reliance' stated: 'In every work of genius we recognize our own rejected thoughts; they come back to us with a certain alienated majesty.'

Colonel Edward M. House wielded an enormous influence in national and international affairs while Woodrow Wilson occupied the White House. Wilson leaned upon Colonel House for secret counsel and advice more than he did upon even members of his own cabinet.

What method did the Colonel use in influencing the President? Fortunately, we know, for House himself revealed it to Arthur D. Howden Smith, and Smith quoted House in an article in *The Saturday Evening Post*.

' "After I got to know the President," House said, "I learned the best way to convert him to an idea was to plant it in his mind casually, but so as to interest him in it – so as to get him thinking about it on his own account. The first time this worked it was an accident. I had been visiting him at the White House and urged a policy on him which he appeared to disapprove. But several days later, at the dinner table, I was amazed to hear him trot out my suggestion as his own.

Did House interrupt him and say, 'That's not your idea. That's mine'? Oh, no. Not House. He was too adroit for that. He didn't care about credit. He wanted results. So he let Wilson continue to feel that the idea was his. House did even more than that. He gave Wilson public credit for these ideas.

Let's remember that everyone we come in contact with is just as human as Woodrow Wilson. So let's use Colonel House's technique.

A man up in the beautiful Canadian province of New Brunswick used this technique on me and won my patronage. I was planning at the time to do some fishing and canoeing in New Brunswick. So I wrote the tourist bureau for information. Evidently my name and address were put on a mailing list, for I was immediately overwhelmed with scores of letters and booklets and printed testimonials from camps and guides. I was bewildered. I didn't know which to choose. Then one camp owner did a clever thing. He sent me the names and telephone numbers of several New York people who had stayed at his camp and he invited me to telephone them and discover for myself what he had to offer.

I found to my surprise that I knew one of the men on his list. I telephoned him, found out what his experience had been, and then wired the camp the date of my arrival.

The others had been trying to sell me on their service, but one let me sell myself. That organization won.

Twenty-five centuries ago, Lao-tse, a Chinese sage, said some things that readers of this book might use today:

'The reason why rivers and seas receive the homage of a hundred mountain streams is that they keep below them. Thus they are able to reign over all the mountain streams. So the sage, wishing to be above men, putteth himself below them; wishing to be before them, he putteth himself behind them. Thus, though his place be above men, they do not feel his weight; though his place be before them, they do not count it an injury.'

PRINCIPLE 7

Let the other person feel that the idea is his or hers.

□ 8 □

A formula that will work wonders for you

Remember that other people may be totally wrong. But they don't think so. Don't condemn them. Any fool can do that. Try to understand them. Only wise, tolerant, exceptional people even try to do that.

There is a reason why the other man thinks and acts as he does. Ferret out that reason – and you have the key to his actions, perhaps to his personality.

Try honestly to put yourself in his place.

If you say to yourself, 'How would I feel, how would I react if I were in his shoes?' you will save yourself time and irritation, for 'by becoming interested in the cause, we are less likely to dislike the effect.' And, in addition, you will sharply increase your skill in human relationships.

'Stop a minute,' says Kenneth M. Goode in his book *How to Turn People Into Gold*, 'stop a minute to contrast your keen interest in your own affairs with your mild concern about anything else. Realize then, that everybody else in the world feels exactly the same way! Then, along with Lincoln and Roosevelt, you will have grasped the only solid foundation for interpersonal relationships; namely, that success in dealing with people depends on a sympathetic grasp of the other persons' viewpoint.'

Sam Douglas of Hempstead, New York, used to tell his wife that she spent too much time working on their lawn, pulling weeds, fertilizing, cutting the grass twice a week when the lawn didn't look any better than it had when they moved into their home four years earlier. Naturally, she was distressed by his remarks, and each time he made such remarks the balance of the evening was ruined.

After taking our course, Mr. Douglas realized how foolish he had been all those years. It never occurred to him that she enjoyed doing that work and she might really appreciate a compliment on her diligence.

One evening after dinner, his wife said she wanted to pull some weeds and invited him to keep her company. He first declined, but then thought better of it and went out after her and began to help her pull weeds. She was visibly pleased, and together they spent an hour in hard work and pleasant conversation.

After that he often helped her with the gardening and complimented her on how fine the lawn looked, what a fantastic job she was doing with a yard where the soil was like concrete. Result: a happier life for both because he had learned to look at things from her point of view – even if the subject was only weeds.

In his book *Getting Through to People*, Dr. Gerald S. Nirenberg commented: 'Cooperativeness in conversation is achieved when you show that you consider the other person's ideas and feelings as important as your own. Starting your conversation by giving the other person the purpose or direction of your conversation, governing what you say by what you would want to hear if you were the listener, and accepting his or her viewpoint will encourage the listener to have an open mind to your ideas.'*

I have always enjoyed walking and riding in a park near my home. Like the Druids of ancient Gaul, I all but worship an oak tree, so I was distressed season after season to see the young trees and shrubs killed off by needless fires. These fires weren't caused by careless smokers. They were almost all caused by youngsters who went out to the park to go native and cook a frankfurter or an egg under the trees. Sometimes, these fires raged so fiercely that the fire department had to be called out to fight the conflagration.

There was a sign on the edge of the park saying that anyone who started a fire was liable to fine and imprisonment, but the sign stood in an unfrequented part of the park, and few of the culprits ever saw it. A mounted policeman was supposed to look after the park; but he didn't take his duties too seriously, and the fires continued to spread season after season. On one occasion, I rushed up to a policeman and told him about a fire spreading rapidly through the park and wanted him to notify the fire department, and he nonchalantly replied that it was none of his business because it wasn't in his precinct! I was desperate, so after that when I went riding, I acted as a self-appointed committee of one to protect the public domain. In the beginning, I am afraid I didn't even attempt to see the other people's point of view. When I saw a fire blazing under the trees, I was so unhappy about it, so eager to do the right thing, that I did

* Dr. Gerald S. Nirenberg, *Getting Through to People* (Englewood Cliffs, N.J. Prentice-Hall, 1963), p.31.

the wrong thing. I would ride up to the boys, warn them that they could be jailed for starting a fire, order with a tone of authority that it be put out; and, if they refused, I would threaten to have them arrested. I was merely unloading my feelings without thinking of their point of view.

The result? They obeyed – obeyed sullenly and with resentment. After I rode on over the hill, they probably rebuilt the fire and longed to burn up the whole park.

With the passing of the years, I acquired a trifle more knowledge of human relations, a little more tact, a somewhat greater tendency to see things from the other person's standpoint. Then, instead of giving orders, I would ride up to a blazing fire and begin something like this:

'Having a good time, boys? What are you going to cook for supper? . . . I loved to build fires myself when I was a boy – and I still love to. But you know they are dangerous here in the park. I know you boys don't mean to do any harm, but other boys aren't so careful. They come along and see that you have built a fire; so they build one and don't put it out when they go home and it spreads among the dry leaves and kills the trees. We won't have any trees here at all if we aren't more careful. You could be put in jail for building this fire. But I don't want to be bossy and interfere with your pleasure. I like to see you enjoy yourselves; but won't you please rake all the leaves away from the fire right now – and you'll be careful to cover it with dirt, a lot of dirt, before you leave, won't you? And the next time you want to have some fun, won't you please build your fire over the hill there in the sandpit? It can't do any harm there. . . . Thanks so much boys. Have a good time.'

What a difference that kind of talk made! It made the boys want to cooperate. No sullenness, no resentment. They hadn't been forced to obey orders. They had saved their faces. They felt better and I felt better because I had handled the situation with consideration for their point of view.

Seeing things through another person's eyes may ease tensions when personal problems become overwhelming. Elizabeth Novak of New South Wales, Australia, was six weeks late with her car payment. 'On a Friday,' she reported, 'I received a nasty phone call from the man who was handling my account informing me that if I did not come up with $122 by Monday morning I could anticipate further action from the company. I had no way of raising the money over the weekend, so when I received his phone call first thing on Monday morning I expected the worst. Instead of becoming upset, I looked at the situation from his point of view. I apologized most sincerely for causing him so much inconvenience and remarked that I must be his most troublesome customer as this was not the first time I was behind in my payments. His tone of voice changed immediately, and he reassured me that I was far from being one of his really troublesome customers. He went on to tell me several examples of how rude his customers sometimes were, how they lied to him and often tried to avoid talking to him at all. I said nothing. I listened and let him pour out his troubles to me. Then, without any suggestion from me, he said it did not matter if I couldn't pay all the money immediately. It would be all right if I paid him $20 by the end of the month and made up the balance whenever it was convenient for me to do so.'

Tomorrow, before asking anyone to put out a fire or buy your product or contribute to your favourite charity, why not pause and close your eyes and try to think the whole thing through from another person's point of view? Ask yourself: 'Why should he or she want to do it?' True, this will take time, but it will avoid making enemies and will get better results – and with less friction and less shoe leather.

'I would rather walk the sidewalk in front of a person's office for two hours before an interview,' said Dean Donham of the Harvard business school, 'than step into that office without a perfectly clear idea of what I was going to say and what that person – from my knowledge of his or her interests and motives – was likely to answer.'

That is so important that I am going to repeat it in italics for the sake of emphasis.

I would rather walk the sidewalk in front of a person's office for two hours before an interview than step into that office without a perfectly clear idea of what I was going to say and what that person – from my knowledge of his or her interests and motives – was likely to answer.

If, as a result of reading this book, you get only one thing – an increased tendency to think always in terms of the other person's point of view, and see things from that person's angle, as well as your own – if you get only one thing from this book, it may easily prove to be one of the stepping-stones of your career.

PRINCIPLE 8

Try honestly to see things from the other person's point of view.

□ **9** □

What everybody wants

Wouldn't you like to have a magic phrase that would stop arguments, eliminate ill feeling, create good will, and make the other person listen attentively?

Yes? All right. Here is it: 'I don't blame you one iota for feeling as you do. If I were you I would undoubtedly feel just as you do.'

An answer like that will soften the most cantankerous old cuss alive. And you can say that and be 100 percent sincere, because if you were the other person you, of course, would feel just as he does. Take Al Capone, for example. Suppose you had inherited the same body and temperament and mind that Al Capone had. Suppose you had his environment and experiences. You would then be precisely what he was – and where he was. For it is those things – and only those things – that made him what he was. The only reason, for example, that you are not a rattlesnake is that your mother and father weren't rattlesnakes.

You deserve very little credit for being what you are – and remember, the people who come to you irritated, bigoted, unreasoning, deserve very little discredit for being what they are. Feel sorry for the poor devils. Pity them. Sympathize with them. Say to yourself: 'There, but for the grace of God, go I.'

Three-fourths of the people you will ever meet are hungering and thirsting for sympathy. Give it to them, and they will love you.

I once gave a broadcast about the author of *Little Women*, Louisa May Alcott. Naturally, I knew she had lived and written her immortal books in Concord, Massachusetts. But, without thinking what I was saying, I spoke of visiting her old home in Concord, New Hampshire. If I had said New Hampshire only once, it might have been forgiven. But, alas and alack! I said it twice. I was deluged with letters and telegrams, stinging messages that swirled around my defenceless head like a swarm of hornets. Many were indignant. A few insulting. One Colonial Dame, who had been reared in Concord, Massachusetts, and who was then living in Philadelphia, vented her scorching wrath upon me. She couldn't have been much more bitter if I had accused Miss Alcott of being a cannibal from New Guinea. As I read the letter, I said to myself, 'Thank God, I am not married to that woman.' I felt like writing and telling her that although I had made a mistake in geography, she had made a far greater mistake in common courtesy. That was to be just my opening sentence. Then I was going to roll up my sleeves and tell her what I really thought. But I didn't. I controlled myself. I realized that any hotheaded fool could do that – and that most fools would do just that.

I wanted to be above fools. So I resolved to try to turn her hostility into friendliness. It would be a challenge, a sort of game I could play. I said to myself, 'After all, if I were she, I would probably feel just as she does.' So, I determined to sympathize with her viewpoint. The next time I was in Philadelphia, I called her on the telephone. The conversation went something like this:

ME: Mrs. So-and-So, you wrote me a letter a few weeks ago, and I want to thank you for it.

SHE: (in incisive, cultured, well-bred tones): To whom have I the honour of speaking?

ME: I am a stranger to you. My name is Dale Carnegie. You listened to a broadcast I gave about Louisa May Alcott a few Sundays ago, and I made the unforgivable blunder of saying that she had lived in Concord, New Hampshire. It was a stupid blunder, and I want to apologize for it. It was so nice of you to take the time to write me.

SHE: I am sorry, Mr. Carnegie, that I wrote as I did. I lost my temper. I must apologize.

ME: No! No! You are not the one to apologize; I am. Any school child would have known better than to have said what I said. I apologized over the air the following Sunday, and I want to apologize to you personally now.

SHE: I was born in Concord, Massachusetts. My family has been prominent in Massachusetts affairs for two centuries, and I am very proud of my native state. I was really quite distressed to hear you say that Miss Alcott had lived in New Hampshire. But I am really ashamed of that letter.

ME: I assure you that you were not one-tenth as distressed as I am. My error didn't hurt Massachusetts, but it did hurt me. It is so seldom that people of your standing and culture take time to write people who speak on the radio, and I do hope you will write again if you detect an error in my talks.

SHE: You know, I really like very much the way you have accepted my criticism. You must be a very nice person. I should like to know you better.

So, because I had apologized and sympathized with her point of view, she began apologizing and sympathizing with my point of view. I had the satisfaction of controlling my temper, the satisfaction of returning kindness for an insult. I got infinitely more fun out of making her like me than I could ever have gotten out of telling her to go and take a jump in the Shuylkill River.

Every man who occupies the White House is faced almost daily with thorny problems in human relations. President Taft was no exception, and he learned from experience the enormous chemical value of sympathy in neutralizing the acid of hard feelings. In his book *Ethics in Service*, Taft gives rather an amusing illustration of how he softened the ire of a disappointed and ambitious mother.

'A lady in Washington,' wrote Taft, 'whose husband had some political influence, came and laboured with me for six weeks or more to appoint her son to a position. She secured the aid of Senators and Congressmen in formidable number and came with them to see that they spoke with emphasis. The place was one requiring technical qualification, and following the recommendation of the head of the Bureau, I appointed somebody else. I then received a letter from the mother, saying that I was most ungrateful, since I declined to make her a happy woman as I could have done by a turn of my hand. She complained further that she had laboured with her state delegation and got all the votes for an administration bill in which I was especially interested and this was the way I had rewarded her.

'When you get a letter like that, the first thing you do is to think how you can be severe with a person who has committed an impropriety, or even been a little impertinent. Then you may compose an answer. Then if you are wise, you will put the letter in a drawer and lock the drawer. Take it out in the course of two days – such communications will always bear two days' delay in answering – and when you take it out after that interval, you will not send it. That is just the course I took. After that, I sat down and wrote her just as polite a letter as I could, telling her I realized a mother's disappointment under such circumstances, but that really the appointment was not left to my mere personal preference, that I had to select a man with technical qualifications, and had, therefore, to follow the recommendations of the head of the Bureau. I expressed the hope that her son would go on to accomplish what she had hoped for him in the position which he then had. That mollified her and she wrote me a note saying she was sorry she had written as she had.

'But the appointment I sent in was not confirmed at once, and after an interval I received a letter which purported to come from her husband, though it was in the same handwriting as all the others. I was therein advised that, due to the nervous prostration that had followed her disappointment in this case, she had to take to her bed and had developed a most serious case of cancer of the stomach. Would I not restore her to health by withdrawing the first name and replacing it by her son's? I had to write another letter, this one to the husband, to say that I hoped the diagnosis would prove to be inaccurate, that I sympathized with him in the sorrow he must have in the serious illness of his wife, but that it was impossible to withdraw the name sent in. The man whom I appointed was confirmed, and within two days after I received that letter, we gave a musicale at the White House. The first two people to greet Mrs. Taft and me were this husband and wife, though the wife had so recently been *in articulo mortis*.'

Jay Mangum represented an elevator-escalator maintenance company in Tulsa, Oklahoma, which had the maintenance contract for the escalators in one of Tulsa's leading hotels. The hotel manager did not want to shut down the escalator for more than two hours at a time because he did not want to inconvenience the hotel's guests. The repair that had to be made would take at least eight hours, and his company did not always have a specially qualified mechanic available at the convenience of the hotel.

When Mr. Mangum was able to schedule a top-flight mechanic for this job, he telephoned the hotel manager and instead of arguing with him to give him the necessary time he said:

'Rick, I know your hotel is quite busy and you would like to keep the escalator shutdown time to a minimum. I understand your concern about this, and we want to do everything possible to accommodate you. However, our diagnosis of the situation shows that if we do not do a complete job now, your escalator may suffer more serious damage and that would cause a much longer shutdown. I know you would not want to inconvenience your guests for several days.'

The manager had to agree that an eight-hour shutdown was more desirable than several days'. By sympathizing with the manager's desire to keep his patrons happy, Mr. Mangum was able to win the hotel manager to his way of thinking easily and without rancour.

Joyce Norris, a piano teacher in St. Louis, Missouri, told of how she had handled a problem piano teachers often have with teenage girls. Babette had exceptionally long fingernails. This is a serious handicap to anyone who wants to develop proper piano-playing habits.

Mrs Norris reported: 'I knew her long fingernails would be a barrier for her in her desire to play well. During our discussion prior to her starting her lessons with me, I did not mention anything to her about her nails. I didn't want to discourage her from taking lessons, and I also knew she would not want to lose that which she took so much pride in and such great care to make attractive.

'After her first lesson, when I felt the time was right, I said: "Babette, you have attractive hands and beautiful fingernails. If you want to play the piano as well as you are capable of and as well as you would like to, you would be surprised how much quicker and easier it would be for you, if you would trim your nails shorter. Just think about it, okay?" She made a face which was definitely negative. I also talked to her mother about this situation, again mentioning how lovely her nails were. Another negative reaction. It was obvious that Babette's beautifully manicured nails were important to her.

'The following week Babette returned for her second lesson. Much to my surprise, the fingernails had been trimmed. I complimented her and praised her for making such a sacrifice. I also thanked her mother for influencing Babette to cut her nails. Her reply was "Oh, I had nothing to do with it. Babette decided to do it on her own, and this is the first time she has ever trimmed her nails for anyone." '

Did Mrs Norris threaten Babette? Did she say she would refuse to teach a student with long fingernails? No, she did not. She let Babette know that her fingernails were a thing of beauty and it would be a sacrifice to cut them. She implied, 'I sympathize with you – I know it won't be easy, but it will pay off in your better musical development.'

Sol Hurok was probably America's number one impresario. For almost half a century he handled artists – such world-famous artists as Chaliapin, Isadora Duncan, and Pavlova. Mr. Hurok told me that one of the first lessons he had learned in dealing with his temperamental stars was the necessity for sympathy, sympathy and more sympathy with their idiosyncrasies.

For three years, he was impresario for Feodor Chaliapin – one of the greatest bassos who ever thrilled the ritzy boxholders at the Metropolitan. Yet Chaliapin was a constant problem. He carried on like a spoiled child. To put it in Mr. Hurok's own inimitable phrase: 'He was a hell of a fellow in every way.'

For example, Chaliapin would call up Mr. Hurok about noon of the day he was going to sing and say, 'Sol, I feel terrible. My throat is like raw hamburger. It is impossible for me to sing tonight.' Did Mr. Hurok argue with him? Oh, no. He knew that an entrepreneur couldn't handle artists that way. So he would rush over to Chaliapin's hotel, dripping with sympathy. 'What a pity,' he would mourn. 'What a pity! My poor fellow. Of course, you cannot sing. I will cancel the engagement at once. It will only cost you a couple of thousand dollars, but that is nothing in comparison to your reputation.'

Then Chaliapin would sigh and say, 'Perhaps you had better come over later in the day. Come at five and see how I feel then.'

At five o'clock, Mr. Hurok would again rush to his hotel, dripping with sympathy. Again he would insist on cancelling the engagement and again Chaliapin would sigh and say, 'Well, maybe you had better come to see me later. I may be better then.'

At seven-thirty the great basso would consent to sing, only with the understanding that Mr. Hurok would walk out on the stage of the Metropolitan and announce that Chaliapin had a very bad cold and was not in good voice. Mr. Hurok would lie and say he would do it, for he knew that was the only way to get the basso out on the stage.

Dr. Arthur I. Gates said in his splendid book *Educational Psychology:* 'Sympathy the human species universally craves. The child eagerly displays his injury; or even inflicts a cut or bruise in order to reap abundant sympathy. For the same purpose adults . . . show their bruises, relate their accidents, illness, especially details of surgical operations. "Self-pity" for misfortunes real or imaginary is, in some measure, practically a universal practice.'

So, if you want to win people to your way of thinking, put in practice . . .

PRINCIPLE 9

Be sympathetic with the other person's ideas and desires.

□ 10 □

An appeal that everybody likes

I was reared on the edge of the Jesse James country out in Missouri, and I visited the James farm at Kearney, Missouri, where the son of Jesse James was then living.

His wife told me stories of how Jesse robbed trains and held up banks and then gave money to the neighbouring farmers to pay off their mortgages.

Jesse James probably regarded himself as an idealist at heart, just as Dutch Schultz, 'Two Gun' Crowley, Al Capone and many other organized crime 'godfathers' did generations later. The fact is that all people you meet have a high regard for themselves and like to be fine and unselfish in their own estimation.

J. Pierpont Morgan observed, in one of his analytical interludes, that a person usually has two reasons for doing a thing: one that sounds good and a real one.

The person himself will think of the real reason. You don't need to emphasize that. But all of us, being idealists at heart, like to think of motives that sound good. So, in order to change people, appeal to the nobler motives.

Is that too idealistic to work in business? Let's see. Let's take the case of Hamilton J. Farrell of the Farrell-Mitchell Company of Glenolden, Pennsylvania. Mr. Farrell had a disgruntled tenant who threatened to move. The tenant's lease still had four months to run; nevertheless, he served notice that he was vacating immediately, regardless of lease.

'These people had lived in my house all winter – the most expensive part of the year,' Mr. Farrell said as he told the story to the class, 'and I knew it would be difficult to rent the apartment again before fall. I could see all that rent income going over the hill and believe me, I saw red.

'Now, ordinarily, I would have waded into that tenant and advised him to read his lease again. I would have pointed out that if he moved, the full balance of his rent would fall due at once – and that I could, *and would* move to collect.

'However, instead of flying off the handle and making a scene, I decided to try other tactics. So I started like this: "Mr. Doe," I said, "I have listened to your story, and I still don't believe you intend to move. Years in the renting business have taught me something about human nature, and I sized you up in the first place as being a man of your word. In fact, I'm so sure of it that I'm willing to take a gamble.

' "Now, here's my proposition. Lay your decision on the table for a few days and think it over. If you come back to me between now and the first of the month, when your rent is due, and tell me you still intend to move, I give you my word I will accept your decision as final. I will privilege you to move and admit to myself I've been wrong in my judgement. But I still believe you're a man of your word and will live up to your contract. For after all, we are either men or monkeys – and the choice usually lies with ourselves!"

'Well, when the new month came around, this gentleman came to see me and paid his rent in person. He and his wife had talked it over, he said – and decided to stay. They had concluded that the only honourable thing to do was to live up to their lease.'

When the late Lord Northcliffe found a newspaper using a picture of him which he didn't want published, he wrote the editor a letter. But did he say, 'Please do not publish that picture of me any more; *I* don't like it'? No, he appealed to a nobler motive. He appealed to the respect and love that all of us have for motherhood. He wrote, 'Please do not publish that picture of me any more. My mother doesn't like it.'

When John D. Rockefeller, Jr., wished to stop newspaper photographers from snapping pictures of his children, he too appealed to the nobler motives. He didn't say: 'I don't want their pictures published.' No, he appealed to the desire, deep in all of us, to refrain from harming children. He said: 'You know how it is, boys. You've got children yourselves, some of you. And you know it's not good for youngsters to get too much publicity.'

When Cyrus H. K. Curtis, the poor boy from Maine, was starting on his meteoric career, which was destined to make him millions as owner of *The Saturday Evening Post* and the *Ladies' Home Journal,* he couldn't afford to pay his contributors the prices that other magazines paid. He couldn't afford to hire first-class authors to write for money alone. So he appealed to their nobler motives. For example, he persuaded even Louisa May Alcott, the immortal author of *Little Women*, to write for him when she was at the flood tide of her fame; and he did it by offering to send a cheque for a hundred dollars, not to her, but to her favourite charity.

Right here the sceptic may say: 'Oh, that stuff is all right for Northcliffe and Rockefeller or a sentimental novelist. But, I'd like to see you make it work with the tough babies I have to collect bills from!'

You may be right. Nothing will work in all cases – and nothing will work with all people. If you are satisfied with the results you are now getting, why change? If you are not satisfied, why not experiment?

At any rate, I think you will enjoy reading this true story told by James L. Thomas, a former student of mine:

Six customers of a certain automobile company refused to pay their bills for servicing. None of the customers protested the entire bill, but each claimed that some one charge was wrong. In each case, the customer had signed for the work done, so the company knew it was right – and said so. That was the first mistake.

Here are the steps the men in the credit department took to collect these overdue bills. Do you suppose they succeeded?

1 They called on each customer and told him bluntly that they had come to collect a bill that was long past due.
2 They made it very plain that the company was absolutely and unconditionally right; therefore he, the customer, was absolutely and unconditionally wrong.
3 They intimated that they, the company, knew more about automobiles than he could ever hope to know. So what was the argument about?
4 Result: They argued.

Did any of these methods reconcile the customer and settle the account? You can answer that one yourself.

At this stage of affairs the credit manager was about to open fire with a battery of legal talent, when fortunately the matter came to the attention of the general manager. The manager investigated these defaulting clients and discovered that they all had the reputation of paying their bills promptly. Something was drastically wrong about the method of collection. So he called in James L. Thomas and told him to collect these 'uncollectable' accounts.

Here, in his own words, are the steps Mr. Thomas took:

1 My visit to each customer was likewise to collect a bill long past due – a bill that we knew was absolutely right. But I didn't say a word about that. I explained I had called to find out what it was the company had done, or failed to do.
2 I made it clear that, until I had heard the customer's story, I had no opinion to offer. I told him the company made no claims to being infallible.
3 I told him I was interested only in his car, and that he knew more about his car than anyone else in the world; that he was the authority on the subject.
4 I let him talk, and I listened to him with all the interest and sympathy that he wanted – and had expected.
5 Finally, when the customer was in a reasonable mood, I put the whole thing up to his sense of fair play. I appealed to the nobler motives. 'First,' I said, 'I want you to know I also feel that this matter has been badly mishandled. You've been inconvenienced and annoyed and irritated by one of our representatives. That should never have happened. I'm sorry and, as a representative of the company, I apologize. As I sat here and listened to your side of the story, I could not help being impressed by your fairness and patience. And now, because you are fair-minded and patient, I am

going to ask you to do something for me. It's something that you can do better than anyone else, something you know more about than anyone else. Here is your bill; I know it is safe for me to ask you to adjust it, just as you would do if you were the president of my company. I am going to leave it all up to you. Whatever you say goes.'

Did he adjust the bill? He certainly did, and got quite a kick out of it. The bills ranged from $150 to $400 – but did the customer give himself the best of it? Yes, one of them did! One of them refused to pay a penny of the disputed charge; but the other five all gave the company the best of it! And here's the cream of the whole thing: we delivered new cars to all six of these customers within the next two years!

'Experience has taught me,' says Mr. Thomas, 'That when no information can be secured about the customer, the only sound basis on which to proceed is to assume that he or she is sincere, honest, truthful and willing and anxious to pay the charges, once convinced they are correct. To put it differently and perhaps more clearly, people are honest and want to discharge their obligations. The exceptions to that rule are comparatively few, and I am convinced that the individuals who are inclined to chisel will in most cases react favourably if you make them feel that you consider them honest, upright and fair.'

PRINCIPLE 10

Appeal to the nobler motives.

□ 11 □

The movies do it. TV does it. Why don't you do it?

Many years ago, the Philadelphia *Evening Bulletin* was being maligned by a dangerous whispering campaign. A malicious rumour was being circulated. Advertisers were being told that the newspaper was no longer attractive to readers because it carried too much advertising and too little news. Immediate action was necessary. The gossip had to be squelched.

But how?

This is the way it was done.

The *Bulletin* clipped from its regular edition all reading matter of all kinds on one average day, classified it, and published it as a book. The book was called *One Day*. It contained 307 pages – as many as a hard-covered book; yet the *Bulletin* had printed all this news and feature material on one day and sold it, not for several dollars, but for a few cents.

The printing of that book dramatized the fact that the *Bulletin* carried an enormous amount of interesting reading matter. It conveyed the facts more vividly, more interestingly, more impressively, than pages of figures and mere talk could have done.

This is the day of dramatization. Merely stating a truth isn't enough. The truth has to be made vivid, interesting, dramatic. You have to use showmanship. The movies do it. Television does it. And you will have to do it if you want attention.

Experts in window display know the power of dramatization. For example, the manufacturers of a new rat poison gave dealers a window display that included two live rats. The week the rats were shown, sales zoomed to five times their normal rate.

Television commercials abound with examples of the use of dramatic techniques in selling products. Sit down one evening in front of your television set and analyze what the advertisers do in each of their presentations. You will note how an antacid medicine changes the colour of the acid in a test tube while its competitor doesn't, how one brand of soap or detergent gets a greasy shirt clean when the other brand leaves it grey. You'll see a car manoeuvre around a series of turns and curves – far better than just being told about it. Happy faces will show contentment with a variety of products. All of these dramatize for the viewer the advantages offered by whatever is being sold – and they do get people to buy them.

You can dramatize your ideas in business or in any other aspect of your life. It's easy. Jim Yeamans, who sells for the NCR company (National Cash Register) in Richmond, Virginia, told how he made a sale by dramatic demonstration.

'Last week I called on a neighbourhood grocer and saw that the cash registers he was using at his checkout counters were very old-fashioned. I approached the owner and told him: 'You are literally throwing away pennies every time a customer goes through your line.' With that I threw a handful of pennies on the floor. He quickly became more attentive. The mere words should have been of interest to him, but the sound of pennies hitting the floor really stopped him. I was able to get an order from him to replace all of his old machines.'

It works in home life as well. When the old-time lover proposed to his sweetheart, did he just use words of love? No! He went down on his knees. That really showed he meant what he said. We don't propose on our knees any more, but many suitors still set up a romantic atmosphere before they pop the question.

Dramatizing what you want works with children as well. Joe B. Fant, Jr., of Birmingham, Alabama, was having difficulty getting his five-year-old boy and three-year-old daughter to pick up their toys, so he invented a 'train.' Joey was the engineer (Captain Casey Jones) on his tricycle. Janet's wagon was attached, and in the evening she loaded all the 'coal' on the caboose (her wagon) and then jumped in while her brother drove her around the room. In this way the room was cleaned up – without lectures, arguments or threats.

Mary Catherine Wolf of Mishawaka, Indiana, was having some problems at work and decided that she had to discuss them with the boss. On Monday morning she requested an appointment with him but was told he was very busy and she should arrange with his secretary for an appointment later in the week. The secretary indicated that his schedule was very tight, but she would try to fit her in.

Ms. Wolf described what happened:

'I did not get a reply from her all week long. Whenever I questioned her, she would give me a reason why the boss could not see me. Friday morning came and I had heard nothing definite. I really wanted to see him and discuss my problems before the weekend, so I asked myself how I could get him to see me.

'What I finally did was this. I wrote him a formal letter. I indicated in the letter that I fully understood how extremely busy he was all week, but it was important that I speak with him. I enclosed a form letter and a self-addressed envelope and asked him to please fill it out or ask his secretary to do it and return it to me. The form letter read as follows:

Ms. Wolf – I will be able to see you on — at — a.m./p.m. I will give you — minutes of my time.

'I put this letter in his in-basket at 11 a.m. At 2 p.m. I checked my mailbox. There was my self-addressed envelope. He had answered my form letter himself and indicated he could see me that afternoon and could give me ten minutes of his time. I met with him, and we talked for over an hour and resolved my problems.

'If I had not dramatized to him the fact that I really wanted to see him, I would probably be still waiting for an appointment.'

James B. Boynton had to present a lengthy market report. His firm had just finished an exhaustive study for a leading brand of cold cream. Data were needed immediately about the competition in this market; the prospective customer was one of the biggest – and most formidable – men in the advertising business.

And his first approach failed almost before he began.

'The first time I went in,' Mr. Boynton explains, 'I found myself sidetracked into a futile discussion of the methods used in the investigation. He argued and I argued. He told me I was wrong, and I tried to prove that I was right.

'I finally won my point, to my own satisfaction – but my time was up, the interview was over, and I still hadn't produced results.

'The second time, I didn't bother with tabulations of figures and data. I went to see this man, I dramatized my facts.

'As I entered his office, he was busy on the phone. While he finished his conversation, I opened a suitcase and dumped thirty-two jars of cold cream on top of his desk – all products he knew – all competitors of his cream.

'On each jar, I had a tag itemizing the results of the trade investigation. And each tag told its story briefly, dramatically.

'What happened?

'There was no longer an argument. Here was something new, something different. He picked up first one then another of the jars of cold cream and read the information on the tag. A friendly conversation developed. He asked additional questions. He was intensely interested. He had originally given me only ten minutes to present my facts, but ten minutes passed, twenty minutes, forty minutes, and at the end of an hour we were still talking.

'I was presenting the same facts this time that I had presented previously. But this time I was using dramatization, showmanship – and what a difference it made.'

PRINCIPLE 11

Dramatize your ideas.

☐ 12 ☐

When nothing else works, try this

Charles Schwab had a mill manager whose people weren't producing their quota of work.

'How is it,' Schwab asked him, 'that a manager as capable as you can't make this mill turn out what it should?'

'I don't know,' the manager replied. 'I've coaxed the men, I've pushed them, I've sworn and cussed, I've threatened them with damnation and being fired. But nothing works. They just won't produce.'

This conversation took place at the end of the day, just before the night shift came on. Schwab asked the manager for a piece of chalk, then, turning to the nearest man, asked: 'How many heats did your shift make today?'

'Six.'

Without another word, Schwab chalked a big figure '6' on the floor, and walked away.

When the night shift came in, they saw the '6' and asked what it meant.

'The big boss was in here today,' the day people said. 'He asked us how many heats we made, and we told him six. He chalked it on the floor.'

The next morning Schwab walked through the mill again. The night shift had rubbed out '6' and replaced it with a big '7.'

When the day shift reported for work the next morning, they saw a big '7' chalked on the floor. So the night shift thought they were better than the day shift, did they? Well, they would show the night shift a thing or two. The crew pitched in with enthusiasm, and when they quit that night, they left behind them an enormous, swaggering '10'. Things were stepping up.

Shortly this mill, which had been lagging way behind in production, was turning out more work than any other mill in the plant.

The principle?

Let Charles Schwab say it in his own words: 'The way to get things done,' says Schwab, 'is to stimulate competition. I do not mean in a sordid money-getting way, but in the desire to excel.'

The desire to excel! The challenge! Throwing down the gauntlet! An infallible way of appealing to people of spirit.

Without a challenge, Theodore Roosevelt would never have been President of the United States. The Rough Rider, just back from Cuba, was picked for governor of New York State. The opposition discovered he was no longer a legal resident of the state, and Roosevelt, frightened, wished to withdraw. Then Thomas Collier Platt, then U. S. Senator from New York, threw down the challenge. Turning suddenly on Theodore Roosevelt, he cried in a ringing voice: 'Is the hero of San Juan Hill a coward?'

Roosevelt stayed in the fight – and the rest is history. A challenge not only changed his life; it had a real effect upon the future of his nation.

'All men have fears, but the brave put down their fears and go forward, sometimes to death, but always to victory' was the motto of the King's Guard in ancient Greece. What greater challenge can be offered than the opportunity to overcome those fears?

When Al Smith was the governor of New York, he was up against it. Sing Sing, at the time the most notorious penitentiary west of Devil's Island, was without a warden. Scandals had been sweeping through the prison walls, scandals and ugly rumours. Smith needed a strong man to rule Sing Sing – an iron man. But who? He sent for Lewis E. Lawes of New Hampton.

'How about going up to take charge of Sing Sing?' he said jovially when Lawes stood before him. 'They need a man up there with experience.'

Lawes was flabbergasted. He knew the dangers of Sing Sing. It was a political appointment, subject to the vagaries of political whims. Wardens had come and gone – one lasted only three weeks. He had a career to consider. Was it worth the risk?

Then Smith, who saw his hesitation, leaned back in his chair and smiled. 'Young fellow,' he said, 'I don't blame you for being scared. It's a tough spot. It'll take a big person to go up there and stay.'

So he went. And he stayed. He stayed, to become the most famous warden of his time. His book *20,000 Years in Sing Sing* sold into the hundred of thousands of copies. His broadcasts on the air and his stories of prison life have inspired dozens of movies. His 'humanizing' of criminals wrought miracles in the way of prison reform.

'I have never found,' said Harvey S. Firestone, founder of the great Firestone Tyre and Rubber Company, 'that pay and pay alone would either bring together or hold good people. I think it was the game itself.'

Frederic Herzberg, one of the great behavioural scientists, concurred. He studied in depth the work attitudes of thousands of people ranging from factory workers to senior executives. What do you think he found to be the most motivating factor – the one facet of the jobs that was most stimulating? Money? Good working conditions? Fringe benefits? No – not any of those. The one major factor that motivated people was the work itself. If the work was exciting and interesting, the worker looked forward to doing it and was motivated to do a good job.

That is what every successful person loves: the game. The chance for self-expression. The chance to prove his or her worth, to excel, to win. That is what makes foot-races, and hog-calling, and pie-eating contests. The desire to excel. The desire for a feeling of importance.

PRINCIPLE 12

Throw down a challenge.

PART THREE

☐ **IN A NUTSHELL** ☐

WIN PEOPLE TO YOUR OWN WAY OF THINKING

PRINCIPLE 1

The only way to get the best of an argument is to avoid it.

PRINCIPLE 2

Show respect for the other person's opinions. Never say, 'You're wrong.'

PRINCIPLE 3

If you are wrong, admit it quickly and emphatically.

PRINCIPLE 4

Begin in a friendly way.

PRINCIPLE 5

Get the other person saying 'yes, yes' immediately.

PRINCIPLE 6

Let the other person do a great deal of the talking.

PRINCIPLE 7

Let the other person feel that the idea is his or hers.

PRINCIPLE 8

Try honestly to see things from the other person's point of view.

145

PRINCIPLE 9

Be sympathetic with the other person's ideas and desires.

PRINCIPLE 10

Appeal to the nobler motives.

PRINCIPLE 11

Dramatize your ideas.

PRINCIPLE 12

Throw down a challenge.

Part Four

BE A LEADER:

HOW TO CHANGE PEOPLE

WITHOUT GIVING OFFENCE

OR AROUSING RESENTMENT

□ 1 □

If you must find fault, this is the way to begin

A friend of mine was a guest at the White House for a weekend during the administration of Calvin Coolidge. Drifting into the President's private office, he heard Coolidge say to one of his secretaries, 'That's a very pretty dress you are wearing this morning, and you are a very attractive young woman.'

That was probably the most effusive praise Silent Cal had ever bestowed upon a secretary in his life. It was so unusual, so unexpected, that the secretary blushed in confusion. Then Coolidge said, 'Now, don't get stuck up. I just said that to make you feel good. From now on, I wish you would be a little more careful with your punctuation.'

His method was probably a bit obvious, but the psychology was superb. It is always easier to listen to unpleasant things after we have heard some praise of our good points.

A barber lathers a man before he shaves him; and that is precisely what McKinley did back in 1896, when he was running for President. One of the prominent Republicans of that day had written a campaign speech that he felt was just a trifle better than Cicero and Patrick Henry and Daniel Webster all rolled into one. With great glee, this chap read his immortal speech aloud to McKinley. The speech had its fine points, but it just wouldn't do. McKinley didn't want to hurt the man's feelings. He must not kill the man's splendid enthusiasm, and yet he had to say 'no'. Note how adroitly he did it.

'My friend, that is a splendid speech, a magnificent speech,' McKinley said. 'No one could have prepared a better one. There are many occasions on which it would be precisely the right thing to say, but is it quite suitable to this particular occasion? Sound and sober as it is from your standpoint, I must consider its effect from the party's standpoint. Now go home and write a speech along the lines I indicate, and send me a copy of it.'

He did just that. McKinley blue-pencilled and helped him rewrite his second speech, and he became one of the effective speakers of the campaign.

Here is the second most famous letter that Abraham Lincoln ever wrote. (His most famous one was written to Mrs. Bixby, expressing his sorrow for the death of the five sons she had lost in battle.) Lincoln probably dashed this

149

letter off in five minutes; yet it sold at public auction in 1926 for twelve thousand dollars, and that, by the way, was more money than Lincoln was able to save during half a century of hard work. The letter was written to General Joseph Hooker on April 26, 1863, during the darkest period of the Civil War. For eighteen months, Lincoln's generals had been leading the Union Army from one tragic defeat to another. Nothing but futile, stupid human butchery. The nation was appalled. Thousands of soldiers had deserted from the army, and even the Republican members of the Senate had revolted and wanted to force Lincoln out of the White House. 'We are now on the brink of destruction,' Lincoln said. 'It appears to me that even the Almighty is against us. I can hardly see a ray of hope.' Such was the period of black sorrow and chaos out of which this letter came.

I am printing the letter here because it shows how Lincoln tried to change an obstreperous general when the very fate of the nation could have depended upon the general's action.

This is perhaps the sharpest letter Abe Lincoln wrote after he became President; yet you will note that he praised General Hooker before he spoke of his grave faults.

Yes, they were grave faults, but Lincoln didn't call them that. Lincoln was more conservative, more diplomatic. Lincoln wrote: 'There are some things in regard to which I am not quite satisfied with you.' Talk about tact! And diplomacy!

Here is the letter addressed to General Hooker:

> I have placed you at the head of the Army of the Potomac. Of course, I have done this upon what appears to me to be sufficient reasons, and yet I think it best for you to know that there are some things in regard to which I am not quite satisfied with you.
>
> I believe you to be a brave and skillful soldier, which, of course, I like. I also believe you do not mix politics with your profession, in which you are right. You have confidence in yourself, which is a valuable if not an indispensable quality.
>
> You are ambitious, which, within reasonable bounds, does good rather than harm. But I think that during General Burnside's command of the army you have taken counsel of your ambition and thwarted him as much as you could, in which you did a great wrong to the country and to a most meritorious and honourable brother officer.
>
> I have heard, in such a way as to believe it, of your recently saying that both the army and the Government needed a dictator. Of course, it was not for this, but in spite of it, that I have given you command.
>
> Only those generals who gain successes can set up as dictators. What I now ask of you is military success and I will risk the dictatorship.
>
> The Government will support you to the utmost of its ability, which is neither more nor less than it has done and will do for all commanders. I

much fear that the spirit which you have aided to infuse into the army, of criticizing their commander and withholding confidence from him, will now turn upon you. I shall assist you, as far as I can, to put it down.

Neither you nor Napoleon, if he were alive again, could get any good out of an army while such spirit prevails in it, and now beware of rashness. Beware of rashness, but with energy and sleepless vigilance, go forward and give us victories.

You are not a Coolidge, a McKinley or a Lincoln. You want to know whether this philosophy will operate for you in everyday business contacts. Will it? Let's see. Let's take the case of W. P. Gaw, of the Wark Company, Philadelphia.

The Wark Company had contracted to build and complete a large office building in Philadelphia by a certain specified date. Everything was going along well; the building was almost finished, when suddenly the subcontractor making the ornamental bronze work to go on the exterior of this building declared that he couldn't make delivery on schedule. What! An entire building held up! Heavy penalties! Distressing losses! All because of one man!

Long-distance telephone calls. Arguments! Heated conversations! All in vain. Then Mr. Gaw was sent to New York to beard the bronze lion in his den.

'Do you know you are the only person in Brooklyn with your name?' Mr. Gaw asked the president of the subcontracting firm shortly after they were introduced. The president was surprised. 'No, I didn't know that.'

'Well,' said Mr. Gaw, 'when I got off the train this morning, I looked in the telephone book to get your address, and you're the only person in the Brooklyn phone book with your name.'

'I never knew that,' the subcontractor said. He checked the phone book with interest. 'Well, it's an unusual name,' he said proudly. 'My family came from Holland and settled in New York almost two hundred years ago.' He continued to talk about his family and his ancestors for several minutes. When he finished that, Mr. Gaw complimented him on how large a plant he had and compared it favourably with a number of similar plants he had visited. 'It is one of the cleanest and neatest bronze factories I ever saw.' said Gaw.

'I've spent a lifetime building up this business,' the subcontractor said, 'and I am rather proud of it. Would you like to take a look around the factory?'

During this tour of inspection, Mr. Gaw complimented the other man on his system of fabrication and told him how and why it seemed superior to those of some of his competitors. Gaw commented on some unusual machines, and the subcontractor announced that he himself had invented those machines. He spent considerable time showing Gaw how they operated and the superior work they turned out. He insisted on taking his visitor to lunch. So far, mind you, not a word had been said about the real purpose of Gaw's visit.

After lunch, the subcontractor said, 'Now, to get down to business. Naturally,

I know why you're here. I didn't expect that our meeting would be so enjoyable. You can go back to Philadelphia with my promise that your material will be fabricated and shipped, even if other orders have to be delayed.'

Mr. Gaw got everything that he wanted without even asking for it. The material arrived on time, and the building was completed on the day the completion contract specified.

Would this have happened had Mr. Gaw used the hammer-and-dynamite method generally employed on such occasions?

Dorothy Wrublewski, a branch manager of the Fort Monmouth, New Jersey, Federal Credit Union, reported to one of our classes how she was able to help one of her employees become more productive.

'We recently hired a young lady as a teller trainee. Her contact with our customers was very good. She was accurate and efficient in handling individual transactions. The problem developed at the end of the day when it was time to balance out.

'The head teller came to me and strongly suggested that I fire this woman. "She is holding up everyone else because she is so slow in balancing out. I've shown her over and over, but she can't get it. She's got to go."

'The next day I observed her working quickly and accurately when handling the normal everyday transactions, and she was very pleasant with our customers.

'It didn't take long to discover why she had trouble balancing out. After the office closed, I went over to talk with her. She was obviously nervous and upset. I praised her for being so friendly and outgoing with the customers and complimented her for the accuracy and speed used in that work. I then suggested we review the procedure we use in balancing the cash drawer. Once she realized I had confidence in her, she easily followed my suggestions and soon mastered this function. We have had no problems with her since then.'

Beginning with praise is like the dentist who begins his work with Novocain. The patient still gets a drilling, but the Novocain is pain-killing. A leader will use . . .

PRINCIPLE 1

Begin with praise and honest appreciation.

How to criticize – and not be hated for it

Charles Schwab was passing through one of his steel mills one day at noon when he came across some of his employees smoking. Immediately above their heads was a sign that said 'No Smoking'. Did Schwab point to the sign and say, 'Can't you read?' Oh, no not Schwab. He walked over to the men, handed each one a cigar, and said, 'I'll appreciate it, boys, if you will smoke these on the outside.' They knew that he knew that they had broken a rule – and they admired him because he said nothing about it and gave them a little present and made them feel important. Couldn't keep from loving a man like that, could you?

John Wanamaker used the same technique. Wanamaker used to make a tour of his great store in Philadelphia every day. Once he saw a customer waiting at a counter. No one was paying the slightest attention to her. The salespeople? Oh, they were in a huddle at the far end of the counter laughing and talking among themselves. Wanamaker didn't say a word. Quietly slipping behind the counter, he waited on the woman himself and then handed the purchase to the salespeople to be wrapped as he went on his way.

Public officials are often criticized for not being accessible to their constituents. They are busy people, and the fault sometimes lies in overprotective assistants who don't want to overburden their bosses with too many visitors. Carl Langford, who has been mayor of Orlando, Florida, the home of Disney World, for many years, frequently admonished his staff to allow people to see him. He claimed he had an 'open-door' policy; yet the citizens of his community were blocked by secretaries and administrators when they called.

Finally the mayor found the solution. He removed the door from his office! His aides got the message, and the mayor has had a truly open administration since the day his door was symbolically thrown away.

Simply changing one three-letter word can often spell the difference between failure and success in changing people without giving offence or arousing resentment.

Many people begin their criticism with sincere praise followed by the word 'but' and ending with a critical statement. For example, in trying to change a child's careless attitude toward studies, we might say, 'We're really proud of you, Johnnie, for raising your grades this term. *But* if you had worked harder on your algebra, the results would have been better.'

In this case, Johnnie might feel encouraged until he heard the word 'but'. He might then question the sincerity of the original praise. To him, the praise seemed only to be a contrived lead-in to a critical inference of failure. Credibility would be strained, and we probably would not achieve our objectives of changing Johnnie's attitude toward his studies.

This could be easily overcome by changing the word 'but' to 'and'. 'We're really proud of you, Johnnie, for raising your grades this term, *and* by continuing the same conscientious efforts next term, your algebra grade can be up with all the others.'

Now, Johnnie would accept the praise because there was no follow-up of an inference of failure. We have called his attention to the behaviour we wished to change indirectly, and the chances are he will try to live up to our expectations.

Calling attention to one's mistakes indirectly works wonders with sensitive people who may resent bitterly any direct criticism. Marge Jacob of Woonsocket, Rhode Island, told one of our classes how she convinced some sloppy construction workers to clean up after themselves when they were building additions to her house.

For the first few days of the work, when Mrs. Jacob returned from her job, she noticed that the yard was strewn with the cut ends of lumber. She didn't want to antagonize the builders, because they did excellent work. So after the workers had gone home, she and her children picked up and neatly piled all the lumber debris in a corner. The following morning she called the foreman to one side and said, 'I'm really pleased with the way the front lawn was left last night; it is nice and clean and does not offend the neighbours.' From that day forward the workers picked up and piled the debris to one side, and the foreman came in each day seeking approval of the condition the lawn was left in after a day's work.

One of the major areas of controversy between members of the army reserves and their regular army trainers is haircuts. The reservists consider themselves civilians (which they are most of the time) and resent having to cut their hair short.

Master Sergeant Harley Kaiser of the 542nd USAR School addressed himself to this problem when he was working with a group of reserve noncommissioned officers. As an old-time regular-army master sergeant, he might have been expected to yell at his troops and threaten them. Instead he chose to make his point indirectly.

'Gentlemen,' he started, 'you are leaders. You will be most effective when you lead by example. You must be the example for your men to follow. You know what the army regulations say about haircuts. I am going to get my hair cut today, although it is still much shorter than some of yours. You look at yourself in the mirror, and if you feel you need a haircut to be a good example, we'll arrange time for you to visit the post barbershop.'

The result was predictable. Several of the candidates did look in the mirror and went to the barbershop that afternoon and received 'regulation' haircuts. Sergeant Kaiser commented the next morning that he already could see the development of leadership qualities in some of the members of the squad.

On March 8, 1887, the eloquent Henry Ward Beecher died. The following Sunday, Lyman Abbott was invited to speak in the pulpit left silent by Beecher's passing. Eager to do his best, he wrote, rewrote and polished his sermon with the meticulous care of a Flaubert. Then he read it to his wife. It was poor – as most written speeches are. She might have said, if she had had less judgement, 'Lyman, that is terrible. That'll never do. You'll put people to sleep. It reads like an encyclopaedia. You ought to know better than that after all the years you have been preaching. For heaven's sake, why don't you talk like a human being? Why don't you act natural? You'll disgrace yourself if you ever read that stuff.'

That's what she *might* have said. And, if she had, you know what would have happened. And she knew too. So, she merely remarked that it would make an excellent article for the *North American Review*. In other words, she praised it and at the same time subtly suggested that it wouldn't do as a speech. Lyman Abbott saw the point, tore up his carefully prepared manuscript and preached without even using notes.

An effective way to correct others' mistakes is . . .

PRINCIPLE 2

Call attention to people's mistakes indirectly.

☐ **3** ☐

Talk about your own mistakes first

My niece, Josephine Carnegie, had come to New York to be my secretary. She was nineteen, had graduated from high school three years previously, and her business experience was a trifle more than zero. She became one of the most proficient secretaries west of Suez, but in the beginning, she was – well, susceptible to improvement. One day when I started to criticize her, I said to myself: 'Just a minute, Dale Carnegie; just a minute. You are twice as old as Josephine. You have had ten thousand times as much business experience. How can you possibly expect her to have your viewpoint, your judgement, your initiative – mediocre though they may be? And just a minute, Dale, what were you doing at nineteen? Remember the asinine mistakes and blunders you made? Remember the time you did this . . . and that . . .?'

After thinking the matter over, honestly and impartially, I concluded that Josephine's batting average at nineteen was better than mine had been – and that, I'm sorry to confess, isn't paying Josephine much of a compliment.

So after that, when I wanted to call Josephine's attention to a mistake, I used to begin by saying, 'You have made a mistake, Josephine, but the Lord knows, it's no worse than many I have made. You were not born with judgement. That comes only with experience, and you are better than I was at your age. I have been guilty of so many stupid, silly things myself, I have very little inclination to criticize you or anyone. But don't you think it would have been wiser if you had done so and so?'

It isn't nearly so difficult to listen to a recital of your faults if the person criticizing begins by humbly admitting that he, too, is far from impeccable.

E. G. Dillistone, an engineer in Brandon, Manitoba, Canada, was having problems with his new secretary. Letters he dictated were coming to his desk for signature with two or three spelling mistakes per page. Mr. Dillistone reported how he handled this:

'Like many engineers, I have not been noted for my excellent English or spelling. For years I have kept a little black thumb-index book for words I had trouble spelling. When it became apparent that merely pointing out the errors was not going to cause my secretary to do more proofreading and dictionary work, I resolved to take another approach. When the next letter came to my attention that had errors in it, I sat down with the typist and said:

' "Somehow this word doesn't look right. It's one of the words I always have had trouble with. That's the reason I started this spelling book of mine. [I opened the book to the appropriate page.] Yes, here it is. I'm very conscious of my spelling now because people do judge us by our letters and misspellings make us look less professional."

'I don't know whether she copied my system or not, but since that conversation, her frequency of spelling errors has been significantly reduced.'

The polished Prince Bernhard von Bülow learned the sharp necessity of doing this back in 1909. Von Bülow was then the Imperial Chancellor of Germany, and on the throne sat Wilhelm II – Wilhelm, the haughty; Wilhelm, the arrogant; Wilhelm, the last of the German Kaisers, building an army and navy that he boasted could whip their weight in wildcats.

Then an astonishing thing happened. The Kaiser said things, incredible things, things that rocked the continent and started a series of explosions heard around the world. To make matters infinitely worse, the Kaiser made silly, egotistical, absurd announcements in public, he made them while he was a guest in England, and he gave his royal permission to have them printed in the *Daily Telegraph*. For example, he declared that he was the only German who felt friendly toward the English; that he was constructing a navy against the menace of Japan; that he, and he alone, had saved England from being humbled in the dust by Russia and France; that it had been *his* campaign plan that enabled England's Lord Roberts to defeat the Boers in South Africa; and so on and on.

No other such amazing words had ever fallen from the lips of a European king in peacetime within a hundred years. The entire continent buzzed with the fury of a hornet's nest. England was incensed. German statesmen were aghast. And in the midst of all this consternation, the Kaiser became panicky and suggested to Prince von Bülow, the Imperial Chancellor, that he take the blame. Yes, he wanted von Bülow to announce that it was all his responsibility, that he had advised his monarch to say these incredible things.

'But Your Majesty,' von Bülow protested, 'it seems to me utterly impossible that anybody either in Germany or England could suppose me capable of having advised Your Majesty to say any such thing.'

The moment those words were out of von Bülow's mouth, he realized he had made a grave mistake. The Kaiser blew up.

'You consider me a donkey,' he shouted, 'capable of blunders you yourself could never have committed!'

Von Bülow knew that he ought to have praised before he condemned; but since that was too late, he did the next best thing. He praised after he had criticized. And it worked a miracle.

'I'm far from suggesting that,' he answered respectfully. 'Your Majesty surpasses me in many respects; not only, of course, in naval and military knowledge, but above all, in natural science. I have often listened in admiration when Your Majesty explained the barometer, or wireless telegraphy, or the Roentgen rays. I am shamefully ignorant of all branches of natural science, have no notion of chemistry or physics, and am quite incapable of explaining the simplest of natural phenomena. But,' von Bülow continued, 'in compensation, I possess some historical knowledge and perhaps certain qualities useful in politics, especially in diplomacy.'

The Kaiser beamed. Von Bülow had praised him. Von Bülow had exalted him and humbled himself. The Kaiser could forgive anything after that. 'Haven't I always told you,' he exclaimed with enthusiasm, 'that we complete one another famously? We should stick together, and we will!'

He shook hands with von Bülow, not once, but several times. And later in the day he waxed so enthusiastic that he exclaimed with doubled fists, 'If anyone says anything to me against Prince von Bülow, *I shall punch him in the nose.*'

Von Bülow saved himself in time – but, canny diplomat that he was, he nevertheless had made one error: he should have *begun* by talking about his own shortcomings and Wilhelm's superiority – not by intimating that the Kaiser was a half-wit in need of a guardian.

If a few sentences humbling oneself and praising the other party can turn a haughty, insulted Kaiser into a staunch friend, imagine what humility and praise can do for you and me in our daily contacts. Rightfully used, they will work veritable miracles in human relations.

Admitting one's own mistakes – even when one hasn't corrected them – can help convince somebody to change his behaviour. This was illustrated more recently by Clarence Zerhusen of Timonium, Maryland, when he discovered his fifteen-year-old son was experimenting with cigarettes.

'Naturally, I didn't want David to smoke,' Mr. Zerhusen told us, 'but his mother and I smoked cigarettes; we were giving him a bad example all the time. I explained to Dave how I started smoking at about his age and how the nicotine had gotten the best of me and now it was nearly impossible for me to stop. I reminded him how irritating my cough was and how he had been after me to give up cigarettes not many years before.

'I didn't exhort him to stop or make threats or warn him about their dangers. All I did was point out how I was hooked on cigarettes and what it had meant to me.

'He thought about it for a while and decided he wouldn't smoke until he had graduated from high school. As the years went by David never did start smoking and has no intention of ever doing so.

'As a result of that conversation I made the decision to stop smoking cigarettes myself, and with the support of my family, I have succeeded.'

A good leader follows this principle:

PRINCIPLE 3

Talk about your own mistakes before criticizing the other person.

☐ **4** ☐

No one likes to take orders

I once had the pleasure of dining with Miss Ida Tarbell, the dean of American biographers. When I told her I was writing this book, we began discussing this all-important subject of getting along with people, and she told me that while she was writing her biography of Owen D. Young, she interviewed a man who had sat for three years in the same office with Mr. Young. This man declared that during all that time he had never heard Owen D. Young give a direct order to anyone. He always gave suggestions, not orders. Owen D. Young never said, for example, 'Do this or do that,' or 'Don't do this or don't do that.' He would say, 'You might consider this,' or 'Do you think that would work?' Frequently he would say, after he had dictated a letter, 'What do you think of this?' In looking over a letter of one of his assistants, he would say, 'Maybe if we were to phrase it this way it would be better.' He always gave people the opportunity to do things themselves; he never told his assistants to do things; he let them do them, let them learn from their mistakes.

A technique like that makes it easy for a person to correct errors. A technique like that saves a person's pride and gives him or her a feeling of importance. It encourages cooperation instead of rebellion.

Resentment caused by a brash order may last a long time – even if the order was given to correct an obviously bad situation. Dan Santarelli, a teacher at a vocational school in Wyoming, Pennsylvania, told one of our classes how one of his students had blocked the entrance way to one of the school's shops by illegally parking his car in it. One of the other instructors stormed into the classroom and asked in an arrogant tone, 'Whose car is blocking the driveway?' When the student who owned the car responded, the instructor screamed: 'Move that car and move it right now, or I'll wrap a chain around it and drag it out of there.'

Now that student was wrong. The car should not have been parked there. But from that day on, not only did that student resent the instructor's action, but all the students in the class did everything they could to give the instructor a hard time and make his job unpleasant.

How could he have handled it differently? If he had asked in a friendly way, 'Whose car is in the driveway?' and then suggested that if it were moved, other cars could get in and out, the student would have gladly moved it and neither he nor his classmates would have been upset and resentful.

Asking questions not only makes an order more palatable; it often stimulates the creativity of the persons whom you ask. People are more likely to accept an order if they have had a part in the decision that caused the order to be issued.

When Ian Macdonald of Johannesburg, South Africa, the general manager of a small manufacturing plant specializing in precision machine parts, had the opportunity to accept a very large order, he was convinced that he would not meet the promised delivery date. The work already scheduled in the shop and the short completion time needed for this order made it seem impossible for him to accept the order.

Instead of pushing his people to accelerate their work and rush the order through, he called everybody together, explained the situation to them, and told them how much it would mean to the company and to them if they could make it possible to produce the order in time. Then he started asking questions:

'Is there anything we can do to handle this order?'

'Can anyone think of different ways to process it through the shop that will make it possible to take the order?'

'Is there any way to adjust our hours or personnel assignments that would help?'

The employees came up with many ideas and insisted that he take the order. They approached it with a 'We can do it' attitude, and the order was accepted, produced and delivered on time.

An effective leader will use . . .

PRINCIPLE 4

Ask questions instead of giving direct orders.

□ **5** □

Let the other person save face

Years ago the General Electric Company was faced with the delicate task of removing Charles Steinmetz from the head of a department. Steinmetz, a genius of the first magnitude when it came to electricity, was a failure as the head of the calculating department. Yet the company didn't dare offend the man. He was indispensable – and highly sensitive. So they gave him a new title. They made him Consulting Engineer of the General Electric Company – a new title for work he was already doing – and let someone else head up the department.

Steinmetz was happy.

So were the officers of G.E. They had gently manoeuvred their most temperamental star, and they had done it without a storm – by letting him save face.

Letting one save face! How important, how vitally important that is! And how few of us ever stop to think of it! We ride roughshod over the feelings of others, getting our own way, finding fault, issuing threats, criticizing a child or an employee in front of others, without even considering the hurt to the other person's pride. Whereas a few minutes' thought, a considerate word or two, a genuine understanding of the other person's attitude, would go so far toward alleviating the sting!

Let's remember that the next time we are faced with the distasteful necessity of discharging or reprimanding an employee.

'Firing employees is not much fun. Getting fired is even less fun.' (I'm quoting now from a letter written me by Marshall A. Granger, a certified public accountant.) 'Our business is mostly seasonal. Therefore we have to let a lot of people go after the income tax rush is over.

'It's a byword in our profession that no one enjoys wielding the axe. Consequently, the custom has developed of getting it over as soon as possible, and usually in the following way: "Sit down, Mr. Smith. The season's over, and we don't seem to see any more assignments for you. Of course, you understood you were only employed for the busy season anyhow, etc., etc." '

'The effect on these people is one of disappointment and a feeling of being "let down". Most of them are in the accounting field for life, and they retain no particular love for the firm that drops them so casually.

'I recently decided to let our seasonal personnel go with a little more tact and consideration. So I call each one in only after carefully thinking over his or her work during the winter. And I've said something like this: "Mr. Smith, you've done a fine job (if he has). That time we sent you to Newark, you had a tough assignment. You were on the spot, but you came through with flying colours, and we want you to know the firm is proud of you. You've got the stuff – you're going a long way, wherever you're working. This firm believes in you, and is rooting for you, and we don't want you to forget it." '

'Effect? The people go away feeling a lot better about being fired. They don't feel "let down". They know if we had work for them, we'd keep them on. And when we need them again, they come to us with a keen personal affection.'

At one session of our course, two class members discussed the negative effects of faultfinding versus the positive effects of letting the other person save face.

Fred Clark of Harrisburg, Pennsylvania, told of an incident that occurred in his company: 'At one of our production meetings, a vice president was asking very pointed questions of one of our production supervisors regarding a production process. His tone of voice was aggressive and aimed at pointing out faulty performance on the part of the supervisor. Not wanting to be embarrassed in front of his peers, the supervisor was evasive in his responses. This caused the vice president to lose his temper, berate the supervisor and accuse him of lying.

'Any working relationship that might have existed prior to this encounter was destroyed in a few brief moments. This supervisor, who was basically a good worker, was useless to our company from that time on. A few months later he left our firm and went to work for a competitor, where I understand he is doing a fine job.'

Another class member, Anna Mazzone, related how a similar incident had occurred at her job – but what a difference in approach and results! Ms. Mazzone, a marketing specialist for a food packer, was given her first major assignment – the test-marketing of a new product. She told the class: 'When the results of the test came in, I was devastated. I had made a serious error in my planning, and the entire test had to be done all over again. To make this worse, I had no time to discuss it with my boss before the meeting in which I was to make my report on the project.

'When I was called on to give the report, I was shaking with fright. I had all I could do to keep from breaking down, but I resolved I would not cry and have all those men make remarks about women not being able to handle a management job because they are too emotional. I made my report briefly and stated that due to an error I would repeat the study before the next meeting. I sat down, expecting my boss to blow up.

'Instead, he thanked me for my work and remarked that it was not unusual for a person to make an error on a new project and that he had confidence that the repeat survey would be accurate and meaningful to the company. He assured me, in front of all my colleagues, that he had faith in me and knew I had done my best, and that my lack of experience, not my lack of ability, was the reason for the failure.

'I left that meeting with my head up in the air and with the determination that I would never let that boss of mine down again.'

Even if we are right and the other person is definitely wrong, we only destroy ego by causing someone to lose face. The legendary French aviation pioneer and author Antoine de Saint-Exupéry wrote: 'I have no right to say or do anything that diminishes a man in his own eyes. What matters is not what I think of him, but what he thinks of himself. Hurting a man in his dignity is a crime.'

A real leader will always follow . . .

PRINCIPLE 5

Let the other person save face.

How to spur people on to success

Pete Barlow was an old friend of mine. He had a dog-and-pony act and spent his life travelling with circuses and vaudeville shows. I loved to watch Pete train new dogs for his act. I noticed that the moment the dog showed the slightest improvement, Pete patted and praised him and gave him meat and made a great to-do about it.

That's nothing new. Animal trainers have been using that same technique for centuries.

Why, I wonder, don't we use the same common sense when trying to change people that we use when trying to change dogs? Why don't we use meat instead of a whip? Why don't we use praise instead of condemnation? Let us praise even the slightest improvement. That inspires the other person to keep on improving.

In his book, *I Ain't Much, Baby – But I'm All I Got*, the psychologist Jess Lair comments: 'Praise is like sunlight to the warm human spirit; we cannot flower and grow without it. And yet, while most of us are only too ready to apply to others the cold wind of criticism, we are somehow reluctant to give our fellow the warm sunshine of praise.'*

I can look back at my own life and see where a few words of praise have sharply changed my entire future. Can't you say the same thing about your life? History is replete with striking illustrations of the sheer witchery of praise.

For example, many years ago a boy of ten was working in a factory in Naples. He longed to be a singer, but his first teacher discouraged him. 'You can't sing,' he said. 'You haven't any voice at all. It sounds like the wind in the shutters.'

But his mother, a poor peasant woman, put her arms about him and praised him and told him she knew he could sing, she could already see an improvement, and she went barefoot in order to save money to pay for his music lessons. That peasant mother's praise and encouragement changed that boy's life. His name was Enrico Caruso, and he became the greatest and most famous opera singer of his age.

In the early eighteenth century, a young man in London aspired to be a

* Jess Lair, *I Ain't Much, Baby – But I'm All I Got* (Greenwich, Conn.: Fawcett, 1976), p. 248.

writer. But everything seemed to be against him. He had never been able to attend school more than four years. His father had been flung in jail because he couldn't pay his debts, and this young man often knew the pangs of hunger. Finally, he got a job pasting labels on bottles of blacking in a rat-infested warehouse, and he slept at night in a dismal attic room with two other boys – guttersnipes from the slums of London. He had so little confidence in his ability to write that he sneaked out and mailed his first manuscript in the dead of night so nobody would laugh at him. Story after story was refused. Finally the great day came when one was accepted. True, he wasn't paid a shilling for it, but one editor had praised him. One editor had given him recognition. He was so thrilled that he wandered aimlessly around the streets with tears rolling down his cheeks.

The praise, the recognition, that he received through getting one story in print, changed his whole life, for if it hadn't been for that encouragement, he might have spent his entire life working in rat-infested factories. You may have heard of that boy. His name was Charles Dickens.

Another boy in London made his living as a clerk in a dry-goods store. He had to get up at five o'clock, sweep out the store, and slave for fourteen hours a day. It was sheer drudgery and he despised it. After two years, he could stand it no longer, so he got up one morning and, without waiting for break-fast, tramped fifteen miles to talk to his mother, who was working as a housekeeper.

He was frantic. He pleaded with her. He wept. He swore he would kill himself if he had to remain in the shop any longer. Then he wrote a long, pathetic letter to his old schoolmaster, declaring that he was heartbroken, that he no longer wanted to live. His old schoolmaster gave him a little praise and assured him that he really was very intelligent and fitted for finer things and offered him a job as a teacher.

That praise changed the future of that boy and made a lasting impression on the history of English literature. For that boy went on to write innumerable best-selling books and made over a million dollars with his pen. You've probably heard of him. His name: H. G. Wells.

Use of praise instead of criticism is the basic concept of B. F. Skinner's teachings. This great contemporary psychologist has shown by experiments with animals and with humans that when criticism is minimized and praise emphasized, the good things people do will be reinforced and the poorer things will atrophy for lack of attention.

John Ringelspaugh of Rocky Mount, North Carolina, used this in dealing with his children. It seemed that, as in so many families, mother and dad's chief form of communication with the children was yelling at them. And, as in so many cases, the children became a little worse rather than better after each such session – and so did the parents. There seemed to be no end in sight for this problem.

Mr. Ringelspaugh determined to use some of the principles he was learning in our course to solve this situation. He reported: 'We decided to try praise instead of harping on their faults. It wasn't easy when all we could see were the negative things they were doing; it was really tough to find things to praise. We managed to find something, and within the first day or two some of the really upsetting things they were doing quit happening. Then some of their other faults began to disappear. They began capitalizing on the praise we were giving them. They even began going out of their way to do things right. Neither of us could believe it. Of course, it didn't last forever, but the norm reached after things levelled off was so much better. It was no longer necessary to react the way we used to. The children were doing far more right things than wrong ones.' All of this was a result of praising the slightest improvement in the children rather than condemning everything they did wrong.

This works on the job too. Keith Roper of Woodland Hills, California, applied this principle to a situation in his company. Some material came to him in his print shop which was of exceptionally high quality. The printer who had done this job was a new employee who had been having difficulty adjusting to the job. His supervisor was upset about what he considered a negative attitude and was seriously thinking of terminating his services.

When Mr. Roper was informed of this situation, he personally went over to the print shop and had a talk with the young man. He told him how pleased he was with the work he had just received and pointed out it was the best work he had seen produced in that shop for some time. He pointed out exactly why it was superior and how important the young man's contribution was to the company.

Do you think this affected that young printer's attitude toward the company? Within days there was a complete turnabout. He told several of his co-workers about the conversation and how someone in the company really appreciated good work. And from that day on, he was a loyal and dedicated worker.

What Mr. Roper did was not just flatter the young printer and say, 'You're good.' He specifically pointed out how his work was superior. Because he had singled out a specific accomplishment, rather than just making general flattering remarks, his praise became much more meaningful to the person to whom it was given. Everybody likes to be praised, but when praise is specific, it comes across as sincere – not something the other person may be saying just to make one feel good.

Remember, we all crave appreciation and recognition, and will do almost anything to get it. But nobody wants insincerity. Nobody wants flattery.

Let me repeat: The principles taught in this book will work only when they come from the heart. I am not advocating a bag of tricks. I am talking about a new way of life.

Talking about changing people. If you and I will inspire the people with whom we come in contact to a realization of the hidden treasures they possess, we can do far more than change people. We can literally transform them.

Exaggeration? Then listen to these sage words from William James, one of the most distinguished psychologists and philosophers America has ever produced:

> Compared with what we ought to be, we are only half awake. We are making use of only a small part of our physical and mental resources. Stating the thing broadly, the human individual thus lives far within his limits. He possesses powers of various sorts which he habitually fails to use.

Yes, you who are reading these lines possess powers of various sorts which you habitually fail to use; and one of these powers you are probably not using to the fullest extent is your magic ability to praise people and inspire them with a realization of their latent possibilities.

Abilities wither under criticism; they blossom under encouragement. To become a more effective leader of people, apply . . .

PRINCIPLE 6

Praise the slightest improvement and praise every improvement. Be 'hearty in your approbation and lavish in your praise.'

☐ **7** ☐

Give a dog a good name

What do you do when a person who has been a good worker begins to turn in shoddy work? You can fire him or her, but that really doesn't solve anything. You can berate the worker, but this usually causes resentment. Henry Henke, a service manager for a large truck dealership in Lowell, Indiana, had a mechanic whose work had become less than satisfactory. Instead of bawling him out or threatening him, Mr. Henke called him into his office and had a heart-to-heart talk with him.

'Bill,' he said, 'you are a fine mechanic. You have been in this line of work for a good number of years. You have repaired many vehicles to the customers' satisfaction. In fact, we've had a number of compliments about the good work you have done. Yet, of late, the time you take to complete each job has been increasing and your work has not been up to your own old standards. Because you have been such an outstanding mechanic in the past, I felt sure you would want to know that I am not happy with this situation, and perhaps jointly we could find some way to correct the problem.'

Bill responded that he hadn't realized he had been falling down in his duties and assured his boss that the work he was getting was not out of his range of expertise and he would try to improve in the future.

Did he do it? You can be sure he did. He once again became a fast and thorough mechanic. With that reputation Mr. Henke had given him to live up to, how could he do anything else but turn out work comparable to that which he had done in the past.

'The average person,' said Samuel Vauclain, then president of the Baldwin Locomotive Works, 'can be led readily if you have his or her respect and if you show that you respect that person for some kind of ability.'

In short, if you want to improve a person in a certain respect, act as though that particular trait were already one of his or her outstanding characteristics. Shakespeare said 'Assume a virtue, if you have it not.' And it might be well to assume and state openly that other people have the virtue you want them to develop. Give them a fine reputation to live up to, and they will make prodigious efforts rather than see you disillusioned.

Georgette Leblanc, in her book *Souvenirs, My life with Maeterlinck*, describes the startling transformation of a humble Belgian Cinderella.

'A servant girl from a neighbouring hotel brought my meals,' she wrote. 'She was called "Marie the Dishwasher" because she had started her career as a scullery assistant. She was a kind of monster, cross-eyed, bandy-legged, poor in flesh and spirit.

'One day, while she was holding my plate of macaroni in her red hand, I said to her point-blank, "Marie, you do not know what treasures are within you." '

'Accustomed to holding back her emotion, Marie waited for a few moments, not daring to risk the slightest gesture for fear of a catastrophe. Then she put the dish on the table, sighed and said ingenuously, "Madame, I would never have believed it." She did not doubt, she did not ask a question. She simply went back to the kitchen and repeated what I had said, and such is the force of faith that no one made fun of her. From that day on, she was even given a certain consideration. But the most curious change of all occurred in the humble Marie herself. Believing she was the tabernacle of unseen marvels, she began taking care of her face and body so carefully that her starved youth seemed to bloom and modestly hide her plainness.

'Two months later, she announced her coming marriage with the nephew of the chef. "I'm going to be a lady," she said, and thanked me. A small phrase had changed her entire life.'

Georgette Leblanc had given 'Marie the Dishwasher' a reputation to live up to – and that reputation had transformed her.

Bill Parker, a sales representative for a food company in Daytona Beach, Florida, was very excited about the new line of products his company was introducing and was upset when the manager of a large independent food market turned down the opportunity to carry it in his store. Bill brooded all day over this rejection and decided to return to the store before he went home that evening and try again.

'Jack,' he said, 'since I left this morning I realized I hadn't given you the entire picture of our new line, and I would appreciate some of your time to tell you about the points I omitted. I have respected the fact that you are always willing to listen and are big enough to change your mind when the facts warrant a change.'

Could Jack refuse to give him another hearing? Not with that reputation to live up to.

One morning Dr. Martin Fitzhugh, a dentist in Dublin, Ireland, was shocked when one of his patients pointed out to him that the metal cup holder which she was using to rinse her mouth was not very clean. True, the patient drank from the paper cup, not the holder, but it certainly was not professional to use tarnished equipment.

When the patient left, Dr. Fitzhugh retreated to his private office to write a note to Bridgit, the charwoman, who came twice a week to clean his office. He wrote:

My dear Bridgit,

I see you so seldom, I thought I'd take the time to thank you for the fine job of cleaning you've been doing. By the way, I thought I'd mention that since two hours, twice a week, is a very limited amount of time, please feel free to work an extra half hour from time to time if you feel you need to do those 'once-in-a-while' things like polishing the cup holders and the like. I, of course, will pay you for the extra time.

'The next day, when I walked into my office,' Dr. Fitzhugh reported, 'my desk had been polished to a mirror-like finish, as had my chair, which I nearly slid out of. When I went into the treatment room I found the shiniest, cleanest chrome-plated cup holder I have ever seen nestled in its receptacle. I had given my charwoman a fine reputation to live up to, and because of this small gesture she outperformed all her past efforts. How much additional time did she spend on this? That's right – none at all.'

There is an old saying: 'Give a dog a bad name and you may as well hang him.' But give him a good name – and see what happens!

When Mrs. Ruth Hopkins, a fourth-grade teacher in Brooklyn, New York, looked at her class roster the first day of school, her excitement and joy of starting a new term was tinged with anxiety. In her class this year she would have Tommy T., the school's most notorious 'bad boy'. His third-grade teacher had constantly complained about Tommy to colleagues, the principal and anyone else who would listen. He was not just mischievous; he caused serious discipline problems in the class, picked fights with the boys, teased the girls, was fresh to the teacher, and seemed to get worse as he grew older. His only redeeming feature was his ability to learn rapidly and master the school work easily.

Mrs. Hopkins decided to face the 'Tommy problem' immediately. When she greeted her new students, she made little comments to each of them: 'Rose, that's a pretty dress you are wearing,' 'Alicia, I hear you draw beautifully.' When she came to Tommy, she looked him straight in the eyes and said, 'Tommy, I understand you are a natural leader. I'm going to depend on you to help me make this class the best class in the fourth grade this year.' She reinforced this over the first few days by complimenting Tommy on everything he did and commenting on how this showed what a good student he was. With that reputation to live up to, even a nine-year-old couldn't let her down – and he didn't.

If you want to excel in that difficult leadership role of changing the attitude or behaviour of others, use . . .

PRINCIPLE 7

Give the other person a fine reputation to live up to.

□ **8** □

Make the fault seem easy to correct

A bachelor friend of mine, about forty years old, became engaged, and his fiancée persuaded him to take some belated dancing lessons. 'The Lord knows I needed dancing lessons,' he confessed as he told me the story, 'for I danced just as I did when I first started twenty years ago. The first teacher I engaged probably told me the truth. She said I was all wrong; I would just have to forget everything and begin all over again. But that took the heart out of me. I had no incentive to go on. So I quit her.

'The next teacher may have been lying, but I liked it. She said nonchalantly that my dancing was a bit old-fashioned perhaps, but the fundamentals were all right, and she assured me I wouldn't have any trouble learning a few new steps. The first teacher had discouraged me by emphasizing my mistakes. This new teacher did the opposite. She kept praising the things I did right and minimizing my errors. "You have a natural sense of rhythm," she assured me. "You really are a natural-born dancer." Now my common sense tells me that I always have been and always will be a fourth-rate dancer; yet, deep in my heart, I still like to think that *maybe* she meant it. To be sure, I was paying her to say it; but why bring that up?'

'At any rate, I know I am a better dancer than I would have been if she hadn't told me I had a natural sense of rhythm. That encouraged me. That gave me hope. That made me want to improve.'

Tell your child, your spouse, or your employee that he or she is stupid or dumb at a certain thing, has no gift for it, and is doing it all wrong, and you have destroyed almost every incentive to try to improve. But use the opposite technique – be liberal with your encouragement, make the thing seem easy to do, let the other person know that you have faith in his ability to do it, that he has an undeveloped flair for it – and he will practise until the dawn comes in the window in order to excel.

Lowell Thomas, a superb artist in human relations, used this technique. He gave you confidence, inspired you with courage and faith. For example, I spent a weekend with Mr. and Mrs. Thomas; and on Saturday night, I was asked to sit in on a friendly bridge game before a roaring fire. Bridge? Oh, no! No! Not me. I knew nothing about it. The game had always been a black mystery to me. No! No! Impossible!

'Why, Dale, it is no trick at all,' Lowell replied. 'There is nothing to bridge except memory and judgement. You've written articles on memory. Bridge will be a cinch for you. It's right up your alley.'

And presto, almost before I realized what I was doing, I found myself for the first time at a bridge table. All because I was told I had a natural flair for it and the game was made to seem easy.

Speaking of bridge reminds me of Ely Culbertson, whose books on bridge have been translated into a dozen languages and have sold more than a million copies. Yet he told me he never would have made a profession out of the game if a certain young woman hadn't assured him he had a flair for it.

When he came to America in 1922, he tried to get a job teaching in philosophy and sociology, but he couldn't.

Then he tried selling coal, and he failed at that.

He had tried selling coffee, and he failed at that, too.

He had played some bridge, but it had never occurred to him in those days that someday he would teach it. He was not only a poor card player, but he was also very stubborn. He asked so many questions and held so many post-mortem examinations that no one wanted to play with him.

Then he met a pretty bridge teacher, Josephine Dillon, fell in love and married her. She noticed how carefully he analyzed his cards and persuaded him that he was a potential genius at the card table. It was that encouragement and that alone, Culbertson told me, that caused him to make a profession of bridge.

Clarence M. Jones, one of the instructors of our course in Cincinnati, Ohio, told how encouragement and making faults seem easy to correct completely changed the life of his son.

'In 1970 my son David, who was then fifteen years old, came to live with me in Cincinnati. He had led a rough life. In 1958 his head was cut open in a car accident, leaving a very bad scar on his forehead. In 1960 his mother and I were divorced and he moved to Dallas, Texas, with his mother. Until he was fifteen he had spent most of his school years in special classes for slow learners in the Dallas school system. Possibly because of the scar, school administrators had decided he was brain-injured and could not function at a normal level. He was two years behind his age group, so he was only in the seventh grade. Yet he did not know his multiplication tables, added on his fingers and could barely read.

'There was one positive point. He loved to work on radio and TV sets. He wanted to become a TV technician. I encouraged this and pointed out that he needed maths to qualify for the training. I decided to help him become proficient in this subject. We obtained four sets of flash cards: multiplication, division, addition and subtraction. As we went through the cards, we put the correct answers in a discard stack. When David missed one, I gave him the correct answer and then put the card in the repeat stack until there were no cards left. I made a big deal out of each card he got right, particularly if he had missed it previously. Each night we would go through the repeat stack until there were no cards left. Each night we timed the exercise with a stop watch. I promised him that when he could get all the cards correct in eight minutes with no incorrect answers, we would quit doing it every night. This seemed an impossible goal to David. The first night it took 52 minutes, the second night, 48, then 45, 44, 41, then under 40 minutes. We celebrated each reduction. I'd call in my wife, and we would both hug him and we'd all dance a jig. At the end of the month he was doing all the cards perfectly in less than eight minutes. When he made a small improvement he would ask to do it again. He had made the fantastic discovery that learning was easy and fun.

'Naturally his grades in algebra took a jump. It is amazing how much easier algebra is when you can multiply. He astonished himself by bringing home a B in maths. That had never happened before. Other changes came with almost unbelievable rapidity. His reading improved rapidly, and he began to use his natural talents in drawing. Later in the school year his science teacher assigned him to develop an exhibit. He chose to develop a highly complex series of models to demonstrate the effect of levers. It required skill not only in drawing and model making but in applied mathematics. The exhibit took first prize in his school's science fair and was entered in the city competition and won third prize for the entire city of Cincinnati.

'That did it. Here was a kid who had flunked two grades, who had been told he was "brain-damaged", who had been called "Frankenstein" by his classmates and told his brains must have leaked out of the cut on his head. Suddenly he discovered he could really learn and accomplish things. The result? From the last quarter of the eighth grade all the way through high school, he never failed to make the honour roll; in high school he was elected to the national honour society. Once he found learning was easy, his whole life changed.'

If you want to help others to improve, remember . . .

PRINCIPLE 8

Use encouragement. Make the fault seem easy to correct.

☐ 9 ☐

Making people glad to do what you want

Back in 1915, America was aghast. For more than a year, the nations of Europe had been slaughtering one another on a scale never before dreamed of in all the bloody annals of mankind. Could peace be brought about? No one knew. But Woodrow Wilson was determined to try. He would send a personal representative, a peace emissary, to counsel with the warlords of Europe.

William Jennings Bryan, secretary of state, Bryan, the peace advocate, longed to go. He saw a chance to perform a great service and make his name immortal. But Wilson appointed another man, his intimate friend and adviser Colonel Edward M. House; and it was House's thorny task to break the unwelcome news to Bryan without giving him offence.

'Bryan was distinctly disappointed when he heard I was to go to Europe as the peace emissary,' Colonel House records in his diary. 'He said he had planned to do this himself . . .'

'I replied that the President thought it would be unwise for anyone to do this officially, and *that his going would attract a great deal of attention* and people would wonder why he was there . . .'

You see the intimation? House practically told Bryan that he was *too important* for the job – and Bryan was satisfied.

Colonel House, adroit, experienced in the ways of the world, was following one of the important rules of human relations: *Always make the other person happy about doing the thing you suggest.*

Woodrow Wilson followed that policy even when inviting William Gibbs McAdoo to become a member of his cabinet. That was the highest honour he could confer upon anyone, and yet Wilson extended the invitation in such a way as to make McAdoo feel doubly important. Here is the story in McAdoo's own words: 'He [Wilson] said that he was making up his cabinet and that he would be very glad if I would accept a place in it as Secretary of the Treasury. He had a delightful way of putting things; he created the impression that by accepting this great honour I would be doing him a favour.'

Unfortunately, Wilson didn't always employ such tact. If he had, history might have been different. For example, Wilson didn't make the Senate and the Republican Party happy by entering the United States in the League of Nations. Wilson refused to take such prominent Republican leaders as Elihu Root or Charles Evans Hughes or Henry Cabot Lodge to the peace conference with him. Instead, he took along unknown men from his own party. He snubbed the Republicans, refused to let them feel that the League was their idea as well as his, refused to let them have a finger in the pie; and, as a result of this crude handling of human relations, wrecked his own career, ruined his health, shortened his life, caused America to stay out of the League, and altered the history of the world.

Statesmen and diplomats aren't the only ones who use this make-a-person-happy-to-do-things-you-want-them-to-do approach. Dale O. Ferrier of Fort Wayne, Indiana, told how he encouraged one of his young children to willingly do the chore he was assigned.

'One of Jeff's chores was to pick up pears from under the pear tree so the person who was mowing underneath wouldn't have to stop to pick them up. He didn't like this chore, and frequently it was either not done at all or it was done so poorly that the mower had to stop and pick up several pears that he had missed. Rather than have an eyeball-to-eyeball confrontation about it, one day I said to him: "Jeff, I'll make a deal with you. For every bushel basket full of pears you pick up, I'll pay you one dollar. But after you are finished, for every pear I find left in the yard, I'll take away a dollar. How does that sound?" As you would expect, he not only picked up all of the pears, but I had to keep an eye on him to see that he didn't pull a few off the trees to fill up some of the baskets.'

I knew a man who had to refuse many invitations to speak, invitations extended by friends, invitations coming from people to whom he was obligated; and yet he did it so adroitly that the other person was at least contented with his refusal. How did he do it? Not by merely talking about the fact that he was too busy and too-this and too-that. No, after expressing his appreciation of the invitation and regretting his inability to accept it, he suggested a substitute speaker. In other words, he didn't give the other person any time to feel unhappy about the refusal. He immediately changed the other person's thoughts to some other speaker who could accept the invitation.

Gunter Schmidt, who took our course in West Germany, told of an employee in the food store he managed who was negligent about putting the proper price tags on the shelves where the items were displayed. This caused confusion and customer complaints. Reminders, admonitions, confrontations with her about this did not do much good. Finally, Mr. Schmidt called her into his office and told her he was appointing her Supervisor of Price Tag Posting for the entire store and she would be responsible for keeping all of the shelves properly tagged. This new responsibility and title changed her attitude completely, and she fulfilled her duties satisfactorily from then on.

Childish? Perhaps. But that is what they said to Napoleon when he created the Legion of Honour and distributed 15,000 crosses to his soldiers and made eighteen of his generals 'Marshals of France' and called his troops the 'Grand Army'. Napoleon was criticized for giving 'toys' to war-hardened veterans, and Napoleon replied, 'Men are ruled by toys.'

This technique of giving titles and authority worked for Napoleon and it will work for you. For example, a friend of mine, Mrs. Ernest Gent of Scarsdale, New York, was troubled by boys running across and destroying her lawn. She tried coaxing. Neither worked. Then she tried giving the worst sinner in the gang a title and a feeling of authority. She made him her 'detective' and put him in charge of keeping all trespassers off her lawn. That solved her problem. Her 'detective' built a bonfire in the backyard, heated an iron red hot, and threatened to brand any boy who stepped on the lawn.

The effective leader should keep the following guidelines in mind when it is necessary to change attitudes or behaviour:

1 Be sincere. Do not promise anything that you cannot deliver. Forget about the benefits to yourself and concentrate on the benefits to the other person.
2 Know exactly what it is you want the other person to do.
3 Be empathetic. Ask yourself what is it the other person really wants.
4 Consider the benefits that person will receive from doing what you suggest.
5 Match those benefits to the other person's wants.
6 When you make your request, put it in a form that will convey to the other person the idea that he personally will benefit. We could give a curt order like this: 'John, we have customers coming in tomorrow and I need the stockroom cleaned out. So sweep it out, put the stock in neat piles on the shelves and polish the counter.' Or we could express the same idea

by showing John the benefits he will get from doing the task: 'John, we have a job that should be completed right away. *If it is done now, we won't be faced with it later.* I am bringing some customers in tomorrow to show our facilities. I would like to show them the stockroom, but it is in poor shape. If you could sweep it out, put the stock in neat piles on the shelves, and polish the counter, it would make us look efficient, and *you will have done your part to provide a good company image.'*

Will John be happy about doing what you suggest? Probably not very happy, but happier than if you had not pointed out the benefits. Assuming you know that John has pride in the way his stockroom looks and is interested in contributing to the company image, he will be more likely to be cooperative. It also will have been pointed out to John that the job would have to be done eventually and by doing it now, he won't be faced with it later.

It is naïve to believe you will always get a favourable reaction from other persons when you use these approaches, but the experience of most people shows that you are more likely to change attitudes this way than by not using these principles – and if you increase your successes by even a mere 10 percent, you have become 10 percent more effective as a leader than you were before – and that is *your* benefit.

People are more likely to do what you would like them to do when you use . . .

PRINCIPLE 9

Make the other person happy about doing the thing you suggest.

PART FOUR

□ IN A NUTSHELL □

BE A LEADER
A leader's job often includes changing your people's attitudes and behaviour. Some suggestions to accomplish this:

PRINCIPLE 1

Begin with praise and honest appreciation.

PRINCIPLE 2

Call attention to people's mistakes indirectly.

PRINCIPLE 3

Talk about your own mistakes before criticizing the other person.

PRINCIPLE 4

Ask questions instead of giving direct orders.

PRINCIPLE 5

Let the other person save face.

PRINCIPLE 6

Praise the slightest improvement and praise every improvement. Be 'hearty in your approbation and lavish in your praise.'

PRINCIPLE 7

Give the other person a fine reputation to live up to.

> **PRINCIPLE 8**
>
> Use encouragement. Make the fault seem easy to correct.
>
> **PRINCIPLE 9**
>
> Make the other person happy about doing the thing you suggest.

A shortcut to distinction

by Lowell Thomas

This biographical information about Dale Carnegie was written as an introduction to the original edition of How to Win Friends and Influence People. *It is reprinted in this edition to give the readers additional background on Dale Carnegie.*

It was a cold January night in 1935, but the weather couldn't keep them away. Two thousand five hundred men and women thronged into the grand ballroom of the Hotel Pennsylvania in New York. Every available seat was filled by half-past seven. At eight o'clock, the eager crowd was still pouring in. The spacious balcony was soon jammed. Presently even standing space was at a premium, and hundreds of people, tired after navigating a day in business, stood up for an hour and a half that night to witness – what?

A fashion show?

A six-day bicycle race or a personal appearance by Clark Gable?

No. These people had been lured there by a newspaper ad. Two evenings previously, they had seen this full-page announcement in the New York *Sun* staring them in the face:

Learn to Speak Effectively
Prepare for Leadership

Old stuff? Yes, but believe it or not, in the most sophisticated town on earth, during a depression with 20 percent of the population on relief, twenty-five hundred people had left their homes and hustled to the hotel in response to that ad.

The people who responded were of the upper economic strata – executives, employers and professionals.

These men and women had come to hear the opening gun of an ultramodern, ultrapractical course in 'Effective Speaking and Influencing Men in Business' – a course given by the Dale Carnegie Institute of Effective Speaking and Human Relations.

Why were they there, these twenty-five hundred business men and women?

Because of a sudden hunger for more education because of the depression?

Apparently not, for this same course had been playing to packed houses in New York City every season for the preceding twenty-four years. During that time, more than fifteen thousand business and professional people had been trained by Dale Carnegie. Even large, sceptical, conservative organizations such as the Westinghouse Electric Company, the McGraw-Hill Publishing Company, the Brooklyn Union Gas Company, the Brooklyn Chamber of Commerce, the American Institute of Electrical Engineers and the New York Telephone Company have had this training conducted in their own offices for the benefit of their members and executives.

The fact that these people, ten or twenty years after leaving grade school, high school or college, come and take this training is a glaring commentary on the shocking deficiencies of our educational system.

What do adults really want to study? That is an important question; and, in order to answer it, the University of Chicago, the American Association for Adult Education, and the United Y.M.C.A. Schools made a survey over a two-year period.

That survey revealed that the prime interest of adults is health. It also revealed that their second interest is in developing skill in human relationships – they want to learn the technique of getting along with and influencing other people. They don't want to listen to a lot of high-sounding talk about psychology; they want suggestions they can use immediately in business, in social contacts and in the home.

So that was what adults wanted to study, was it?

'All right,' said the people making the survey. 'Fine. If that is what they want, we'll give it to them.'

Looking around for a textbook, they discovered that no working manual had ever been written to help people solve their daily problems in human relationships.

Here was a fine kettle of fish! For hundreds of years, learned volumes had been written on Greek and Latin and higher mathematics – topics about which the average adult doesn't give two hoots. But on the one subject on which he has a thirst for knowledge, a veritable passion for guidance and help – nothing!

This explained the presence of twenty-five hundred eager adults crowding into the grand ballroom of the Hotel Pennsylvania in response to a newspaper advertisement. Here, apparently, at last was the thing for which they had long been seeking.

Back in high school and college, they had poured over books, believing that knowledge alone was the open sesame to financial and professional rewards.

But a few years in the rough-and-tumble of business and professional life had brought sharp disillusionment. They had seen some of the most important business successes won by men who possessed, in addition to their knowledge, the ability to talk well, to win people to their way of thinking, and to 'sell' themselves and their ideas.

They soon discovered that if one aspired to wear the captain's cap and navigate the ship of business, personality and the ability to talk are more important than a knowledge of Latin verbs or a sheepskin from Harvard.

The advertisement in the New York *Sun* promised that the meeting would be highly entertaining. It was.

Eighteen people who had taken the course were marshalled in front of the loudspeaker – and fifteen of them were given precisely seventy-five seconds each to tell his or her story. Only seventy-five seconds of talk, then 'bang' went the gavel, and the chairman shouted, 'Time! Next speaker!'

The affair moved with the speed of a herd of buffalo thundering across the plains. Spectators stood for an hour and a half to watch the performance.

The speakers were a cross section of life: several sales representatives, a chain store executive, a baker, the president of a trade association, two bankers, an insurance agent, an accountant, a dentist, an architect, a druggist who had come from Indianapolis to New York to take the course, a lawyer who had come from Havana in order to prepare himself to give one important three-minute speech.

The first speaker bore the Gaelic name Patrick J. O'Haire. Born in Ireland, he attended school for only four years, drifted to America, worked as a mechanic, then as a chauffeur.

Now, however, he was forty, he had a growing family and needed more money, so he tried selling trucks. Suffering from an inferiority complex that, as he put it, was eating his heart out, he had to walk up and down in front of an office half a dozen times before he could summon up enough courage to open the door. He was so discouraged as a salesman that he was thinking of going back to working with his hands in a machine shop, when one day he received a letter inviting him to an organization meeting of the Dale Carnegie Course in Effective Speaking.

He didn't want to attend. He feared he would have to associate with a lot of college graduates, that he would be out of place.

His despairing wife insisted that he go, saying, 'It may do you some good, Pat. God knows you need it.' He went down to the place where the meeting was to be held and stood on the sidewalk for five minutes before he could generate enough self-confidence to enter the room.

The first few times he tried to speak in front of the others, he was dizzy with fear. But as the weeks drifted by, he lost all fear of audiences and soon found that he loved to talk – the bigger the crowd, the better. And he also lost his fear of individuals and of his superiors. He presented his ideas to them, and soon he had been advanced into the sales department. He had become a valued and much liked member of his company. This night, in the Hotel Pennsylvania, Patrick O'Haire stood in front of twenty-five thousand people and told a gay, rollicking story of his achievements. Wave after wave of laughter swept over the audience. Few professional speakers could have equalled his performance.

The next speaker, Godfrey Meyer, was a grey-headed banker, the father of eleven children. The first time he had attempted to speak in class, he was literally struck dumb. His mind refused to function. His story is a vivid illustration of how leadership gravitates to the person who can talk.

He worked on Wall Street, and for twenty-five years he had been living in Clifton, New Jersey. During that time, he had taken no active part in community affairs and knew perhaps five hundred people.

Shortly after he had enrolled in the Carnegie course, he received his tax bill and was infuriated by what he considered unjust charges. Ordinarily, he would have sat at home and fumed, or he would have taken it out in grousing to his neighbours. But instead, he put on his hat that night, walked into the town meeting, and blew off steam in public.

As a result of that talk of indignation, the citizens of Clifton, New Jersey, urged him to run for the town council. So for weeks he went from one meeting to another, denouncing waste and municipal extravagance.

There were ninety-six candidates in the field. When the ballots were counted, lo, Godfrey Meyer's name led all the rest. Almost overnight, he had become a public figure among the forty thousand people in his community. As a result of his talks, he made eighty times more friends in six weeks than he had been able to previously in twenty-five years.

And his salary as councilman meant that he got a return of 1,000 percent a year on his investment in the Carnegie course.

The third speaker, the head of a large national association of food manufacturers, told how he had been unable to stand up and express his ideas at meetings of a board of directors.

As a result of learning to think on his feet, two astonishing things happened. He was soon made president of his association, and in that capacity, he was obliged to address meetings all over the United States. Excerpts from his talks were put on the Associated Press wires and printed in newspapers and trade magazines throughout the country.

In two years, after learning to speak more effectively, he received more free publicity for his company and its products than he had been able to get previously with a quarter of a million dollars spent in direct advertising. This speaker admitted that he had formerly hesitated to telephone some of the more important business executives in Manhattan and invite them to lunch with him. But as a result of the prestige he had acquired by his talks, these same people telephoned him and invited him to lunch and apologized to him for encroaching on his time.

The ability to speak is a shortcut to distinction. It puts a person in the limelight, raises one head and shoulders above the crowd. And the person who can speak acceptably is usually given credit for an ability out of all proportion to what he or she really possesses.

Dale Carnegie

A movement for adult education has been sweeping over the nation; and the most spectacular force in that movement was Dale Carnegie, a man who listened to and critiqued more talks by adults that has any other man in captivity. According to a cartoon by 'Believe-It-or-Not' Ripley, he had criticized 150,000 speeches. If that grand total doesn't impress you, remember that it meant one talk for almost every day that has passed since Columbus discovered America. Or, to put it in other words, if all the people who had spoken before him had used only three minutes and had appeared before him in succession, it would have taken ten months, listening day and night, to hear them all.

Dale Carnegie's own career, filled with sharp contrasts, was a striking example of what a person can accomplish when obsessed with an original idea and afire with enthusiasm.

Born on a Missouri farm ten miles from a railway, he never saw a streetcar until he was twelve years old; yet by the time he was forty-six, he was familiar with the far-flung corners of the earth, everywhere from Hong Kong to Hammerfest; and at one time, he approached closer to the North Pole than Admiral Byrd's headquarters at Little America was to the South Pole.

This Missouri lad who had once picked strawberries and cut cockleburs for five cents an hour became the highly paid trainer of the executives of large corporations in the art of self-expression.

This erstwhile cowboy who had once punched cattle and branded calves and ridden fences out in western South Dakota later went to London to put on shows under the patronage of the royal family.

This chap who was a total failure the first half-dozen times he tried to speak in public later became my personal manager. Much of my success has been due to training under Dale Carnegie.

Young Carnegie had to struggle for an education, for hard luck was always battering away at the old farm in northwest Missouri with a flying tackle and a body slam. Year after year, the '102' River rose and drowned the corn and swept away the hay. Season after season, the fat hogs sickened and died from cholera, the bottom fell out of the market for cattle and mules, and the bank threatened to foreclose the mortgage.

Sick with discouragement, the family sold out and bought another farm near the State Teachers' College at Warrensburgh, Missouri. Board and room could be had in town for a dollar a day, but young Carnegie couldn't afford it. So he stayed on the farm and commuted on horseback three miles to college each day. At home, he milked the cows, cut the wood, fed the hogs, and studied his Latin verbs by the light of a coal-oil lamp until his eyes blurred and he began to nod.

Even when he got to bed at midnight, he set the alarm for three o'clock. His father bred pedigreed Duroc-Jersey hogs – and there was danger, during the bitter cold nights, that the young pigs would freeze to death: so they were put in a basket, covered with a gunny sack, and set behind the kitchen stove.

True to their nature, the pigs demanded a hot meal at 3 a.m. So when the alarm went off, Dale Carnegie crawled out of the blankets, took the basket of pigs out to their mother, waited for them to nurse, and then brought them back to the warmth of the kitchen stove.

There were six hundred students in State Teachers' College, and Dale Carnegie was one of the isolated half-dozen who couldn't afford to board in town. He was ashamed of the poverty that made it necessary for him to ride back to the farm and milk the cows every night. He was ashamed of his coat, which was too tight, and his trousers, which were too short. Rapidly developing an inferiority complex, he looked about for some shortcut to distinction. He soon saw that there were certain groups in college that enjoyed influence and prestige – the football and baseball players and the chaps who won the debating and public-speaking contests.

Realizing that he had no flair for athletics, he decided to win one of the speaking contests. He spent months preparing his talks. He practised as he sat in the saddle galloping to college and back; he practised his speeches as he milked the cows; and then he mounted a bale of hay in the barn and with great gusto and gestures harangued the frightened pigeons about the issues of the day.

But in spite of all this earnestness and preparation, he met with defeat after defeat. He was eighteen at the time – sensitive and proud. He became so discouraged, so depressed, that he even thought of suicide. And then suddenly he began to win, not one contest, but every speaking contest in college.

Other students pleaded with him to train them; and they won also.

After graduating from college, he started selling correspondence courses to the ranchers among the sand hills of western Nebraska and eastern Wyoming. In spite of all his boundless energy and enthusiasm, he couldn't make the grade. He became so discouraged that he went to his hotel room in Alliance, Nebraska, in the middle of the day, threw himself across the bed, and wept in despair. He longed to go back to college, he longed to retreat from the harsh battle of life; but he couldn't. So he resolved to go to Omaha and get another job. He didn't have the money for a railroad ticket, so he travelled on a freight train, feeding and watering two carloads of wild horses in return for his passage. After landing in south Omaha, he got a job selling bacon and soap and lard for Armour and Company. His territory was up among the Badlands and the cow and Indian country of western South Dakota. He covered his territory by freight train and stage coach and horseback and slept in pioneer hotels where the only partition between the rooms was a sheet of muslin. He studied books on salesmanship, rode bucking bronchos, played poker with the Indians, and learned how to collect money. And when, for example, an inland storekeeper couldn't pay cash for the bacon and hams he had ordered, Dale Carnegie would take a dozen pairs of shoes off his shelf, sell the shoes to the railroad men, and forward the receipts to Armour and Company.

He would often ride a freight train a hundred miles a day. When the train stopped to unload freight, he would dash uptown, see three or four merchants, get his orders; and when the whistle blew, he would dash down the street again lickety-split and swing onto the train while it was moving.

Within two years, he had taken an unproductive territory that had stood in the twenty-fifth place and had boosted it to first place among all the twenty-nine car routes leading out of south Omaha. Armour and Company offered to promote him, saying: 'You have achieved what seemed impossible.' But he refused the promotion and resigned, went to New York, studied at the American Academy of Dramatic Arts, and toured the country, playing the role of Dr. Harley in *Polly of the Circus*.

He would never be a Booth or a Barrymore. He had the good sense to recognize that. So back he went to sales work, selling automobiles and trucks for the Packard Motor Car Company.

He knew nothing about machinery and cared nothing about it. Dreadfully unhappy, he had to scourge himself to his task each day. He longed to have time to study, to write the books he had dreamed about writing back in college. So he resigned. He was going to spend his days writing stories and novels and support himself by teaching in a night school.

Teaching what? As he looked back and evaluated his college work, he saw that his training in public speaking had done more to give him confidence, courage, poise and the ability to meet and deal with people in business than had all the rest of his college courses put together. So he urged the Y.M.C.A. schools in New York to give him a chance to conduct courses in public speaking for people in business.

What? Make orators out of business people? Absurd. The Y.M.C.A. people knew. They had tried such courses – and they had always failed. When they refused to pay him a salary of two dollars a night, he agreed to teach on a commission basis and take a percentage of the net profits – if there were any profits to take. And inside of three years they were paying him thirty dollars a night on that basis – instead of two.

The course grew. Other 'Ys' heard of it, then other critics. Dale Carnegie soon became a glorified circuit rider covering New York, Philadelphia, Baltimore and later London and Paris. All the textbooks were too academic and impractical for the business people who flocked to his courses. Because of this he wrote his own book entitled *Public Speaking and Influencing Men in Business*. It became the official text of all the Y.M.C.A.s as well as of the American Bankers' Association and the National Credit Men's Association.

Dale Carnegie claimed that all people can talk when they get mad. He said that if you hit the most ignorant man in town on the jaw and knock him down, he would get on his feet and talk with an eloquence, heat and emphasis that would have rivalled that world famous orator William Jennings Bryan at the height of his career. He claimed that almost any person can speak acceptably in public if he or she has self-confidence and an idea that is boiling and stewing within.

The way to develop self-confidence, he said, is to do the thing you fear to do and get a record of successful experiences behind you. So he forced each class member to talk at every session of the course. The audience is sympathetic. They are all in the same boat; and, by constant practice, they develop a courage, confidence and enthusiasm that carry over into their private speaking.

Dale Carnegie would tell you that he made a living all these years, not by teaching public speaking – that was incidental. His main job was to help people conquer their fears and develop courage.

He started out at first to conduct merely a course in public speaking, but the students who came were business men and women. Many of them hadn't seen the inside of a classroom in thirty years. Most of them were paying their tuition on the instalment plan. They wanted results and they wanted them quick – results that they could use the next day in business interviews and in speaking before groups.

So he was forced to be swift and practical. Consequently, he developed a system of training that is unique – a striking combination of public speaking, salesmanship, human relations and applied psychology.

A slave to no hard-and-fast rules, he developed a course that is as real as the measles and twice as much fun.

When the classes terminated, the graduates formed clubs of their own and continued to meet fortnightly for years afterwards. One group of nineteen in Philadelphia met twice a month during the winter season for seventeen years. Class members frequently travel fifty or a hundred miles to attend classes. One student used to commute each week from Chicago to New York.

Professor William James of Harvard used to say that the average person develops only 10 percent of his latent mental ability. Dale Carnegie, by helping business men and women to develop their latent possibilities, created one of the most significant movements in adult education.

Lowell Thomas 1936

HOW TO STOP WORRYING

AND START LIVING

This book is dedicated to a man who doesn't need to read it

LOWELL THOMAS

Contents

Preface

How this book was written – and why

In 1909, I was one of the unhappiest lads in New York. I was selling motor trucks for a living. I didn't know what made a motor truck run. That wasn't all: I didn't want to know. I despised my job. I despised living in a cheap furnished room on West Fifty-sixth Street – a room infested with cockroaches. I still remember that I had a bunch of neckties hanging on the walls; and when I reached out of a morning to get a fresh necktie, the cockroaches scattered in all directions. I despised having to eat in cheap, dirty restaurants that were also probably infested with cockroaches.

I came home to my lonely room each night with a sick headache – a headache bred and fed by disappointment, worry, bitterness, and rebellion. I was rebelling because the dreams I had nourished back in my college days had turned into nightmares. Was this life? Was this the vital adventure to which I had looked forward so eagerly? Was this all life would ever mean to me – working at a job I despised, living with cockroaches, eating vile food – and with no hope for the future? . . . I longed for leisure to read, and to write books I had dreamed of writing back in my college days.

I knew I had everything to gain and nothing to lose by giving up the job I despised. I wasn't interested in making a lot of money, but I was interested in making a lot of living. In short, I had come to the Rubicon – to the moment of decision which faces most young people when they start out in life. So I made my decision – and that decision completely altered my future. It has made the rest of my life happy and rewarding beyond my most utopian aspirations.

My decision was this: I would give up the work I loathed; and, since I had spent four years studying in the State Teachers College at Warrensburg, Missouri, preparing to teach, I would make my living teaching adult classes in night schools. Then I would have my days free to read books, prepare lectures, write novels and short stories. I wanted 'to live to write and write to live.'

What subject should I teach to adults at night? As I looked back and evaluated my own college training, I saw that the training and experience I

192

had had in public speaking had been of more practical value to me in business – and in life – than everything else I had studied in college all put together. Why? Because it has wiped out my timidity and lack of self-confidence and given me the courage and assurance to deal with people. It had also made clear that leadership usually gravitates to the man who can get up and say what he thinks.

I applied for a position teaching public speaking in the night extension courses both at Columbia University and New York University, but these universities decided they could struggle along without my help.

I was disappointed then – but I now thank God that they did turn me down, because I started teaching in Y.M.C.A. night schools, where I had to show concrete results and show them quickly. What a challenge that was! These adults didn't come to my classes because they wanted college credits or social prestige. They came for one reason only: they wanted to solve their problems. They wanted to be able to stand up on their feet and say a few words at a business meeting without fainting from fright. Salesmen wanted to be able to call on a tough customer without having to walk around the block three times to get up courage. They wanted to develop poise and self-confidence. They wanted to get ahead in business. They wanted to have more money for their families. And since they were paying their tuition on an instalment basis – and they stopped paying if they didn't get results – and since I was being paid, not a salary, but a percentage of the profits, I had to be practical if I wanted to eat.

I felt at the time that I was teaching under a handicap, but I realize now that I was getting priceless training. I *had to motivate* my students, I *had* to help them *solve their problems*. I *had to make each session so inspiring that they wanted to continue coming*.

It was exciting work. I loved it. I was astounded at how quickly these businessmen developed self-confidence and how quickly many of them secured promotions and increased pay. The classes were succeeding far beyond my most optimistic hopes. Within three seasons, the Y.M.C.A.s, which had refused to pay me five dollars a night in salary, were paying me thirty dollars a night on a percentage basis. At first, I taught only public speaking, but, as the years went by, I saw that these adults also needed the ability to win friends and influence people. Since I couldn't find an adequate textbook on human relations, I wrote one myself. It was written – no, it wasn't written in the usual way. It grew and *evolved* out of the experiences of the adults in these classes. I called it *How to Win Friends and Influence People*.

Since it was written solely as a textbook for my own adult classes, and since I had written four others books that no one had ever heard of, I never dreamed that it would have a large sale: I am probably one of the most astonished authors now living.

As the years went by, I realized that another one of the biggest problems of these adults was *worry*. A large majority of my students were businessmen

– executives, salesmen, engineers, accountants: a cross section of all the trades and professions – and most of them had problems! There were women in the classes – businesswomen and housewives. They, too, had problems! Clearly, what I needed was a textbook on how to conquer worry – so again I tried to find one. I went to New York's great public library at Fifth Avenue and Forty-second Street and discovered to my astonishment that this library had only twenty-two books listed under the title WORRY. I also noticed, to my amusement, that it had one hundred eighty-nine books listed under WORMS. *Almost nine times as many books about worms as about worry!* Astounding, isn't it? Since worry is one of the biggest problems facing mankind, you would think, wouldn't you, that every high school and college in the land would give a course on 'How to Stop Worrying'? Yet, if there is even one course on that subject in any college in the land, I have never heard of it. No wonder David Seabury said in his book *How to Worry Successfully*: 'We come to maturity with as little preparation for the pressures of experience as a bookworm asked to do a ballet.'

The result? More than half of our hospital beds are occupied by people with nervous and emotional troubles.

I looked over these twenty-two books on worry reposing on the shelves of the New York Public Library. In addition, I purchased all the books on worry I could find; yet I couldn't discover even one that I could use as a text in my course for adults. So I resolved to write one myself.

I began preparing myself to write this book seven years ago. How? By reading what the philosophers of all ages have said about worry. I also read hundreds of biographies, all the way from Confucius to Churchill. I also interviewed scores of prominent people in many walks of life, such as Jack Dempsey, General Omar Bradley, General Mark Clark, Henry Ford, Eleanor Roosevelt, and Dorothy Dix. But that was only a beginning.

I also did something else that was far more important than the interviews and the reading. I worked for five years in a laboratory for conquering worry – a laboratory conducted in our own adult classes. As far as I know, it was the first and only laboratory of its kind in the world. This is what we did. We gave students a set of rules on how to stop worrying and asked them to apply these rules in their own lives and then talk to the class on the results they had obtained. Others reported on techniques they had used in the past.

As a result of this experience, I presume that I have listened to more talks on 'How I Conquered Worry' than has any other individual who ever walked this earth. In addition, I *read* hundreds of other talks on 'How I Conquered Worry' – talks that were sent to me by mail – talks that had won prizes in our classes that are held throughout the world. So this book didn't come out of an ivory tower. Neither is it an academic preachment on how worry *might* be conquered. Instead, I have tried to write a fast-moving, concise, *documented report on how worry has been conquered by thousands of adults.* One thing is certain: this book is practical. You can set your teeth in it.

'Science,' said the French philosopher Valéry, 'is a collection of successful recipes.' That is what this book is: a collection of successful and time-tested recipes to rid our lives of worry. However, let me warn you: you won't find anything new in it, but you will find much that is not generally applied. And when it comes to that, you and I don't need to be told anything new. We already know enough to lead perfect lives. We have all read the golden rule and the Sermon on the Mount. Our trouble is not ignorance, but inaction. The purpose of this book is to restate, illustrate, streamline, air-condition, and glorify a lot of ancient and basic truths – and kick you in the shins and make you do something about applying them.

You didn't pick up this book to read about how it was written. You are looking for action. All right, let's go. Please read Parts One and Two of this book – and if by that time you don't feel that you have acquired a new power and a new inspiration to stop worry and enjoy life – then toss this book away. It is no good for you.

Dale Carnegie

Nine suggestions on how to get the most out of this book

1 If you wish to get the most out of this book, there is one indispensable requirement, one essential infinitely more important than any rules or techniques. Unless you have this one fundamental requisite a thousand rules on how to study will avail little. And if you do have this cardinal endowment, then you can achieve wonders without reading any suggestions for getting the most out of a book.

What is this magic requirement? *Just this: a deep, driving desire to learn, a vigorous determination to stop worrying and start living.*

How can you develop such an urge? By constantly reminding yourself of how important these principles are to you. Picture to yourself how their mastery will aid you in living a richer, happier life. Say to yourself over and over: 'My peace of mind, my happiness, my health, and perhaps even my income will, in the long run, depend largely on applying the old, obvious, and eternal truths taught in this book.'

2 Read each chapter rapidly at first to get a bird's-eye view of it. You will probably be tempted then to rush on to the next one. But don't. Unless you are reading merely for entertainment. But if you are reading because you want to stop worrying and start living, then go back and *reread each chapter thoroughly*. In the long run, this will mean saving time and getting results.

3 *Stop frequently in your reading to think over what you are reading.* Ask yourself just how and when you can apply each suggestion. That kind of reading will aid you far more than racing ahead like a whippet chasing a rabbit.

4 *Read with a red crayon, pencil, or pen in your hand; and when you come across a suggestion that you feel you can use, draw a line beside it.* If it is a four-star suggestion, then underscore every sentence, or mark it with 'XXXX.' Marking and underscoring a book make it more interesting, and far easier to review rapidly.

5 I know a woman who has been office manager for a large insurance concern for fifteen years. She reads every month all the insurance contracts her company issues. Yes, she reads the same contracts over month after month, year after year. Why? Because experience has taught her that that is the only way she can keep their provisions clearly in mind.

I once spent almost two years writing a book on public speaking; and yet I find I have to keep going back over it from time to time in order to remember what I wrote in my own book. The rapidity with which we forget is astonishing.

So, if you want to get a real, lasting benefit out of this book, don't imagine that skimming through it once will suffice. After reading it thoroughly, you ought to spend a few hours reviewing it every month. Keep it on your desk in front of you every day. Glance through it often. Keep constantly impressing yourself with the rich possibilities for improvement that still lie in the offing. Remember that the use of these principles can be made habitual and unconscious only by a constant and vigorous campaign of review and application. There is no other way.

6 Bernard Shaw once remarked' 'If you teach a man anything, he will never learn.' Shaw was right. *Learning is an active process. We learn by doing. So, if you desire to master the principles you are studying in this book, do something about them. Apply these rules at every opportunity.* If you don't, you will forget them quickly. Only knowledge that is used sticks in your mind.

You will probably find it difficult to apply these suggestions all the time. I know, because I wrote this book, and yet frequently I find it difficult to apply everything I have advocated here. So, as you read this book, remember that you are not merely trying to acquire information. You are attempting to form new habits. Ah yes, you are attempting a new way of life. That will require time and persistence and daily application.

So refer to these pages often. Regard this as a working handbook on conquering worry; and when you are confronted with some trying problem – don't get all stirred up. Don't do the natural thing, the impulsive thing. That is usually wrong. Instead, turn to these pages and review the paragraphs you have underscored. Then try these new ways and watch them achieve magic for you.

7 *Offer your family members a quarter every time they catch you violating one of the principles advocated in this book. They will break you!*

8 Please turn to page 343 of this book and read how the Wall Street banker, H. P. Howell, and old Ben Franklin corrected their mistakes. Why don't you use the Howell and Franklin techniques to check up on your application of the principles discussed in this book? If you do, two things will result.

First, you will find yourself engaged in an educational process that is both intriguing and priceless.

Second, you will find that your ability to stop worrying and start living will grow and spread like a green bay tree.

9 Keep a diary – a diary in which you ought to record your triumphs in the application of these principles. Be specific. Give names, dates, results. Keeping such a record will inspire you to greater efforts; and how fascinating these entries will be when you chance upon them some evening, years from now!

☐ IN A NUTSHELL ☐

1. Develop a deep, driving desire to master the principles of conquering worry.
2. Read each chapter twice before going on to the next one.
3. As you read, stop frequently to ask yourself how you can apply each suggestion.
4. Underscore each important idea.
5. Review this book each month.
6. Apply these principles at every opportunity. Use this volume as a working handbook to help you solve your daily problems.
7. Make a lively game out of your learning by offering some friend a quarter every time you are caught violating one of these principles.
8. Check up each week on the progress you are making. Ask yourself what mistakes you have made, what improvement, what lessons you have learned for the future.
9. Keep a diary in the back of this book showing how and when you have applied these principles.

Part One

FUNDAMENTAL FACTS YOU SHOULD

KNOW ABOUT WORRY

□ 1 □

Live in 'Day-tight Compartments'

In the spring of 1871, a young man picked up a book and read twenty-one words that had a profound effect on his future. A medical student at the Montreal General Hospital, he was worried about passing the final examination, worried about what to do, where to go, how to build up a practice, how to make a living.

The twenty-one words that this young medical student read in 1871 helped him to become the most famous physician of his generation. He organized the world-famous Johns Hopkins School of Medicine. He became Regius Professor of Medicine at Oxford – the highest honour that can be bestowed upon any medical man in the British Empire. He was knighted by the King of England. When he died, two huge volumes containing 1466 pages were required to tell the story of his life.

His name was Sir William Osler. Here are the twenty-one words that he read in the spring of 1871 – twenty-one words from Thomas Carlyle that helped him lead a life free from worry: *'Our main business is not to see what lies dimly at a distance, but to do what lies clearly at hand.'*

Forty-two years later, on a soft spring night when the tulips were blooming on the campus, this man, Sir William Osler, addressed the students of Yale University. He told those Yale students that a man like himself who had been a professor in four universities and had written a popular book was supposed to have 'brains of a special quality'. He declared that that was untrue. He said that his intimate friends knew that his brains were 'of the most mediocre character'.

What, then, was the secret of his success? He stated that it was owing to what he called living in 'day-tight compartments'. What did he mean by that? A few months before he spoke at Yale, Sir William Osler had crossed the Atlantic on a great ocean liner where the captain, standing on the bridge, could press a button and – presto! – there was a clanging of machinery and various parts of the ship were immediately shut off from one another – shut off into watertight compartments. 'Now each one of you,' Dr. Osler said to those Yale students, 'is a much more marvellous organization than the great liner, and bound on a longer voyage. What I urge is that you so learn to control the machinery as to live with 'day-tight compartments' as the most certain way to ensure safety on the voyage. Get on the bridge, and see that at least the great bulkheads are in working order. Touch a button and hear, at every level of your life, the iron doors shutting out the Past – the dead yesterdays. Touch another and shut off, with a metal curtain, the Future – the unborn tomorrows. Then you are safe – safe for today! ... Shut off the past! Let the dead past bury its dead ... Shut out the yesterdays which have lighted fools the way to dusty death ... The load of tomorrow, added to that of yesterday, carried today, makes the strongest falter. Shut off the future as tightly as the past ... The future is today ... There is no tomorrow. The day of man's salvation is now. Waste of energy, mental distress, nervous worries dog the steps of a man who is anxious about the future ... Shut close, then, the great fore and aft bulkheads, and prepare to cultivate the habit of a life of "day-tight compartments".'

Did Dr. Osler mean to say that we should not make any effort to prepare for tomorrow? No. Not at all. But he did go on in that address to say that the best possible way to prepare for tomorrow is to concentrate with all your intelligence, all your enthusiasm, on doing today's work superbly today. That is the only possible way you can prepare for the future.

Sir William Osler urged the students at Yale to begin the day with Christ's prayer: 'Give us this day our daily bread.'

Remember that that prayer asks only for *today's* bread. It doesn't complain about the stale bread we had to eat yesterday; and it doesn't say: 'Oh God, it has been pretty dry out in the wheat belt lately and we may have another drought – and then how will I get bread to eat next fall – or suppose I lose my job – oh, God, how could I get bread then?'

No, this prayer teaches us to ask for *today's* bread only. Today's bread is the only kind of bread you can possibly eat.

Years ago, a penniless philosopher was wandering through a stony country where the people had a hard time making a living. One day a crowd gathered about him on a hill, and he gave what is probably the most-quoted speech ever delivered anywhere at any time. This speech contains twenty-six words that have gone ringing down across the centuries: 'Take therefore no thought for the morrow; for the morrow shall take thought for the things of itself. Sufficient unto the day is the evil thereof.'

Many men have rejected those words of Jesus: 'Take no thought for the morrow.' They have rejected those words as a counsel of perfection, as a bit of mysticism. 'I *must* take thought for the morrow," they say. 'I *must* take out insurance to protect my family. I *must* lay aside money for my old age. I *must* plan and prepare to get ahead.'

Right! Of course you must. The truth is that those words of Jesus, translated over three hundred years ago, don't mean today what they meant during the reign of King James. Three hundred years ago the word *thought* frequently meant anxiety. Modern versions of the Bible quote Jesus more accurately as saying: 'Have no anxiety for the tomorrow.'

By all means take thought for the tomorrow, yes, careful thought and planning and preparation. But have no anxiety.

During the Second World War, our military leaders *planned* for the morrow, but they could not afford to have any anxiety. 'I have supplied the best men with the best equipment we have,' said Admiral Ernest J. King, who directed the United States Navy, 'and have given them what seems to be the wisest mission. That is all I can do.

'If a ship has been sunk,' Admiral King went on, 'I can't bring it up. If it is going to be sunk, I can't stop it. I can use my time much better working on tomorrow's problem than by fretting about yesterday's. Besides, if I let those things get me, I wouldn't last long.'

Whether in war or peace, the chief difference between good thinking and bad thinking is this: good thinking deals with causes and effects and leads to logical, constructive planning; bad thinking frequently leads to tension and nervous breakdown.

I had the privilege of interviewing Arthur Hays Sulzberger, publisher (1935–1961) of one of the most famous newspapers in the world, *The New York Times*. Mr. Sulzberger told me that when the Second World War flamed across Europe, he was so stunned, so worried about the future, that he found it impossible to sleep. He would frequently get out of bed in the middle of the night, take some canvas and tubes of paint, look in the mirror, and try to paint a portrait of himself. He didn't know anything about painting, but he painted anyway, to get his mind off his worries. Mr. Sulzberger told me that he was never able to banish his worries and find peace until he had adopted as his motto five words from a church hymn: *One step enough for me*.

Lead, kindly Light . . .
Keep thou my feet: I do not ask to see
The distant scene; one step enough for me.

At about the same time, a young man in uniform – somewhere in Europe – was learning the same lesson. His name was Ted Bengermino, of Baltimore, Maryland – and he had worried himself into a first-class case of combat fatigue.

'In April, 1945,' wrote Ted Bengermino, 'I had worried until I had developed what doctors call a 'spasmodic transverse colon' – a condition that produced intense pain. If the war hadn't ended when it did, I am sure I would have had a complete physical breakdown.

'I was utterly exhausted. I was a Graves Registration, non-commissioned Officer for the 94th Infantry Division. My work was to help set up and maintain records of all men killed in action, missing in action, and hospitalized. I also had to help disinter the bodies of both Allied and enemy soldiers who had been killed and hastily buried in shallow graves during the pitch of the battle. I had to gather up the personal effects of these men and see that they were sent back to parents or closest relatives who would prize these personal effects so much. I was constantly worried for fear we might be making embarrassing and serious mistakes. I was worried about whether or not I would come though all this. I was worried about whether I would live to hold my only child in my arms – a son of sixteen months, whom I had never seen. I was so worried and exhausted that I lost thirty-four pounds. I was so frantic that I was almost out of my mind. I looked at my hands. They were hardly more than skin and bones. I was terrified at the thought of going home a physical wreck. I broke down and sobbed like a child. I was so shaken that tears welled up every time I was alone. There was one period soon after the Battle of the Bulge started that I wept so often that I almost gave up hope of ever being a normal human being again.

'I ended up in an Army dispensary. An Army doctor gave me some advice which has completely changed my life. After giving me a thorough physical examination, he informed me that my troubles were mental. *'Ted,'* he said, *'I want you to think of your life as an hourglass. You know there are thousands of grains of sand in the top of the hourglass; and they all pass slowly and evenly through the narrow neck in the middle. Nothing you or I could do would make more than one grain of sand pass through this narrow neck without impairing the hourglass. You and I and everyone else are like this hourglass. When we start in the morning, there are hundreds of tasks which we feel that we must accomplish that day, but if we do not take them one at a time and let them pass through the day slowly and evenly, as do the grains of sand passing through the narrow neck of the hourglass, then we are bound to break our own physical or mental structure.'*

'I have practiced that philosophy ever since that memorable day that an Army doctor gave it to me. "One grain of sand at a time ... One task at a time." That advice saved me physically and mentally during the war; and it has also helped me in my present position of Public Relations and Advertising Director for the Adcrafters Printing & Offset Co., Inc. I found the same problems arising in business that had arisen during the war: a score of things that had to be done at once – and there was little time to do them. We were low in stocks. We had new forms to handle, new stock arrangements, changes of address, opening and closing offices, and so on. Instead of getting taut and nervous, I remembered what the doctor had told me. "One grain of sand at a time. One task at a time." By repeating these words to myself over and over, I accomplished my tasks in a more efficient manner and I did my work without the confused and jumbled feeling that had almost wrecked me on the battlefield.'

One of the most appalling comments on our present way of life is that at one time half of all the beds in our hospitals were reserved for patients with nervous or mental troubles, patients who had collapsed under the crushing burden of accumulated yesterdays and fearful tomorrows. Yet a vast majority of those people could have avoided those hospitals – could have led happy, useful lives – if they had only heeded the words of Jesus: *'Have no anxiety about the morrow*'; or the words of Sir William Osler: '*Live in day-tight compartments.*'

You and I are standing this very second at the meeting place of two eternities: the vast past that has endured forever, and the future that is plunging on to the last syllable of recorded time. We can't possibly live in either of those eternities – no, not even for one split second. But, by trying to do so, we can wreck both our bodies and our minds. So let's be content to live the only time we can possibly live: from now until bedtime. 'Anyone can carry his burden, however hard, until nightfall,' wrote Robert Louis Stevenson. 'Anyone can do his work, however hard, for one day. Anyone can live sweetly, patiently, lovingly, purely, till the sun goes down. And this is all that life really means.'

Yes, that is all that life requires of us; but Mrs. E. K. Shields, of Saginaw, Michigan, was driven to despair – even to the brink of suicide – before she learned to live just till bedtime. 'In 1937, I lost my husband,' Mrs. Shields said as she told be her story. 'I was very depressed – and almost penniless. I wrote my former employer, Mr. Leon Roach, of the Roach-Fowler Company of Kansas City, and got my old job back. I had formerly made my living selling World Books to rural and town school boards, I had sold my car two years previously when my husband became ill; but I managed to scrape together enough money to put a down payment on a used car and started out to sell books again.

'I had thought that getting back on the road would help relieve my depression; but driving alone and eating alone was almost more than I could take. Some of the territory was not very productive, and I found it hard to make those car payments, small as they were.

'In the spring of 1938, I was working out of Versailles, Missouri. The schools were poor, the roads bad; I was so lonely and discouraged that at one time I even considered suicide. It seemed that success was impossible. I had nothing to live for. I dreaded getting up each morning and facing life. I was afraid of everything: afraid I could not meet the car payments; afraid I could not pay my room rent; afraid I would not have enough to eat. I was afraid my health was failing and I had no money for a doctor. All that kept me from suicide were the thoughts that my sister would be deeply grieved, and that I did not have enough money to pay my funeral expenses.

'Then one day I read an article that lifted me out of my despondence and gave me the courage to go on living. I shall never cease to be grateful for one inspiring sentence in that article. It said: "Every day is a new life to a wise man." I typed that sentence and pasted it on the windshield of my car, where I saw it every minute I was driving. I found it wasn't so hard to live only one day at a time. I learned to forget the yesterdays and to not-think of the tomorrows. Each morning I said to myself, "Today is a new life."

'I have succeeded in overcoming my fear of loneliness, my fear of want. I am happy and fairly successful now and have a lot of enthusiasm and love for life. I know now that I shall never again be afraid, regardless of what life hands me. I know now that I don't have to fear the future. I know now that I can

live one day at a time – and that "Every day is a new life to a wise man." '
Who do you suppose wrote this verse:

Happy the man, and happy he alone,
He, who can call to-day his own:
He who, secure within, can say:
"To-morrow, do thy worst, for I have liv'd to-day."

Those words sound modern, don't they? Yet they were written thirty years before Christ was born, by the Roman poet Horace.

One of the most tragic things I know about human nature is that all of us tend to put off living. We are all dreaming of some magical rose garden over the horizon – instead of enjoying the roses that are blooming outside our windows today.

Why are we such fools – such tragic fools?

'How strange it is, our little procession of life!' wrote Stephen Leacock. 'The child says, "When I am a big boy." But what is that? The big boy says, "When I grow up." And then, grown up, he says, "When I get married." But to be married, what is that after all? The thought changes to "When I'm able to retire." And then, when retirement comes, he looks back over the landscape traversed; a cold wind seems to sweep over it; somehow he has missed it all, and it is gone. Life, we learn too late, is in the living, in the tissue of every day and hour.'

The late Edward S. Evans of Detroit almost killed himself with worry before he learned that life 'is in the living, in the tissue of every day and hour.' Brought up in poverty, Edward Evans made his first money by selling newspapers, then worked as a grocer's clerk. Later, with seven people dependent upon him for bread and butter, he got a job as an assistant librarian. Small as the pay was, he was afraid to quit. Eight years passed before he could summon up the courage to start out on his own. But once he started, he built up an original investment of fifty-five borrowed dollars into a business of his own that made him twenty thousand dollars a year. Then came a frost, a killing frost. He endorsed a big note for a friend – and the friend went bankrupt. Quickly on top of that disaster came another: the bank in which he had all his money collapsed. He not only lost every cent he had, but was plunged into debt for sixteen thousand dollars. His nerves couldn't take it. 'I couldn't sleep or eat,' he told me. 'I became strangely ill. *Worry* and *nothing but worry*,' he said, *'brought on this illness*. One day as I was walking down the street, I fainted and fell on the sidewalk. I was no longer able to walk. I was put to bed and my body broke out in boils. These boils turned inward until just lying in bed was agony. I grew weaker every day. Finally my doctor told me that I had only two more weeks to live. I was shocked. I drew up my will, and then lay back in bed to await my end. No use now to struggle or worry. I gave up, relaxed, and went to sleep. I hadn't slept two hours in succession for weeks; but now with my earthly problems drawing to an end,

I slept like a baby. My exhausting weariness began to disappear. My appetite returned. I gained weight.

'A few weeks later, I was able to walk with crutches. Six weeks later, I was able to go back to work. I had been making twenty thousand dollars a year; but I was glad now to get a job for thirty dollars a week. I got a job selling blocks to put behind the wheels of automobiles when they are shipped by freight. I had learned my lesson now. No more worry for me – no more regret about what had happened in the past – no more dread of the future. I concentrated all my time, energy, and enthusiasm into selling those blocks.'

Edward S. Evans shot up fast now. In a few years, he was president of the company – the Evans Products Company. It has been listed on the New York Stock Exchange for years. If you ever fly over Greenland you many land on Evans Field – a flying field named in his honour. Yet Edward S. Evans never would have achieved these victories if he hadn't learned to live in day-tight compartments.

You will recall that the White Queen said: 'The rule is jam tomorrow and jam yesterday but never jam today.' Most of us are like that – stewing about yesterday's jam and worrying about tomorrow's jam – instead of spreading today's jam thick on our bread right now.

Even the great French philosopher, Montaigne, made that mistake. 'My life,' he said, 'has been full of terrible misfortunes most of which never happened,' So has mine – so has yours.

'Think,' said Dante, 'that this day will never dawn again.' Life is slipping away with incredible speed. We are racing through space at the rate of nineteen miles every second. *Today* is our most precious possession. *It is our only sure possession.*

That is the philosophy of Lowell Thomas. I recently spent a weekend at his farm; and I noticed that he had these words from Psalm cxviii framed and hanging on the walls of his broadcasting studio where he would see them often:

This is the day which the Lord hath made:
we will rejoice and be glad in it.

The writer John Ruskin had on his desk a simple piece of stone on which was carved one word: TODAY. And while I haven't a piece of stone on my desk, I do have a poem pasted on my mirror where I can see it when I shave every morning – a poem that Sir William Osler always kept on his desk – a poem written by the famous Indian dramatist, Kalidasa:

SALUTATION TO THE DAWN

Look to this day!
For it is life, the very life of life.
In its brief course

Lie all the verities and realities of your existence:
    The bliss of growth
      The glory of action
        The splendour of beauty,
For yesterday is but a dream
And tomorrow is only a vision,
But today well lived makes every yesterday a dream of happiness
And every tomorrow a vision of hope.
Look well, therefore, to this day!
Such is the salutation to the dawn.

So, the first thing you should know about worry is this: if you want to keep it out of your life, do what Sir William Osler did –

1 Shut the iron doors on the past and the future. Live in Day-tight Compartments.

Why not ask yourself these questions, and write down the answers?

1 Do I tend to put off living in the present in order to worry about the future, or to yearn for some 'magical rose garden over the horizon'?

2 Do I sometimes embitter the present by regretting things that happened in the past – that are over and done with?

3 Do I get up in the morning determined to 'Seize the day' – to get the utmost out of these twenty-four hours?

4 Can I get more out of life by 'living in day-tight compartments'?

5 When shall I start to do this? Next week? . . . Tomorrow? . . . *Today*?

□ **2** □

A magic formula for solving worry situations

Would you like a quick, sure-fire recipe for handling worry situations – a technique you can start using right away, before you go any further in reading this book?

Then let me tell you about the method worked out by Willis H. Carrier, the brilliant engineer who launched the air-conditioning industry, and who headed the world-famous Carrier Corporation, in Syracuse, New York. It is one of the best techniques I ever heard of for solving worry problems, and I got it from Mr. Carrier personally when we were having lunch together one day at the Engineers' Club in New York.

'When I was a young man,' Mr. Carrier said, 'I worked for the Buffalo Forge Company in Buffalo, New York. I was handed the assignment of installing a gas-cleaning device in a plant of the Pittsburgh Plate Glass Company at Crystal City, Missouri – a plant costing millions of dollars. The purpose of this installation was to remove the impurities from the gas so it could be burned without injuring the engines. This method of cleaning gas was new. It had been tried only once before – and under different conditions. In my work at Crystal City, Missouri, unforeseen difficulties arose. It worked after a fashion – but not well enough to meet the guarantee we had made.

'I was stunned by my failure. It was almost as if someone had struck me a blow on the head. My stomach, my insides, began to twist and turn. For a while I was so worried I couldn't sleep.

'Finally, common sense reminded me that worry wasn't getting me anywhere; so I figured out a way to handle my problem without worrying. It worked superbly. I have been using this same anti-worry technique for more than thirty years. It is simple. Anyone can use it. It consists of three steps:

'Step I. *I analyzed the situation fearlessly and honestly and figured out what was the worst that could possibly happen as a result of this failure.* No one was going to jail me or shoot me. That was certain. True, there was also a chance that I would lose my position; and there was also a chance that my employers would have to remove the machinery and lose the twenty thousand dollars we had invested.

'Step II. *After figuring out what was the worst that could possibly happen, I reconciled myself to accepting it, if necessary.* I said to myself: This failure will be a blow to my record, and it might possibly mean the loss of my job; but if it does, I can always get another position. Conditions could be much worse; and as far as my employers are concerned – well, they realize that we are experimenting with a new method of cleaning gas, and if this experience costs them twenty thousand dollars, they can stand it. They can charge it up to research, for it is an experiment.

'After discovering the worst that could possibly happen and reconciling myself to accepting it, if necessary, an extremely important thing happened: I immediately relaxed and felt a sense of peace that I hadn't experienced in days.

'Step III. *From that time on, I calmly devoted my time and energy to trying to improve upon the worst which I had already accepted mentally.*

'I now tried to figure out ways and means by which I might reduce the loss of twenty thousand dollars that we faced. I made several tests and finally figured out that if we spent another five thousand for additional equipment, our problem would be solved. We did this, and instead of the firm losing twenty thousand, we made fifteen thousand.

'I probably would never have been able to do this if I had kept on worrying, because one of the worst features about worrying is that it destroys our ability to concentrate. When we worry, our minds jump here and there and everywhere, and we lose all power of decision. However, when we force ourselves to face the worst and accept it mentally, we then eliminate all these vague imaginings and put ourselves in a position in which we are able to concentrate on our problem.

'This incident that I have related occurred many years ago. It worked so superbly that I have been using it ever since; and, as a result, my life has been almost completely free from worry.'

Now, why is Willis H. Carrier's magic formula so valuable and so practical, psychologically speaking? Because it yanks us down out of the great grey clouds in which we fumble around when we are blinded by worry. It plants our feet good and solid on the earth. We know where we stand. And if we haven't solid ground under us, how in creation can we ever hope to think anything through?

Professor William James, the father of applied psychology, has been dead since 1910. But if he were alive today, and could hear this formula for facing the worst, he would heartily approve it. How do I know that? Because he told his own students: 'Be willing to have it so ... Be willing to have it so,' he said, *because* '... acceptance of what has happened is the first step to overcoming the consequences of any misfortune.'

The same idea was expressed by Lin Yutang in his widely read book, *The Importance of Living*. 'True peace of mind,' said this Chinese philosopher, 'comes from accepting the worst. Psychologically, I think, it means a release of energy.'

That's it, exactly! Psychologically, it means a new release of energy! When we have accepted the worst, we have nothing more to lose. And that automatically means – we have *everything* to gain! 'After facing the worst,' Willis H. Carrier reported, 'I immediately relaxed and felt a sense of peace that I hadn't experienced in days. From that time on, I was able to *think*.'

Makes sense, doesn't it? Yet millions of people have wrecked their lives in angry turmoil, because they refused to accept the worst; refused to try to improve upon it; refused to salvage what they could from the wreck. Instead of trying to reconstruct their fortunes, they engaged in a bitter and 'violent contest with experience' – and ended up victims of that brooding fixation known as melancholia.

Would you like to see how someone else adopted Willis H. Carrier's magic formula and applied it to his own problem? Well, here is one example, from a New York oil dealer who was a student in my classes.

'I was being blackmailed!' this student began. 'I didn't believe it was possible

– I didn't believe it could happen outside of the movies – but I was actually being blackmailed! What happened was this: the oil company of which I was the head had a number of delivery trucks and a number of drivers. At that time, war regulations were strictly in force, and we were rationed on the amount of oil we could deliver to any one of our customers. I didn't know it, but it seems that certain of our drivers had been delivering oil short to our regular customers, and then reselling the surplus to customers of their own.

'The first inkling I had of these illegitimate transactions was when a man who claimed to be a government inspector came to see me one day and demanded hush money. He had got documentary proof of what our drivers had been doing, and he threatened to turn this proof over to the District Attorney's office if I didn't cough up.

'I knew, of course, that I had nothing to worry about – personally, at least. But I also knew that the law says a firm is responsible for the action of its employees. What's more, I knew that if the case came to court, and it was aired in the newspapers, the bad publicity would ruin my business. And I was proud of my business – it had been founded by my father twenty-four years before.

'I was so worried I was sick! I didn't eat or sleep for three days and nights. I kept going around in crazy circles. Should I pay the money – five thousand dollars – or should I tell this man to go ahead and do his damnedest? Either way I tried to make up my mind, it ended in nightmare.

'Then, on Sunday night, I happened to pick up the booklet on *How to Stop Worrying*, which I had been given in my Carnegie class in public speaking. I started to read it, and came across the story of Willis H. Carrier. "Face the worst," it said. So I asked myself, "What is the worst that can happen if I refuse to pay up, and these blackmailers turn their records over to the District Attorney?"

'The answer to that was: "The ruin of my business – that's the worst that can happen. I can't go to jail. All that can happen is that I shall be ruined by the publicity."

'I then said to myself, "All right, the business *is* ruined. I accept that mentally. What happens next?"

'Well, with my business ruined, I would probably have to look for a job. That wasn't bad. I knew a lot about oil – there were several firms that might be glad to employ me . . . I began to feel better. The blue funk I had been in for three days and nights began to lift a little. My emotions calmed down . . . And to my astonishment, I was able to *think*.

'I was clearheaded enough now to face Step III – *improve on the worst*. As I thought of solutions, an entirely new angle presented itself to me. If I told my attorney the whole situation, he might find a way out which I hadn't thought of. I know it sounds stupid to say that this hadn't even occurred to me before – but of course I hadn't been thinking, I had only been *worrying*! I immediately made up my mind that I would see my attorney first thing in the morning – and then I went to bed and slept like a log!

'How did it end? Well, the next morning my lawyer told me to go and see the District Attorney and tell him the truth. I did precisely that. When I finished I was astonished to hear the D.A. say that this blackmail racket had been going on for months and that the man who claimed to be a "government agent" was a crook wanted by the police. What a relief to hear all this after I had tormented myself for three days and nights wondering whether I should hand over five thousand dollars to this professional swindler!

'This experience taught me a lasting lesson. Now, whenever I face a pressing problem that threatens to worry me, I give it what I call "the old Willis H. Carrier formula".'

If you think Willis H. Carrier had troubles – listen: you ain't heard nothin' yet. Here is the story of Earl P. Haney, of Winchester, Massachusetts. Here is the story as he told it to me himself on November 17, 1948, in the Hotel Statler in Boston.

'Back in the twenties,' he said, 'I was so worried that ulcers began eating the lining of my stomach. One night, I had a terrible hemorrhage. I was rushed to a hospital connected with the School of Medicine of Northwestern University of Chicago. My weight dropped from 175 pounds to 90 pounds. I was so ill I was warned not even to lift my hand. Three doctors, including a celebrated ulcer specialist, said my case was "incurable". I lived on alkaline powders and a tablespoonful of half milk and half cream every hour. A nurse put a rubber tube down into my stomach every night and every morning and pumped out the contents.

'This went on for months . . . Finally, I said to myself: "Look here, Earl Haney, if you have nothing to look forward to except a lingering death, you might as well make the most of the little time you have left. You have always wanted to travel around the world before you die; so if you are ever going to do it, you'll have to do it now."

'When I told my physicians I was going to travel around the world and pump out my own stomach twice a day, they were shocked. Impossible! They had never heard of such a thing. They warned me that if I started around the world, I would be buried at sea. "No, I won't," I replied. "I have promised my relatives that I will be buried in the family plot at Broken Bow, Nebraska. So I am going to take my casket with me."

'I arranged for a casket, put it aboard ship, and then made arrangements with the steamship company – in the event of my death – to put my corpse in a freezing compartment and keep it there till the liner returned home. I set out on my trip, imbued with the spirit of old Omar:

Ah, make the most of what we yet may spend,
Before we too into the Dust descend;

Dust into Dust, and under Dust, to lie,
Sans Wine, sans Song, sans Singer, and – sans End!

'The moment I boarded the S. S. *President Adams* in Los Angeles and headed for the Orient, I felt better. I gradually gave up my alkaline powders and my stomach pump. I was soon eating all kinds of foods – even strange native mixtures and concoctions that were guaranteed to kill me. As the weeks went by, I even smoked long, black cigars and drank highballs. I enjoyed myself more than I had in years! We ran into monsoons and typhoons which should have put me in my casket, if only from fright – but I got an enormous kick out of all this adventure.

'I played games aboard the ship, sang songs, made new friends, stayed up half the night. When we reached China and India, I realized that the business cares that I had faced back home were paradise compared to the poverty and hunger in the Orient. I stopped all my senseless worrying and felt fine. When I got back to America, I had gained ninety pounds and I had almost forgotten I had ever had a stomach ulcer. I had never felt better in my life. I went back to business and haven't been ill a day since.'

Earl P. Haney told me he realizes now that he was unconsciously using the selfsame principles that Willis H. Carrier used to conquer worry.

'First, I asked myself, "What is the worst that could possibly happen?" The answer was death.

'Second, I prepared myself to accept death. I had to. There was no choice. The doctors said my case was hopeless.

'Third, I tried to improve the situation by getting the utmost enjoyment out of life for the short time I had left . . . *If*,' he continued, 'if I had gone on worrying after boarding that ship, I have no doubt that I would have made the return voyage inside my coffin. But I relaxed – and I forgot all my troubles. And this calmness of mind gave me a new burst of energy which actually saved my life.'

So, Rule 2 is: If you have a worry problem, apply the magic formula of Willis H. Carrier by doing these three things –

1 Ask yourself, 'What is the worst that can possibly happen?'
2 Prepare to accept it if you have to.
3 Then calmly proceed to improve on the worst.

☐ 3 ☐

What worry may do to you

Those who do not know how to fight worry die young.
DR. ALEXIS CARREL

Many years ago, a neighbour rang my doorbell one evening and urged me and my family to be vaccinated against smallpox. He was only one of thousands of volunteers who were ringing doorbells all over New York City. Frightened people stood in lines for hours at a time to be vaccinated. Vaccination stations were opened not only in all hospitals, but also in firehouses, police precincts, and in large industrial plants. More than two thousand doctors and nurses worked feverishly day and night, vaccinating crowds. The cause of all this excitement? Eight people in New York City had smallpox – and two had died. Two deaths out of a population of almost eight million.

Now, I had lived in New York for many, many years; and no one had ever yet rung my doorbell to warn me against the emotional sickness of worry – an illness that, during the same time period, had caused ten thousand times more damage than smallpox.

No doorbell ringer has ever warned me that one person out of ten now living in these United States will have a nervous breakdown – induced in the vast majority of cases by worry and emotional conflicts. So I am writing this chapter to ring your doorbell and warn you.

The great Nobel prize winner in medicine, Dr. Alexis Carrel, said, 'Businessmen who do not know how to fight worry die young.' And so do housewives and horse doctors and bricklayers.

A few years ago, I spent my vacation motoring through Texas and New Mexico with Dr. O. F. Gober – one of the medical executives of the Santa Fe railway. His exact title was chief physician of the Gulf, Colorado and Santa Fe Hospital Association. We got to talking about the effects of worry, and he said: 'Seventy percent of all patients who come to physicians could cure themselves if they only got rid of their fears and worries. Don't think for a moment that I mean that their ills are imaginary,' he said. 'Their ills are as real as a throbbing toothache and sometimes a hundred times more serious. I refer to such illnesses as nervous indigestion, some stomach ulcers, heart

214

disturbances, insomnia, some headaches, and some types of paralysis.

'These illnesses are real. I know what I am talking about,' said Dr. Gober, 'for I myself suffered from a stomach ulcer for twelve years.'

'Fear causes worry. Worry makes you tense and nervous and affects the nerves of your stomach and actually changes the gastric juices of your stomach from normal to abnormal and often leads to stomach ulcers.'

Dr. Joseph F. Montague, author of the book *Nervous Stomach Trouble*, says much the same thing. He says: 'You do not get stomach ulcers from what you eat. You get ulcers from what is eating you.'

Dr. W. C. Alvarez, of the Mayo Clinic, said: 'Ulcers frequently flare up or subside according to the hills and valleys of emotional stress.'

That statement was backed up by a study of 15,000 patients treated for stomach disorders at the Mayo Clinic. Four out of five had no physical basis whatever for their stomach illnesses. Fear, worry, hate, supreme selfishness, and the inability to adjust themselves to the world of reality – these were largely the causes of their stomach illnesses and stomach ulcers . . . Stomach ulcers can kill you. According to *Life* magazine, they now stand tenth in our list of fatal diseases.

I recently had some correspondence with Dr. Harold C. Habein of the Mayo Clinic. He read a paper at the annual meeting of the American Association of Industrial Physicians and Surgeons, saying that he had made a study of 176 business executives whose average age was 44.3 years. *He reported that slightly more than a third of these executives suffered from one of three ailments peculiar to high-tension living – heart disease, digestive-tract ulcers, and high blood pressure.* Think of it – a third of our business executives are wrecking their bodies with heart disease, ulcers, and high blood pressure before they even reach forty-five. What price success! And they aren't even buying success! Can any man possibly be a success who is paying for business advancement with stomach ulcers and heart trouble? What shall it profit a man if he gains the whole world – and loses his health? Even if he owned the whole world, he could sleep in only one bed at a time and eat only three meals a day. Even a new employee can do that – and probably sleep more soundly and enjoy his food more than a high-powered executive. Frankly, I would rather be a carefree person with no responsibility than wreck my health at forty-five by trying to run a railroad or a cigarette company.

The best-known cigarette manufacturer in the world dropped dead from heart failure while trying to take a little recreation in the Canadian woods. He amassed millions – and fell dead at sixty-one. He probably traded years of his life for what is called 'business success'.

In my estimation, this cigarette executive with all his millions was not half as successful as my father – a Missouri farmer – who died at eight-nine, without a dollar.

The famous Mayo brothers declared that more than half of our hospital beds are occupied by people with nervous troubles. Yet, when the nerves of these people are studied under a high-power microscope in a post-mortem examination, their nerves in most cases are apparently as healthy as the nerves of Jack Dempsey. Their 'nervous troubles' are caused not by a physical deterioration of the nerves, but by emotions of futility, frustration, anxiety, worry, fear, defeat, despair. Plato said that 'the greatest mistake physicians make is that they attempt to cure the body without attempting to cure the mind; yet the mind and body are one and should not be treated separately!'

It took medical science twenty-three hundred years to recognize this great truth. We are just now beginning to develop a new kind of medicine called *psychosomatic* medicine – a medicine that treats both the mind and the body. It is high time we are doing that, for medical science has largely wiped out the terrible *diseases caused by physical germs* – diseases such as smallpox, cholera, yellow fever, and scores of other scourges that swept untold millions into untimely graves. But medical science has been unable to cope with the mental and physical wrecks caused, not by germs, but by emotions of worry, fear, hate, frustration, and despair. Casualties caused by these emotional diseases are mounting and spreading with catastrophic rapidity. One out of every six of our young men called up by the draft in the Second World War was rejected for psychiatric reasons.

What causes insanity? No one knows all the answers. But it is highly probable that in many cases fear and worry are contributing factors. The anxious and harassed individual who is unable to cope with the harsh world of reality breaks off all contact with his environment and retreats into a private dream world of his own making, and this solves his worry problems.

I have on my desk a book by Dr. Edward Podolsky entitled *Stop Worrying and Get Well*. Here are some chapter titles in that book:

WHAT WORRY DOES TO THE HEART
HIGH BLOOD PRESSURE IS FED BY WORRY
RHEUMATISM CAN BE CAUSED BY WORRY
WORRY LESS FOR YOUR STOMACH'S SAKE
HOW WORRY CAN CAUSE A COLD
WORRY AND THE THYROID
THE WORRYING DIABETIC

Another illuminating book about worry is *Man Against Himself* by Dr. Karl Menninger, one of the 'Mayo brothers of psychiatry'. Dr. Menninger's book will not give you any rules about how to avoid worry; but it will give you a startling revelation of how we destroy our bodies and minds by anxiety, frustration, hatred, resentment, rebellion, and fear. You will probably find a copy in your public library.

Worry can make even the most stolid person ill. General Grant discovered that during the closing days of the Civil War. The story goes like this: Grant had been besieging Richmond for nine months. General Lee's troops, ragged and hungry, were beaten. Entire regiments were deserting at a time. Others were holding prayer meetings in their tents – shouting, weeping, and seeing visions. The end was close. Lee's men set fire to the cotton and tobacco warehouses in Richmond, burned the arsenal, and fled from the city at night while towering flames roared up into darkness. Grant was in hot pursuit, banging away at the Confederates from both sides and the rear, while Sheridan's cavalry was heading them off in front, tearing up railway lines and capturing supply trains.

Grant, half blind with a violent sick headache, fell behind his army and stopped at a farmhouse. 'I spent the night,' he records in his *Memoirs*, 'in bathing my feet in hot water and mustard, and putting mustard plasters on my wrists and the back part of my neck, hoping to be cured by morning.'

The next morning, he was cured instantaneously. And the thing that cured him was not a mustard plaster, but a horseman galloping down the road with a letter from Lee, saying he wanted to surrender.

'When the officer [bearing the message] reached me,' Grant wrote, 'I was still suffering with the sick headache, but the instant I saw the contents of the note, I was cured.'

Obviously it was Grant's worries, tensions, and emotions that made him ill. He was cured instantly the moment his emotions took on the hue of confidence, achievement, and victory.

Seventy years later, Henry Morgenthau, Jr., Secretary of the Treasury in Franklin D. Roosevelt's cabinet, discovered that worry could make him so ill that he was dizzy. He records in his diary that he was terribly worried when the President, in order to raise the price of wheat, bought 4,400,000 bushels in one day. He says in his diary: 'I felt literally dizzy while the thing was going on. I went home and went to bed for two hours after lunch.'

If I want to see what worry does to people, I don't have to go to a library or a physician. I can look out of the window of my home where I am writing this book; and I can see, within one block, one house where worry caused nervous breakdown – and another house where a man worried himself into diabetes. When the stock market went down, the sugar in his blood and urine went up.

When Montaigne, the illustrious French philosopher, was elected Mayor of his home town – Bordeaux – he said to his fellow citizens: 'I am willing to take your affairs into my hands but not into my liver and lungs.'

This neighbour of mine took the affairs of the stock market into his blood stream – and almost killed himself.

If I want to be reminded of what worry does to people, I don't need to look at my neighbours' houses. I can look at this very room where I am writing now and be reminded that a former owner of this house worried himself into an untimely grave.

Worry can put you into a wheelchair with rheumatism and arthritis.

Dr. Russell L. Cecil, a world-recognized authority on arthritis, has listed four of the commonest conditions that bring on arthritis:

1. Marital shipwreck.
2. Financial disaster and grief.
3. Loneliness and worry.
4. Long-cherished resentments.

Naturally, these four emotional situations are far from being the only causes of arthritis. There are many different kinds of arthritis – due to various causes. But, to repeat, the *commonest conditions* that bring on arthritis are the four listed by Dr. Russell L. Cecil. For example, a friend of mine was so hard hit during the Depression that the gas company shut off the gas and the bank foreclosed the mortgage on the house. His wife suddenly had a painful attack of arthritis – and, in spite of medicine and diets, the arthritis continued until their financial situation improved.

Worry can even cause tooth decay. Dr. William I. L. McGonigle said in an address before the American Dental Association that 'unpleasant emotions such as those caused by worry, fear, nagging . . . may upset the body's calcium balance and cause tooth decay.' Dr. McGonigle told of a patient of his who had always had a perfect set of teeth until he began to worry over his wife's sudden illness. During the three weeks she was in the hospital, he developed nine cavities – cavities brought on by worry.

Have you ever seen a person with an acutely overactive thyroid? I have, and I can tell you they tremble; they shake; they look like someone half scared to death – and that's about what it amounts to. The thyroid gland, the gland that regulates the body, has been thrown out of kilter. It speeds up the heart – the whole body is roaring away at full blast like a furnace with all of its drafts wide open. And if this isn't checked, by operation or treatment, the victim may die, may 'burn himself out'.

Some time ago I went to Philadelphia with a friend of mine who suffered from this condition. We consulted Dr. Israel Bram, a famous specialist who has been treating this type of ailment for thirty-eight years. Here is the advice he had hanging on the wall of his waiting room – painted on a large wooden sign. I copied it down on the back of an envelope while I was waiting:

RELAXATION AND RECREATION

The most relaxing recreating forces are a healthy
religion, sleep, music, and laughter.
Have faith in God – learn to sleep well –
Love good music – see the funny side of life –
And health and happiness will be yours.

The first question he asked this friend of mine was: 'What emotional disturbance brought on this condition?' He warned my friend that, if he didn't stop worrying, he could get other complications: heart trouble, stomach ulcers, or diabetes. 'All of these diseases,' said that eminent doctor, 'are cousins, first cousins.'

When I interviewed film star Merle Oberon, she told me that she refused to worry because she knew that worry would destroy her chief asset on the motion-picture screen: her good looks.

'When I first tried to break into the movies,' she told me, 'I was worried and scared. I had just come from India, and I didn't know anyone in London, where I was trying to get a job. I saw a few producers, but none of them hired me; and the little money I had began to give out. For two weeks I lived on nothing but crackers and water. I was not only worried now. I was hungry. I said to myself, "Maybe you're a fool. Maybe you will *never* break into the movies. After all, you have no experience, you've never acted at all – what have you to offer but a rather pretty face?"

'I went to the mirror. And when I looked in that mirror, I saw what worry was doing to my looks! I saw the lines it was forming. I saw the anxious expression. So I said to myself, "You've got to stop this at once! You can't afford to worry. The only thing you have to offer at all is your looks, and worry will ruin them!" '

Few things can age and sour a woman and destroy her looks as quickly as worry. Worry curdles the expression. It makes us clench our jaws and lines our faces with wrinkles. It forms a permanent scowl. It may turn the hair grey, and, in some cases, even make it fall out. It can ruin the complexion – it can bring on all kinds of skin rashes, eruptions and pimples.

Heart disease is the number-one killer in America today. During the Second World War, almost a third of a million men were killed in combat; but during the same period, heart disease killed two million civilians – and one million of those casualties were caused by the kind of heart disease that is brought on by worry and high-tension living. Yes, heart disease is one of the chief reasons why Dr. Alexis Carrel said: 'Businessmen who do not know how to fight worry die young.'

'The Lord may forgive us our sins,' said William James, 'but the nervous system never does.'

Here is a startling and almost incredible fact: more Americans commit suicide each year than die from the five most common communicable diseases.

Why? The answer is largely: 'Worry'.

When the cruel Chinese war lords wanted to torture their prisoners, they would tie their prisoners hand and foot and put them under a bag of water that constantly dripped ... dripped ... dripped ... day and night. These drops of water constantly falling on the head finally became like the sound of hammer blows – and drove men insane. This same method of torture was used during the Spanish Inquisition and in German concentration camps under Hitler.

Worry is like the constant drip, drip, rip of water; and the constant drip, drip, drip of worry often drives men to insanity and suicide.

When I was a country lad in Missouri, I was half scared to death by listening to Billy Sunday describe the hell-fires of the next world. But he never mentioned the hell-fires of physical agony that worriers may have to face here and now. For example, if you are a chronic worrier, you may be stricken someday with one of the most excruciating pains ever endured by man: angina pectoris.

Do you love life? Do you want to live long and enjoy good health? Here is how you can do it. I am quoting Dr. Alexis Carrel again: He said, *'Those who keep the peace of their inner selves in the midst of the tumult of the modern city are immune from nervous diseases.'*

Can you keep the peace of your inner self in the midst of the tumult of a modern city? If you are a normal person, the answer is, 'yes'. 'Emphatically yes.' Most of us are stronger than we realize. We have inner resources that we have probably never tapped. As Thoreau said in his immortal book, *Walden*: 'I know of no more encouraging fact than the unquestionable ability of man to elevate his life by a conscious endeavor . . . If one advances confidently in the direction of his dreams, and endeavors to live the life he has imagined, he will meet with a success unexpected in common hours.'

Surely, many of the readers of this book have as much willpower and as many inner resources as has Olga K. Jarvey, of Coeur d'Alene, Idaho. She discovered that under the most tragic circumstances she could banish worry. I firmly believe that you and I can also – if we apply the old, old truths discussed in this volume. Here is Olga K. Jarvey's story as she wrote it for me: 'Eight and a half years ago, I was condemned to die – a slow, agonizing death – of cancer. The best medical brains of the country, the Mayo brothers, confirmed the sentence. I was at a dead-end street, the ultimate gaped at me! I was young. I did not want to die! In my desperation, I phoned my doctor at Kellogg and cried out to him the despair in my heart. Rather impatiently he upbraided me, "What's the matter, Olga, haven't you any fight in you? Sure, you will die if you keep on crying. Yes, the worst has overtaken you. O.K. – face the facts! Quit worrying! And then do something about it!" Right then and there I took an oath, an oath so solemn that the nails sank deep into my flesh and cold chills ran down my spine: *'I am not going to worry! I am not going to cry! And if there is anything to mind over matter, I am going to win! I am going to LIVE!"*

'The usual amount of X-rays in such advanced cases was, at that time, $10^1/_2$ minutes a day for 30 days. They gave me X-ray for $14^1/_2$ minutes a day for 49 days; and although my bones stuck out of my emaciated body like rocks on a barren hillside, and although my feet were like lead, *I did not worry!* Not once did I cry! I *smiled*! Yes, I actually *forced* myself to smile.

'I am not so idiotic as to imagine that merely smiling can cure cancer. But I do believe that a cheerful mental attitude helps the body fight disease. At any rate, I experienced one of the miracle cures of cancer. I have never been healthier than in the last few years, thanks to those challenging, fighting words: "Face the facts: Quit worrying; then do something about it!" '

I am going to close this chapter by repeating its title: the words of Dr. Alexis Carrel: *'Those who do not know how to fight worry die young.'*

The followers of the prophet Mohammed often had verses from the Koran tattooed on their breasts. I would like to have the title of this chapter tattooed on the breast of every reader of this book: 'Those who do not know how to fight worry die young.'

Was Dr. Carrel speaking of *you*?

Could be.

□ **IN A NUTSHELL** □

FUNDAMENTAL FACTS YOU SHOULD KNOW ABOUT WORRY

RULE 1: If you want to avoid worry, do what Sir William Osler did: Live in 'day-tight compartments.' Don't stew about the future. Just live each day until bedtime.

RULE 2: The next time Trouble – with a Capital T – backs you up in a corner, try the magic formula of Willis H. Carrier:

    a. Ask yourself, 'What is the worst that can possibly happen if I can't solve my problem?'

    b. Prepare yourself mentally to accept the worst – if necessary.

    c. Then calmly try to improve upon the worst – which you have already mentally agreed to accept.

RULE 3: Remind yourself of the exorbitant price you can pay for worry in terms of your health. 'Those who do not know how to fight worry die young.'

Part Two

BASIC TECHNIQUES IN ANALYZING

WORRY

□ 4 □

How to analyze and solve worry problems

I keep six honest serving-men
(They taught me all I knew):
Their names are What and Why and When
And How and Where and Who.

— RUDYARD KIPLING

Will the magic formula of Willis H. Carrier, described in Part One, Chapter 2, solve *all* worry problems? No, of course not.

Then what *is* the answer? The answer is that we must equip ourselves to deal with different kinds of worries by learning the three basic steps of problem analysis. The three steps are:

1 Get the facts.
2 Analyze the facts.
3 Arrive at a decision – and then act on that decision.

Obvious stuff? Yes. Aristotle taught it – and used it. And you and I must use it too if we are going to solve the problems that are harassing us and turning our days and nights into veritable hells.

Let's take the first rule: *Get the facts.* Why is it so important to get the facts? Because unless we have the facts we can't possibly even attempt to solve our problems intelligently. Without the facts, all we can do is stew around in confusion. My idea? No, that was the idea of the late Herbert E. Hawkes, Dean of Columbia College, Columbia University, for twenty-two years. He had helped two hundred thousand students solve their worry problems; and he told me that *'confusion is the chief cause of worry'*. He put it this way – he said: 'Half the worry in the world is caused by people trying to make decisions before they have sufficient knowledge on which to base a decision. For example,' he said, 'if I have a problem which has to be faced at three o'clock next Tuesday, I refuse to even try to make a decision about it until next Tuesday arrives. In the meantime, I concentrate on getting all the facts that bear on the problem. I don't worry,' he said. 'I don't agonize over my problem.

I don't lose sleep. I simply concentrate on getting the facts. And by the time Tuesday rolls around, if I've got all the facts the problem usually solves itself!'

I asked Dean Hawkes if this meant he had licked worry entirely. 'Yes,' he said, 'I think I can honestly say that my life is now almost totally devoid of worry. I have found,' he went on, 'that if a man will devote his time to securing facts in an impartial, objective way, his worries will usually evaporate in the light of knowledge.'

Let me repeat that: *'If a man will devote his time to securing facts in an impartial, objective way, his worries will usually evaporate in the light of knowledge.'*

But what do most of us do? If we bother with facts at all – and Thomas Edison said in all seriousness, 'There is no expedient to which a man will not resort to avoid the labour of thinking' – if we bother with facts at all, we hunt like bird dogs after the facts that bolster up what we *already* think – and ignore all the others! We want only the facts that justify our acts – the facts that fit in conveniently with our wishful thinking and justify our preconceived prejudices!

As André Maurois put it: 'Everything that is in agreement with our personal desires seems true. Everything that is not puts us into a rage.'

Is it any wonder, then, that we find it so hard to get at the answers to our problems? Wouldn't we have the same trouble trying to solve a second-grade arithmetic problem, if we went ahead on the assumption that two plus two equals five? Yet there are a lot of people in this world who make life a hell for themselves and others by insisting that two plus two equals five – or maybe five hundred!

What can we do about it? We have to keep our emotions out of our thinking; and, as Dean Hawkes put it, we must secure the facts in 'an impartial, objective' manner.

That is not an easy task when we are worried. When we are worried, our emotions are riding high. But here are two ideas that I have found helpful when trying to step aside from my problems, in order to see the facts in a clear, objective manner.

1. When trying to get the facts, I pretend that I am collecting this information not for myself, but for some other person. This helps me to take a cold, impartial view of the evidence. This helps me eliminate my emotions.

2. While trying to collect the facts about the problem that is worrying me, I sometimes pretend that I am a lawyer preparing to argue the other side of the issue. In other words, I try to get all the facts against myself – all the facts that are damaging to my wishes, all the facts I don't like to face.

Then I write down both my side of the case and the other side of the case – and I generally find that the truth lies somewhere in between these two extremities.

Here is the point I am trying to make. Neither you nor I nor Einstein nor the Supreme Court of the United States is brilliant enough to reach an intelligent decision on any problem without first getting the facts. Thomas Edison knew that. At the time of his death, he had two thousand five hundred notebooks filled with facts about the problems he was facing.

So Rule 1 for solving our problems is: *Get the facts*. Let's do what Dean Hawkes did: let's not even attempt to solve our problems without first collecting all the facts in an impartial manner.

However, getting all the facts in the world won't do us any good until we analyze them and interpret them.

I have found from costly experience that it is much easier to analyze the facts after writing them down. In fact, merely writing the facts on a piece of paper and stating our problem clearly goes a long way toward helping us reach a sensible decision. As Charles Kettering puts it: 'A problem well stated is a problem half solved.'

Let me show you all this as it works out in practice. Since the Chinese say one picture is worth ten thousand words, suppose I show you a picture of how one man put exactly what we are talking about into concrete action.

Let's take the case of Galen Litchfield – a man I have known for several years; one of the most successful American businessmen in the Far East. Mr. Litchfield was in China in 1942, when the Japanese invaded Shanghai. And here is his story as he told it to me while a guest in my home:

'Shortly after the Japanese bombed Pearl Harbor,' Galen Litchfield began, 'they came swarming into Shanghai. I was the manager of the Asia Life Assurance Company in Shanghai. They sent us an "army liquidator" – he was really an admiral – and gave me orders to assist this man in liquidating our assets. I didn't have any choice in the matter. I could cooperate – or else. And the "or else" was certain death.

'I went through the motions of doing what I was told, because I had no alternative. But there was one block of securities, worth $750,000, which I left off the list I gave to the admiral. I left that block of securities off the list because they belonged to our Hong Kong organization and had nothing to do with the Shanghai assets. All the same, I feared I might be in hot water if the Japanese found out what I had done. And they soon found out.

'I wasn't in the office when the discovery was made, but my head accountant was there. He told me that the Japanese admiral flew into a rage, and stamped and swore, and called me a thief and a traitor! I had defied the Japanese army! I knew what that meant. I would be thrown into the Bridgehouse!

'The Bridgehouse! The torture chamber of the Japanese Gestapo! I had had personal friends who had killed themselves rather than be taken to that prison. I had had other friends who had died in that place after ten days of questioning and torture. Now I was slated for the Bridgehouse myself!

'What did I do? I heard the news on Sunday afternoon. I suppose I should have been terrified. And I would have been terrified if I hadn't had a definite technique for solving my problems. For years, whenever I was worried I had always gone to my typewriter and written down two questions – and the answers to these questions:

'1. *What am I worrying about?*
'2. *What can I do about it?*

'I used to try to answer those questions without writing them down. But I stopped that years ago. I found that writing down both the questions and the answers clarifies my thinking. So, that Sunday afternoon, I went directly to my room at the Shanghai Y.M.C.A., and got out my typewriter. I wrote:

'1. What am I worrying about?

I am afraid I will be thrown into the Bridgehouse tomorrow morning.

'Then I typed out the second question:
'2. What can I do about it?

'I spent hours thinking out and writing down the four courses of action I could take – and what the probable consequence of each action would be.

1 I can try to explain to the Japanese admiral. But he doesn't speak English. If I try to explain to him through an interpreter, I may stir him up again. That might mean death, for he is cruel, would rather dump me in the Bridgehouse than bother talking about it.
2 I can try to escape. Impossible. They keep track of me all the time. I have to check in and out of my room at the Y.M.C.A. If I try to escape, I'll probably be captured and shot.
3 I can stay here in my room and not go near the office again. If I do, the Japanese admiral will be suspicious, will probably send soldiers to get me and throw me into the Bridgehouse without giving me a chance to say a word.
4 I can go down to the office as usual on Monday morning. If I do, there is a chance that the Japanese admiral may be so busy that he will not think of what I did. Even if he does think of it, he may have cooled off and may not bother me. If this happens, I am all right. Even if he does bother me, I'll still have a chance to try to explain to him. So, going down to the office as usual on Monday morning, and acting as if nothing had gone wrong, gives me two chances to escape the Bridgehouse.

'As soon I as thought it all out and decided to accept the fourth plan – to go down to the office as usual on Monday morning – I felt immensely relieved.

'When I entered the office next morning, the Japanese admiral sat there with a cigarette dangling from his mouth. He glared at me as he always did; and said nothing. Six weeks later – thank God – he went back to Tokyo and my worries were ended.

'As I have already said, I probably saved my life by sitting down that Sunday afternoon and writing out all the various steps I could take and then writing down the probable consequence of each step and calmly coming to a decision.

If I hadn't done that, I might have floundered and hesitated and done the wrong thing on the spur of the moment. If I hadn't thought out my problem and come to a decision, I would have been frantic with worry all Sunday afternoon. I wouldn't have slept that night. I would have gone down to the office Monday morning with a harassed and worried look; and that alone might have aroused the suspicion of the Japanese admiral and spurred him to act.

'Experience has proved to me, time after time, the enormous value of arriving at a decision. It is the failure to arrive at a fixed purpose, the inability to stop going round and round in maddening circles, that drives men to nervous breakdowns and living hells. I find that fifty percent of my worries vanishes once I arrive at a clear, definite decision; and another forty percent usually vanishes once I start to carry out that decision.

'So I banish about ninety percent of my worries by taking these four steps:

'1 Writing down precisely what I am worrying about.
'2 Writing down what I can do about it.
'3 Deciding what to do.
'4 Starting immediately to carry out that decision.'

Galen Litchfield became the Far Eastern Director for Starr, Park and Freeman Inc., representing large insurance and financial interests. This made him one of the most important American businessmen in Asia; and he confessed to me that he owed a large part of his success to this method of analyzing worry and meeting it head-on.

Why is his method so superb? Because it is efficient, concrete, and goes directly to the heart of the problem. On top of all that, it is climaxed by the third and indispensable rule: *Do something about it.* Unless we carry out our action, all our fact-finding and analysis is whistling upwind – it's a sheer waste of energy.

William James said this: 'When once a decision is reached and execution is the order of the day, dismiss absolutely all responsibility and care about the outcome.' (In this case, William James undoubtedly used the word 'care' as a synonym for 'anxiety'.) He meant – once you have made a careful decision based on facts, *go into action*. Don't stop to reconsider. Don't begin to hesitate, worry and retrace your steps. Don't lose yourself in self-doubting which begets other doubts. Don't keep looking back over your shoulder.

I once asked Waite Phillips, one of Oklahoma's most prominent oil men, how he carried out decisions. He replied: 'I find that to keep thinking about our problems beyond a certain point is bound to create confusion and worry. There comes a time when any more investigation and thinking are harmful. There comes a time when we must decide and act and never look back.'

Why don't you employ Galen Litchfield's technique to one of your worries right now?

Here is question No. 1 – *What am I worrying about?* (Please pencil the answer to that question in the space below.)

Question No 2 – *What can I do about it?* (Please write your answer to that question in the space below.)

Question No. 3 – *Here is what I am going to do about it.*

Question No. 4 – *When am I going to start doing it?*

□ **5** □

How to eliminate fifty percent of your business worries

If you are in business, you are probably saying to yourself right now: 'The title of this chapter is ridiculous. I have been running my business for nineteen years; and I certainly know the answers if anybody does. The idea of anybody trying to tell me how I an eliminate fifty percent of my business worries – it's absurd!'

Fair enough – I would have felt exactly the same way myself a few years ago if I had seen this title on a chapter. It promises a lot – and promises are cheap.

Let's be very frank about it: *maybe I won't* be able to help you eliminate fifty percent of your business worries. In the last analysis, no one can do that, except yourself. But what I *can* do is to show you how other people have done it – and leave the rest up to you!

You may recall that in chapter 3 of this book I quote the world-famous Dr. Alexis Carrel as saying: 'Those who do not know how to fight worry die young.'

Since worry is that serious, wouldn't you be satisfied if I could help you eliminate even ten percent of your worries? ... Yes? ... Good! Well, I am going to show you how one business executive eliminated not fifty percent of his worries, but seventy-five percent of all the time he formerly spent in conferences, trying to solve business problems.

Furthermore, I am not going to tell you this story about a 'Mr. Jones' or a 'Mr. X' or 'a man I know in Ohio' – vague stories that you can't check up on. It concerns a very real person – Leon Shimkin, a former partner and general manager of one of the foremost publishing houses in these United States: Simon and Schuster, Rockefeller Center, New York.

Here is Leon Shimkin's experience in his own words.

'For fifteen years I spent almost half of every business day holding conferences, discussing problems. Should we do this or that – or nothing at all? We would get tense; twist in our chairs; walk the floor, argue and go around in circles. When night came, I would be utterly exhausted. I fully expected to go on doing this sort of thing for the rest of my life. I had been doing it for fifteen years, and it never occurred to me that there was a better way of doing it. If anyone had told me that I could eliminate three fourths of all the time I spent in those worried conferences, and three fourths of my nervous strain – I would have thought he was a wild-eyed, slap-happy, armchair optimist. Yet I devised a plan that did just that. I have been using this plan for eight years. It has performed wonders for my efficiency, my health, and my happiness.

'It sounds like magic – but like all magic tricks, it is extremely simple when you see how it is done.

'Here is the secret: First, I immediately stopped the procedure I had been using in my conferences for fifteen years – a procedure that began with my troubled associates reciting all the details of what had gone wrong, and ending up by asking: "What shall we do?" Second, I made a new rule – a rule that everyone who wishes to present a problem to me must first prepare and submit a memorandum answering these four questions:

'Question 1: *What is the problem?*

('In the old days we used to spend an hour or two in a worried conference without anyone's knowing specifically and concretely what the real problem was. We used to work ourselves into a lather discussing our troubles without ever troubling to write out specifically what our problem was.)

'Question 2: *What is the cause of the problem?*

('As I look back over my career, I am appalled at the wasted hours I have spent in worried conferences without ever trying to find out clearly the conditions which lay at the root of the problem.)

'Question 3: *What are all the possible solutions of the problem?*

('In the old days, one man in the conference would suggest one solution. Someone else would argue with him. Tempers would flare. We would often get clear off the subject, and at the end of the conference no one would have written down all the various things we could do to attack the problem.)

'Question 4: *What solution do you suggest?*

('I used to go into a conference with a man who had spent hours worrying about a situation and going around in circles without ever once thinking through all possible solutions and then writing down, "This is the solution I recommend."

'My associates rarely come to me now with their problems. Why? Because they have discovered that in order to answer those four questions they have to get all the facts and think their problems through. And after they have done that they find, in three fourths of the cases, they don't have to consult me at all, because the proper solution has popped out like a piece of bread popping out from an electric toaster. Even in those cases where consultation is necessary, the discussion takes about one third the time formerly required, because it proceeds along an orderly, logical path to a reasoned conclusion.

'Much less time is now consumed in the house of Simon and Schuster in *worrying* and *talking* about what is wrong; and a lot more *action* is obtained toward making those things right.'

My friend Frank Bettger, one of the top insurance men in America, told me he not only reduced his business worries, but nearly doubled his income, by a similar method.

'Years ago,' said Frank Bettger, 'when I first started to sell insurance, I was filled with a boundless enthusiasm and love for my work. Then something happened. I became so discouraged that I despised my work and thought of giving it up. I think I would have quit – if I hadn't got the idea, one Saturday morning, of sitting down and trying to get at the root of my worries.

'1. I asked myself first, *"Just what is the problem?"* The problem was: *that I was not getting high enough returns for the staggering amount of calls I was making.* I seemed to do pretty well at selling a prospect, until the moment came for closing a sale. Then the customer would say, "Well, I'll think it over, Mr. Bettger. Come and see me again." It was the time I wasted on these follow-up calls that was causing my depression.

'2. I asked myself, *"What are the possible solutions?"* But to get the answer to that one, I had to study the facts. I got out my record book for the last twelve months and studied the figures.

'*I made an astounding discovery!* Right there in black and white, I discovered that seventy percent of my sales had been closed on the very first interview! Twenty-three percent of my sales had been closed on the second interview! And only *seven percent of my sales* had been closed on those third, fourth, fifth, etc., interviews, which were running me ragged and taking up time. In other words, I was wasting fully one half of my working day on a part of my business which was responsible for only seven per cent of my sales!

'3: *"What is the answer?"* The answer was obvious. I immediately cut out all visits beyond the second interview, and spent the extra time building up new prospects. The results were unbelievable. In a very short time, I had doubled the cash value of every visit I made.'

As I said, Frank Bettger became one of the best-known life-insurance salesmen in the country. But he was on the point of giving up. He was on the point of admitting failure – until *analyzing* the problem gave him a boost on the road to success.

Can you apply these questions to *your* business problems? To repeat my challenge – they *can* reduce your worries by fifty percent. Here they are again:

1. What is the problem?
2. What is the CAUSE of the problem?
3. What are all possible solutions to the problem?
4. What solution do you suggest?

☐ **IN A NUTSHELL** ☐

RULE 1: Get the facts. Remember that Dean Hawkes of Columbia University said that 'half the worry in the world is caused by people trying to make decisions before they have sufficient knowledge on which to base a decision.'

RULE 2: After carefully weighing all the facts, come to a decision.

RULE 3: Once a decision is carefully reached, act! Get busy carrying out your decision – and dismiss all anxiety about the outcome.

RULE 4: When you, or any of your associates, are tempted to worry about a problem, write out and answer the following questions:

   a. What is the problem?

   b. What is the cause of the problem?

   c. What are all possible solutions?

   d. What is the best solution?

Part Three

HOW TO BREAK THE WORRY HABIT

BEFORE IT BREAKS YOU

□ 6 □

How to crowd worry out of your mind

I shall never forget one night when Marion J. Douglas was a student in one of my classes. (I have not used his real name. He requested me, for personal reasons, not to reveal his identity.) But here is his real story as he told it to the class. He told us how tragedy had struck at his home, not once, but twice. The first time he had lost his five-year-old daughter, a child he adored. He and his wife thought they couldn't endure that first loss; but, as he said, 'Ten months later God gave us another little girl – and she died in five days.'

This double bereavement was almost too much to bear. 'I couldn't take it,' this father told us. 'I couldn't sleep, I couldn't eat. I couldn't rest or relax. My nerves were utterly shaken and my confidence gone.' At last he went to doctors; one recommended sleeping pills and another recommended a trip. He tried both, but neither remedy helped. He said, 'My body felt as if it were encased in a vice, and the jaws of the vice were being drawn tighter and tighter.' The tension of grief – if you have ever been paralyzed by sorrow, you know what he meant.

'But thank God, I had one child left – a four-year-old son. He gave me the solution to my problem. One afternoon as I sat around feeling sorry for myself, he asked: "Daddy, will you build a boat for me?" I was in no mood to build a boat; in fact, I was in no mood to do anything. But my son is a persistent little fellow! I had to give in.

'Building that toy boat took about three hours. By the time it was finished, I realized that those three hours spent building that boat were the first hours of mental relaxation and peace I had had in months!

'That discovery jarred me out of my lethargy and caused me to do a bit of thinking – the first real thinking I had done in months. I realized that it is difficult to worry while you are busy doing something that requires planning and thinking. In my case, building the boat had knocked worry out of the ring. So I resolved to keep busy.

'The following night, I went from room to room in the house, compiling a list of jobs that ought to be done. Scores of items needed to be repaired: bookcases, stair steps, storm windows, window shades, knobs, locks, leaky faucets. Astonishing as it seems, in the course of two weeks I had made a list of 242 items that needed attention.

'During the last two years I have completed most of them. Besides, I have filled my life with stimulating activities. Two nights per week I attend adult-education classes in New York. I have gone in for civic activities in my home town and I am now chairman of the school board. I attend scores of meetings. I help collect money for the Red Cross and other activities. I am so busy now that I have no time for worry.'

No time for worry! That is exactly what Winston Churchill said when he was working eighteen hours a day at the height of the war. When he was asked if he worried about his tremendous responsibilities, he said, 'I'm too busy. I have no time for worry.'

Charles Kettering was in the same fix when he started out to invent a self-starter for automobiles. Mr. Kettering was, until his retirement, vice-president of General Motors in charge of the world-famous General Motors Research Corporation. But in those days, he was so poor that he had to use the hayloft of a barn as a laboratory. To buy groceries, he had to use fifteen hundred dollars that his wife had made by giving piano lessons; later, he had to borrow five hundred dollars on his life insurance. I asked his wife if she wasn't worried at a time like that. 'Yes,' she replied, 'I was so worried I couldn't sleep; but Mr. Kettering wasn't. He was too absorbed in his work to worry.'

The great scientist, Pasteur, spoke of 'the peace that is found in libraries and laboratories.' Why is peace found there? Because the men in libraries and laboratories are usually too absorbed in their tasks to worry about themselves. Research men rarely have nervous breakdowns. They haven't time for such luxuries.

Why does such a simple thing as keeping busy help to drive out anxiety? Because of a law – one of the most fundamental laws every revealed by psychology. And that law is: that it is utterly impossible for any human mind, no matter how brilliant, to think of more than *one thing* at any given time. You don't quite believe it? Very well, then, let's try an experiment.

Suppose you lean back right now, close your eyes, and try, at the same instant, to think of the Statue of Liberty and of what you plan to do tomorrow morning. (Go ahead, try it.)

You found out, didn't you, that you could focus on either thought *in turn*, but never on both simultaneously? Well, the same thing is true in the field of emotions. We cannot be pepped up and enthusiastic about doing something exciting and feel dragged down by worry at the very same time. One kind of emotion drives out the other. And it was that simple discovery that enabled Army psychiatrists to perform such miracles during the Second World War.

When men came out of battle so shaken by the experience that they were called 'psychoneurotic', Army doctors prescribed 'Keep 'em busy' as a cure.

Every waking minute of these nerve-shocked men was filled with activity – usually outdoor activity, such as fishing, hunting, playing ball, golf, taking pictures, making gardens, and dancing. They were given no time for brooding over their terrible experiences.

'Occupational therapy' is the term now used by psychiatry when work is prescribed as though it were a medicine. It is not new. The old Greek physicians were advocating it five hundred years before Christ was born!

The Quakers were using it in Philadelphia in Ben Franklin's time. A man who visited a Quaker sanitarium in 1774 was shocked to see that the patients who were mentally ill were busy spinning flax. He thought these poor unfortunates were being exploited – until the Quakers explained that they found that their patients actually improved when they did a little work. It was soothing to the nerves.

Any psychiatrist will tell you that work – keeping busy – is one of the best anaesthetics ever known for sick nerves. Henry W. Longfellow found that out for himself when he lost his young wife. His wife had been melting some sealing wax at a candle one day, when her clothes caught on fire. Longfellow heard her cries and tried to reach her in time; but she died from the burns. For a while, Longfellow was so tortured by the memory of that dreadful experience that he nearly went insane; but, fortunately for him, his three small children needed his attention. In spite of his own grief, Longfellow undertook to be father and mother to his children. He took them for walks, told them stories, played games with them, and immortalized their companionship in his poem *The Children's Hour*. He also translated Dante; and all these duties combined kept him so busy that he forgot himself entirely, and regained his peace of mind. As Tennyson declared when he lost his most intimate friend, Arthur Hallam, 'I must lose myself in action, lest I wither in despair.'

Most of us have little trouble 'losing ourselves in action' while we have our noses to the grindstone and are doing our day's work. But the hours after work – they are the dangerous ones. Just when we're free to enjoy our own leisure, and ought to be happiest – that's when the blue devils of worry attack us. That's when we begin to wonder whether we're getting anywhere in life; whether we're in a rut; whether the boss 'meant anything' by that remark he made today; or whether we're losing our sex appeal.

When we are not busy, our minds tend to become a near-vacuum. Every student of physics knows that 'nature abhors a vacuum'. The nearest thing to a vacuum that you and I will probably ever see is the inside of an incandescent electric-light bulb. Break that bulb – and nature forces air in to fill the theoretically empty space.

Nature also rushes in to fill the vacant mind. With what? Usually with emotions. Why? Because emotions of worry, fear, hate, jealousy, and envy are driven by primeval vigour and the dynamic energy of the jungle. Such emotions are so violent that they tend to drive out of our minds all peaceful, happy thoughts and emotions.

James L. Mursell, professor of education, Teachers College, Columbia, put it very well when he said: 'Worry is most apt to ride you ragged not when

241

you are in action, but when the day's work is done. Your imagination can run riot then and bring up all sorts of ridiculous possibilities and magnify each little blunder. At such a time,' he continued, 'your mind is like a motor operating without its load. It races and threatens to burn out its bearings or even to tear itself to bits. The remedy for worry is to get completely occupied doing something constructive.'

But you don't have to be a college professor to realize this truth and put it into practice. During the Second World War, I met a housewife from Chicago who told me how she discovered for herself that 'the remedy for worry is to get completely occupied doing something constructive.' I met this woman and her husband in the dining car while I was travelling from New York to my farm in Missouri.

This couple told me that their son had joined the armed forces the day after Pearl Harbor. The woman told me that she had almost wrecked her health worrying over that only son. Where was he? Was he safe? Or in action? Would he be wounded? Killed?

When I asked her how she overcame her worry, she replied: 'I got busy.' She told me that at first she had dismissed her maid and tried to keep busy by doing all her housework herself. But that didn't help much. 'The trouble was,' she said, 'that I could do my housework almost mechanically, without using my mind. So I kept on worrying while making the beds and washing the dishes. I realized I needed some new kind of work that would keep me busy both mentally and physically every hour of the day. So I took a job as a saleswoman in a large department store.

'That did it,' she said. 'I immediately found myself in a whirlwind of activity: customers swarming around me, asking for prices, sizes, colours. Never a second to think of anything except my immediate duty; and when night came, I could think of nothing except getting off my aching feet. As soon as I ate dinner, I fell into bed and instantly became unconscious. I had neither the time nor the energy to worry.'

She discovered for herself what John Cowper Powys meant when he said, in *The Art of Forgetting the Unpleasant*: 'A certain comfortable security, a certain profound inner peace, a kind of happy numbness, soothes the nerves of the human animal when absorbed in its allotted task.'

And what a blessing that it is so! Osa Johnson, one of the world's most famous women explorers, told me how she found release from worry and grief. You may have read the story of her life. It is called *I Married Adventure*. If any woman ever married adventure, she certainly did. Martin Johnson married her when she was sixteen and lifted her feet off the sidewalks of Chanute, Kansas, and set them down on the wild jungle trails of Borneo. For a quarter of a century, this Kansas couple travelled all over the world, making motion pictures of the vanishing wild life of Asia and Africa. Some years later, they were on a lecture tour, showing their famous films. They took a plane out of Denver, bound for the Coast. The plane plunged into a mountain.

Martin Johnson was killed instantly. The doctors said Osa would never leave her bed again. But they didn't know Osa Johnson. Three months later, she was in a wheelchair, lecturing before large audiences. In fact, she addressed over a hundred audiences that season – all from a wheelchair. When I asked her why she did it, she replied: 'I did it so that I would have no time for sorrow and worry.'

Osa Johnson had discovered the same truth that Tennyson had sung about a century earlier: 'I must lose myself in action, lest I wither in despair.'

Admiral Byrd discovered this same truth when he lived all alone for five months in a shack that was literally buried in the great glacial icecap that covers the South Pole – an icecap that holds nature's oldest secrets – an icecap covering an unknown continent larger than the United States and Europe combined. Admiral Byrd spent five months there alone. No other living creature of any kind existed within a hundred miles. The cold was so intense that he could hear his breath freeze and crystallize as the wind blew it past his ears. In his book, *Alone*, Admiral Byrd tells all about those five months he spent in bewildering and soul-shattering darkness. The days were as black as the nights. He had to keep busy to preserve his sanity.

'At night,' he says, 'before blowing out the lantern, I formed the habit of blocking out the morrow's work. It was a case of assigning myself an hour, say, to the Escape Tunnel, half an hour to leveling drift, an hour to straightening up the fuel drums, an hour to cutting bookshelves in the walls of the food tunnel, and two hours to renewing a broken bridge in the man-hauling sledge . . .

'It was wonderful,' he says, 'to be able to dole out time in this way. I brought me an extraordinary sense of command over myself . . .' And he adds, 'Without that or an equivalent, the days would have been without purpose; and without purpose they would have ended, as such days always end, in disintegration.'

Note that last again: *'Without purpose, the days would have ended, as such days always end, in disintegration.'**

If you and I are worried, let's remember that we can use good old-fashioned work as a medicine. That was said by no less an authority than the late Dr. Richard C. Cabot, formerly professor of clinical medicine at Harvard. In his book *What Men Live By*, Dr. Cabot says, 'As a physician, I have had the happiness of seeing work cure many persons who have suffered from trembling palsy of the soul which results from overmastering doubts, hesitations, vacillation and fear . . . Courage given us by our work is like the self-reliance which Emerson has made forever glorious.'

If you and I don't keep busy – if we sit around and brood – we will hatch out a whole flock of what Charles Darwin used to call the 'wibber gibbers'. And the 'wibber gibbers' are nothing but old-fashioned gremlins that will run us hollow and destroy our power of action and our power of will.

---

* From *Alone*, by Richard E. Byrd. Copyright, 1938, by Richard E. Byrd. Courtesy of G. P. Putnam's Sons.

I knew a businessman in New York who fought the 'wibber gibbers' by getting so busy that he had no time to fret and stew. His name is Tremper Longman. He was a student in one of my classes; and his talk on conquering worry was so interesting, so impressive, that I asked him to have a late supper with me after class; and we sat in a restaurant until long past midnight, discussing his experiences. Here is the story he told me: 'Eighteen years ago, I was so worried I had insomnia. I was tense, irritated, and jittery. I felt I was headed for a nervous breakdown.

'I had reason to be worried. I was treasurer of the Crown Fruit and Extract Company. We had half a million dollars invested in strawberries packed in gallon tins. For twenty years, we had been selling these gallon tins of strawberries to manufacturers of ice cream. Suddenly our sales stopped because the big ice-cream makers, such as National Dairy and Borden's, were rapidly increasing their production and were saving money and time by buying strawberries packed in barrels.

'Not only were we left with half a million dollars in berries we couldn't sell, but we were also under contract to buy a million dollars more of strawberries in the next twelve months! We had already borrowed $350,000 from the banks. We couldn't possibly pay off or renew these loans. No wonder I was worried!

'I rushed out to Watsonville, California, where our factory was located, and tried to persuade our president that conditions had changed, that we were facing ruin. He refused to believe it. He blamed our New York office for all the trouble – poor salesmanship.

'After days of pleading, I finally persuaded him to stop packing more strawberries and to sell our new supply on the fresh berry market in San Francisco. That almost solved our problems. I should have been able to stop worrying then; but I couldn't. Worry is a habit; and I had that habit.

'When I returned to New York, I began worrying about everything; the cherries we were buying in Italy, the pineapples we were buying in Hawaii, and so on. I was tense, jittery, couldn't sleep; and, as I have already said, I was heading for a nervous breakdown.

'In despair, I adopted a way of life that cured my insomnia and stopped my worries. I got busy. I got so busy with problems demanding all my faculties that I had no time to worry. I had been working seven hours a day. I now began working fifteen and sixteen hours a day. I got down to the office every morning at eight o'clock and stayed there every night until almost midnight. I took on new duties, new responsibilities. When I got home at midnight, I was so exhausted when I fell in bed that I became unconscious in a few seconds.

'I kept up this program for about three months. I had broken the habit of worry by that time, so I returned to a normal working day of seven or eight hours. This event occurred eighteen years ago. I have never been troubled with insomnia or worry since then.'

George Bernard Shaw was right. He summed it all up when he said: '*The secret of being miserable is to have the leisure to bother about whether you are happy or not.*' So don't bother to think about it! Spit on your hands and get busy. Your blood will start circulating; your mind will start ticking – and pretty soon this whole positive upsurge of life in your body will drive worry from your mind. *Get* busy. *Keep* busy. It's the cheapest kind of medicine there is on this earth – and one of the best.

To break the worry habit, here is Rule 1:

Keep busy. The worried person must lose himself in action,
lest he wither in despair.

☐ 7 ☐

Don't let the beetles get you down

Here is a dramatic story that I'll probably remember as long as I live. It was told to me by Robert Moore, of Maplewood, New Jersey.

'I learned the biggest lesson of my life in March, 1945,' he said. 'I learned it under 276 feet of water off the coast of Indo-China. I was one of eighty-eight men aboard the submarine *Baya* S.S. 318. We had discovered by radar that a small Japanese convoy was coming our way. As daybreak approached, we submerged to attack. I saw through the periscope a Japanese destroyer escort, a tanker, and a mine layer. We fired three torpedoes at the destroyer escort, but missed. Something went haywire in the mechanics of each torpedo. The destroyer, not knowing that she had been attacked, continued on. We were getting ready to attack the last ship, the mine layer, when suddenly she turned and came directly at us. (A Japanese plane had spotted us under sixty feet of water and had radioed our position to the Japanese mine layer.) We went down to 150 feet, to avoid detection, and rigged for a depth charge. We put extra bolts on the hatches; and, in order to make our sub absolutely silent, we turned off the fans, the cooling system, and all electrical gear.

'Three minutes later, all hell broke loose. Six depth charges exploded all around us and pushed us down to the ocean floor – a depth of 276 feet. We were terrified. To be attacked in less than a thousand feet of water is dangerous

– less than five hundred is almost always fatal. And we were being attacked in a trifle more than half of five thousand feet of water – just knee-deep, as far as safety was concerned. For fifteen hours, that Japanese mine layer kept dropping depth charges. If a depth charge explodes within seventeen feet of a sub, the concussion will blow a hole in it. Scores of these depth charges exploded within fifty feet of us. We were ordered "to secure" – to lie quietly in our bunks and remain calm. I was so terrified I could hardly breathe. "This is death." I kept saying to myself over and over. "This is death! . . . This is death!" With the fans and cooling system turned off, the air inside the sub was over a hundred degrees; but I was so chilled with fear that I put on a sweater and a fur-lined jacket; and still I trembled with cold. My teeth chattered. I broke out in a cold, clammy sweat. The attack continued for fifteen hours. Then ceased suddenly. Apparently the Japanese mine layer had exhausted its supply of depth charges, and steamed away. Those fifteen hours of attack seemed like fifteen million years. All my life passed before me in review. I remembered all the bad things I had done, all the little absurd things I had worried about. I had been a bank clerk before I joined the Navy. I had worried about the long hours, the poor pay, the poor prospects of advancement. I had worried because I couldn't own my own home, couldn't buy a new car, couldn't buy my wife nice clothes. How I hated my old boss, who was always nagging and scolding! I remembered how I would come home at night sore and grouchy and quarrel with my wife over trifles. I had worried about a scar on my forehead – a nasty cut from an auto accident.

'How big all those worries seemed years ago! But how absurd they seemed when depth charges were threatening to blow me to kingdom come. I promised myself then and there that if I ever saw the sun and the stars again, I would never, never worry again. Never! Never!! Never!!! I learned more about the art of living in those fifteen terrible hours in that submarine than I had learned by studying books for four years in Syracuse University.'

We often face the major disasters of life bravely – and then let the trifles, the 'pains in the neck', get us down. For example, Samuel Pepys tells in his *Diary* about seeing Sir Harry Vane's head chopped off in London. As Sir Harry mounted the platform, he was not pleading for his life, but was pleading with the executioner not to hit the painful boil on his neck!

That was another thing that Admiral Byrd discovered down in the terrible cold and darkness of the polar nights – that his men fussed more about the 'pains in the neck' than about the big things. They bore, without complaining, the dangers, the hardships, and the cold that was often eighty degrees below zero. 'But,' says Admiral Byrd, 'I know of bunk-mates who quit speaking because each suspected the other of inching his gear into the other's allotted space; and I knew of one who could not eat unless he could find a place in the mess hall out of sight of the Fletcherist who solemnly chewed his food twenty-eight times before swallowing.

'In a polar camp,' says Admiral Byrd, 'little things like that have the power to drive people to the edge of insanity and cause 'half the heartaches in the world'.

At least, that is what the authorities say. For example, Judge Joseph Sabath of Chicago, after acting as arbiter in more than forty thousand unhappy marriages, declared: 'Trivialities are at the bottom of most marital unhappiness'; and Frank S. Hogan, former District Attorney of New York County, says, 'Fully half the cases in our criminal courts originate in little things. Barroom bravado, domestic wrangling, an insulting remark, a disparaging word, a rude action – those are the little things that lead to assault and murder. Very few of us are cruelly and greatly wronged. It is the small blows to our self-esteem, the indignities, the little jolts to our vanity, which cause half the heartaches in the world.'

When Eleanor Roosevelt was first married, she 'worried for days' because her new cook had served a poor meal. 'But if that happened now,' Mrs. Roosevelt said, 'I would shrug my shoulders and forget it.' Good. That is acting like an adult emotionally. Even Catherine the Great, an absolute autocrat, used to laugh the thing off when the cook spoiled a meal.

Mrs. Carnegie and I had dinner at a friend's house in Chicago. While carving the meat, he did something wrong. I didn't notice it; and I wouldn't have cared even if I had noticed it. But his wife saw it and jumped down his throat right in front of us. 'John,' she cried, 'watch what you are doing! Can't you ever learn to serve properly!'

Then she said to us: 'He is always making mistakes. He just doesn't try. Maybe he didn't try to carve; but I certainly give him credit for trying to live with her for twenty years. Frankly, I would rather have eaten a couple of hot dogs with mustard – in an atmosphere of peace – than to have dined on Peking duck and shark fins while listening to her scolding.

Shortly after that experience, Mrs. Carnegie and I had some friends at our home for dinner. Just before they arrived, Mrs. Carnegie found that three of the napkins didn't match the tablecloth.

'I rushed to the cook,' she told me later, 'and found that the other three napkins had gone to the laundry. The guests were at the door. There was no time to change. I felt like bursting into tears! All I could think was, "Why did this stupid mistake have to spoil my whole evening?" Then I thought – well – why let it? I went in to dinner, determined to have a good time. And I did. I would much rather our friends think I'm a sloppy housekeeper,' she told me, 'than a nervous, bad-tempered one. And anyhow, as far as I could make out, no one noticed the napkins!'

A well-known legal maxim says: *De minimis non curat lex* – 'the law does not concern itself with trifles.' And neither should the worrier – if he wants peace of mind.

Much of the time, all we need to overcome the annoyance of trifles is to affect a shifting of emphasis – set up a new, and pleasurable, point of view in the mind. My friend Homer Croy, who wrote *They Had to See Paris* and a dozen other books, gives a wonderful example of how this can be done. He used to be driven half crazy, while working on a book, by the rattling of the radiators in his New York apartment. The steam would bang and sizzle – and he would sizzle with irritation as he sat at his desk.

'Then,' says Homer Croy, 'I went with some friends on a camping expedition. While listening to the limbs crackling in the roaring fire, I thought how much they sounded like the crackling of the radiators. Why should I like one and hate the other? When I went home I said to myself, "The crackling of the limbs in the fire was a pleasant sound; the sound of the radiators is about the same – I'll go to sleep and not worry about the noise." *And I did.* For a few days I was conscious of the radiators; but soon I forgot all about them.

'And so it is with many petty worries. We dislike them and get into a stew, all because we exaggerate their importance. . . .'

Disraeli said: 'Life is too short to be little.' 'Those words,' said André Maurois in *This Week* magazine, 'have helped me through many a painful experience: often we allow ourselves to be upset by small things we should despise and forget . . . Here we are on this earth, with only a few more decades to live, and we lose many irreplaceable hours brooding over grievances that, in a year's time, will be forgotten by us and by everybody. No, let us devote our life to worthwhile actions and feelings, to great thoughts, real affections and enduring undertakings. For life is too short to be little.'

Even so illustrious a figure as Rudyard Kipling forgot at times that 'Life is too short to be little.' The result? He and his brother-in-law fought the most famous court battle in the history of Vermont – a battle so celebrated that a book has been written about it: *Rudyard Kipling's Vermont Feud.*

The story goes like this: Kipling married a Vermont girl, Caroline Balestier, built a lovely home in Brattleboro, Vermont; settled down and expected to spend the rest of his life there. His brother-in-law, Beatty Balestier, became Kipling's best friend. The two of them worked and played together.

Then Kipling bought some land from Balestier, with the understanding that Balestier would be allowed to cut hay off it each season. One day, Balestier found Kipling laying out a flower garden on this hayfield. His blood boiled. He hit the ceiling. Kipling fired right back. The air over the Green Mounts of Vermont turned blue!

A few days later, when Kipling was riding his bicycle, his brother-in-law drove a wagon and a team of horses across the road suddenly and forced Kipling to take a spill. And Kipling – the man who wrote, 'If you can keep your head when all about you are losing theirs and blaming it on you' – he lost his own head, and swore out a warrant for Balestier's arrest! A sensational trial followed. Reporters from the big cities poured into the town. The news flashed around the world. Nothing was settled. This quarrel caused Kipling and his wife to abandon their American home for the rest of their lives. All that worry and bitterness over a mere trifle! A load of hay.

Pericles said, twenty-four centuries ago: 'Come, gentlemen, we sit too long on trifles.' We do, indeed!

Here is one of the most interesting stories that Dr. Harry Emerson Fosdick ever told – a story about the battles won and lost by a giant of the forest:

> On the slope of Long's Peak in Colorado lies the ruin of a gigantic tree. Naturalists tell us that it stood for some four hundred years. It was a seedling when Columbus landed at San Salvador, and half grown when the Pilgrims settled at Plymouth. During the course of its long life it was struck by lightning fourteen times, and the innumerable avalanches and storms of four centuries thundered past it. It survived them all. In the end, however, an army of beetles attacked the tree and leveled it to the ground. The insects ate their way through the bark and gradually destroyed the inner strength of the tree by their tiny but incessant attacks. A forest giant which age had not withered, nor lightning blasted, nor storms subdued, fell at last before beetles so small that a man could crush them between his forefinger and his thumb.

Aren't we all like that battling giant of the forest? Don't we manage somehow to survive the rare storms and avalanches and lightning blasts of life, only to let our hearts be eaten out by little beetles of worry – little beetles that could be crushed between a finger and a thumb?

I travelled through the Teton National Park, in Wyoming, with Charles Seifred, highway superintendent for the state of Wyoming, and some of his friends. We were all going to visit the John D. Rockefeller estate in the park. But the car in which I was riding took a wrong turn, got lost, and drove up to the entrance of the estate an hour after the other cars had gone in. Mr. Seifred had the key that unlocked the private gate, so he waited in the hot, mosquito-infested woods for an hour until we arrived. The mosquitoes were enough to drive a saint insane. But they couldn't triumph over Charles Seifred. While waiting for us, he cut a limb off an aspen tree – and made a whistle of it. When we arrived, was he cussing the mosquitoes? No, he was playing his whistle. I have kept that whistle as a memento of a man who knew how to put trifles in their place.

To break the worry habit before it breaks you, here is Rule 2:

Let's not allow ourselves to be upset by small things we should despise and forget. Remember 'Life is too short to be little.'

□ 8 □

A law that will outlaw many of your worries

As a child, I grew up on a Missouri farm; and one day, while helping my mother pit cherries. I began to cry. My mother said, 'Dale, what in the world are you crying about?' I blubbered, 'I'm afraid I am going to be buried alive!'

I was full of worries in those days. When thunderstorms came, I worried for fear I would be killed by lightning. When hard times came, I worried for fear we wouldn't have enough to eat. I worried for fear I would go to hell when I died. I was terrified for fear an older boy, Sam White, would cut off my big ears – as he threatened to do. I worried for fear girls would laugh at me if I tipped my hat to them. I worried for fear no girl would ever be willing to marry me. I worried about what I would say to my wife immediately after we were married. I imagined that we would be married in some country church, and then get in a surrey with fringe on the top and ride back to the farm . . . but how would I be able to keep the conversation going on that ride back to the farm? How? How? I pondered over that earth-shaking problem for many an hour as I walked behind the plough.

As the years went by, I gradually discovered that ninety-nine percent of the things I worried about never happened.

For example, as I have already said, I was once terrified of lightning; but I now know that the chances of my being killed by lightning in any one year are, according to the National Safety Council, only one in three hundred and fifty thousand.

My fear of being buried alive was even more absurd: I don't imagine that – even back in the days before embalming was the rule – that one person in ten million was buried alive; yet I once cried for fear of it.

One person out of every eight dies of cancer. If had wanted something to worry about, I should have worried about cancer – instead of being killed by lightning or being buried alive.

To be sure, I have been talking about the worries of youth and adolescence. But many of our adult worries are almost as absurd. You and I could probably eliminate nine tenths of our worries right now if we would cease fretting long enough to discover whether, *by the law of averages*, there was any real justification for our worries.

The most famous insurance company on earth – Lloyd's of London – has made countless millions of dollars out of the tendency of everybody to worry about things that rarely happen. Lloyd's of London bets people that the disasters they are worrying about will never occur. However, *they don't call it betting. They call it insurance. But it is really betting based on the law of averages.* This great insurance firm has been going strong for over two hundred years; and unless human nature changes, it will still be going strong fifty centuries from now by insuring shoes and ships and sealing wax against disasters that, *by the law of averages*, don't happen nearly so often as people imagine.

If we examine the law of averages, we will often be astounded at the facts we uncover. For example, if I knew that during the next five years I would have to fight in a battle as bloody as the Battle of Gettysburg, I would be terrified. I would take out all the life insurance I could get. I would draw up my will and set all my earthly affairs in order. I would say, 'I'll probably never live through that battle, so I had better make the most of the few years I have left.' Yet the facts are that, according to the law of averages, it is just as dangerous, just as fatal, to try to live from age fifty to age fifty-five in peacetime as it was to fight in the Battle of Gettysburg. What I am trying to say is this: in times of peace, just as many people die per thousand between the ages of fifty and fifty-five as were killed per thousand among the 163,000 soldiers who fought at Gettysburg.

I wrote several chapters of this book at James Simpson's Num-Ti-Gah Lodge, on the shore of Bow Lake in the Canadian Rockies. While stopping there one summer, I met Mr. and Mrs. Herbert H. Salinger, of San Francisco. Mrs. Salinger, a poised, serene woman, gave me the impression that she had never worried. One evening in front of the roaring fireplace, I asked her if she had ever been troubled by worry. 'Troubled by it?' she said. 'My life was almost *ruined* by it. Before I learned to conquer worry, I lived through eleven years of self-made hell. I was irritable and hot-tempered. I lived under terrific tension. I would take the bus every week from my home in San Mateo to shop in San Francisco. But even while shopping, I worried myself into a dither: maybe I had left the electric iron connected on the ironing board. Maybe the house had caught fire. Maybe the maid had run off and left the children. Maybe they had been out on their bicycles and been killed by a car. In the midst of my shopping, I would often worry myself into a cold perspiration and rush out and take the bus home to see if everything was all right. No wonder my first marriage ended in disaster.

'My second husband is a lawyer – a quiet, analytical man who never worries about anything. When I became tense and anxious, he would say to me, "Relax. Let's think this out . . . What are you really worrying about? Let's examine the law of averages and see whether or not it is likely to happen."

'For example, I remember the time we were driving from Alburquerque, New Mexico, to the Carlsbad Caverns – driving on a dirt road – when we were caught in a terrible rainstorm.

'The car was slithering and sliding. We couldn't control it. I was positive we would slide off into one of the ditches that flanked the road; but my husband kept repeating to me: "I am driving very slowly. Nothing serious is likely to happen. Even if the car does slide into the ditch, by the law of averages, we won't be hurt." His calmness and confidence quieted me.

'One summer we were on a camping trip in the Touquin Valley of the Canadian Rockies. One night, we were camping seven thousand feet above sea level, when a storm threatened to tear our tents to shreds. The tents were tied with guy ropes to a wooden platform. The outer tent shook and trembled and screamed and shrieked in the wind. I expected every minute to see our tent torn loose and hurled through the sky. I was terrified! But my husband kept saying: "Look, my dear, we are travelling with Brewsters' guides. Brewsters know what they are doing. They have been pitching tents in these mountains for sixty years. This tent has been here for many seasons. It hasn't blown down yet and, by the law of averages, it won't blow away tonight; and even if it does, we can take shelter in another tent. So relax . . ." I did; and I slept soundly the balance of the night.

'A few years ago an infantile-paralysis epidemic swept over our part of California. In the old days, I would have been hysterical. But my husband persuaded me to act calmly. We took all the precautions we could: we kept our children away from crowds, away from school and the movies. By consulting the Board of Health, we found out that even during the worst infantile-paralysis epidemic that California had ever known up to that time, only 1835 children had been stricken in the entire state of California. And that the usual number was around two hundred or three hundred. Tragic as those figures are, we nevertheless felt that, according to the law of averages, the chances of any one child being stricken were remote.

' "By the law of averages, it won't happen." That phrase has destroyed ninety percent of my worries; and it has made the past twenty years of my life beautiful and peaceful beyond my highest expectations.'

It has been said that nearly all of our worries and unhappiness come from our imagination and not from reality. As I look back across the decades, I can see that that is where most of my worries came from also. Jim Grant told me that that had been his experience, too. He owned the James A. Grant Distributing Company, of New York City. He ordered from ten to fifteen carloads of Florida oranges and grapefruit at a time. He told me that he used to torture himself with such thoughts as: What if there's a train wreck? What if my fruit is strewn all over the countryside? What if a bridge collapses as my cars are going across it? Of course, the fruit was insured; but he feared that if he didn't deliver his fruit on time, he might risk the loss of his market. He worried so much that he feared he had stomach ulcers and went to a doctor. The doctor told him there was nothing wrong with him except jumpy nerves. 'I saw the light then,' he said,'and began to ask myself questions. I said to myself: "Look here, Jim Grant, how many fruit cars have you handled over the years?" The answer was: "About twenty-five thousand." Then I asked myself: "How many of those cars were ever wrecked?" The answer was: "Oh – maybe five. Then I said to myself: "Only five – out of twenty-five thousand? Do you know what that means? A ratio of five thousand to one! In other words, by the law of averages, based on experience, the chances are five thousand to one against one of your cars ever being wrecked. So what are you worried about?"

'Then I said to myself: "Well, a bridge may collapse!" Then I asked myself: "How many cars have you actually lost from a bridge collapsing?" The answer was – "None". Then I said to myself: "Aren't you a fool to be worrying yourself into stomach ulcers over a bridge which has never yet collapsed, and over a railroad wreck when the chances are five thousand to one against it!

'When I looked at it that way,' Jim Grant told me, 'I felt pretty silly. I decided then and there to let the law of averages do the worrying for me – and I have not been troubled with my "stomach ulcer" since!'

When Al Smith was Governor of New York, I heard him answer the attacks of his political enemies by saying over and over: 'Let's examine the record . . . let's examine the record.' Then he proceeded to give the facts. The next time you and I are worrying about what may happen, let's take a tip from wise old Al Smith: let's examine the record and see what basis there is, if any, for our gnawing anxieties. That is precisely what Frederick J. Mahlstedt did when he feared he was lying in his grave. Here is his story as he told it to one of our classes in New York:

'Early in June, 1944, I was lying in a slit trench near Omaha Beach. I was with the 999th Signal Service Company, and we had just "dug in" in Normandy. As I looked around at that slit trench – just a rectangular hole in the ground – I said to myself, "This looks just like a grave. I couldn't help saying to myself, *"Maybe this is my grave."* When the German bombers began coming over at 11 p.m., and the bombs started falling, I was scared stiff. For the first two or three nights I couldn't sleep at all. By the fourth or fifth night, I was almost a nervous wreck. I knew that if I didn't do something, I would go stark crazy. So I reminded myself that five nights had passed, and I was still alive; and so was every man in our outfit. Only two had even been injured, and they had been hurt, not by German bombs, but by falling flak, from our own antiaircraft guns. I decided to stop worrying by doing something constructive. So I built a thick wooden roof over my slit trench, to protect myself from flak. I thought of the vast area over which my unit was spread. I told myself that the only way I could be killed in that deep, narrow slit trench was by a direct hit; and I figured out that the chance of a direct hit on me was not one in ten thousand. After a couple of nights of looking at it in this way, I calmed down and slept even through the bomb raids!'

The United States Navy used the statistics of the law of averages to buck up the morale of their men. One ex-sailor told me that when he and his shipmates were assigned to high-octane tankers, they were worried stiff. They all believed that if a tanker loaded with high-octane gasoline was a hit by a torpedo, it exploded and blew everybody to kingdom come.

But the U.S. Navy knew otherwise; so the Navy issued exact figures, showing that out of one hundred tankers hit by torpedoes, sixty stayed afloat; and of the forty that did sink, only five sank in less than ten minutes. That meant time to get off the ship – it also meant casualties were exceedingly small. Did this help morale? 'This knowledge of the law of averages wiped out my jitters,' said Clyde W. Maas, of St. Paul, Minnesota – the man who told this story. 'The whole crew felt better. We knew we had a chance; and that, by the law of averages, we probably wouldn't be killed.'

To break the worry habit before it breaks you – here is Rule 3:

'Let's examine the record.' Let's ask ourselves: 'What are the chances, according to the law of averages, that this event I am worrying about will ever occur?'

□ **9** □

Cooperate with the inevitable

When I was a little boy, I was playing with some of my friends in the attic of an old, abandoned log house in northwest Missouri. As I climbed down out of the attic, I rested my feet on a window sill for a moment – and then jumped. I had a ring on my left forefinger; and as I jumped, the ring caught on a nailhead and tore off my finger.

I screamed. I was terrified. I was positive I was going to die. But after the hand healed, I never worried about it for one split second. What would have been the use? I accepted the inevitable.

Now I often go for a month at a time without even thinking about the fact that I have only three fingers and a thumb on my left hand.

A few years ago, I met a man who was running a freight elevator in one of the downtown office buildings in New York. I noticed that his left hand had been cut off at the wrist. I asked him if the loss of that hand bothered him. He said, 'Oh, no, I hardly ever think about it. I am not married; and the only time I ever think about it is when I try to thread a needle.'

It is astonishing how quickly we can accept almost any situation – if we have to – and adjust ourselves to it and forget about it.

I often think of an inscription on the ruins of a fifteenth-century cathedral in Amsterdam, Holland. This inscription says in Flemish: 'It is so. It cannot be otherwise.'

As you and I march across the decades of times, we are going to meet a lot of unpleasant situations that are so. They cannot be otherwise. We have our choice. We can either accept them as inevitable and adjust ourselves to them, or we can ruin our lives with rebellion and maybe end up with a nervous breakdown.

Here is a bit of sage advice from one of my favourite philosophers, William James. *'Be willing to have it so,;* he said. *'Acceptance of what has happened is the first step to overcoming the consequences of any misfortune.'* Elizabeth Connley, of Portland, Oregon, had to find that out the hard way. Here is a letter that she wrote me: 'On the very day that America was celebrating the victory of our armed forces in North Africa,' the letter says, 'I received a telegram from the War Department: my nephew – the person I loved most – was missing in action. A short time later, another telegram arrived saying he was dead.

'I was prostrate with grief. Up to that time, I had felt that life had been very good to me. I had a job I loved. I had helped to raise this nephew. He represented to me all that was fine and good in young manhood. I had felt that all the bread I had cast upon the waters was coming back to me as cake! . . . Then came this telegram. My whole world collapsed. I felt there was nothing left to live for. I neglected my work; neglected my friends. I let everything go. I was bitter and resentful. Why did my loving nephew have to be taken? Why did this good boy – with life all before him – why did he have to be killed? I couldn't accept it. My grief was so overwhelming that I decided to give up my work, and go away and hide myself in my tears and bitterness.

'I was clearing out my desk, getting ready to quit, when I came across a letter that I had forgotten – a letter from this nephew who had been killed, a letter he had written to me when my mother had died a few years ago. 'Of course, we will all miss her,' the letter said, 'and especially you. But I know you'll carry on. Your own personal philosophy will make you do that. I shall never forget the beautiful truths you taught me. Wherever I am, or how far apart we may be, I shall always remember that you taught me to smile, and to take whatever comes, like a man.'

'I read and reread that letter. It seemed as if he were there beside me speaking to me. He seemed to be saying to me: "Why don't you do what you taught me to do? Carry on, no matter what happens. Hide your private sorrows under a smile and carry on."

'So, I went back to my work. I stopped being bitter and rebellious. I kept saying to myself: "It is done. I can't change it. But I can and will carry on as he wished me to do." I threw all my mind and strength into my work. I wrote letters to soldiers – to other people's boys. I joined am adult-education class at night – seeking out new interests and making new friends. I can hardly believe the change that has come over me. I have ceased mourning over the past that is forever gone. I am living each day now with joy – just as my nephew would have wanted me to do. I have made peace with life. I have accepted my fate. I am now living a fuller and more complete life than I have ever known.'

Elizabeth Connley learned what all of us will have to learn sooner or later: namely, that we must accept and cooperate with the inevitable. 'It is so. It cannot be otherwise.' That is not an easy lesson to learn. Even kings on their thrones have to keep reminding themselves of it. The late George V had these framed words hanging on the wall of his library in Buckingham Palace: 'Teach me neither to cry for the moon nor over spilt milk.' The same thought is expressed by Schopenhauer in this way: 'A good supply of resignation is of the first importance in providing for the journey of life.'

Obviously, circumstances alone do not make us happy or unhappy. It is the way we react to circumstances that determines our feelings. Jesus said that the kingdom of heaven is within you. That is where the kingdom of hell is, too.

We can all endure disaster and tragedy and triumph over them – if we have to. We may not think we can, but we have surprisingly strong inner resources that will see us through if we will only make use of them. We are stronger than we think.

The late Booth Tarkington always said: 'I could take anything that life could force upon me except one thing: blindness. I could never endure that.'

Then one day, when he was along in his sixties, Tarkington glanced down at the carpet on the floor. The colours were blurred. He couldn't see the pattern. He went to a specialist. He learned the tragic truth: he was losing his sight. One eye was nearly blind; the other would follow. That which he feared most had come upon him.

And how did Tarkington react to this 'worst of all disasters'? Did he feel, 'This is it! This is the end of my life'? No, to his amazement, he felt quite gay. He even called upon his humour. Floating 'specks' annoyed him; they would swim across his eyes and cut off his vision. Yet when the largest of these specks would swim across his sight, he would say, 'Hello! There's Grandfather again! Wonder where he's going on this fine morning!'

How could fate ever conquer a spirit like that? The answer is it couldn't. When total darkness closed in, Tarkington said, 'I found I could take the loss of my eyesight, just as a man can take anything else. If I lost *all five* of my senses, I know I could live on inside my mind. For it is in the mind we can see, and in the mind we live, whether we know it or not.'

In the hope of restoring his eyesight, Tarkington had to go through more than twelve operations within one year. With *local* anaesthetic! Did he rail against this? He knew it had to be done. He knew he couldn't escape it, so the only way to lessen his suffering was to take it with grace. He refused a private room at the hospital and went into a ward, where he could be with other people who had troubles, too. He tried to cheer them up. And when he had to submit to repeated operations – fully conscious of what was being done to his eyes – he tried to remember how fortunate he was. 'How wonderful!' he said. 'How wonderful, that science now has the skill to operate on anything so delicate as the human eye!'

The average man would have been a nervous wreck if he had had to endure more than twelve operations and blindness. Yet Tarkington said, 'I would not exchange this experience for a happier one.' It taught acceptance. It taught him that nothing life could bring him was beyond his strength to endure. It taught him, as John Milton discovered, that 'It is not miserable to be blind, it is only miserable not to be able to endure blindness.'

Margaret Fuller, the famous New England feminist, once offered as her credo: 'I accept the Universe!'

When grouchy old Thomas Carlyle heard that in England, he snorted 'By gad, she'd better!' Yes, and by gad, you and I had better accept the inevitable, too!

If we rail and kick against it and grow bitter, we won't change the inevitable; but we will change ourselves. I know. I have tried it.

I once refused to accept an inevitable situation with which I was confronted. I played the fool and railed against it, and rebelled. I turned my nights into hells of insomnia. I brought upon myself everything I didn't want. Finally, after a year of self-torture, I had to accept what I knew from the outset I couldn't possibly alter.

I should have cried out years ago with old Walt Whitman:

Oh, to confront night, storms, hunger,
Ridicule, accident, rebuffs as the trees and animals do.

I spent twelve years working with cattle; yet I never saw a Jersey cow running a temperature because the pasture was burning up from a lack of rain or because of sleet and cold or because her boy friend was paying too much attention to another heifer. The animals confront night, storms, and hunger calmly; so they never have nervous breakdowns or stomach ulcers; and they never go insane.

Am I advocating that we simply bow down to *all* the adversities that come our way? Not by a long shot! That is mere fatalism. As long as there is a chance that we can save a situation, let's fight! But when common sense tells us that we are up against something that is so – and cannot be otherwise – then, in the name of our sanity, let's not 'look before and after and pine for what is not.'

The late Dean Hawkes of Columbia University told me that he had taken a Mother Goose rhyme as one of his mottoes:

For every ailment under the sun,
There is a remedy, or there is none;
If there be one, try to find it;
If there be none, never mind it.

While writing this book, I interviewed a number of the leading business executives of America; and I was impressed by the fact that they cooperated with the inevitable and led lives singularly free from worry. If they hadn't done that, they would have cracked under the strain. Here are a few examples of what I mean:

J. C. Penney, founder of the nation-wide chain of Penney stores, said to me: 'I wouldn't worry if I lost every dollar I have because I don't see what is to be gained by worrying. I do the best job I possibly can; and leave the results in the laps of the gods.'

Henry Ford told me much the same thing. 'When I can't handle events,' he said, 'I let them handle themselves.'

When I asked K. T. Keller, then president of the Chrysler Corporation, how he kept from worrying, he replied: 'When I am up against a tough situation, if I can do anything about it, I do it. If I can't, I just forget it. I never worry about the future, because I know no man living can possibly figure out what is going to happen in the future. There are so many forces that will affect that future! Nobody can tell what prompts those forces – or understand them. So why worry about them?' K. T. Keller would be embarrassed if you told him he is a philosopher. He is just a good businessman, yet he has stumbled on the same philosophy that Epictetus taught in Rome nineteen centuries ago. 'There is only one way to happiness,' Epictetus taught the Romans, 'and that is to cease worrying about things which are beyond the power of our will.'

Sarah Bernhardt, the 'divine Sarah', was an illustrious example of a woman who knew how to cooperate with the inevitable. For half a century, she had been the reigning queen of the theatre on four continents – the best-loved actress on earth. Then when she was seventy-one and broke – she had lost all her money – her physician, Professor Pozzi of Paris, told her he would have to amputate her leg. While crossing the Atlantic, she had fallen on deck during a storm, and injured her leg severely. Phlebitis developed. Her leg shrank. The pain became so intense that the doctor felt her leg had to be amputated. he was almost afraid to tell the stormy, tempestuous 'divine Sarah' what had to be done. He fully expected that the terrible news would set off an explosion of hysteria. But he was wrong. Sarah looked at him a moment, and then said quietly, 'If it has to be, it has to be.' It was fate.

As she was being wheeled away to the operating room her son stood weeping. She waved to him with a gay gesture and said cheerfully: 'Don't go away. I'll be right back.'

On the way to the operating room she recited a scene from one of her plays. Someone asked her if she were doing this to cheer herself up. She said: 'No, to cheer up the doctors and nurses. It will be a strain on them.'

After recovering from the operation, Sarah Bernhardt went on touring the world and enchanting audiences for another seven years.

'When we stop fighting the inevitable,' said Elsie MacCormick in a *Reader's Digest* article, 'we release energy which enables us to create a richer life.'

No one living has enough emotion and vigour to *fight* the inevitable and, at the same time, enough left over to create a new life. Choose one or the other. You can either bend with the inevitable sleetstorms of life – or you can resist them and break!

I saw that happen on a farm I own in Missouri. I planted a score of trees on that farm. At first, they grew with astonishing rapidity. Then a sleetstorm encrusted each twig and branch with a heavy coating of ice. Instead of bowing gracefully to their burden, these trees proudly resisted and broke and split under the load – and had to be destroyed. They hadn't learned the wisdom of the forests of the North. I have travelled hundreds of miles through the evergreen forests of Canada. Yet I have never seen a spruce or a pine broken by sleet or ice. These evergreen forests know how to bend, how to bow down their branches, how to cooperate with the inevitable.

The masters of jujitsu teach their pupils to 'bend like the willow; don't resist like the oak.'

Why do you think your automobile tyres stand up on the road and take so much punishment? At first, the tyre manufacturers tried to make a tyre that would resist the shocks of the road. It was soon cut to ribbons. Then they made a tyre that would absorb the shocks of the road. That tyre could 'take it'. You and I will last longer, and enjoy smoother riding, if we learn to absorb the shocks and jolts along the rocky road of life.

What will happen to you and me if we resist the shocks of life instead of absorbing them? What will happen if we refuse to 'bend like the willow' and insist on resisting like the oak? The answer is easy. We will set up a series of inner conflicts. We will be worried, tense, strained, and neurotic.

If we go still further and reject the harsh world of reality and retreat into a dream world of our own making, we will then be insane.

During the war, millions of frightened soldiers had either to accept the inevitable or break under the strain. To illustrate, let's take the case of William H. Casselius, of Glendale, New York. Here is a prize-winning talk he gave before one of my classes in New York:

'Shortly after I joined the Coast Guard, I was assigned to one of the hottest spots on this side of the Atlantic. I was made a supervisor of explosives. Imagine it. Me! A cracker salesman becoming a supervisor of explosives! The very thought of finding yourself standing on top of thousands of tons of TNT is enough to chill the marrow in a cracker salesman's bones. I was given only two days of instruction; and what I learned filled me with even more terror. I'll never forget my first assignment. On a dark, cold, foggy day, I was given my orders on the open pier of Caven Point, Bayonne, New Jersey.

'I was assigned to Hold No. 5 on my ship. I had to work down in that hold with five longshoremen. They had strong backs, but they knew nothing whatever about explosives. And they were loading blockbusters, each one of which contained a ton of TNT – enough explosive to blow that old ship to kingdom come. These blockbusters were being lowered by two cable slings. I kept saying to myself: Suppose one of those cables slipped – or broke! Oh, boy! Was I scared! I trembled. My mouth was dry. My knees sagged. My heart pounded. But I couldn't run away. That would be desertion. I would be disgraced – my parents would be disgraced – and I might be shot for desertion. I couldn't run. I had to stay. I kept looking at the careless way those longshoremen were handling those blockbusters. The ship might blow up any minute. After an hour or more of spine-chilling terror, I began to use a little common sense. I gave myself a good talking to. I said, "Look here! So you are blown up. So what! You will never know the difference! It will be an easy way to die. Much better than dying by cancer. Don't be a fool. You can't expect to live forever! You've got to do this job – or be shot. So you might as well do it."

'I talked to myself like that for hours; and I began to feel at ease. Finally, I overcame my worry and fears by forcing myself to accept the inevitable situation.

'I'll never forget that lesson. Every time I am tempted now to worry about something I can't possibly change, I shrug my shoulders and say, "Forget it." I find that it works – even for a cracker salesman.' Horray! Let's give three cheers and one cheer more for the cracker salesman of the *Pinafore*.

Outside of the crucifixion of Jesus, the most famous death scene in all history was the death of Socrates. Ten thousand centuries from now, men will still be reading and cherishing Plato's immortal description of it – one of the most moving and beautiful passages in all literature. Certain men of Athens – jealous and envious of old barefooted Socrates – trumped up charges against him and had him tried and condemned to death. When the friendly jailer gave Socrates the poison cup to drink, the jailer said: *'Try to bear lightly what needs must be.'* Socrates did. He faced death with a calmness and resignation that touched the hem of divinity.

'Try to bear lightly what needs must be.' Those words were spoken 399 years before Christ was born; but this worrying old world needs those words today more than ever before: *'Try to bear lightly what needs must be.'*

I have been reading practically every book and magazine article I could find that dealt even remotely with banishing worry . . . Would you like to know what is the best single bit of advice about worry that I have ever discovered in all that reading? Well, here it is – summed up in twenty-seven words – words that you and I ought to paste on our bathroom mirrors, so that each time we wash our faces we could also wash away all worry from our minds. This priceless prayer was written by Dr. Reinhold Niebuhr.

> God grant me the serenity
> To accept the things I cannot change,
> The courage to change the things I can;
> And the wisdom to know the difference.

To break the worry habit before it breaks you, Rule 4 is:

> Cooperate with the inevitable.

☐ 10 ☐

Put a 'stop-loss' order on your worries

Would you like to know how to make money in Wall Street? Well, so would a million other people – and if I knew the answer, this book would sell for ten thousand dollars a copy. However, there's one good idea that some successful operators use. This story was told to me by Charles Roberts, an investment counsellor.

'I originally came up to New York from Texas with twenty thousand dollars which my friends had given me to invest in the stock market,' Charles Roberts told me. 'I thought,' he continued, 'that I knew the ropes in the stock market; but I lost every cent. True, I made a lot of profit on some deals; but I ended up by losing everything.'

'I did not mind so much losing my own money,' Mr. Roberts explained, 'but I felt terrible about having lost my friends' money, even though they could well afford it. I dreaded facing them again after our venture had turned out so unfortunately, but, to my astonishment, they not only were good sports about it but proved to be incurable optimists.

'I knew I had been trading on a hit-or-miss basis and depending largely on luck and other people's opinions. I had been "playing the stock market by ear."

'I began to think over my mistakes and I determined that before I went back into the market again, I would try to find out what it was all about. So I sought out and became acquainted with one of the most successful speculators who ever lived: Burton S. Castles. I believed I could learn a great deal from him because he had long enjoyed the reputation of being successful year after year and I knew that such a career was not the result of mere chance or luck.

'He asked me a few questions about how I had traded before and then told me what I believe is the most important principle in trading. He said, "I put a stop-loss order on every market commitment I make. If I buy a stock at, say, fifty dollars a share, I immediately place a stop-loss order on it at forty-five." That means that when and if the stock should decline as much as five points below its cost, it would be sold automatically, thereby limiting the loss to five points.

' "If your commitments are intelligently made in the first place," the old master continued, "your profits will average ten, twenty-five, or even fifty points. Consequently, by limiting your losses to five points, you can be wrong more than half of the time and still make plenty of money."

'I adopted that principle immediately and have used it ever since. It has saved my clients and me many thousands of dollars.

'After a while I realized that the stop-loss principle could be used in other ways besides in the stock market. I began to place stop-loss orders on other worries besides financial ones. I began to place a stop-loss order on any and every kind of annoyance and resentment that came to me. It has worked like magic.

'For example, I often have a luncheon date with a friend who is rarely on time. In the old days, he used to keep me stewing around for half my lunch hour before he showed up. Finally, I told him about my stop-loss orders on my worries. I said, "Bill, my stop-loss order on waiting for you is exactly ten minutes. If you arrive more than ten minutes late, our luncheon engagement will be sold down the river – and I'll be gone." '

Man alive! How I wish I had had the sense, years ago, to put stop-loss orders on my impatience, on my temper, on my desire for self-justification, on my regrets, and on all my mental and emotional strains. Why didn't I have the horse sense to size up every situation that threatened to destroy my peace of mind and say to myself: 'See here, Dale Carnegie, this situation is worth just so much fussing about – and no more'? . . . Why didn't I?

However, I must give myself credit for a little sense on one occasion, at least. And it was a serious occasion, too – a crisis in my life – a crisis when I stood watching my dreams and my plans for the future and the work of years vanish into thin air. It happened like this. In my early thirties, I had decided to spend my life writing novels. I was going to be a second Frank Norris or Jack London or Thomas Hardy. I was so in earnest that I spent two years in Europe – where I could live cheaply with dollars during the period of wild, printing-press money that followed the First World War. I spent two years there, writing my magnum opus. I called it *The Blizzard*. The title was a natural, for the reception it got among publishers was as cold as any blizzard that ever howled across the plains of the Dakotas. When my literary agent told me it was worthless, that I had no gift, no talent, for fiction, my heart almost stopped. I left his office in a daze. I couldn't have been more stunned if he had hit me across the head with a club. I was stupefied. I realized that I was standing at the crossroads of life, and had to make a tremendous decision. What should I do? Which way should I turn? Weeks passed before I came out of the daze. At that time I had never heard of the phrase 'put a stop-loss order on your worries'. But as I look back now, I can see that I did just that. I wrote off my two years of sweating over that novel for just what they were worth – a noble experiment – and went forward from there. I returned to my work of organizing and teaching adult-education classes, and wrote biographies in my spare time – biographies and nonfiction books such as the one you are reading now.

Am I glad now that I made that decision? Glad? Every time I think about it now I feel like dancing in the street for sheer joy! I can honestly say that I have never spent a day or an hour since, lamenting the fact that I am not another Thomas Hardy.

One night a century ago, when a screech owl was screeching in the woods along the shores of Walden Pond, Henry Thoreau dipped his goose quill into his homemade ink and wrote in his diary: 'The cost of a thing is the amount of what I call life, which is required to be exchanged for it immediately or in the long run.'

To put it another way: we are fools when we overpay for a thing in terms of what it takes out of our very existence.

Yet that is precisely what Gilbert and Sullivan did. They knew how to create gay words and gay music, but they knew distressingly little about how to create gaiety in their own lives. They created some of the loveliest light operas that ever delighted the world: *Patience, Pinafore, The Mikado*. But they couldn't control their tempers. They embittered their years over nothing more than the price of a carpet! Sullivan ordered a new carpet for the theatre they had bought. When Gilbert saw the bill, he hit the roof. They battled it out in court, and never spoke to one another again as long as they lived. When Sullivan wrote the music for a new production, he mailed it to Gilbert; and when Gilbert wrote the words, he mailed it back to Sullivan. Once they had to make a curtain call together, but they stood on opposite sides of the stage and bowed in different directions, so they wouldn't see one another. They hadn't the sense to put a stop-loss order on their resentment, as Lincoln did.

Once, during the Civil War, when some of Lincoln's friends were denouncing his bitter enemies, Lincoln said: 'You have more of a feeling of personal resentment than I have. Perhaps I have too little of it; but I never thought it paid. A man doesn't have the time to spend half his life in quarrels. If any man ceases to attack me, I never remember the past against him.'

I wish an old Aunt of mine – Aunt Edith – had had Lincoln's forgiving spirit. She and Uncle Frank lived on a mortgaged farm that was infested with cockleburs and cursed with poor soil and ditches. They had tough going – had to squeeze every nickel. But Aunt Edith loved to buy a few curtains and other small items to brighten up their bare home. She bought these small luxuries on credit at Dan Eversole's drygoods store in Maryville, Missouri. Uncle Frank worried about their debts. He had a farmer's horror of running up bills, so he secretly told Dan Eversole to stop letting his wife buy on credit. When she heard that, she hit the roof – and she was still hitting the roof about it almost fifty years after it had happened. I have heard her tell the story – not once, but many times. The last time I ever saw her, she was in her late seventies. I said to her: 'Aunt Edith, Uncle Frank did wrong to humiliate you; but don't you honestly feel that your complaining about it almost half a century after it happened is infinitely worse than what he did?' (I might as well have said it to the moon.)

Aunt Edith paid dearly for the grudges and bitter memories that she nourished. She paid for them with her own peace of mind.

When Benjamin Franklin was seven years old, he made a mistake that he remembered for seventy years. When he was a lad of seven, he fell in love with a whistle. He was so excited about it that he went into the toyshop, piled all his coppers on the counter, and demanded the whistle without even asking its price. 'I then came home,' he wrote to a friend seventy years later, 'and went whistling all over the house, much pleased with my whistle.' But when his older brothers and sisters found out that he had paid far more for his whistle than he should have paid, they gave him the horse laugh; and, as he said, 'I cried with vexation.'

Years later, when Franklin was a world-famous figure, and Ambassador to France, he still remembered that the fact that he had paid too much for his whistle had caused him 'more chagrin than the whistle gave him pleasure'.

But the lesson it taught Franklin was cheap in the end. 'As I grew up,' he said, 'and came into the world and observed the actions of men, I thought I met with many, very many, who gave *too much for the whistle*. In short, I conceive that a great part of the miseries of mankind are brought upon them by the false estimates they have made of the value of things, and by their *giving too much for their whistles*.'

Gilbert and Sullivan paid too much for their whistle. So did Aunt Edith. So did Dale Carnegie – on many occasions. And so did the immortal Leo Tolstoy, author of two of the world's greatest novels, *War and Peace* and *Anna Karenina*. According to *The Encyclopaedia Britannica*, Leo Tolstoy was, during the last twenty years of his life, 'probably the most venerated man in the whole world.' For twenty years before he died – from 1890 to 1910 – an unending stream of admirers made pilgrimages to his home in order to catch a glimpse of his face, to hear the sound of his voice, or even touch the hem of his garment. Every sentence he uttered was taken down in a notebook, almost as if it were a 'divine revelation'. But when it came to living – to ordinary living – well, Tolstoy had even less sense at seventy than Franklin had at seven! He had no sense at all.

Here's what I mean. Tolstoy married a girl he loved very dearly. In fact, they were so happy together that they used to get on their knees and pray to God to let them continue their lives in such sheer, heavenly ecstasy. But the girl Tolstoy married was jealous by nature. She used to dress herself up as a peasant and spy on his movements, even out in the woods. They had fearful rows. She became so jealous, even of her own children, that she grabbed a gun and shot a hole in her daughter's photograph. She even rolled on the floor with an opium bottle held to her lips, and threatened to commit suicide, while the children huddled in a corner of the room and screamed with terror.

And what did Tolstoy do? Well, I don't blame the man for up and smashing the furniture – he had good provocation. But he did far worse than that. He kept a diary! Yes, a diary, in which he placed all the blame on his wife! That was his 'whistle'! He was determined to make sure that coming generations would exonerate *him* and put the blame on his wife. And what did his wife do, in answer to this? Why, she tore pages out of his diary and burned them, of course. She started a diary of her own, in which she made *him* the villain. She even wrote a novel, entitled *Whose Fault?*, in which she depicted her husband as a household fiend and herself as a martyr.

All to what end? Why did these two people turn the only home they had into what Tolstoy himself called 'a lunatic asylum'? Obviously, there were several reasons. One of those reasons was their burning desire to impress you and me. Yes, we are the posterity whose opinion they were worried about! Do we give a hoot in Hades about which one was to blame? No, we are too concerned with our own problems to waste a minute thinking about the Tolstoys. What a price these two wretched people paid for their whistle! Fifty years of living in a veritable hell – just because neither of them had the sense to say: 'Stop!' Because neither of them had enough judgement of values to say, 'Let's put a stop-loss order on this thing instantly. We are squandering our lives. Let's say "Enough" now!'

Yes, I honestly believe that this is one of the greatest secrets to true peace of mind – a decent sense of values. And I believe we could annihilate fifty percent of all our worries at once if we could develop a sort of private gold standard – a gold standard of what things are worth to us in terms of our lives.

So, to break the worry habit before it breaks you, here is Rule 5:

Whenever we are tempted to throw good money after bad in terms of human living, let's stop and ask ourselves these three questions:

1. How much does this thing I am worrying about really matter to me?

2. At what point shall I set a 'stop-loss' order on this worry – and forget it?
3. Exactly how much shall I pay for this whistle? Have I already paid more than it is worth?

□ **11** □

Don't try to saw sawdust

As I write this sentence, I can look out of my window and see some dinosaur tracks in my garden – dinosaur tracks embedded in shale and stone. I purchased those dinosaur tracks from the Peabody Museum of Yale University; and I have a letter from the curator of the Peabody Museum, saying that those tracks were made 180 million years ago. Even a Mongolian idiot wouldn't dream of trying to go back 180 million years to change those tracks. Yet that would not be any more foolish than worrying because we can't go back and change what happened 180 seconds ago – and a lot of us are doing just that. To be sure, we may do something to *modify the effects* of what happened 180 seconds ago, but we can't possibly change the event that occurred then.

There is only one way on God's green footstool that the past can be constructive; and that is by calmly analyzing our past mistakes and profiting by them – and forgetting them.

I know that is true; but have I always had the courage and sense to do it? To answer that question, let me tell you about a fantastic experience I had years ago. I let more than three hundred thousand dollars slip through my fingers without making a penny's profit. It happened like this: I launched a large-scale enterprise in adult education, opened branches in various cities, and spent money lavishly in overhead and advertising. I was so busy with teaching that I had neither the time nor the desire to look after finances. I was too naive to realize that I needed an astute business manager to watch expenses.

Finally, after about a year, I discovered a sobering and shocking truth. I discovered that in spite of our enormous intake, we had not netted any profit whatever. After discovering that, I should have done two things. First, I should have had the sense to do what George Washington Carver did when he lost forty thousand dollars in a bank crash – the savings of a lifetime. When someone asked him if he knew he was bankrupt, he replied, 'Yes, I heard' – and went on with his teaching. He wiped the loss out of his mind so completely that he never mentioned it again.

Here is the second thing I should have done: I should have analyzed my mistakes and learned a lasting lesson.

But frankly, I didn't do either one of these things. Instead, I went into a tailspin of worry. For months I was in a daze. I lost sleep and I lost weight. Instead of learning a lesson from this enormous mistake, I went right ahead and did the same thing again on a smaller scale!

It is embarrassing for me to admit all this stupidity; but I discovered long ago that 'it is easier to teach twenty what were good to be done than to be one of the twenty to follow mine own teaching.'

How I wish that I had had the privilege of attending the George Washington High School here in New York and studying under Dr. Paul Brandwine – the same teacher who taught Allen Saunders, of New York!

Mr. Saunders told me that the teacher of his hygiene class, Dr. Paul Brandwine, taught him one of the most valuable lessons he had ever learned. 'I was only in my teens,' said Allen Saunders as he told me the story, 'but I was a worrier even then. I used to stew and fret about the mistakes I had made. If I turned in an examination paper, I used to lie awake and chew my fingernails for fear I hadn't passed. I was always living over the things I had done, and wishing I'd done them differently; thinking over the things I had said, and wishing I'd said them better.

'Then one morning, our class filed into the science laboratory, and there was the teacher, Dr. Paul Brandwine, with a bottle of milk prominently displayed on the edge of the desk. We all sat down, staring at the milk, and wondering what it had to do with the hygiene course he was teaching. Then, all of a sudden, Dr. Paul Brandwine stood up, swept the bottle of milk with a crash into the sink – and shouted: "Don't cry over spilt milk!"

'He then made us all come to the sink and look at the wreckage. "Take a good look," he told us, "because I want you to remember this lesson the rest of your lives. That milk is gone – you can see it's down the drain; and all the fussing and hair-pulling in the world won't bring back a drop of it. With a little thought and prevention, that milk might have been saved. but it's too late now – all we can do is write it off, forget it, and go on to the next thing."

'That one little demonstration,' Allen Saunders told me, 'stuck with me long after I'd forgotten my solid geometry and Latin. In fact, it taught me more about practical living than anything else in my four years of high school. It taught me to keep from spilling milk if I could; but to forget it completely, once it was spilled and had gone down the drain.'

Some readers are going to snort at the idea of making so much over a hackneyed proverb like 'Don't cry over spilt milk.' I know it is trite, commonplace, and a platitude. I know you have heard it a thousand times. But I also know that these hackneyed proverbs contain the very essence of the distilled wisdom of all ages. They have come out of the fiery experience of the human race and have been handed down through countless generations. If you were to read everything that has ever been written about worry by the great scholars of all time, you would never read anything more basic or more profound than such hackneyed proverbs as 'Don't cross your bridges until you come to them' and 'Don't cry over spilt milk.' If we only applied those two proverbs – instead of snorting at them – we wouldn't need this book at all. In fact, if we applied most of the old proverbs, we would lead almost perfect lives. However, knowledge isn't power until it is applied; and the purpose of this book is not to tell you something new. The purpose of this book is to remind you of what you already know and to kick you in the shins and inspire you to do something about applying it.

I have always admired a man like the late Fred Fuller Shedd, who had a gift for stating an old truth in a new and picturesque way. While editor of the *Philadelphia Bulletin* and addressing a college graduating class, he asked: 'How many of you ever sawed wood? Let's see your hands. Most of them had. Then he inquired: 'How many of you have ever sawed *sawdust*?' No hands went up.

'Of course, you can't saw sawdust!' Mr. Shedd exclaimed. 'It's already sawed! And it's the same with the past. When you start worrying about things that are over and done with, you're merely trying to saw sawdust.'

When Connie Mack, the grand old man of baseball, was eighty-one years old, I asked him if he had ever worried over games that were lost.

'Oh, yes, I used to,' Connie Mack told me. 'But I got over that foolishness long years ago. I found out it didn't get me anywhere at all. You can't grind any grain he said, 'with water that has already gone down the creek.'

No, you can't grind any grain – and you can't saw any logs with water that has already gone down the creek. But you can saw wrinkles in your face and ulcers in your stomach.

I had dinner with Jack Dempsey one Thanksgiving; and he told me over the turkey and cranberry sauce about the fight in which he lost the heavyweight championship to Tunney. Naturally, it was a blow to his ego. 'In the midst of that fight,' he told me, 'I suddenly realized I had become an old man . . . At the end of the tenth round, I was still on my feet, but that was about all. My face was puffed up and cut, and my eyes were nearly closed . . . I saw the referee raise Gene Tunney's hand in token of victory . . . I was no longer champion of the world. I started back in the rain – back through the crowd to my dressing room. As I passed, some people tried to grab my hand. Others had tears in their eyes.

'A year later, I fought Tunney again. But it was no use. I was through forever. It was hard to keep from worrying about it all, but I said to myself, "I'm not going to live in the past or cry over spilt milk. I am going to take this blow on the chin and not let it floor me." '

And that is precisely what Jack Dempsey did. How? By saying to himself over and over, 'I won't worry about the past'? No, that would merely have forced him to think of his past worries. He did it by accepting and writing off his defeat and then concentrating on plans for the future. He did it by running the Jack Dempsey Restaurant on Broadway and the Great Northern Hotel on 57th Street. He did it by promoting prize fights and giving boxing exhibitions. He did it by getting so busy on something constructive that he had neither the time nor the temptation to worry about the past. 'I have had a better time during the last ten years,' Jack Dempsey said, 'than I had when I was champion.'

Mr. Dempsey told me that he had not read many books; but, without knowing it, he was following Shakespeare's advice: 'Wise men ne'er sit and wail their loss, but cheerily seek how to redress their harms.'

As I read history and biography and observe people under trying circumstances, I am constantly astonished and inspired by some people's ability to write off their worries and tragedies and go on living fairly happy lives.

I once paid a visit to Sing Sing, and the thing that astonished me most was that the prisoners there appeared to be about as happy as the average person on the outside. I commented on it to Lewis E. Lawes – then warden of Sing Sing – and he told me that when criminals first arrive at Sing Sing, they are likely to be resentful and bitter. But after a few months, the majority of the more intelligent ones write off their misfortunes and settle down and accept prison life calmly and make the best of it. Warden Lawes told me about one Sing Sing prisoner – a gardener – who *sang* as he cultivated the vegetables and flowers inside the prison walls.

That Sing Sing prisoner who sang as he cultivated the flowers showed a lot more sense than most of us do. He knew that

> The Moving Finger writes; and, having writ,
> Moves on: nor all your Piety nor Wit
>   Shall lure it back to cancel half a Line,
> Nor all your Tears wash out a Word of it.

So why waste the tears? Of course, we have been guilty of blunders and absurdities! And so what? Who hasn't? Even Napoleon lost one third of all the important battles he fought. Perhaps our batting average is no worse than Napoleon's. Who knows?

And, anyhow, all the king's horses and all the king's men can't put the past together again. So let's remember Rule 6:

> Don't try to saw sawdust.

☐ IN A NUTSHELL ☐

HOW TO BREAK THE WORRY HABIT BEFORE IT BREAKS YOU

RULE 1: Crowd worry out of your mind by keeping busy. Plenty of action is one of the best therapies ever devised for curing 'wibber gibbers'.

RULE 2: Don't fuss about trifles. Don't permit little things – the mere termites of life – to ruin your happiness.

RULE 3: Use the law of averages to outlaw your worries. Ask yourself: 'What are the odds against this thing's happening at all?'

RULE 4: Cooperate with the inevitable. If you know a circumstance is beyond your power to change or revise, say to yourself: 'It is so; it cannot be otherwise.'

RULE 5: Put a 'stop-loss' order on your worries. Decide just how much anxiety a thing may be worth – and refuse to give it any more.

RULE 6: Let the past bury its dead. Don't saw sawdust.

Part Four

SEVEN WAYS TO CULTIVATE A

MENTAL ATTITUDE THAT WILL

BRING YOU PEACE AND HAPPINESS

☐ 12 ☐

Eight words that can transform your life

A few years ago, I was asked to answer this question on a radio programme: 'What is the biggest lesson you have ever learned?'

That was easy: by far the most vital lesson I have ever learned is the importance of what we think. If I knew what you think, I would know what you are. Our thoughts make us what we are. Our mental attitude is the X factor that determines our fate. Emerson said: 'A man is what he thinks about all day long.' . . . How could he possibly be anything else?

I now know with a conviction beyond all doubt that the biggest problem you and I have to deal with – in fact, almost the *only* problem we have to deal with – is choosing the right thoughts. If we can do that, we will be on the highroad to solving all our problems. The great philosopher who ruled the Roman Empire, Marcus Aurelius, summed it up in eight words – *eight words that can determine your destiny: 'Our life is what our thoughts make it.'*

Yes, if we think happy thoughts, we will be happy. If we think miserable thoughts, we will be miserable. If we think fear thoughts, we will be fearful. If we think sickly thoughts, we will probably be ill. If we think failure, we will certainly fail. If we wallow in self-pity, everyone will want to shun us and avoid us. 'You are not,' said Norman Vincent Peale, 'you are not what you think you are, but what you *think*, you are.'

Am I advocating an habitual Pollyanna attitude toward all our problems? No, unfortunately, life isn't so simple as all that. But I am advocating that we assume a *positive* attitude instead of a negative attitude. In other words, we need to be concerned about our problems, but not worried. What is the difference between concern and worry? Let me illustrate. Every time I cross the traffic-jammed streets of New York, I am concerned about what I am doing – but not worried. Concern means realizing what the problems are and calmly taking steps to meet them. Worrying means going around in maddening, futile circles.

A man can be concerned about his serious problems and still walk with his chin up and a carnation in his buttonhole. I have seen Lowell Thomas do just that. I once had the privilege of being associated with Lowell Thomas in presenting his famous films on the Allenby-Lawrence campaigns in World War I. He and his assistants had photographed the war on half a dozen fronts; and, best of all, had brought back a pictorial record of T. E. Lawrence and his colourful Arabian army, and a film record of Allenby's conquest of the Holy Land. His illustrated talks entitled 'With Allenby in Palestine and Lawrence in Arabia' were a sensation in London – and around the world. The London opera season was postponed for six weeks so that he could continue telling his tale of high adventure and showing his pictures at Covent Garden Royal Opera House. After his sensational success in London came a triumphant tour of many countries. Then he spent two years preparing a film record of life in India and Afghanistan. After a lot of incredibly bad luck, the impossible happened: he found himself broke in London. I was with him at the time. I remember we had to eat cheap meals at the Lyons' Corner House restaurants. We couldn't have eaten even there if Mr. Thomas had not borrowed money from a Scotsman – James McBey, the renowned artist. Here is the point of the story: even when Lowell Thomas was facing huge debts and severe disappointments, he was concerned, but not worried. He knew that if he let his reverses get him down, he would be worthless to everyone, including his creditors. So each morning before he started out, he bought a flower, put it in his buttonhole, and went swinging down Oxford Street with his head high and his step spirited. He thought positive, courageous thoughts and refused to let defeat defeat him. To him, being licked was all a part of the game – the useful training you had to expect if you wanted to get to the top.

Our mental attitude has an almost unbelievable effect even on our physical powers. The famous British psychiatrist, J. A. Hadfield, gives a striking illustration of that fact in his splendid 54-page booklet: *The Psychology of Power*. 'I asked three men,' he writes, 'to submit themselves to test the effect of mental suggestion on their strength, which was measured by gripping a dynamometer.' He told them to grip the dynamometer with all their might. He had them do this under three different sets of conditions.

When he tested them under normal waking conditions, their average grip was 101 pounds.

When he tested them after he had hypnotized them and told them that they were very weak, they could grip only 29 pounds – less than a third of their normal strength. (One of these men was a prize fighter; and when he was told under hypnosis that he was weak, he remarked that his arm felt 'tiny, just like a baby's.')

When Captain Hadfield then tested these men a third time, telling them under hypnosis that they were very strong, they were able to grip an average of 142 pounds. When their minds were filled with positive thoughts of strength, they increased their actual physical powers almost fifty percent.

Such is the incredible power of our mental attitude.

To illustrate the magic power of thought, let me tell you one of the most astounding stories in the annals of America. I could write a book about it; but let's be brief. On a frosty October night, shortly after the close of the Civil War, a homeless, destitute woman, who was little more than a wanderer on the face of the earth, knocked at the door of 'Mother' Webster, the wife of a retired captain, living in Amesbury, Massachusetts.

Opening the door, 'Mother' Webster saw a frail little creature, 'scarcely more than a hundred pounds of frightened skin and bones.' The stranger, a Mrs. Glover, explained she was seeking a home where she could think and work out a great problem that absorbed her day and night.

'Why not stay here?' Mrs. Webster replied. 'I'm all alone in this big house.'

Mrs. Glover might have remained indefinitely with 'Mother' Webster if the latter's son-in-law, Bill Ellis, hadn't come up from New York for a vacation. When he discovered Mrs. Glover's presence, he shouted: 'I'll have no vagabonds in this house'; and he shoved this homeless woman out of the door. A driving rain was falling. She stood shivering in the rain for a few minutes, and then started down the road, looking for shelter.

Here is the astonishing part of the story. That 'vagabond' whom Bill Ellis put out of his house was destined to have as much influence on the thinking of the world as any other woman who ever walked this earth. She is now known to millions of devoted followers as Mary Baker Eddy – the founder of Christian Science.

Yet, until this time, she had known little in life except sickness, sorrow, and tragedy. Her first husband died shortly after their marriage. Her second husband had deserted her and eloped with a married woman. He later died in a poorhouse. She had only one child, a son; and she was forced, because of poverty, illness, and jealousy, to give him up when he was four years old. She lost all track of him and never saw him again for thirty-one years.

Because of her own ill health, Mrs. Eddy had been interested for years in what she called 'the science of mind healing'. But the dramatic turning point in her life occurred in Lynn, Massachusetts. Walking downtown one cold day, she slipped and fell on the icy pavement – and was knocked unconscious. Her spine was so injured that she was convulsed with spasms. Even the doctor expected her to die. If by some miracle she lived, he declared that she would never walk again.

Lying on what was supposed to be her deathbed, Mary Baker Eddy opened her Bible, and was led, she declared, by divine guidance to read these words from Saint Matthew: 'And, behold, they brought to him a man sick of the palsy, lying on a bed: and Jesus . . . said unto the sick of the palsy; Son, be of good cheer; thy sins be forgiven thee . . . Arise, take up thy bed, and go unto thine house. And he arose, and departed to his house.'

These words of Jesus, she declared, produced within her such a strength, such a faith, such a surge of healing power, that she 'immediately got out of bed and walked.'

'That experience,' Mrs. Eddy declared, 'was the falling apple that led me to the discovery of how to be well myself, and how to make others so . . . I gained the scientific certainty that all causation was Mind, and every effect a mental phenomenon.'

Such was the way in which Mary Baker Eddy became the founder and high priestess of a new religion: Christian Science – the only great religious faith ever established by a woman – a religion that has encircled the globe.

You are probably saying to yourself by now: 'This man Carnegie is proselytizing for Christian Science.' No. you are wrong. I am not a Christian Scientist. But the longer I live, the more deeply I am convinced of the tremendous power of thought. As a result of many years spent in teaching adults, I know men and women can banish worry, fear, and various kinds of illnesses, and can transform their lives by changing their thoughts. I know! I know!! I know!!! I have seen such incredible transformations performed hundreds of times. I have seen them so often that I no longer wonder at them.

For example, one of these incredible transformations which illustrate the power of thought happened to one of my students. He had a nervous breakdown. What brought it on? Worry. This student told me, 'I worried about everything: I worried because I was too thin; because I thought I was losing my hair; because I feared I would never make enough money to get married; because I felt I would never make a good father; because I feared I was losing the girl I wanted to marry; because I felt I was not living a good life. I worried about the impression I was making on other people. I worried because I thought I had stomach ulcers. I could no longer work; I gave up my job. I built up tension inside me until I was like a boiler without a safety valve. The pressure got so unbearable that something had to give – and it did. If you have ever had a nervous breakdown, pray God that you never do, for no pain of the body can exceed the excruciating pain of an agonized mind.

'My breakdown was so severe that I couldn't talk even to my own family. I had no control over my thoughts. I was filled with fear. I would jump at the slightest noise. I avoided everybody. I would break out crying for no apparent reason at all.

'Every day was one of agony. I felt that I was deserted by everybody – even God. I was tempted to jump into the river and end it all.

'I decided instead to take a trip to Florida, hoping that a change of scene would help me. As I stepped on the train, my father handed me a letter and told me not to open it until I reached Florida. I landed in Florida during the height of the tourist season. Since I couldn't get in a hotel, I rented a sleeping room in a garage. I tried to get a job on a tramp freighter out of Miami, but had no luck. So I spent my time at the beach. I was more wretched in Florida than I had been at home; so I opened the envelope to see what Dad had written. His note said, "Son, you are 1500 miles from home, and you don't feel any different, do you? I knew you wouldn't, because you took with you the one thing that is the cause of all your trouble, that is, yourself. There is nothing wrong with either your body or your mind. It is not the situations you have met that have thrown you; it is what you think of these situations. 'As a man thinketh in his heart, so is he.' When you realize that, son, come home, for you will be cured."

'Dad's letter made me angry. I was looking for sympathy, not instruction. I was so mad that I decided then and there that I would never go home. That night as I was walking down one of the side streets of Miami, I came to a church where services were going on. Having no place to go, I drifted in and listened to a sermon on the text: "He who conquers his spirit is mightier than he who taketh a city." Sitting in the sanctity of the house of God and hearing the same thoughts that my Dad had written in his letter – all this swept the accumulated litter out of my brain. I was able to think clearly and sensibly for the first time in my life. I realized what a fool I had been. I was shocked to see myself in my true light: here I was, wanting to change the whole world and everyone in it – when the only thing that needed changing was the focus of the lens of the camera which was my mind.

'The next morning I packed and started home. A week later I was back on the job. Four months later I married the girl I had been afraid of losing. We now have a happy family of five children. God has been good to me both materially and mentally. At the time of the breakdown I was a night foreman of a small department handling eighteen people. I am now superintendent of carton manufacture in charge of over four hundred and fifty people. Life is much fuller and friendlier. I believe I appreciate the true values of life now. When moments of uneasiness try to creep in (as they will in everyone's life) I tell myself to get that camera back in focus, and everything is O.K.

'I can honestly say that I am glad I had the breakdown, because I found out the hard way what power our thoughts can have over our mind and our body. Now I can make my thoughts work for me instead of against me. I can see now that Dad was right when he said it wasn't outward situations that had caused all my suffering, but what I thought of those situations. And as soon as I realized that, I was cured – and stayed cured.' Such was the experience of this student.

I am deeply convinced that our peace of mind and the joy we get out of living depends not on where we are, or what we have, or who we are, but solely upon our mental attitude. Outward conditions have very little to do with it. For example, let's take the case of old John Brown, who was hanged for seizing the United States arsenal at Harpers Ferry and trying to incite the slaves to rebellion. He rode away to the gallows, sitting on his coffin. The jailer who rode beside him was nervous and worried. But old John Brown was calm and cool. Looking up at the Blue Ridge mountains of Virginia, he exclaimed, 'What a beautiful country! I never had an opportunity to really see it before.'

Or take the case of Robert Falcon Scott and his companions – the first Englishmen ever to reach the South Pole. Their return trip was probably the cruellest journey ever undertaken by man. Their food was gone – and so was their fuel. They could no longer march because a howling blizzard roared down over the rim of the earth for eleven days and nights – a wind so fierce and sharp that it cut ridges in the polar ice. Scott and his companions knew they were going to die; and they had brought a quantity of opium along for just such an emergency. A big dose of opium, and they could all lie down to pleasant dreams, never to wake again. But they ignored the drug, and died 'singing ringing songs of cheer'. We know they did because of a farewell letter found with their frozen bodies by a searching party, eight months later.

Yes, if we cherish creative thoughts of courage and calmness, we can enjoy the scenery while sitting on our coffin, riding to the gallows; or we can fill our tents with 'ringing songs of cheer', while starving and freezing to death.

Milton in his blindness discovered that same truth three hundred years ago:

The mind is its own place, and in itself
Can make a heaven of Hell, a hell of Heaven.

Napoleon and Helen Keller are perfect illustrations of Milton's statement: Napoleon had everything men usually crave – glory, power, riches – yet he said at Saint Helena, 'I have never known six happy days in my life'; while Helen Keller – blind, deaf, dumb – declared: 'I have found life so beautiful.'

If half a century of living has taught me anything at all, it has taught me that 'Nothing can bring you peace but yourself.'

I am merely trying to repeat what Emerson said so well in the closing words of his essay on 'Self-Reliance': 'A political victory, a rise in rents, the recovery of your sick, or the return of your absent friend, or some other quite external event, raises your spirits, and you think good days are preparing for you. Do not believe it. It can never be so. Nothing can bring you peace but yourself.'

Epictetus, the great Stoic philosopher, warned that we ought to be more concerned about removing wrong thoughts from the mind than about removing 'tumours and abscesses from the body'.

Epictetus said that nineteen centuries ago, but modern medicine would back him up. Dr. G. Canby Robinson declared that four out of five patients admitted to Johns Hopkins Hospital were suffering from conditions brought on in part by emotional strains and stresses. This was often true even in cases of organic disturbances. 'Eventually,' he declared, 'these trace back to maladjustments to life and its problems.'

Montaigne, the great French philosopher, adopted these seventeen words as the motto of his life: 'A man is not hurt so much by what happens, as by his opinion of what happens. And our *opinion* of what happens is entirely up to us.

What do I mean? Have I the colossal effrontery to tell you to your face – when you are mowed down by troubles, and your nerves are sticking out like wires and curling up at the ends – have I the colossal effrontery to tell you that, under those conditions, you can change your mental attitude by an effort of the will? Yes, I mean precisely that! And that is not all. I am going to show you *how* to do it. It may take a little effort, but the secret is simple.

William James, who has never been topped in his knowledge of practical psychology, once made this observation: '*Action seems to follow feeling, but really action and feeling go together; and by regulating the action, which is under the more direct control of the will, we can indirectly regulate the feeling, which is not.*'

In other words, William James tells us that we cannot instantly change our emotions just by 'making up our minds to' – but that we *can* change our actions. And that when we change our actions, we will automatically change our feelings.

'*Thus,*' he explains, '*the sovereign voluntary path to cheerfulness, if your cheerfulness be lost, is to sit up cheerfully and to act and speak as if cheerfulness were already there.*'

Docs that simple trick work? Try it for yourself. Put a big, broad, honest-to-God smile on your face; throw back your shoulders; take a good, deep breath; and sing a snatch of song. If you can't sing, whistle. If you can't whistle, hum. You will quickly discover what William James was talking about – that it is *physically impossible* to remain blue or depressed while you are acting out the symptoms of being radiantly happy!

This is one of the little basic truths of nature that can easily work miracles in all of our lives. I know a woman in California – I won't mention her name – who could wipe out all of her miseries in twenty-four hours if only she knew this secret. She's old, and she's a widow – that's sad, I admit – but does she try to act happy? No; if you ask her how she is feeling, she says, 'Oh, I'm all right' – but the expression on her face and the whine in her voice say, 'Oh, God, if you only knew the troubles I've seen!' She seems to reproach you for being happy in her presence. Hundreds of women are worse off than she is: her husband left her enough insurance to last the rest of her life, and she has married children to give her a home. But I've rarely seen her smile. She complains that all three of her sons-in-law are stingy and selfish – although she is a guest in their homes for months at a time. And she complains that her daughters never give her presents – although she hoards her own money carefully, 'for my old age'. She is a blight on herself and her unfortunate family! But does it have to be so? That is the pity of it – she could change herself from a miserable, bitter, and unhappy old woman into an honoured and beloved member of the family – if she *wanted* to change. And all she would have to do to work this transformation would be to start acting cheerful; start acting as though she had a little love to give away – instead of squandering it all on her own unhappy and embittered self.

H. J. Englert, of Tell City, Indiana, is still alive today because he discovered this secret. Ten years ago Mr. Englert had a case of scarlet fever; and when he recovered, he found he had developed nephritis, a kidney disease. He tried all kinds of doctors, 'even quacks', he informs me, but nothing could cure him.

Then a short time ago, he got other complications. His blood pressure soared. He went to a doctor, and was told that his blood pressure was hitting the top at 214. He was told that it was fatal – that the condition was progressive, and he had better put his affairs in order at once.

'I went home,' he says, 'and made sure that my insurance was all paid up, then I apologized to my Maker for all my mistakes, and settled down to gloomy meditations. I made everyone unhappy. My wife and family were miserable, and I was buried deep in depression myself. However, after a week of wallowing in self-pity, I said to myself, "You're acting like a fool! You may not die for a year yet, so why not try to be happy while you're here?"

'I threw back my shoulders, put a smile on my face, and attempted to act as though everything were normal. I admit it was an effort at first – but I forced myself to be pleasant and cheerful; and this not only helped my family, but it also helped me.

'The first thing I knew, I began to *feel* better – almost as well as I pretended to feel! The improvement went on. And today – months after I was supposed to be in my grave – I am not only happy, well, and alive, but my blood pressure is down! I know one thing for certain: the doctor's prediction would certainly have come true if I had gone on thinking "dying" thoughts of defeat. But I gave my body a chance to heal itself, by nothing in the world but a change of mental attitude!'

Let me ask you a question: If merely acting cheerful and thinking positive thoughts of health and courage could save this man's life, why should you and I tolerate for one minute more our minor glooms and depressions? Why make ourselves, and everyone around us, unhappy and blue, when it is possible for us to start creating happiness by merely acting cheerful?

Years ago, I read a little book that had a lasting and profound effect on my life. It was called *As a Man Thinketh*, by James Allen, and here's what it said:

'A man will find that as he alters his thoughts toward things and other people, things and other people will alter towards him ... Let a man radically alter his thoughts, and he will be astonished at the rapid transformation it will effect in the material conditions of his life. Men do not attract that which they want, but that which they are ... The divinity that shapes our ends is in ourselves. It is our very self ... All that a man achieves is the direct result of his own thoughts ... A man can only rise, conquer and achieve by lifting up his thoughts. He can only remain weak and abject and miserable by refusing to lift up his thoughts.'

According to the book of Genesis, the Creator gave man dominion over the whole wide earth. A mighty big present. But I am not interested in any such superroyal prerogatives. All I desire is dominion over myself – dominion over my thoughts; dominion over my fears; dominion over my mind and over my spirit. And the wonderful thing is that I know that I can attain this dominion to an astonishing degree, any time I want to, by merely controlling my actions – which in turn control my reactions.

So let us remember these words of William James: '*Much of what we call Evil . . . can often be converted into a bracing and tonic good by a simple change of the sufferer's inner attitude from one of fear to one of fight.*'

Let's *fight* for our happiness!

Let's fight for our happiness by following a daily programme of cheerful and constructive thinking. Here is such a programme. It is entitled 'Just for Today'. I found this programme so inspiring that I gave away hundreds of copies. It was written by the late Sibyl F. Partridge. If you and I follow it, we will eliminate most of our worries and increase immeasurably our portion of what the French call *la joie de vivre*.

JUST FOR TODAY

1 Just for today I will be happy. This assumes that what Abraham Lincoln said is true, that 'most folks are about as happy as they make up their minds to be.' Happiness is from within; it is not a matter of externals.

2 Just for today I will try to adjust myself to what is, and not try to adjust everything to my own desires. I will take my family, my business, and my luck as they come and fit myself to them.

3 Just for today I will take care of my body. I will exercise it, care for it, nourish it, not abuse it nor neglect it, so that it will be a perfect machine for my bidding.

4 Just for today I will try to strengthen my mind. I will learn something useful. I will not be a mental loafer. I will read something that requires effort, thought and concentration.

5 Just for today I will exercise my soul in three ways; I will do somebody a good turn and not get found out. I will do at least two things I don't want to do, as William James suggests, just for exercise.

6 Just for today I will be agreeable. I will look as well as I can, dress as becomingly as possible, talk low, act courteously, be liberal with praise, criticize not at all, nor find fault with everything and not try to regulate nor improve anyone.

7. Just for today I will try to live through this day only, not to tackle my whole life problem at once. I can do things for twelve hours that would appall me if I had to keep them up for a lifetime.

8. Just for today I will have a programme. I will write down what I expect to do every hour. I may not follow it exactly, but I will have it. It will eliminate two pests, hurrying and indecision.

9. Just for today I will have a quiet half-hour all by myself and relax. In this half-hour sometimes I will think of God, so as to get a little more perspective into my life.

10. Just for today I will be unafraid, especially I will not be afraid to be happy, to enjoy what is beautiful, to love, and to believe that those I love, love me.

If we want to develop a mental attitude that will bring us peace and happiness, here is Rule 1:

> Think and act cheerfully, and you will feel cheerful.

☐ **13** ☐

The high cost of getting even

One night, years ago, as I was travelling through Yellowstone Park, I sat with other tourists on bleachers facing a dense growth of pine and spruce. Presently the animal which we had been waiting to see, the terror of the forest, the grizzly bear, strode out into the glare of the lights and began devouring the garbage that had been dumped there from the kitchen of one of the park hotels. A forest ranger, Major Martindale, sat on a horse and talked to the excited tourists about bears. He told us that the grizzly bear can whip any other animal in the Western world, with the possible exception of the buffalo and the Kodiak bear; yet I noticed that night that there was one animal, and only one, that the grizzly permitted to come out of the forest and eat with him under the glare of the lights: a skunk. The grizzly knew that he could liquidate a skunk with one swipe of his mighty paw. Why didn't he do it? Because he had found from experience that it didn't pay.

I found that out, too. As a farm boy, I trapped four-legged skunks along the hedgerows in Missouri; and as a man, I encountered a few two-legged skunks on the sidewalks of New York. I have found from sad experience that it doesn't pay to stir up either variety.

When we hate our enemies, we are giving them power over us: power over our sleep, our appetites, our blood pressure, our health, and our happiness. Our enemies would dance with joy if only they knew how they were worrying us, lacerating us, and getting even with us! Our hate is not hurting them at all, but our hate is turning our own days and nights into a hellish turmoil.

Who do you suppose said this: 'If selfish people try to take advantage of you, cross them off your list, but don't try to get even. When you try to get even, you hurt yourself more than you hurt the other fellow'? ... Those words sound as if they might have been uttered by some starry-eyed idealist.

But they weren't. Those words appeared in a bulletin issued by the Police Department of Milwaukee.

How will trying to get even hurt you? In many ways. According to *Life* magazine, it may even wreck your health. 'The chief personality characteristic of persons with hypertension [high blood pressure] is resentment,' said *Life*. 'When resentment is chronic, chronic hypertension and heart trouble follow.'

So you see that when Jesus said, 'Love your enemies,' he was not only preaching sound ethics. He was also preaching twentieth-century medicine. When He said, 'Forgive seventy times seven,' Jesus was telling you and me how to keep from having high blood pressure, heart trouble, stomach ulcers, and many other ailments.

A friend of mine recently had a serious heart attack. Her physician put her to bed and ordered her to refuse to get angry about anything, no matter what happened. Physicians know that if you have a weak heart, a fit of anger *can* kill you. Did I say *can* kill you? A fit of anger *did* kill a restaurant owner, in Spokane, Washington, a few years ago. I have in front of me now a letter from Jerry Swartout, then chief of the police department, Spokane, Washington, saying: 'A few years ago, William Falkaber, a man of sixty-eight who owned a café here in Spokane, killed himself by flying into a rage because his cook insisted on drinking coffee out of his saucer. The café owner was so indignant that he grabbed a revolver and started to chase the cook and fell dead from heart failure – with his hand still gripping the gun. The coroner's report declared that anger had caused the heart failure.'

When Jesus said, 'Love your enemies,' He was also telling us how to improve our looks. I know people – and so do you – whose faces have been wrinkled and hardened by hate and disfigured by resentment. All the cosmetic surgery in Christendom won't improve their looks half so much as would a heart full of forgiveness, tenderness, and love.

Hatred destroys our ability to enjoy even our food. The Bible puts it this way: 'Better is a dinner of herbs where love is, than a stalled ox and hatred therewith.'

Wouldn't our enemies rub their hands with glee if they knew that our hate for them was exhausting us, making us tired and nervous, ruining our looks, giving us heart trouble, and probably shortening our lives?

Even if we can't love our enemies, let's at least love ourselves. Let's love ourselves so much that we won't permit our enemies to control our happiness, our health, and our looks. As Shakespeare put it:

Heat not a furnace for your foe so hot
That it do singe yourself.

When Jesus said that we should forgive our enemies 'seventy times seven', He was also preaching sound business. For example, I have before me as I write a letter I received from George Rona, of Uppsala, Sweden. For years,

George Rona was an attorney in Vienna; but during the Second World War, he fled to Sweden. He had no money, needed work badly. Since he could speak and write several languages, he hoped to get a position as correspondent for some firm engaged in importing or exporting. Most of the firms replied that they had no need of such services because of the war, but they would keep his name on file . . . and so on. One man, however, wrote George Rona a letter saying: 'What you imagine about my business is not true. You are both wrong and foolish. I do not need any correspondent. Even if I did need one, I wouldn't hire you because you can't even write good Swedish. Your letter is full of mistakes.'

When George Rona read that letter, he was as mad as Donald Duck. What did this Swede mean by telling him he couldn't write the language! Why, the letter that this Swede himself had written was full of mistakes! So George Rona wrote a letter that was calculated to burn this man up. Then he paused. He said to himself, 'Wait a minute, now. How do I know this man isn't right? I have studied Swedish, but it's not my native language, so maybe I do make mistakes I don't know anything about. If I do, then I certainly have to study harder if I ever hope to get a job. This man has possibly done me a favour, even though he didn't mean to. The mere fact that he expressed himself in disagreeable terms doesn't alter my debt to him. Therefore, I am going to write him and *thank* him for what he has done.'

So George Rona tore up the scorching letter he had already written, and wrote another that said: 'It was kind of you to go to the trouble of writing to me, especially when you do not need a correspondent. I am sorry I was mistaken about your firm. The reason that I wrote you was that I made inquiry and your name was given me as a leader in your field. I did not know I had made grammatical errors in my letter. I am sorry and ashamed of myself. I will now apply myself more diligently to the study of the Swedish language and try to correct my mistakes. I want to thank you for helping me get started on the road to self-improvement.'

Within a few days, George Rona got a letter from this man, asking Rona to come to see him. Rona went – and got a job. George Rona discovered for himself that 'a soft answer turneth away wrath'.

We may not be saintly enough to love our enemies, but, for the sake of our own health and happiness, let's at least forgive them and forget them. That is the smart thing to do. 'To be wronged or robbed,' said Confucius, 'is nothing unless you continue to remember it.' I once asked General Eisenhower's son, John, if his father ever nourished resentments. 'No,' he replied, 'Dad never wastes a minute thinking about people he doesn't like.'

There is an old saying that a man is a fool who can't be angry, but a man is wise who won't be angry.

That was the policy of William J. Gaynor, a former Mayor of New York. Bitterly denounced by the press, he was shot by a maniac and almost killed. As he lay in the hospital, fighting for his life, he said: 'Every night, I forgive everything and everybody.' Is that too idealistic? Too much sweetness and light? If so, let's turn for counsel to the great German philosopher, Schopenhauer, author of *Studies in Pessimism*. He regarded life as a futile and painful adventure. Gloom dripped from him as he walked; yet out of the depths of his despair, Schopenhauer cried: 'If possible, no animosity should be felt for anyone.'

I once asked Bernard Baruch – the man who was the trusted adviser to six Presidents: Wilson, Harding, Coolidge, Hoover, Roosevelt, and Truman – whether he was ever disturbed by the attacks of his enemies. 'No man can humiliate me or disturb me,' he replied. 'I won't let him.'

No one can humiliate or disturb you and me, either – *unless we let him.*

> Sticks and stones may break my bones,
> But words can never hurt me.

Throughout the ages, mankind has burned its candles before those Christlike individuals who bore no malice against their enemies. I have often stood in the Jasper National Park, in Canada, and gazed upon one of the most beautiful mountains in the Western world – a mountain named in honour of Edith Cavell, the British nurse who went to her death like a saint before a German firing squad on October 12, 1915. Her crime? She had hidden and fed and nursed wounded French and English soldiers in her Belgian home, and had helped them escape into Holland. As the English chaplain entered her cell in the military prison in Brussels that October morning to prepare her for death. Edith Cavell uttered two sentences that have been preserved in bronze and granite: 'I realize that patriotism is not enough. I must have no hatred or bitterness toward anyone.' Four years later, her body was removed to England and memorial services were held in Westminster Abbey. I once spent a year in London; I have often stood before the statue of Edith Cavell opposite the National Portrait Gallery and read her immortal words carved in granite: 'I realize that patriotism is not enough. I must have no hatred or bitterness toward anyone.'

One sure way to forgive and forget our enemies is to become absorbed in some cause infinitely bigger than ourselves. Then the insults and the enmities we encounter won't matter because we will be oblivious of everything but our *cause*. As an example, let's take an intensely dramatic event that was about to take place in the pine woods of Mississippi back in 1918. A lynching! Laurence Jones, a black teacher and preacher, was about to be lynched. Some years ago, I visited the school that Laurence Jones founded – the Piney Woods Country School – and I spoke before the student body. That school is nationally known today, but the incident I am going to relate occurred long before that. It occurred back in the highly emotional days of the First World War. A rumour had spread through central Mississippi that the Germans were arousing the blacks and inciting them to rebellion. Laurence Jones, the man who was about to be lynched, was, as I have already said, a black himself and was accused of helping to arouse his race to insurrection. A group of white men – pausing outside the church – had heard Laurence Jones shouting to his congregation: 'Life is a battle in which every black must gird on his *armour* and *fight* to survive and succeed.'

'Fight!' 'Armour!' Enough! Galloping off into the night, these excited young men recruited a mob, returned to the church, put a rope around the preacher, dragged him for a mile up the road, stood him on a heap of kindling, lighted matches, and were ready to hang him and burn him at the same time, when someone shouted: 'Let's make the blankety-blank-blank talk before he burns. Speech! Speech!' Laurence Jones, standing on the kindling, spoke with a rope around his neck, spoke for his life and his *cause*. He had been graduated from the University of Iowa in 1907. His sterling character, his scholarship, and his musical ability had made him popular with both the students and the faculty. Upon graduation, he had turned down the offer of a hotel man to set him up in business, and had turned down the offer of a wealthy man to finance his musical education. Why? Because he was on fire with a vision. Reading the story of Booker T. Washington's life, he had been inspired to devote his own life to educating the poverty-stricken, illiterate members of his race. So he went to the most backward belt he could find in the South – a spot twenty-five miles south of Jackson, Mississippi. Pawning his watch for $1.65, he started his school in the open woods with a stump for a desk. Laurence Jones told those angry men who were waiting to lynch him of the struggle he had had to educate these unschooled boys and girls and to train them to be good farmers, mechanics, cooks, housekeepers. He told of the white men who had helped him in his struggle to establish Piney Woods Country School – white men who had given him land, lumber, and pigs, cows and money, to help him carry on his educational work.

When Laurence Jones was asked afterward if he didn't hate the men who had dragged him up the road to hang him and burn him, he replied that he was *too busy with his cause* to hate – too *absorbed in something bigger than himself*. '*I have no time to quarrel*', he said, '*no time for regrets, and no man can force me to stoop low enough to hate him.*'

As Laurence Jones talked with sincere and moving eloquence, as he pleaded, not for himself, but his cause, the mob began to soften. Finally, an old Confederate veteran in the crowd said: 'I believe this boy is telling the truth. I know the white men whose names he has mentioned. He is doing a fine work. We have made a mistake. We ought to help him instead of hang him.' The Confederate veteran passed his hat through the crowd and raised a gift of fifty-two dollars and forty cents from the very men who had gathered there to hang the founder of Piney Woods Country School – the man who said: 'I have no time to quarrel, no time for regrets, and no man can force me to stoop low enough to hate him.'

Epictetus pointed out nineteen centuries ago that we reap what we sow and that somehow fate almost always makes us pay for our malefactions. 'In the long run,' said Epictetus, 'every man will pay the penalty for his own misdeeds. The man who remembers this will be angry with no one, indignant with no one, revile no one, blame no one, offend no one, hate no one.'

Probably no other man in American history was ever more denounced and hated and double-crossed than Lincoln. Yet Lincoln, according to Herndon's classic biography, 'never judged men by his like or dislike for them. If any given act was to be performed, he could understand that his enemy could do it just as well as anyone. If a man had maligned him or been guilty of personal ill-treatment, and was the fittest man for the place, Lincoln would give him that place, just as soon as he would give it to a friend . . . I do not think he ever removed a man because he was his enemy or because he disliked him.'

Lincoln was denounced and insulted by some of the very men he had appointed to positions of high power – men like McClellan, Seward, Stanton, and Chase. Yet Lincoln believed, according to Herndon, his law partner, that 'No man was to be eulogized for what he did; or censured for what he did or did not do,' because 'all of us are the children of conditions, of circumstances, of environment, of education, of acquired habits and of heredity molding men as they are and will forever be.'

Perhaps Lincoln was right. If you and I had inherited the same physical, mental, and emotional characteristics that our enemies have inherited, and if life had done to us what it has done to them, we would act exactly as they do. We couldn't possibly do anything else. Let's be charitable enough to repeat the prayer of the Sioux Indians: 'O Great Spirit, keep me from ever judging and criticizing a man until I have walked in his moccasins for two weeks.' So instead of hating our enemies, let's pity them and thank God that life has not made us what they are. Instead of heaping condemnation and revenge upon our enemies, let's give them our understanding, our sympathy, our help, our forgiveness, and our prayers.

I was brought up in a family which read the Scriptures or repeated a verse from the Bible each night and then knelt down and said 'family prayers'. I can still hear my father, in a lonely Missouri farmhouse, repeating these words of Jesus – words that will continue to be repeated as long as man cherishes his ideals: 'Love your enemies, bless them that curse you, do good to them that hate you, and pray for them which despitefully use you, and persecute you.'

My father tried to live those words of Jesus; and they gave him an inner peace that the captains and the kings of earth have often sought for in vain.

To cultivate a mental attitude that will bring you peace and happiness, remember that Rule 2 is:

Let's never try to get even with our enemies, because if
we do we will hurt ourselves far more than we hurt them.
Let's do as General Eisenhower does: let's never waste a
minute thinking about people we don't like.

□ **14** □

If you do this, you will never worry about ingratitude

I recently met a businessman in Texas who was burned up with indignation. I was warned that he would tell me about it within fifteen minutes after I met him. He did. The incident he was angry about had occurred eleven months previously, but he was still burned up about it. He couldn't talk of anything else. He had given his thirty-four employees ten thousand dollars in Christmas bonuses – approximately three hundred dollars each – and no one had thanked him. 'I am sorry,' he complained bitterly, 'that I ever gave them a penny!'

'An angry man,' said Confucius, 'is always full of poison.' This man was so full of poison that I honestly pitied him. He was about sixty years old. Now, life-insurance companies figure that, on the average, we will live slightly more than two thirds of the difference between our present age and eighty. So this man – if he was lucky – probably had about fourteen or fifteen years to live. Yet he had already wasted almost one of his few remaining years by his bitterness and resentment over an event that was past and gone. I pitied him.

Instead of wallowing in resentment and self-pity, he might have asked himself *why* he didn't get any appreciation. Maybe he had underpaid and overworked his employees. Maybe they considered a Christmas bonus not a gift, but something they had earned. Maybe he was so critical and unapproachable that no one dared or cared to thank him. Maybe they felt he gave the bonus because most of the profits were going for taxes, anyway.

On the other hand, maybe the employees were selfish, mean, and ill-mannered. Maybe this. Maybe that. I don't know any more about it than you do. But I do know that Dr. Samuel Johnson said: 'Gratitude is a fruit of great cultivation. You do not find it among gross people.'

Here is the point I am trying to make: *this man made the human and distressing mistake of expecting gratitude.* He just didn't know human nature.

If you saved a man's life, would you expect him to be grateful? You might – but Samuel Leibowitz, who was a famous criminal lawyer before he became a judge, saved *seventy-eight* men from going to the electric chair! How many of these men, do you suppose, stopped to thank Samuel Leibowitz, or ever took the trouble to send him a Christmas card? How many? Guess. . . . That's right – none.

Christ helped ten lepers in one afternoon – but how many of those lepers even stopped to thank Him? Only one. Look it up in Saint Luke. When Christ turned around to His disciples and asked, 'Where are the other nine?' they had all run away. Disappeared without thanks! Let me ask you a question: Why should you and I – or this businessman in Texas – expect more thanks for *our* small favours than was given Jesus Christ?

And when it comes to money matters! Well, that is even more hopeless. Charles Schwab told me that he had once saved a bank cashier who had speculated in the stock market with funds belonging to the bank. Schwab put up the money to save this man from going to the penitentiary. Was the cashier grateful? Oh, yes, for a little while. Then he turned against Schwab and reviled him and denounced him – the very man who had kept him out of jail!

If you gave one of your relatives a million dollars, would you expect him to be grateful? Andrew Carnegie did just that. But if Andrew Carnegie had come back from the grave a little while later, he would have been shocked to find this relative cursing him! Why? Because Old Andy had left 365 million dollars to public charities – and had 'cut him off with one measly million', as he put it.

That's how it goes. Human nature has always been human nature – and it probably won't change in your lifetime. So why not accept it? Why not be as realistic about it as was old Marcus Aurelius, one of the wisest men who ever ruled the Roman Empire. He wrote in his diary one day: 'I am going to meet people today who talk too much – people who are selfish, egotistical, ungrateful. But I won't be surprised or disturbed, for I couldn't imagine a world without such people.'

That makes sense, doesn't it? If you and I go around grumbling about ingratitude, who is to blame? Is it human nature – or is it our ignorance of human nature? Let's not expect gratitude. Then, if we get some occasionally, it will come as a delightful surprise. If we don't get it, we won't be disturbed.

Here is the first point I am trying to make in this chapter: *It is natural for people to forget to be grateful; so, if we go around expecting gratitude, we are headed straight for a lot of heartaches.*

I know a woman in New York who is always complaining because she is lonely. Not one of her relatives wants to go near her – and no wonder. If you visit her she will tell you for hours what she did for her nieces when they were children: she nursed them through the measles and the mumps and the whooping cough; she boarded them for years; she helped to send one of them through business school, and she made a home for the other until she got married.

Do the nieces come to see her? Oh, yes, now and then, out of a spirit of duty. But they dread these visits. They know they will have to sit and listen for hours to half-veiled reproaches. They will be treated to an endless litany of bitter complaints and self-pitying sighs. And when this woman can no longer bludgeon, browbeat, or bully her nieces into coming to see her, she has one of her 'spells'. She develops a heart attack.

Is the heart attack real? Oh, yes. The doctors say she has 'a nervous heart', suffers from palpitations. But the doctors also say they can do nothing for her – her trouble is emotional.

What this woman really wants is love and attention. But she calls it 'gratitude'. And she will never get gratitude or love, because she demands it. She thinks it's her due.

There are thousands of people like her, people who are ill from 'ingratitude', loneliness, and neglect. They long to be loved; but the only way in this world that they can ever hope to be loved is to stop asking for it and to start pouring out love without hope of return.

Does that sound like sheer, impractical, visionary idealism? It isn't. It is just horse sense. It is a good way for you and me to find the happiness we long for. I know. I have seen it happen right in my own family. My own mother and father gave for the joy of helping others. We were poor – always overwhelmed by debts. Yet, poor as we were, my father and mother always managed to send money every year to an orphans' home, The Christian Home in Council Bluffs, Iowa. Mother and Father never visited that home. Probably no one thanked them for their gifts – except by letter – but they were richly repaid, for they had the joy of helping little children – without wishing for or expecting any gratitude in return.

After I left home, I would always send Father and Mother a cheque at Christmas and urge them to indulge in a few luxuries for themselves. But they rarely did. When I came home a few days before Christmas, Father would tell me of the coal and groceries they had bought for some 'widder woman' in town who had a lot of children and no money to buy food and fuel. What joy they got out of these gifts – the joy of giving without expecting anything whatever in return!

I believe my father would almost have qualified for Aristotle's description of the ideal man – the man most worthy of being happy. 'The ideal man,' said Aristotle, 'takes joy in doing favours for others.'

Here is the second point I am trying to make in this chapter: *If we want to find happiness, let's stop thinking about gratitude or ingratitude and give for the inner joy of giving.*

Parents have been tearing their hair about the ingratitude of children for ten thousand years.

Even Shakespeare's King Lear cried out, 'How sharper than a serpent's tooth it is to have a thankless child!'

But why should children be thankful – unless we train them to be? Ingratitude is natural – like weeds. Gratitude is like a rose. It has to be fed and watered and cultivated and loved and protected.

If our children are ungrateful, who is to blame? Maybe we are. If we have never taught them to express gratitude to others, how can we expect them to be grateful to us?

I knew a man in Chicago who had cause to complain of the ingratitude of his stepsons. He slaved in a box factory, seldom earning more than forty dollars a week. He married a widow, and she persuaded him to borrow money and send her two grown sons to college. Out of his salary of forty dollars a week, he had to pay for food, rent, fuel, clothes, and also for the payments on his notes. He did this for four years, working like a coolie, and never complaining.

Did he get any thanks? No; his wife took it all for granted – and so did her sons. They never imagined that they owed their stepfather anything – not even thanks!

Who was to blame? The boys? Yes; but the mother was even more to blame. She thought it was a shame to burden their young lives with a 'sense of obligation'. She didn't want her sons to 'start out under debt'. So she never dreamed of saying: 'What a prince your stepfather is to help you through college!' Instead, she took the attitude: 'Oh, that's the least he can do.'

She thought she was sparing her sons, but, in reality, she was sending them out into life with the dangerous idea that the world owed them a living. And it *was* a dangerous idea – for one of those sons tried to 'borrow' from an employer, and ended up in jail!

We must remember that our children are very much what we make them. For example, my mother's sister – Viola Alexander, of Minneapolis – is a shining example of a woman who has never had cause to complain about the 'ingratitude' of children. When I was a boy, Aunt Viola took her own mother into her home to love and take care of; and she did the same thing for her husband's mother. I can still close my eyes and see those two old ladies sitting before the fire in Aunt Viola's farmhouse. Were they any 'trouble' to Aunt Viola? Oh, often I suppose. But you would never have guessed it from her attitude. She *loved* those old ladies – so she pampered them, and spoiled them, and made them feel at home. In addition, Aunt Viola had six children of her own; but it never occurred to her that she was doing anything especially noble, or deserved any halos for taking these old ladies into her home. To her, it was the natural thing, the right thing, the thing she wanted to do.

Where is Aunt Viola today? Well, she has now been a widow for twenty-odd years, and she has five grown-up children – five separate households – all clamouring to share her, and to have her come and live in their homes! Her children adore her; they never get enough of her. Out of 'gratitude'? Nonsense! It is love – *sheer love*. Those children breathed in warmth and radiant human-kindness all during their childhoods. Is it any wonder that, now that the situation is reversed, they *give back* love?

So let us remember that to raise grateful children, we have to *be* grateful. Let us remember 'little pitchers have big ears' – and watch what we say. To illustrate – the next time we are tempted to belittle someone's kindness in the presence of our children, let's stop. Let's never say: 'Look at these dishcloths Cousin Sue sent for Christmas. She knit them herself. They didn't cost her a cent!' The remark may seem trivial to us – but the children are listening. So, instead, we had better say: 'Look at the hours Cousin Sue spent making these for Christmas! Isn't she nice? Let's write her a thank-you note right now.' And our children may unconsciously absorb the habit of praise and appreciation.

To avoid resentment and worry over ingratitude, here is Rule 3:

A. Instead of worrying about ingratitude, let's expect it. Let's remember that Jesus healed ten lepers in one day – and only one thanked Him. Why should we expect more gratitude than Jesus got?

B. Let's remember that the only way to find happiness is not to expect gratitude, but to give for the joy of giving.

C. Let's remember that gratitude is a 'cultivated' trait; so if we want our children to be grateful, we must train them to be grateful.

☐ 15 ☐

Would you take a million dollars for what you have?

I have known Harold Abbott for years. He lived in Webb City, Missouri. He used to be my lecture manager. One day he and I met in Kansas City and he drove me down to my farm at Belton, Missouri. During that drive, I asked him how he kept from worrying; and he told me an inspiring story that I shall never forget.

'I used to worry a lot,' he said, 'but one spring day in 1934, I was walking down West Dougherty Street in Webb City when I saw a sight that banished all my worries. It all happened in ten seconds, but during those ten seconds I learned more about how to live than I had learned in the previous ten years. For two years I had been running a grocery store in Webb City,' Harold Abbott said, as he told me the story. 'I had not only lost all my savings, but I had incurred debts that took me seven years to pay back. My grocery store had been closed the previous Saturday; and now I was going to the Merchants and Miners Bank to borrow money so I could go to Kansas City to look for a job. I walked like a beaten man. I had lost all my fight and faith. Then suddenly I saw coming down the street a man who had no legs. He was sitting on a little wooden platform equipped with wheels from roller skates. He propelled himself along the street with a block of wood in each hand. I met him just after he had crossed the street and was starting to lift himself up a few inches over the curb to the sidewalk. As he tilted his little wooden platform to an angle, his eyes met mine. He greeted me with a grand smile. "Good morning, sir. It is a fine morning, isn't it?" he said with spirit. As I stood looking at him, I realized how rich I was. I had two legs. I could walk. I felt ashamed of my self-pity. I said to myself if he can be happy, cheerful, and confident without legs, I certainly can with legs. I could already feel my chest lifting. I had intended to ask the Merchants and Miners Bank for only one hundred dollars. But now I had courage to ask for *two* hundred. I had intended to say that I wanted to go to Kansas City to *try* to get a job. But now I announced confidently that I wanted to go to Kansas City to *get* a job. I got the loan; and I got the job.

'I now have the following words pasted on my bathroom mirror, and I read them every morning as I shave:

I had the blues because I had no shoes,
Until upon the street, I met a man who had no feet.

I once asked Eddie Rickenbacker what was the biggest lesson he had learned from drifting about with his companions in life rafts for twenty-one days, hopelessly lost in the Pacific. 'The biggest lesson I learned from that experience,' he said, 'was that if you have all the fresh water you want to drink and all the food you want to eat, you ought never to complain about anything.'

Time ran an article about a sergeant who had been wounded on Guadalcanal. Hit in the throat by a shell fragment, this sergeant had had seven blood transfusions. Writing a note to his doctor, he asked: 'Will I live?' The doctor replied: 'Yes.' He wrote another note, asking: 'Will I be able to talk?' Again the answer was yes. He then wrote another note, saying: *'Then what in the hell am I worrying about?'*

Why don't you stop right now and ask yourself: 'What in the hell am I worrying about?' You will probably find that it is comparatively unimportant and insignificant.

About ninety percent of the things in our lives are right and about ten percent are wrong. If we want to be happy, all we have to do is to concentrate on the ninety percent that are right and ignore the ten percent that are wrong. If we want to be worried and bitter and have stomach ulcers, all we have to do is to concentrate on the ten percent that are wrong and ignore the ninety percent that are glorious.

The words 'Think and Thank' are inscribed in many of the Cromwellian churches of England. These words ought to be inscribed on our hearts, too: 'Think and Thank.' Think of all we have to be grateful for, and thank God for all our boons and bounties.

Jonathan Swift, author of *Gulliver's Travels*, was the most devastating pessimist in English literature. He was so sorry that he had been born that he wore black and fasted on his birthdays; yet, in his despair, this supreme pessimist of English literature praised the great health-giving powers of cheerfulness and happiness. 'The best doctors in the world,' he declared, 'are Doctor Diet, Doctor Quiet, and Doctor Merryman.'

You and I may have the services of 'Doctor Merryman' free every hour of the day by keeping our attention fixed on all the incredible riches we possess – riches exceeding by far the fabled treasures of Ali Baba. Would you sell both your eyes for a billion dollars? What would you take for your two legs? Your hands? Your hearing? Your children? Your family? Add up your assets, and you will find that you won't sell what you have for all the gold ever amassed by the Rockefellers, the Fords and the Morgans combined.

But do we appreciate all this? Ah, no. As Schopenhauer said: 'We seldom think of what we have but always of what we lack.' Yes, the tendency to 'seldom think of what we have but always of what we lack' is the greatest tragedy on earth. It has probably caused more misery than all the wars and diseases in history.

It caused John Palmer to turn 'from a regular guy into an old grouch,' and almost wrecked his home. I know because he told me so.

Mr. Palmer lives in Paterson, New Jersey. 'Shortly after I returned from the Army,' he said, 'I started in business for myself. I worked hard day and night. Things were going nicely. Then trouble started. I couldn't get parts and materials. I was afraid I would have to give up my business. I worried so much that I changed from a regular guy into an old grouch. I became so sour and cross that – well, I didn't know it then; but I now realize that I came very near to losing my happy home. Then one day a young, disabled veteran who works for me said, "Johnny, you ought to be ashamed of yourself. You take on as if you were the only person in the world with troubles. Suppose you do have to shut up shop for a while – so what? You can start up again when things get normal. You've got a lot to be thankful for. Yet you are always growling. Boy, how I wish I were in your shoes! Look at me. I've got only one arm, and half of my face is shot away, and yet I am not complaining: If you don't stop your growling and grumbling, you will lose not only your business, but also your health, your home, and your friends!"

'Those remarks stopped me dead in my tracks. They made me realize how well off I was. I resolved then and there that I would change and be my old self again – and I did.'

A friend of mine, Lucile Blake, had to tremble on the edge of tragedy before she learned to be happy about what she had instead of worrying over what she lacked.

I met Lucile years ago, when we were both studying short-story writing in the Columbia University School of Journalism. Some years ago, she got the shock of her life. She was living then in Tucson, Arizona. She had – well, here is the story as she told it to me:

'I had been living in a whirl: studying the organ at the University of Arizona, conducting a speech clinic in town, and teaching a class in musical appreciation at the Desert Willow Ranch, where I was staying. I was going in for parties, dances, horseback rides under the stars. One morning I collapsed. My heart! "You will have to lie in bed for a year of complete rest," the doctor said. He didn't encourage me to believe I would ever be strong again.

'In bed for a year! To be an invalid – perhaps to die! I was terror-stricken! Why did all this have to happen to me? What had I done to deserve it? I wept and wailed. I was bitter and rebellious. But I did go to bed as the doctor advised. A neighbour of mine, Mr. Rudolf, an artist, said to me, "You think now that spending a year in bed will be a tragedy. But it won't be. You will have time to think and get acquainted with yourself. You will make more spiritual growth in these next few months than you have made during all your previous life." I became calmer, and tried to develop a new sense of values. I read books of inspiration. One day I heard a radio commentator say: "You can express only what is in your own consciousness." I had heard words like these many times before, but now they reached down inside me and took root. I resolved to think only the thoughts I wanted to live by: thoughts of joy, happiness, health. I forced myself each morning, as soon as I awoke, to go over all the things I had to be grateful for. No pain. A lovely young daughter. My eyesight. My hearing. Lovely music on the radio. Time to read. Good food. Good friends. I was so cheerful and had so many visitors that the doctor put up a sign saying that only one visitor at a time would be allowed in my cabin – and only at certain hours.

'Many years have passed since then, and I now lead a full, active life. I am deeply grateful now for that year I spent in bed. It was the most valuable and the happiest year I spent in Arizona. The habit I formed then of counting my blessings each morning still remains with me. It is one of my most precious possessions. I am ashamed to realize that I never really learned to live until I feared I was going to die.'

My dear Lucile Blake, you may not realize it, but you learned the same lesson that Dr. Samuel Johnson learned two hundred years ago. 'The habit of looking on the best side of every event,' said Dr. Johnson, 'is worth more than a thousand pounds a year.'

Those words were uttered, mind you, not by a professional optimist, but by a man who had known anxiety, rags, and hunger for twenty years – and finally became one of the most eminent writers of his generation and the most celebrated conversationalist of all time.

Logan Pearsall Smith packed a lot of wisdom into a few words when he said: 'There are two things to aim at in life: first, to get what you want; and, after that, to enjoy it. Only the wisest of mankind achieve the second.'

Would you like to know how to make even dishwashing at the kitchen sink a thrilling experience? If so, read an inspiring book of incredible courage by Borghild Dahl. It is called *I Wanted to See.*

This book was written by a woman who was practically blind for half a century. 'I had only one eye,' she writes, 'and it was so covered with dense scars that I had to do all my seeing through one small opening in the left of the eye. I could see a book only by holding it up close to my face and by straining my one eye as hard as I could to the left.'

But she refused to be pitied, refused to be considered 'different'. As a child, she wanted to play hopscotch with other children, but she couldn't see the markings. So after the other children had gone home, she got down on the ground and crawled along with her eyes near to the marks. She memorized every bit of the ground where she and her friends played and soon became an expert at running games. She did her reading at home, holding a book of large print so close to her eyes that her eyelashes brushed the pages. She earned two college degrees: an A.B. from the University of Minnesota and a Master of Arts from Columbia University.

She started teaching in the tiny village of Twin Valley, Minnesota, and rose until she became professor of journalism and literature at Augustana College in Sioux Falls, South Dakota. She taught there for thirteen years, lecturing before women's clubs and giving radio talks about books and authors. 'In the back of my mind,' she writes, 'there had always lurked a fear of total blindness. In order to overcome this, I had adopted a cheerful, almost hilarious, attitude toward life.'

Then in 1943, when she was fifty-two years old, a miracle happened: an operation at the famous Mayo Clinic. She could now see forty times as well as she had ever been able to see before.

A new and exciting world of loveliness opened before her. She now found it thrilling even to wash dishes in the kitchen sink. 'I begin to play with the white fluffy suds in the dishpan,' she writes. 'I dip my hands into them and I pick up a ball of tiny soap bubbles. I hold them up against the light, and in each of them I can see the brilliant colours of a miniature rainbow.'

As she looked through the window above the kitchen sink, she saw 'the flapping grey-black wings of the sparrows flying through the thick, falling snow.'

She found such ecstasy looking at the soap bubbles and sparrows that she closed her book with these words: ' "Dear Lord," I whisper, "Our Father in Heaven, I thank Thee. I thank Thee." '

Imagine thanking God because you can wash dishes and see rainbows in bubbles and sparrows flying through the snow!

You and I ought to be ashamed of ourselves. All the days of our years we have been living in a fairyland of beauty, but we have been too blind to see, too satiated to enjoy.

If we want to stop worrying and start living, Rule 4 is:

> Count your blessings – not your troubles!

☐ 16 ☐

Find yourself and be yourself: remember there is no one else on earth like you

I have a letter from Mrs. Edith Allred, of Mount Airy, North Carolina: 'As a child, I was extremely sensitive and shy,' she says in her letter. 'I was always overweight and my cheeks made me look even fatter than I was. I had an old-fashioned mother who thought it was foolish to make clothes look pretty. She always said: "Wide will wear while narrow will tear"; and she dressed me accordingly. I never went to parties; never had any fun; and when I went to school, I never joined the other children in outside activities, not even athletics. I was morbidly shy. I felt I was "different" from everybody else, and entirely undesirable.

'When I grew up, I married a man who was several years my senior. But I didn't change. My in-laws were a poised and self-confident family. They were everything I should have been but simply was not. I tried my best to be like them, but I couldn't. Every attempt they made to draw me out of myself only drove me further into my shell. I became nervous and irritable. I avoided all friends. I got so bad I even dreaded the sound of the doorbell ringing! I was a failure. I knew it; and I was afraid my husband would find it out. So, whenever we were in public, I tried to be gay, and overacted my part. I knew I overacted; and I would be miserable for days afterwards. At last I became so unhappy that I could see no point in prolonging my existence. I began to think of suicide.'

What happened to change this unhappy woman's life? Just a chance remark!

'A chance remark,' Mrs. Allred continued, 'transformed my whole life. My mother-in-law was talking one day of how she brought her children up, and she said, "No matter what happened, I always insisted on their being themselves." . . . "On being themselves." . . . That remark is what did it! In a flash, I realized I had brought all this misery on myself by trying to fit myself into a pattern to which I did not conform.

'I changed overnight! I started being myself. I tried to make a study of my own personality. Tried to find out *what I was*. I studied my strong points. I learned all I could about colours and styles, and dressed in a way that I felt was becoming to me. I reached out to make friends. I joined an organization – a small one at first – and was petrified with fright when they put me on a programme. But each time I spoke, I gained a little courage. It took a long while – but today I have more happiness than I ever dreamed possible. In rearing my own children, I have always taught them the lesson I had to learn from such bitter experience: *No matter what happens, always be yourself!*'

This problem of being willing to be yourself is 'as old as history', says Dr. James Gordon Gilkey, 'and as universal as human life.' This problem of being unwilling to be yourself is the hidden spring behind many neuroses and psychoses and complexes. Angelo Patri has written thirteen books and thousands of syndicated newspaper articles on the subject of child training, and he says: 'Nobody is so miserable as he who longs to be somebody and something other than the person he is in body and mind.'

This craving to be something you are not is especially rampant in Hollywood. Sam Wood, one of Hollywood's best-known directors, said the greatest headache he has with aspiring young actors is exactly this problem: to make them be themselves. They all want to be second-rate Lana Turners or third-rate Clark Gables. 'The public has already had that flavour,' Sam Wood keeps telling them; 'now it wants something else.'

Before he started directing such pictures as *Goodbye, Mr. Chips* and *For Whom the Bell Tolls*, Sam Wood spent years in the real-estate business, developing sales personalities. He declares that the same principles apply in the business world as in the world of moving pictures. You won't get anywhere playing the ape. You can't be a parrot. 'Experience has taught me,' says Sam Wood, 'that it is safest to drop, as quickly as possible, people who pretend to be what they aren't.'

I asked Paul Boynton, then employment director for a major oil company, what is the biggest mistake people make in applying for jobs. He ought to know: he has interviewed more than sixty thousand job seekers; and he has written a book entitled *6 Ways to Get a Job*. He replied: 'The biggest mistake people make in applying for jobs is in not being themselves. Instead of taking their hair down and being completely frank, they often try to give you the answers they think you want.' But it doesn't work, because nobody wants a phony. Nobody ever wants a counterfeit coin.

A certain daughter of a streetcar conductor had to learn that lesson the hard way. She longed to be a singer. But her face was her misfortune. She had a large mouth and protruding buck teeth. When she first sang in public – in a New Jersey night club – she tried to pull down her upper lip to cover her teeth. She tried to act 'glamorous'. The results? She made herself ridiculous. She was headed for failure.

However, there was a man in this night club who heard the girl sing and thought she had talent. 'See here,' he said bluntly, 'I've been watching your performance and I know what it is you're trying to hide. You're ashamed of your teeth!' The girl was embarrassed, but the man continued, 'What of it? Is there any particular crime in having buck teeth? Don't try to hide them! Open your mouth, and the audience will love you when they see you're not ashamed. Besides,' he said shrewdly, 'those teeth you're trying to hide may make your fortune!'

Cass Daley took his advice and forgot about her teeth. *From that time on*, she thought only about her audience. She opened her mouth wide and sang with such gusto and enjoyment that she became a top star in movies and radio. Other comedians tried to copy *her*!

The renowned William James was speaking of people who had never found themselves when he declared that the average person develops only ten percent of his or her latent mental abilities. 'Compared to what we ought to be,' he wrote, 'we are only half awake. We are making use of only a small part of our physical and mental resources. Stating the thing broadly, human individuals thus live far within their limits. They possess powers of various sorts which they habitually fail to use.'

You and I have such abilities, so let's not waste a second worrying because we are not like other people. You are something new in this world. Never before, since the beginning of time, has there ever been anybody exactly like you; and never again throughout all the ages to come will there ever be anybody exactly like you again. The science of genetics informs us that you are what you are largely as a result of twenty-four chromosomes contributed by your father and twenty-four chromosomes contributed by your mother. These forty-eight chromosomes comprise everything that determines what you inherit. In each chromosome there may be, says Amram Scheinfeld, 'anywhere from scores to hundreds of genes – with a single gene, in some cases, able to change the whole life of an individual.' Truly, we are 'fearfully and wonderfully' made.

Even after your mother and father met and mated, there was only one chance in 300,000 billion that the person who is specifically you would be born! In other words, if you had 300,000 billion brothers and sisters, they might have all been different from you. Is all this guesswork? No. It is a scientific fact. If you would like to read more about it, consult *You and Heredity*, by Amram Scheinfeld.

I can talk with conviction about this subject of being yourself because I feel deeply about it. I know what I am talking about. I know from bitter and costly experience. To illustrate: when I first came to New York from the cornfields of Missouri, I enrolled in the American Academy of Dramatic Arts. I aspired to be an actor. I had what I thought was a brilliant idea, a shortcut to success, an idea so simple, so foolproof, that I couldn't understand why thousands of ambitious people hadn't already discovered it. It was this: I would study how the famous actors of that day – John Drew, Walter Hampden, and Otis Skinner – got their effects. Then I would imitate the best points of each one of them and make myself into a shining, triumphant combination of all of them. How silly! How absurd! I had to waste years of my life imitating other people before it penetrated through my thick Missouri skull that I had to be myself, and that I couldn't possibly be anyone else.

That distressing experience ought to have taught me a lasting lesson. But it didn't. Not me. I was too dumb. I had to learn it all over again. Several years later, I set out to write what I hoped would be the best book on public speaking for businessmen that had ever been written. I had the same foolish idea about writing this book that I had formerly had about acting: I was going to *borrow* the ideas of a lot of other writers and put them all in one book – a book that would have everything. So I got scores of books on public speaking and spent a year incorporating their ideas into my manuscript. But it finally dawned on me once again that I was playing the fool. This hodgepodge of other men's ideas that I had written was so synthetic, so dull, that no businessman would ever plod through it. So I tossed a year's work into the wastebasket, and started all over again. This time I said to myself: 'You've got to be Dale Carnegie, with all his faults and limitations. You can't possibly be anybody else.' So I quit trying to be a combination of other men, and rolled up my sleeves and did what I should have done in the first place: I wrote a textbook on public speaking out of my own experiences, observations, and convictions as a speaker and a teacher of speaking. I learned – for all time, I hope – the lesson that Sir Walter Raleigh learned. (I am *not* talking about the Sir Walter who threw his coat in the mud for the Queen to step on. I am talking about the Sir Walter Raleigh who was professor of English literature at Oxford back in 1904.) 'I can't write a book commensurate with Shakespeare,' he said, 'but I can write a book by me.'

Be yourself. Act on the sage advice that Irving Berlin gave the late George Gershwin. When Berlin and Gershwin first met, Berlin was famous but Gershwin was a struggling young composer working for thirty-five dollars a week in Tin Pan Alley. Berlin, impressed by Gershwin's ability, offered Gershwin a job as his musical secretary at almost three times the salary he was then getting. 'But don't take the job,' Berlin advised. 'If you do, you may develop into a second-rate Berlin. But if you insist on being yourself, someday you'll become a first-rate Gershwin.'

Gershwin heeded that warning and slowly transformed himself into one of the significant American composers of his generation.

Charlie Chaplin, Will Rogers, Mary Margaret McBride, Gene Autry, and millions of others had to learn the lesson I am trying to hammer home in this chapter. They had to learn the hard way – just as I did.

When Charlie Chaplin first started making films, the director of the pictures insisted on Chaplin's imitating a popular German comedian of that day. Charlie Chaplin got nowhere until he acted himself. Bob Hope had a similar experience: spent years in a singing-and-dancing act – and got nowhere until he began to wisecrack and be himself. Will Rogers twirled a rope in vaudeville for years without saying a word. He got nowhere until he discovered his unique gift for humour and began to talk as he twirled his rope.

When Mary Margaret McBride first went on the air, she tried to be an Irish comedian and failed. When she tried to be just what she was – a plain country girl from Missouri – she became one of the most popular radio stars in New York.

When Gene Autry tried to get rid of his Texas accent and dressed like city boys and claimed he was from New York, people merely laughed behind his back. But when he started twanging his banjo and singing cowboy ballads, Gene Autry started out on a career that made him the world's most popular cowboy both in pictures and on the radio.

You are something new in this world. Be glad of it. Make the most of what nature gave you. In the last analysis, all art is autobiographical. You can sing only what you are. You can paint only what you are. You must be what your experiences, your environment, and your heredity have made you. For better or for worse, you must cultivate your own little garden. For better or for worse, you must play your own little instrument in the orchestra of life.

As Emerson said in his essay on 'Self-Reliance': 'There is a time in every man's education when he arrives at the conviction that envy is ignorance; that imitation is suicide; that he must take himself for better, for worse, as his portion; that though the wide universe is full of good, no kernel of nourishing corn can come to him but through his toil bestowed on that plot of ground which is given him to till. The power which resides in him is new in nature, and none but he knows what that is which he can do, nor does he know until he has tried.'

That is the way Emerson said it. But here is the way a poet – the late Douglas Malloch – said it:

If you can't be a pine on the top of the hill,
    Be a scrub in the valley – but be

The best little scrub by the side of the rill;
    Be a bush, if you can't be a tree.

If you can't be a bush, be a bit of the grass,
    And some highway happier make;
If you can't be a muskie, then just be a bass –
    But the liveliest bass in the lake!

We can't all be captains, we've got to be crew,
    There's something for all of us here.
There's big work to do and there's lesser to do
    And the task we must do is the near.

If you can't be a highway, then just be a trail,
    If you can't be the sun, be a star;
It isn't by size that you win or you fail –
    Be the best of whatever you are!

To cultivate a mental attitude that will bring us peace and freedom from worry, here is Rule 5:

Let's not imitate others.
Let's find ourselves and be ourselves.

□ **17** □

If you have a lemon, make a lemonade

While writing this book, I dropped in one day at the University of Chicago and asked the Chancellor, Robert Maynard Hutchins, how he kept from worrying. He replied, 'I have always tried to follow a bit of advice given to me by the late Julius Rosenwald, President of Sears, Roebuck and Company: "When you have a lemon, make a lemonade." '

That is what a great educator does. But the fool does the exact opposite. If he finds that life has handed him a lemon, he gives up and says: 'I'm beaten. It is fate. I haven't got a chance.' Then he proceeds to rail against the world and indulge in an orgy of self-pity. But when the wise man is handed a lemon, he says: 'What lesson can I learn from this misfortune? How can I improve my situation? How can I turn this lemon into a lemonade?'

After spending a lifetime studying people and their hidden reserves of power, the great psychologist, Alfred Adler, declared that one of the wonder-filled characteristics of human beings is 'their power to turn a minus into a plus.'

Here is an interesting and stimulating story of a woman I know who did just that. Her name is Thelma Thompson. 'During the war,' she said, as she told me of her experience, 'during the war, my husband was stationed at an Army training camp near the Mojave Desert, in California. I went to live there in order to be near him. I hated the place. I loathed it. I had never before been so miserable. My husband was ordered out on manoeuvres in the Mojave Desert, and I was left in a tiny shack alone. The heat was unbearable – 125 degrees in the shade of a cactus. Not a soul to talk to. The wind blew incessantly, and all the food I ate, and the very air I breathed, were filled with sand, sand, sand!

'I was so utterly wretched, so sorry for myself, that I wrote to my parents. I told them I was giving up and coming back home. I said I couldn't stand it one minute longer. I would rather be in jail! My father answered my letter with just two lines – two lines that will always sing in my memory – two lines that completely altered my life:

Two men looked out from prison bars,
One saw the mud, the other saw the stars.

'I read those two lines over and over. I was ashamed of myself. I made up my mind I would find out what was good in my present situation; I would look for the stars.

'I made friends with the natives, and their reaction amazed me. When I showed interest in their weaving and pottery, they gave me presents of their favourite pieces which they had refused to sell to tourists. I studied the fascinating forms of the cactus and the yuccas and the Joshua trees. I learned about prairie dogs, watched for the desert sunsets, and hunted for seashells that had been left there millions of years ago when the sands of the desert had been an ocean floor.

'What brought about this astonishing change in me? The Mojave Desert hadn't changed. But I had. I had changed my attitude of mind. And by doing so, I transformed a wretched experience into the most exciting adventure of my life. I was stimulated and excited by this new world that I had discovered. I was so excited I wrote a book about it – a novel that was published under the title *Bright Ramparts*. . . . I had looked out of my self-created prison and found the stars.'

Thelma Thompson, you discovered an old truth that the Greeks taught five hundred years before Christ was born: 'The best things are the most difficult.'

Harry Emerson Fosdick repeated it again in the twentieth century: 'Happiness is not mostly pleasure; it is mostly victory.' Yes, the victory that comes from a sense of achievement, of triumph, of turning our lemons into lemonades.

I once visited a happy farmer down in Florida who turned even a poison lemon into lemonade. When he first got his farm, he was discouraged. The land was so wretched he could neither grow fruit nor raise pigs. Nothing thrived there but scrub oaks and rattlesnakes. Then he got his idea. He would turn his liability into an asset: he would make the most of these rattlesnakes. To everyone's amazement, he started canning rattlesnake meat. When I stopped to visit him a few years ago, I found that tourists were pouring in to see his rattlesnake farm at the rate of twenty thousand a year. His business was thriving. I saw poison from the fangs of his rattlers being shipped to laboratories to make antivenom toxin; I saw rattlesnake skins being sold at fancy prices to make women's shoes and handbags. I saw canned rattlesnake meat being shipped to customers all over the world. I bought a picture postcard of the place and mailed it at the local post office of the village, which had been rechristened 'Rattlesnake, Florida,' in honour of a man who had turned a poison lemon into a sweet lemonade.

As I have travelled up and down and back and forth across this nation time after time, it has been my privilege to meet dozens of men and women who have demonstrated 'their power to turn a minus into a plus'.

The late William Bolitho, author of *Twelve Against the Gods*, put it like this: 'The most important thing in life is not to capitalize on your gains. Any fool can do that. The really important thing is to profit from your losses. That requires intelligence; and it makes the difference between a man of sense and a fool.'

Bolitho uttered those words after he had lost a leg in a railway accident. But I know a man who lost both legs and turned his minus into a plus. His name is Ben Fortson. I met him in a hotel elevator in Atlanta, Georgia. As I stepped into the elevator, I noticed this cheerful-looking man, who had both legs missing, sitting in a wheelchair in a corner of the elevator. When the elevator stopped at his floor, he asked me pleasantly if I would step to one corner, so he could manage his chair better. 'So sorry,' he said, 'to inconvenience you' – and a deep, heart-warming smile lighted his face as he said it.

When I left the elevator and went to my room, I could think of nothing but this cheerful cripple. So I hunted him up and asked him to tell me his story.

'It happened in 1929,' he told me with a smile. 'I had gone out to cut a load of hickory poles to stake the beans in my garden. I had loaded the poles on my Ford and started back home. Suddenly one pole slipped under the car and jammed the steering apparatus at the very moment I was making a sharp turn. The car shot over an embankment and hurled me against a tree. My spine was hurt. My legs were paralyzed.

'I was twenty-four when that happened, and I have never taken a step since.'

Twenty-four years old, and sentenced to a wheelchair for the rest of his life! I asked him how he managed to take it so courageously, and he said, 'I didn't.' He said he raged and rebelled. He fumed about his fate. But as the years dragged on, he found that his rebellion wasn't getting him anything except bitterness. 'I finally realized,' he said, 'that other people were kind and courteous to me. So the least I could do was to be kind and courteous to them.'

I asked if he still felt, after all these years, that his accident had been a terrible misfortune, and he promptly said, 'No.' He said, 'I'm almost glad now that it happened.' He told me that after he got over the shock and resentment, he began to live in a different world. He began to read and developed a love for good literature. In fourteen years, he said, he had read at least fourteen hundred books; and those books had opened up new horizons for him and made his life richer than he ever thought possible. He began to listen to good music; and he is now thrilled by great symphonies that would have bored him before. But the biggest change was that he had time to think. 'For the first time in my life,' he said, 'I was able to look at the world and get a real sense of values. I began to realize that most of the things I had been striving for before weren't worthwhile at all.'

As a result of his reading, he became interested in politics, studied public questions, made speeches from his wheelchair! He got to know people and people got to know him. And – still in his wheelchair – he got to be Secretary for the state of Georgia!

While conducting adult-education classes in New York City, I have discovered that one of the major regrets of many adults is that they never went to college. They seem to think that not having a college education is a great handicap. I know that this isn't necessarily true because I have known thousands of successful men who never went beyond high school. So I often tell these students the story of a man I knew who had never finished even grade school. He was brought up in blighting poverty. When his father died, his father's friends had to chip in to pay for the coffin in which he was buried. After his father's death, his mother worked in an umbrella factory ten hours a day and then brought piecework home and worked until eleven o'clock at night.

The boy brought up in these circumstances went in for amateur dramatics put on by a club in his church. He got such a thrill out of acting that he decided to take up public speaking. This led him into politics. By the time he reached thirty, he was elected to the New York State legislature. But he was woefully unprepared for such a responsibility. In fact, he told me that frankly he didn't know what it was all about. He studied the long, complicated bills that he was supposed to vote on – but, as far as he was concerned, those bills might as well have been written in the language of the Choctaw Indians. He was worried and bewildered when he was made a member of the committee on forests before he had ever set foot in a forest. He was worried and bewildered when he was made a member of the State Banking

Commission before he had ever had a bank account. He himself told me that he was so discouraged that he would have resigned from the legislature if he hadn't been ashamed to admit defeat to his mother. In despair he decided to study sixteen hours a day and turn his lemon of ignorance into a lemonade of knowledge. By doing that, he transformed himself from a local politician into a national figure and made himself so outstanding that *The New York Times* called him 'the best-loved citizen of New York'.

I am talking about Al Smith.

Ten years after Al Smith set out his programme of political self-education, he was the greatest living authority on the government of New York State. He was elected Governor of New York for four terms – at that time a record never attained by any other man. In 1928, he was the Democratic candidate for President. Six great universities – including Columbia and Harvard – conferred honorary degrees upon this man who had never gone beyond grade school.

Al Smith himself told me that none of these things would ever have come to pass if he hadn't worked hard sixteen hours a day to turn his minus into a plus.

Nietzsche's formula for the superior man was 'not only to bear up under necessity but to love it.'

The more I have studied the careers of men of achievement the more deeply I have been convinced that a surprisingly large number of them succeeded because they started out with handicaps that spurred them on to great endeavour and great rewards. As William James said: 'Our very infirmities help us unexpectedly.'

Yes, it is highly probable that Milton wrote better poetry because he was blind and that Beethoven composed better music because he was deaf.

Helen Keller's brilliant career was inspired and made possible because of her blindness and deafness.

If Tchaikovsky had not been frustrated – and driven almost to suicide by his tragic marriage – if his own life had not been pathetic, he probably would never have been able to compose his immortal '*Symphonie Pathétique*'.

If Dostoevsky and Tolstoy had not led tortured lives, they would probably never have been able to write their immortal novels.

'If I had not been so great an invalid,' wrote the man who changed the scientific concept of life on earth – 'if I had not been so great an invalid, I should not have done so much work as I have accomplished.' That was Charles Darwin's confession that his infirmities had helped him unexpectedly.

The same day that Darwin was born in England, another baby was born in a log cabin in the forests of Kentucky. He, too, was helped by his infirmities. His name was Lincoln – Abraham Lincoln. If he had been reared in an aristocratic family and had had a law degree from Harvard and a happy married life, he would probably never have found in the depths of his heart the haunting words that he immortalized at Gettysburg, or the sacred poem that he spoke at his second inauguration – the most beautiful and noble phrases ever uttered by a ruler of men: 'With malice toward none; with charity for all . . .'

Harry Emerson Fosdick says in his book, *The Power to See It Through*, 'There is a Scandinavian saying which some of us might well take as a rallying cry for our lives: "The north wind made the Vikings." Wherever did we get the idea that secure and pleasant living, the absence of difficulty, and the comfort of ease, ever of themselves made people either good or happy? Upon the contrary, people who pity themselves go on pitying themselves even when they are laid softly on a cushion, but always in history character and happiness have come to people in all sorts of circumstances, good, bad, and indifferent, when they shouldered their personal responsibility. So, repeatedly the north wind has made the Vikings.'

Suppose we are so discouraged that we feel there is no hope of our ever being able to turn our lemons into lemonade – then here are two reasons why we ought to try, anyway – two reasons why we have everything to gain and nothing to lose.

Reason one: We may succeed.

Reason two: Even if we don't succeed, the mere attempt to turn our minus into a plus will cause us to look forward instead of backward; it will replace negative thoughts with positive thoughts; it will release creative energy and spur us to get so busy that we won't have either the time or the inclination to mourn over what is past and forever gone.

Once when Ole Bull, the world-famous violinist, was giving a concert in Paris, the A string on his violin suddenly snapped. But Ole Bull simply finished the melody on three strings. 'That is life,' says Harry Emerson Fosdick, 'to have your A string snap and finish on three strings.'

That is not only life. It is *more* than life. It is life triumphant!

If I had the power to do so, I would have these words of William Bolitho carved in eternal bronze and hung in every schoolhouse in the land:

The most important thing in life is not to capitalize on your gains. Any fool can do that. The really important thing is to profit from your losses. That requires intelligence; and it makes the difference between a man of sense and a fool.

So, to cultivate a mental attitude that will bring us peace and happiness, let's do something about Rule 6:

When fate hands us a lemon, let's try to make a lemonade.

□ 18 □

How to cure depression in fourteen days

When I started writing this book, I offered a two-hundred-dollar prize for the most helpful and inspiring true story on 'How I Conquered Worry'.

The three judges for this contest were: Eddie Rikenbacker, president, Eastern Air Lines; Dr. Stewart W. McClelland, president, Lincoln Memorial University; H. V. Kaltenborn, radio news analyst. However, we received two stories so superb that the judges found it impossible to choose between them. So we divided the prize. Here is one of the stories that tied for first prize – the story of C. R. Burton (who worked for Whizzer Motor Sales of Springfield, Missouri).

'I lost my mother when I was nine years old, and my father when I was twelve,' Mr. Burton wrote me. 'My father was killed, but my mother simply walked out of the house one day nineteen years ago; and I have never seen her since. Neither have I ever seen my two little sisters that she took with her. She never even wrote me a letter until after she had been gone seven years. My father was killed in an accident three years after Mother left. He and a partner had bought a café in a small Missouri town; and while Father was away on a business trip, his partner sold the café for cash and skipped out. A friend wired Father to hurry back home; and in his hurry, Father was killed in a car accident at Salinas, Kansas. Two of my father's sisters, who were poor and old and sick, took three of the children into their homes. Nobody wanted me and my little brother. We were left at the mercy of the town. We were haunted by the fear of being called orphans and treated as orphans. Our fears soon materialized, too. I lived for a little while with a poor family in town. But times were hard and the head of the family lost his job, so they couldn't afford to feed me any longer. Then Mr. and Mrs. Loftin took me to live with them on their farm eleven miles from town. Mr. Loftin was seventy years old, and sick in bed with shingles. He told me I could stay there "as long as I didn't lie, didn't steal, and did as I was told." Those three orders became my Bible. I lived by them strictly. I started to school, but the first week found me at home, bawling like a baby. The other children picked on me and poked fun at my big nose and said I was dumb and called me an "orphan brat". I was hurt so badly that I wanted to fight them; but Mr. Loftin, the farmer who had taken me in said to me: "Always remember that it takes a bigger man to walk away from a fight than it does to stay and fight." I didn't fight until one day a kid picked up some chicken manure from the schoolhouse yard and threw it in my face. I beat the hell out of him; and made a couple of friends. They said he had it coming to him.

'I was proud of a new cap that Mrs. Loftin had bought me. One day one of the big girls jerked it off my head and filled it with water and ruined it. She said she filled it with water so that "the water would wet my thick skull and keep my popcorn brains from popping."

'I never cried at school, but I used to bawl it out at home. Then one day Mrs. Loftin gave me some advice that did away with all troubles and worries and turned my enemies into friends. She said, "Ralph, they won't tease you and call you an 'orphan brat' any more if you will get interested in them and see how much you can do for them." I took her advice. I studied hard; and though I soon headed the class, I was never envied because I went out of my way to help them.

'I helped several of the boys write their themes and essays. I wrote complete debates for some of the boys. One lad was ashamed to let his folks know that I was helping him. So he used to tell his mother he was going possum hunting. Then he would come to Mr. Loftin's and tie his dogs up in the barn while I helped him with his lessons. I wrote book reviews for one lad and I spent several evenings helping one of the girls on her math.

'Death struck our neighbourhood. Two elderly farmers died and one woman was deserted by her husband. I was the only male in four families. I helped these widows for two years. On my way to and from school, I stopped at their farms, cut wood for them, milked their cows, and fed and watered their stock. I was now blessed instead of cursed. I was accepted as a friend by everyone. They showed me their real feelings when I returned home from the Navy. More than two hundred farmers came to see me the first day I was home. Some of them drove as far as eighty miles, and their concern for me was really sincere. Because I have been busy and happy trying to help other people, I have few worries; and I haven't been called an "orphan brat" now for thirteen years.'

Hooray for C. R. Burton! He knows how to win friends! And he also knows how to conquer worry and enjoy life.

So did the late Dr. Frank Loope, of Seattle, Washington. He was an invalid for twenty-three years. Arthritis. Yet Stuart Whithouse of the *Seattle Star* wrote me, saying, 'I interviewed Dr. Loope many times; and *I have never known a man more unselfish or a man who got more out of life.*'

How did this bed-ridden invalid get so much out of life? I'll give you two guesses. Did he do it by complaining and criticizing? No. . . . By wallowing in self-pity and demanding that he be the centre of attention and everyone cater to him? No. . . . Still wrong. He did it by adopting as his slogan the motto of the Prince of Wales: *'Ich dien'* – 'I serve'. He accumulated the names and addresses of other invalids and cheered both them and himself by writing happy, encouraging letters. In fact, he organized a letter-writing club for invalids and got them writing letters to one another. Finally he formed a national organization called The Shut-in Society.

As he lay in bed, he wrote an average of fourteen hundred letters a year and brought joy to thousands of invalids by getting radios and books for shut-ins.

What was the chief difference between Dr. Loope and a lot of other people? Just this: Dr. Loope had the inner glow of a man with a purpose, a mission. He had the joy of knowing that he was being used by an idea far nobler and more significant than himself, instead of being, as Shaw put it, 'a self-centred, little clod of ailments and grievances complaining that the world would not devote itself to making him happy.'

Here is the most astonishing statement that I ever read from the pen of a great psychiatrist. This statement was made by Alfred Adler. He used to say to his melancholia patients: 'You can be cured in fourteen days if you follow this prescription. Try to think every day how you can please someone.'

That statement sounds so incredible that I feel I ought to try to explain it by quoting a couple of pages from Dr. Adler's splendid book, *What Life Should Mean to You*:

Melancholia is like a long-continued rage and reproach against others, though for the purpose of gaining care, sympathy and support, the patient seems only to be dejected about his own guilt. A melancholiac's first memory is generally something like this: 'I remember I wanted to lie on the couch, but my brother was lying there. I cried so much that he had to leave.'

Melancholiacs are often inclined to revenge themselves by committing suicide, and my doctor's first care is to avoid giving them an excuse for suicide. I myself try to relieve the whole tension by proposing to them, as the first rule in treatment, 'Never do anything you don't like.' This seems to be very modest, but I believe that it goes to the root of the whole trouble. If a melancholiac is able to do anything he wants, whom can he accuse? What has he got to revenge himself for? 'If you want to go to the theater,' I tell him, 'or to go on a holiday, do it. If you find on the way that you don't want to, stop it.' It is the best situation any one could be in. It gives a satisfaction to his striving for superiority. He is like God and can do what he pleases. On the other hand, it does not fit very easily into his style of life. He wants to dominate and accuse others and if they agree with him there is no way of dominating them. This rule is a great relief and I have never had a suicide among my patients.

Generally the patient replies, 'But there is nothing I like doing.' I have prepared for this answer, because I have heard it so often. 'Then refrain from doing anything you dislike,' I say. Sometimes, however, he will reply, 'I should like to stay in bed all day.' I know that, if I allow it, he will no longer want to do it. I know that, if I hinder him, he will start a war. I always agree.

This is one rule. Another attacks their style of life still more directly. I tell them, *'You can be cured in fourteen days if you follow this prescription. Try to think every day how you can please some one.'* See what this means to them. They are occupied with the thought, 'How can I worry some one?' The answers are very interesting. Some say, 'This will be very easy for me. I have done it all my life.' They have never done it. I ask them to think it over. They do not think it over. I tell them, 'You can make use of all the time you spend when you are unable to go to sleep by thinking how you can please some one, and it will be a big step forward in your health.' When I see them next day, I ask them, 'Did you think over what I suggested?' They answer, 'Last night I went to sleep as soon as I got into bed.' All this must be done, of course, in a modest, friendly manner, without a hint of superiority.

Others will answer, 'I could never do it. I am so worried.' I tell them, 'Don't stop worrying; but at the same time you can think now and then of others.' I want to direct their interest always towards their fellows. Many say, 'Why should I please others? Others do not try to please me.' 'You must think of your health,' I answer. 'The others will suffer later on.' It is extremely rare that I have found a patient who said, 'I have thought over what you suggested.' All my efforts are devoted towards increasing the social interest of the patient. I know that the real reason for his malady is his lack of co-operation and I want him to see it too. As soon as he can connect himself with his fellow men on an equal and co-operative footing, he is cured. . . . The most important task imposed by religion has always been 'Love thy neighbor.' . . . It is the individual who is not interested in his fellow man who has the greatest difficulties in life and provides the greatest injury to others. It is from among such individuals that all human failures spring. . . . All that we demand of a human being, and the highest praise we can give him, is that he should be a good fellow worker, a friend to all other men, and a true partner in love and marriage.

Dr. Adler urges us to do a good deed every day. And what is a good deed? 'A good deed,' said the prophet Mohammed, 'is one that brings a smile of joy to the face of another.'

Why will doing a good deed every day produce such astounding effects on the doer? Because trying to please others will cause us to stop thinking of ourselves: the very thing that produces worry and fear and melancholia.

Mrs. William T. Moon, who operated the Moon Secretarial School in New York, didn't have to spend two weeks thinking how she could please someone in order to banish her melancholy. She went Alfred Adler one better – no, she went Adler *thirteen* better. She banished her melancholy, not in fourteen days, but in *one* day, by thinking how she could please a couple of orphans.

It happened like this: 'In December, five years ago,' said Mrs. Moon, 'I was engulfed in a feeling of sorrow and self-pity. After several years of happy married life, I had lost my husband. As the Christmas holidays approached, my sadness deepened. I had never spent a Christmas alone in all my life; and I dreaded to see this Christmas come. Friends had invited me to spend Christmas with them. But I did not feel up to any gaiety. I knew I would be a wet blanket at any party. So, I refused their kind invitations. As Christmas Eve approached, I was more and more overwhelmed with self-pity. True, I should have been thankful for many things, as all of us have many things for which to be thankful. The day before Christmas, I left my office at three o'clock in the afternoon and started walking aimlessly up Fifth Avenue, hoping that I might banish my self-pity and melancholy. The avenue was jammed with gay and happy crowds – scenes that brought back memories of happy years that were gone. I just couldn't bear the thought of going home to a lonely and empty apartment. I was bewildered. I didn't know what to do. I couldn't keep the tears back. After walking aimlessly for an hour or so, I found myself in front of a bus terminal. I remembered that my husband and I had often boarded an unknown bus for adventure, so I boarded the first bus I found at the station. After crossing the Hudson River and riding for some time, I heard the bus conductor say, "Last stop, lady." I got off. I didn't even know the name of the town. It was a quiet, peaceful little place. While waiting for the next bus home, I started walking up a residential street. As I passed a church, I heard the beautiful strains of "Silent Night". I went in. The church was empty except for the organist. I sat down unnoticed in one of the pews. The lights from the gaily decorated Christmas tree made the decorations seem like myriads of stars dancing in the moonbeams. The long-drawn cadences of the music – and the fact that I had forgotten to eat since morning – made me drowsy. I was weary and heavy-laden, so I drifted off to sleep.

'When I awoke, I didn't know where I was. I was terrified. I saw in front of me two small children who had apparently come in to see the Christmas tree. One, a little girl, was pointing at me and saying, "I wonder if Santa Claus brought her." These children were also frightened when I awoke. I told them that I wouldn't hurt them. They were poorly dressed. I asked them where their mother and daddy were. "We ain't got no mother and daddy," they said. Here were two little orphans much worse off then I had ever been. They made me feel ashamed of my sorrow and self-pity. I showed them the Christmas tree and then took them to a drugstore and we had some refreshments, and I bought them some candy and a few presents. My loneliness vanished as if by magic. These two orphans gave me the only real happiness and self-forgetfulness that I had had in months. As I chatted with them, I realized how lucky I had been. I thanked God that all my Christmases as a child had been bright with parental love and tenderness. Those two little orphans did far more for me than I did for them. That experience showed me again the necessity of making other people happy in order to be happy ourselves. I found that happiness is contagious. By giving, we receive. By helping someone and giving out love, I had conquered worry and sorrow and self-pity, and felt like a new person. And I was a new person – not only then, but in the years that followed.'

I could fill a book with stories of people who forgot themselves into health and happiness. For example, let's take the case of Margaret Tayler Yates, one of the most popular women in the United States Navy.

Mrs. Yates is a writer of novels, but none of her mystery stories is half so interesting as the true story of what happened to her that fateful morning when the Japanese struck our fleet at Pearl Harbor. Mrs. Yates had been an invalid for more than a year: bad heart. She spent twenty-two out of every twenty-four hours in bed. The longest journey that she undertook was a walk into the garden to take a sunbath. Even then, she had to lean on the maid's arm as she walked. She herself told me that in those days she expected to be an invalid for the balance of her life. 'I would never have really lived again,' she told me, 'if the Japanese had not struck Pearl Harbor and jarred me out of my complacency.

'When this happened,' Mrs. Yates said, as she told her story, 'everything was chaos and confusion. One bomb struck so near my home, the concussion threw me out of bed. Army trucks rushed out to Hickam Field, Scofield Barracks, and Kaneohe Bay Air Station, to bring Army and Navy wives and children to the public schools. There the Red Cross telephoned those who had extra rooms to take them in. The Red Cross workers knew that I had a telephone beside my bed, so they asked me to be a clearinghouse of information. So I kept track of where Army and Navy wives and children were being housed, and all Navy and Army men were instructed by the Red Cross to telephone me to find out where their families were.

'I soon discovered that my husband, Commander Robert Raleigh Yates, was safe. I tried to cheer up the wives who did not know whether their husbands had been killed; and I tried to give consolation to the widows whose husbands had been killed – and they were many. Two thousand, one hundred and seventeen officers and enlisted men in the Navy and Marine Corps were killed and 960 were reported missing.

'At first I answered these phone calls while lying in bed. Then I answered them sitting up in bed. Finally, I got so busy, so excited, that I forgot all about my weakness and got out of bed and sat by a table. By helping others who were much worse off than I was, I forgot all about myself; and I have never gone back to bed again except for my regular eight hours of sleep each night. I realize now that if the Japanese had not struck at Pearl Harbor, I would probably have remained a semi-invalid all my life. I was comfortable in bed. I was constantly waited on, and I now realize that I was unconsciously losing my will to rehabilitate myself.

'The attack on Pearl Harbor was one of the greatest tragedies in American history, but as far as I was concerned, it was one of the best things that ever happened to me. That terrible crisis gave me strength that I never dreamed I possessed. It took my attention off myself and focused it on others. It gave me something big and vital and important to live for. I no longer had time to think about myself or care about myself.'

A third of the people who rush to psychiatrists for help could probably cure themselves if they could only do as Margaret Yates did: get interested in helping others. My idea? No, that is approximately what Carl Jung said. And he ought to know – if anybody does. He said: 'About one third of my patients are suffering from no clinically definable neurosis, but from the senselessness and emptiness of their lives.' To put it another way, they are trying to thumb a ride through life – and the parade passes them by. So they rush to a psychiatrist with their petty, senseless, useless lives. Having missed the boat, they stand on the wharf, blaming everyone except themselves and demanding that the world cater to their self-centred desires.

You may be saying to yourself now: 'Well, I am not impressed by these stories. I myself could get interested in a couple of orphans I met on Christmas Eve; and if I had been at Pearl Harbor, I would gladly have done what Margaret Tayler Yates did. But with me things are different: I live an ordinary humdrum life. I work at a dull job eight hours a day. Nothing dramatic ever happens to me. How can I get interested in helping others? And why should I? What is there in it for me?'

A fair question. I'll try to answer it. However humdrum your existence may be, you surely meet *some* people every day of your life. What do you do about them? Do you merely stare through them, or do you try to find out what it is that makes them tick? How about the postman, for example – he travels hundreds of miles every year, delivering your mail; but have you ever taken the trouble to find out where *he* lives, or ask to see a snapshot of his wife and his kids? Did you ever ask him if he gets tired, or if he ever gets bored?

What about the grocery boy, the newspaper vendor, the chap at the corner who polishes your shoes? These people are human – bursting with troubles, and dreams, and private ambitions. They are also bursting for the chance to share them with someone. But do you ever let them? Do you ever show an eager, honest interest in them or their lives? That's the sort of thing I mean. You don't have to become a Florence Nightingale or a social reformer to help improve the world – your own private world; you can start tomorrow morning with the people you meet!

What's in it for you? Much greater happiness! Greater satisfaction, and pride in yourself! Aristotle called this kind of attitude 'enlightened selfishness'. Zoroaster said, 'Doing good to others is not a duty. It is a joy, for it increases your own health and happiness.' And Benjamin Franklin summed it up very simply – 'When you are good to others,' said Franklin, 'you are best to yourself.'

'No discovery of modern psychology,' wrote Henry C. Link, director of the Psychological Service Center in New York, 'is, in my opinion, so important as its scientific proof of the necessity of self-sacrifice or discipline to self-realization and happiness.'

Thinking of others will not only keep you from worrying about yourself; it will also help you to make a lot of friends and have a lot of fun. How? Well, I once asked Professor William Lyon Phelps, of Yale, how he did it; and here is what he said:

'I never go into a hotel or a barbershop or a store without saying something agreeable to everyone I meet. I try to say something that treats them as an individual – not merely a cog in a machine. I sometimes compliment the girl who waits on me in the store by telling her how beautiful her eyes are – or her hair. I will ask a barber if he doesn't get tired standing on his feet all day. I'll ask him how he came to take up barbering – how long he has been at it and how many heads of hair he has cut. I'll help him figure it out. I find that taking an interest in people makes them beam with pleasure. I frequently shake hands with a redcap who has carried my grip. It gives him a new lift and freshens him up for the whole day. One extremely hot summer day, I went into a dining car of the New Haven Railway to have lunch. The crowded car was almost like a furnace and the service was slow. When the steward finally got around to handing me the menu, I said: "The boys back there cooking in that hot kitchen certainly must be suffering today." The steward began to curse. His tones were bitter. At first, I thought he was angry. "Good God Almighty," he exclaimed. "people come in here and complain about the food. They kick about the slow service and growl about the heat and the prices. I have listened to their criticism for nineteen years and you are the first person and the only person that has ever expressed any sympathy for the cooks back there in the boiling kitchen. I wish to God we had more passengers like you."

'The steward was astounded because I had thought of the cooks as human beings, and not merely as a cog in the organization of a great railway. What people want,' continued Professor Phelps, 'is a little attention as human beings. When I meet a man on the street with a beautiful dog, I always comment on the dog's beauty. As I walk on and glance back over my shoulder, I frequently see the man petting and admiring the dog. My appreciation has renewed his appreciation.

'One time in England, I met a shepherd, and expressed my sincere admiration for his big, intelligent sheep dog. I asked him to tell me how he trained the dog. As I walked away, I glanced back over my shoulder and saw the dog standing with his paws on the shepherd's shoulders and the shepherd was petting him. By taking a little interest in the shepherd and his dog, I made the shepherd happy, I made the dog happy and I made myself happy.'

Can you imagine a man who goes around shaking hands with porters and expressing sympathy for the cooks in the hot kitchen – and telling people how much he admires their dogs – can you imagine a man like that being sour and worried and needing the services of a psychiatrist? You can't, can you? No, of course not. A Chinese proverb puts it this way: 'A bit of fragrance always clings to the hand that gives you roses.'

You didn't have to tell that to Billy Phelps of Yale. He knew it. He lived it. If you are a man, skip this paragraph. It won't interest you. It tells how a worried, unhappy girl got several men to propose to her. The girl who did that is a grandmother now. A few years ago, I spent the night in her and her husband's home. I had been giving a lecture in her town; and the next morning she drove me about fifty miles to catch a train on the main line of the New York Central. We got to talking about winning friends, and she said: 'Mr. Carnegie, I am going to tell you something that I have never confessed to anyone before – not even to my husband.' She told me that she had been reared in a social-register family in Philadelphia. 'The tragedy of my girlhood and young womanhood,' she said, 'was our poverty. We could never entertain the way the other girls in my social set entertained. My clothes were never of the best quality. I outgrew them and they didn't fit and they were often out of style. I was so humiliated, so ashamed, that I often cried myself to sleep. Finally, in sheer desperation, I hit upon the idea of always asking my partner at dinner parties to tell me about his experience, his ideas, and his plans for the future. I didn't ask these questions because I was especially interested in the answers. I did it solely to keep my partner from looking at my poor clothes. But a strange thing happened: as I listened to these young men talk and learned more about them, I really became interested in listening to what they had to say. I became so interested that I myself sometimes forgot about my clothes. But the astounding thing to me was this: since I was a good listener and encouraged the boys to talk about themselves, I gave them happiness and I gradually became the most popular girl in our social group and three of these men proposed marriage to me.'

Some people who read this chapter are going to say: 'All this talk about getting interested in others is a lot of damn nonsense! Sheer religious pap! None of that stuff for me! I am going to put money in my purse. I am going to grab all I can get – and grab it now – and to hell with the other dumb clucks!'

Well, if that is your opinion, you are entitled to it; but if you are right, then all the great philosophers and teachers since the beginning of recorded history – Jesus, Confucius, Buddha, Plato, Aristotle, Socrates, Saint Francis – were all wrong. But since you may sneer at the teachings of religious leaders, let's turn for advice to a couple of atheists. First, let's take the late A. E. Housman, professor at Cambridge University, and one of the most distinguished scholars of his generation. In 1936, he gave an address at Cambridge University on 'The Name and Nature of Poetry'. In that address, he declared that 'the greatest truth ever uttered and the most profound moral discovery of all time were these words of Jesus: "He that findeth his life shall lose it: and he that loseth his life for my sake shall find it." '

We have heard preachers say that all our lives. But Housman was an atheist, a pessimist, a man who contemplated suicide; and yet he felt that the man who thought only of himself wouldn't get much out of life. He would be miserable. But the man who forgot himself in service to others would find the joy of living.

If you are not impressed by what A. E. Housman said, let's turn for advice to the most distinguished American atheist of the twentieth century: Theodore Dreiser. Dreiser ridiculed all religions as fairy tales and regarded life as 'a tale told by an idiot, full of sound and fury, signifying nothing.' Yet Dreiser advocated the one great principle that Jesus taught – service to others. 'If he [man] is to extract any joy out of his span,' Dreiser said, 'he must think and plan to make things better not only for himself but for others, since joy for himself depends upon his joy in others and theirs in him.'

If we are going 'to make things better for others' – as Dreiser advocated – let's be quick about it. Time is a-wastin'. 'I shall pass this way but once. Therefore any good that I can do or any kindness that I can show – let me do it now. Let me not defer nor neglect it, for I shall not pass this way again.'

So if you want to banish worry and cultivate peace and happiness, here is Rule 7:

> Forget yourself by becoming interested in others.
> Every day do a good deed that will put a smile of
> joy on someone's face.

☐ IN A NUTSHELL ☐

SEVEN WAYS TO CULTIVATE A MENTAL ATTITUDE THAT WILL BRING YOU
PEACE AND HAPPINESS

RULE 1: Let's fill our minds with thoughts of peace, courage, health, and hope, for 'our life is what our thoughts make it'.

RULE 2: Let's never try to get even with our enemies, because if we do we will hurt ourselves far more than we hurt them. Let's do as General Eisenhower does: let's never waste a minute thinking about people we don't like.

RULE 3: *A.* Instead of worrying about ingratitude, let's expect it. Let's remember that Jesus healed ten lepers in one day – and only one thanked Him. Why should we expect more gratitude than Jesus got?
B. Let's remember that the only way to find happiness is not to expect gratitude – but to give for the joy of giving.
C. Let's remember that gratitude is a 'cultivated' trait; so if we want our children to be grateful, we must train them to be grateful.

RULE 4: Count your blessings – not your troubles!

RULE 5: Let's not imitate others. Let's find ourselves and be ourselves, for 'envy is ignorance' and 'imitation is suicide'.

RULE 6: When fate hands us a lemon, let's try to make a lemonade.

RULE 7: Let's forget our own unhappiness – by trying to create a little happiness for others. 'When you are good to others, you are best to yourself.'

Part Five

THE PERFECT WAY TO CONQUER WORRY

How my mother and father conquered worry

As I have said, I was born and brought up on a Missouri farm. Like most farmers of that day, my parents had pretty hard scratching. My mother had been a country schoolteacher and my father had been a farm hand working for twelve dollars a month. Mother made not only my clothes, but also the soap with which we washed our clothes.

We rarely had any cash – except once a year when we sold our hogs. We traded our butter and eggs at the grocery store for flour, sugar, coffee. When I was twelve years old, I didn't have as much as fifty cents a year to spend on myself. I can still remember the day we went to a Fourth-of-July celebration and Father gave me ten cents to spend as I wished. I felt the wealth of the Indies was mine.

I walked a mile to attend a one-room country school. I walked when the snow was deep and the thermometer shivered around twenty-eight degrees below zero. Until I was fourteen, I never had any rubbers or overshoes. During the long, cold winters, my feet were always wet and cold. As a child I never dreamed that anyone had dry, warm feet during the winter.

My parents slaved sixteen hours a day, yet we constantly were oppressed by debts and harassed by hard luck. One of my earliest memories is watching the flood waters of the 102 River rolling over our corn and hayfields, destroying everything. The floods destroyed our crops six years out of seven. Year after year, our hogs died of cholera and we burned them. I can close my eyes now and recall the pungent odour of burning hog flesh.

One year, the floods didn't come. We raised a bumper corn crop, bought feed cattle, and fattened them with our corn. But the floods might just as well have drowned our corn that year, for the price of fat cattle fell on the Chicago market; and after feeding and fattening the cattle, we got only thirty dollars more for them than what we had paid for them. Thirty dollars for a whole year's work!

No matter what we did, we lost money. I can still remember the mule colts that my father bought. We fed them for three years, hired men to break them, then shipped them to Memphis, Tennessee – and sold them for less than what we had paid for them three years previously.

After ten years of hard, gruelling work, we were not only penniless; we were heavily in debt. Our farm was mortgaged. Try as hard as we might, we couldn't even pay the interest on the mortgage. The bank that held the mortgage abused and insulted my father and threatened to take his farm away from him. Father was forty-seven years old. After more than thirty years of hard work, he had nothing but debts and humiliation. It was more than he could take. He worried. His health broke. He had no desire for food; in spite of the hard physical work he was doing in the field all day, he had to take medicine to give him an appetite. He lost flesh. The doctor told my mother that he would be dead within six months. Father was so worried that he no longer wanted to live. I have often heard my mother say that when Father went to the barn to feed the horses and milk the cows, and didn't come back as soon as she expected, she would go out to the barn, fearing that she would find his body dangling from the end of a rope. One day as he returned home from Maryville, where the banker had threatened to foreclose the mortgage, he stopped his horses on a bridge crossing the 102 River, got off the wagon, and stood for a long time looking down at the water, debating with himself whether he should jump in and end it all.

Years later, Father told me that the only reason he didn't jump was because of my mother's deep, abiding, and joyous belief that if we loved God and kept His commandments everything would come out all right. Mother was right. Everything did come out all right in the end. Father lived forty-two happy years longer, and died in 1941, at the age of eighty-nine.

During all those years of struggle and heartache, my mother never worried. She took all her troubles to God in prayer. Every night before we went to bed, Mother would read a chapter from the Bible; frequently Mother or Father would read these comforting words of Jesus: 'In my Father's house are many mansions. . . . I go to prepare a place for you . . . that where I am, there ye may be also.' Then we all knelt down before our chairs in that lonely Missouri farmhouse and prayed for God's love and protection.

When William James was professor of philosophy at Harvard, he said, 'Of course, the sovereign cure for worry is religious faith.'

You don't have to go to Harvard to discover that. My mother found that out on a Missouri farm. Neither flood nor debts nor disaster could suppress her happy, radiant, and victorious spirit. I can still hear her singing as she worked:

Peace, peace, wonderful peace,
Flowing down from the Father above,
Sweep over my spirit forever I pray
In fathomless billows of love.

My mother wanted me to devote my life to religious work. I thought seriously of becoming a foreign missionary. Then I went away to college; and gradually, as the years passed, a change came over me. I studied biology, science, philosophy, and comparative religions. I read books on how the Bible was written. I began to question many of its assertions. I began to doubt many of the narrow doctrines taught by the country preachers of that day. I was bewildered. Like Walt Whitman, I 'felt the curious, abrupt questionings stir within me.' I didn't know what to believe. I saw no purpose in life. I stopped praying. I became an agnostic. I believed that all life was planless and aimless. I believed that human beings had no more divine purpose than had the dinosaurs that roamed the earth two hundred million years ago. I felt that someday the human race would perish – just as the dinosaurs had. I knew that science taught that the sun was slowly cooling and that when its temperature fell even ten percent, no form of life could exist on earth. I sneered at the idea of a beneficent God who had created man in His own likeness. I believed that the billions upon billions of suns whirling through black, cold, lifeless space had been created by blind force. Maybe they had never been created at all. Maybe they had existed forever – just as time and space have always existed.

Do I profess to know the answers to all those questions now? No. No man has ever been able to explain the mystery of the universe – the mystery of life. We are surrounded by mysteries. The operation of your body is a profound mystery. So is the electricity in your home. So is the flower in the crannied wall. So is the green grass outside your window. Charles F. Kettering, the guiding genius of General Motors Research Laboratories, gave Antioch College thirty thousand dollars a year out of his own pocket to try to discover why grass is green. He declared that if we knew how grass is able to transform sunlight, water, and carbon dioxide into food sugar, we could transform civilization.

Even the operation of the engine in your car is a profound mystery. General Motors Research Laboratories have spent years of time and millions of dollars trying to find out how and why a spark in the cylinder sets off an explosion that makes your car run.

The fact that we don't understand totally the mysteries of our bodies or electricity or a gas engine doesn't keep us from using and enjoying them. The fact that I don't understand the mysteries of prayer and religion no longer keeps me from enjoying the richer, happier life that religion brings. At long last, I realize the wisdom of Santayana's words: 'Man is not made to understand life, but to live it.'

I have gone back – well, I was about to say that I had gone *back* to religion; but that would not be accurate. I have gone *forward* to a new concept of religion. I no longer have the faintest interest in the differences in creeds that divide the churches. But I am tremendously interested in what religion does for me, just as I am interested in what electricity and good food and water do for me. They help me to lead a richer, fuller, happier life. But religion does far more than that. It brings me spiritual values. It gives me, as William James put it, *'a new zest for life . . . more life, a larger, richer, more satisfying life.'* It gives me faith, hope, and courage. It banishes tensions, anxieties, fears, and worries. It gives purpose to my life – and direction. It vastly improves my happiness. It gives me abounding health. It helps me to create for myself 'an oasis of peace amidst the whirling sands of life.'

Francis Bacon was right when he said, over three hundred years ago: 'A little philosophy inclineth man's mind to atheism; but depth in philosophy bringeth men's minds about to religion.'

I can remember the days when people talked about the conflict between science and religion. But no more. The newest of all sciences – psychiatry – is teaching what Jesus taught. Why? Because psychiatrists realize that prayer and a strong religious faith will banish the worries, the anxieties, the strains and fears that cause more than half of all our ills. They know, as one of their leaders, Dr. A. A. Brill, said: 'Anyone who is truly religious does not develop a neurosis.'

If religion isn't true, then life is meaningless. It is a tragic farce.

I interviewed Henry Ford a few years prior to his death. Before I met him, I had expected him to show the strains of the long years he had spent in building up and managing one of the world's greatest businesses. So I was surprised to see how calm and well and peaceful he looked at seventy-eight. When I asked him if he ever worried, he replied, 'No. I believe God is managing affairs and that He doesn't need any advice from me. With God in charge, I believe that everything will work out for the best in the end. So what is there to worry about?'

Today, even many psychiatrists are becoming modern evangelists. They are not urging us to lead religious lives to avoid hell-fires in the next world, but they are urging us to lead religious lives to avoid the hell-fires of stomach ulcer, angina pectoris, nervous breakdowns, and insanity. As an example of what our psychologists and psychiatrists are teaching, read *The Return to Religion*, by Dr. Henry C. Link.

Yes, the Christian religion is an inspiring, health-giving activity. Jesus said: 'I came that ye might have life and have it more abundantly.' Jesus denounced and attacked the dry forms and dead rituals that passed for religion in His day. He was a rebel. He preached a new kind of religion – a religion that threatened to upset the world. That is why He was crucified. He preached that religion should exist for man – not man for religion; that the Sabbath was made for man – not man for the Sabbath. He talked more about fear than He did about sin. *The wrong kind of fear is a sin* – a sin against your health, a sin against the richer, fuller, happier, courageous life that Jesus advocated. Emerson spoke of himself as a 'Professor of the Science of Joy'. Jesus, too, was a teacher of 'the Science of Joy'. He commanded His disciples to 'rejoice and leap for joy.'

Jesus declared that there were only two important things about religion: loving God with all our heart, and our neighbour as ourselves. Any man who does that is religious, regardless of whether he knows it. My father-in-law, Henry Price, of Tulsa, Oklahoma, is a good example. He tries to live by the golden rule; and he is incapable of doing anything mean, selfish, or dishonest. However, he doesn't attend church, and regards himself as an agnostic. Nonsense! What makes a man a Christian? I'll let John Baillie answer that. He was a distinguished professor who taught theology at the University of Edinburgh. He said: 'What makes a man a Christian is neither his intellectual acceptance of certain ideas, nor his conformity to a certain rule, but his possession of a certain Spirit, and his participation in a certain Life.'

If that makes a man a Christian, then Henry Price is a noble one.

William James – the father of modern psychology – wrote to his friend, Professor Thomas Davidson, saying that as the years went by, he found himself 'less and less able to get along without God'.

Earlier in this book I mentioned that when the judges tried to pick the best story on worry sent in by my students, they had so much difficulty in choosing between two outstanding stories that the prize money was split. Here is the second story that tied for first prize – the unforgettable experience of a woman who had to find out the hard way that 'she couldn't get along without God'.

I am calling this woman Mary Cushman, although that is not her actual name. She has children and grandchildren who might be embarrassed to see her story in print, so I agreed to disguise her identity. However, the woman herself is real – very real. Here is how her story goes:

'During the Depression,' she said, 'my husband's average salary was eighteen dollars a week. Many times we didn't have even that because he didn't get paid when he was ill – and that was often. He had a series of minor accidents; he also had mumps, scarlet fever, and repeated attacks of flu. We lost the little house that we had built with our own hands. We owed fifty dollars at the grocery store – and had five children to feed. I took in washing and ironing from the neighbours, and bought secondhand clothes from the Salvation Army store and made them over for my children to wear. I made myself ill with worry. One day the grocer to whom we owed fifty dollars accused my eleven-year-old boy of stealing a couple of pencils. My son wept as he told me about it. I knew he was honest and sensitive – and I knew that he had been disgraced and humiliated in front of other people. That was the straw that broke my back. I thought of all the misery we had endured, and I couldn't see any hope for the future. I must have become temporarily insane with worry, for I shut off my washing machine, took my little five-year-old daughter into the bedroom, and plugged up the windows and cracks with paper and rags. My little girl said to me, "Mommy, what are you doing?" And I answered, "There's a little draft in here." Then I turned on the gas heater we had in the bedroom – and didn't light it. As I lay down on the bed with my daughter beside me, she said, "Mommy, this is funny – we just got up a little while ago!" But I said, "Never mind, we'll take a little nap." Then I closed my eyes, listening to the gas escape from the heater. I shall never forget the smell of that gas. . . .

'Suddenly I thought I heard music. I listened. I had forgotten to turn the radio off in the kitchen. It didn't matter now. But the music kept on, and presently I heard someone singing an old hymn:

What a Friend we have in Jesus,
All our sins and griefs to bear!
What a privilege to carry
Everything to God in prayer.
Oh, what peace we often forfeit
Oh, what needless pains we bear
All because we do not carry
Everything to God in prayer!

'As I listened to that hymn, I realized that I had made a tragic mistake. I had tried to fight all my terrible battles alone. I had not taken everything to God in prayer. . . . I jumped up, turned off the gas, opened the door, and raised the windows.

'I wept and prayed all the rest of that day. Only I didn't pray for help – instead I poured out my soul in thanksgiving to God for the blessings He had given me: five splendid children – all of them healthy and fine, strong in body and mind. I promised God that never again would I prove so ungrateful. And I have kept that promise.

'Even after we lost our home, and had to move into a little country school-house that we rented for five dollars a month, I thanked God for that schoolhouse; I thanked Him for the fact that I at least had a roof to keep us warm and dry. I thanked God honestly that things were not worse – and I believe that He heard me. For in time things improved – oh, not overnight; but as the Depression lightened, we made a little more money. I got a job as a hat-check girl in a large country club, and sold stockings as a side line. To help put himself through college, one of my sons got a job on a farm, milked thirteen cows morning and night. Today my children are grown up and married; I have three fine grandchildren. And, as I look back on that terrible day when I turned on the gas, I thank God over and over that I "woke up" in time. What joys I would have missed if I had carried out that act! How many wonderful years I would have forfeited forever! Whenever I hear now of someone who wants to end his life, I feel like crying out: "Don't do it! Don't!" The blackest moments we live through can only last a little time – and then comes the future. . . .'

On the average, someone commits suicide in these United States every thirty-five minutes. On the average, someone goes insane every hundred and twenty seconds. Most of these suicides – and probably many of the tragedies of insanity – could have been prevented if these people had only had the solace and peace that are found in religion and prayer.

One of the most distinguished of psychiatrists, Dr. Carl Jung, says on page 264 of his book *Modern Man in Search of a Soul*, 'During the past thirty years, people from all the civilized countries of the earth have consulted me. I have treated many hundreds of patients. Among all my patients in the second half of life – that is to say, over thirty-five – there has not been one whose problem in the last resort was not that of finding a religious outlook on life. It is safe to say that every one of them fell ill because he had lost that which the living religions of every age have given to their followers, and none of them has been really healed who did not regain his religious outlook.'

That statement is so significant I want to repeat it in *bold type*.

Dr. Carl Jung said:

During the past thirty years, people from all the civilized countries of the earth have consulted me. I have treated many hundreds of patients. Among all my patients in the second half of life – that is to say, over thirty-five – there has not been one whose problem in the last resort was not that of finding a religious outlook on life. It is safe to say that every one of them fell ill because he had lost that which the living religions of every age have given to their followers, and none of them has been really healed who did not regain his religious outlook.

William James said approximately the same thing: *'Faith is one of the forces by which men live,'* he declared, *'and the total absence of it means collapse.'*

The late Mahatma Gandhi, the greatest Indian leader since Buddha, would have collapsed if he had not been inspired by the sustaining power of prayer. How do I know? Because Gandhi himself said so. 'Without prayer,' he wrote, 'I should have been a lunatic long ago.'

Thousands of people could give similar testimony. My own father – well, as I have already said, my own father would have drowned himself had it not been for my mother's prayers and faith. Probably thousands of the tortured souls who are now screaming in our insane asylums could have been saved if they had only turned to a higher power for help instead of trying to fight life's battles alone.

When we are harassed and reach the limit of our own strength, many of us then turn in desperation to God – 'There are no atheists in foxholes.' But why wait till we are desperate? Why not renew our strength every day? Why wait even until Sunday? For years I have had the habit of dropping into empty churches on *weekday afternoons*. When I feel that I am too rushed and hurried to spare a few minutes to think about spiritual things, I say to myself: 'Wait a minute, Dale Carnegie, wait a minute. Why all the feverish hurry and rush, little man? You need to pause and acquire a little perspective.' At such times, I frequently drop into the first church that I find open. Although I am a Protestant, I frequently, on weekday afternoons, drop into St. Patrick's Cathedral on Fifth Avenue, and remind myself that I'll be dead in another thirty years, but that the great spiritual truths that all churches teach are eternal. I close my eyes and pray. I find that doing this calms my nerves, rests my body, clarifies my perspective, and helps me revalue my values. May I recommend this practice to you?

During the past six years that I have been writing this book I have collected hundreds of examples and concrete cases of how men and women conquered fear and worry by prayer. I have in my filing cabinet folders bulging with case histories. Let's take as a typical example the story of a discouraged and disheartened book salesman, John R. Anthony, of Houston, Texas. Here is his story as he told it to me.

'Twenty-two years ago I closed my private law office to become state representative of an American lawbook company. My speciality was selling a set of lawbooks to lawyers – a set of books that were almost indispensable.

'I was ably and thoroughly trained for the job. I knew all the direct sales talks, and the convincing answers to all possible objections. Before calling on a prospect, I familiarized myself with his rating as an attorney, the nature of his practice, his politics and hobbies. During my interview, I used that information with ample skill. Yet, something was wrong. I just couldn't get orders!

'I grew discouraged. As the days and weeks passed, I doubled and redoubled my efforts, but was still unable to close enough sales to pay my expenses. A sense of fear and dread grew within me. I became afraid to call on people. Before I could enter a prospect's office, that feeling of dread flared up so strong that I would pace up and down the hallway outside the door – or go out of the building and circle the block. Then, after losing much valuable time and feigning enough courage by sheer willpower to crash the office door, I feebly turned the doorknob with trembling hand – half hoping my prospect would not be in!

'My sales manager threatened to stop my advances if I didn't send in more orders. My wife at home pleaded with me for money to pay the grocery bill for herself and our three children. Worry seized me. Day by day I grew more desperate. I didn't know what to do. As I have already said, I had closed my private law office at home and had given up my clients. Now I was broke. I didn't have the money to pay even my hotel bill. Neither did I have the money to buy a ticket back home; nor did I have the courage to return home a beaten man, even if I had had the ticket. Finally, at the miserable end of another bad day, I trudged back to my hotel room – for the last time, I thought. So far as I was concerned, I was thoroughly beaten. Heartbroken, depressed, I didn't know which way to turn. I hardly cared whether I lived or died. I was sorry I had ever been born. I had nothing but a glass of hot milk that night for dinner. Even that was more than I could afford. I understood that night why desperate men raise a hotel window and jump. I might have done it myself if I had had the courage. I began wondering what was the purpose of life. I didn't know. I couldn't figure it out.

'Since there was no one else to turn to, I turned to God. I began to pray. I implored the Almighty to give me light and understanding and guidance through the dark, dense wilderness of despair that had closed in about me. I asked God to help me get orders for my books and to give me money to feed my wife and children. After that prayer, I opened my eyes and saw a Gideon Bible that lay on the dresser in that lonely hotel room. I opened it and read those beautiful, immortal promises of Jesus that must have inspired countless generations of lonely, worried, and beaten men throughout the ages – a talk that Jesus gave to His disciples about how to keep from worrying:

> Take no thought for your life, what ye shall eat, or what ye shall drink; nor yet for your body, what ye shall put on. Is not the life more than meat, and the body than raiment? Behold the fowls of the air: for they sow not, neither do they reap, nor gather into barns; yet your heavenly Father feedeth them. Are ye not much better than they? . . . But seek ye first the kingdom of God, and his righteousness; and all these things shall be added unto you.

'As I prayed and as I read those words, a miracle happened: my nervous tension fell away. My anxieties, fears, and worries were transformed into heart-warming courage and hope and triumphant faith.

'I was happy, even though I didn't have enough money to pay my hotel bill. I went to bed and slept soundly – free from care – as I had not done for many years.

'Next morning, I could hardly hold myself back until the offices of my prospects were open. I approached the office door of my first prospect that beautiful, cold, rainy day with a bold and positive stride. I turned the doorknob with a firm and steady grip. As I entered, I made a beeline for my man, energetically, chin up, and with appropriate dignity, all smiles, and saying, "Good morning, Mr. Smith! I'm John R. Anthony of the All-American Lawbook Company!"

' "Oh, yes, yes," he replied, smiling, too, as he rose from his chair with outstretched hand. "I'm glad to see you. Have a seat!"

'I made more sales that day than I had made in weeks. That evening I proudly returned to my hotel like a conquering hero! I felt like a new man. And I *was* a new man, because I had a new and victorious mental attitude. No dinner of hot milk that night. No, sir! I had a steak with all the fixin's. From that day on, my sales zoomed.

'I was born anew that desperate night twenty-two years ago in a little hotel in Amarillo, Texas. My outward situation the next day was the same as it had been through my weeks of failure, but a tremendous thing had happened inside me. I had suddenly become aware of my relationship with God. A mere man alone can easily be defeated, but a man alive with the power of God within him is invincible. I know. I saw it work in my own life.

' "Ask, and it shall be given you; seek, and ye shall find; knock, and it shall be opened unto you." '

When Mrs. L. G. Beaird, of Highland, Illinois, was faced with stark tragedy, she discovered that she could find peace and tranquillity by kneeling down and saying, 'Oh, Lord, Thy will, not mine, be done.'

'One evening our telephone rang,' she writes in a letter that I have before me now. 'It rang fourteen times before I had the courage to pick up the receiver. I knew it must be the hospital, and I was terrified. I feared that our little boy was dying. He had meningitis. He had already been given penicillin, but it made his temperature fluctuate, and the doctors feared that the disease had travelled to his brain and might cause the development of a brain tumour – and death. The phone call *was* just what I feared. The hospital was calling; the doctor wanted us to come immediately.

'Maybe you can picture the anguish my husband and I went through, sitting in the waiting room. Everyone else had his baby, but we sat there with empty arms, wondering if we would ever hold our little fellow again. When we were finally called into the doctor's private office, the expression on his face filled our hearts with terror. His words brought even more terror. He told us that there was only one chance in four that our baby would live. He said that if we knew another doctor, to please call him in on the case.

'On the way home my husband broke down and, doubling up his fist, hit the steering wheel, saying, "Betts, I can't give that little guy up." Have you ever seen a man cry? It isn't a pleasant experience. We stopped the car and, after talking things over, decided to stop in church and pray that if it was God's will to take our baby, we would resign our will to His. I sank in the pew and said with tears rolling down my cheeks, "Not my will but Thine be done."

'The moment I uttered those words, I felt better. A sense of peace that I hadn't felt for a long time came over me. All the way home, I kept repeating, "O God, Thy will, not mine, be done." I slept soundly that night for the first time in a week. The doctor called a few days later and said that Bobby had passed the crisis. I thank God for the strong and healthy four-year-old boy we have today.'

I know men who regard religion as something for women and children and preachers. They pride themselves on being 'he-men' who can fight their battles alone.

How surprised they might be to learn that some of the most famous 'he-men' in the world pray every day. For example, 'he-man' Jack Dempsey told me that he never went to bed without saying his prayers. He told me that he never ate a meal without first thanking God for it. He told me that he prayed every day when he was training for a bout, and that when he was fighting, he always prayed just before the bell sounded for each round. 'Praying,' he said, 'helped me fight with courage and confidence.'

'He-man' Connie Mack told me that he couldn't go to sleep without saying his prayers.

'He-man' Eddie Rickenbacker told me that he believed his life had been saved by prayer. He prayed every day.

'He-man' Edward R. Stettinius, former high official of General Motors and United States Steel, and former Secretary of State, told me that he prayed for wisdom and guidance every morning and night.

'He-man' J. Pierpont Morgan, the greatest financier of his age, often went alone to Trinity Church, at the head of Wall Street, on Saturday afternoons and knelt in prayer.

When 'he-man' Eisenhower flew to England to take supreme command of the British and American forces, he took only one book on the plane with him – the Bible.

'He-man' General Mark Clark told me that he read his Bible every day during the war and knelt down in prayer. So did Chiang Kai-shek, and General Montgomery – 'Monty of El Alamein'. So did Lord Nelson at Trafalgar. So did General Washington, Robert E. Lee, Stonewall Jackson, and scores of other great military leaders.

These 'he-men' discovered the truth of William James's statement: 'We and God have business with each other; and in opening ourselves to His influence, our deepest destiny is fulfilled.'

A lot of 'he-men' are discovering that. Seventy-two million Americans are church members now – an all-time record. As I said before, even the scientists are turning to religion. Take, for example, Dr. Alexis Carrel, who wrote *Man, the Unknown* and won the greatest honour that can be bestowed upon any scientist, the Nobel Prize. Dr. Carrel said in a *Reader's Digest* article: 'Prayer is the most powerful form of energy one can generate. It is a force as real as terrestrial gravity. As a physician, I have seen men, after all other therapy had failed, lifted out of disease and melancholy by the serene effort of prayer.... Prayer like radium is a source of luminous, self-generating energy.... In prayer, human beings seek to augment their finite energy by addressing themselves to the Infinite source of all energy. When we pray, we link ourselves with the inexhaustible motive power that spins the universe. We pray that a part of this power be apportioned to our needs. Even in asking, our human deficiencies are filled and we arise strengthened and repaired.... Whenever we address God in fervent prayer, we change both soul and body for the better. It could not happen that any man or woman could pray for a single moment without some good result.'

Admiral Byrd knew what it meant to 'link ourselves with the inexhaustible motive power that spins the universe.' His ability to do that pulled him through the most trying ordeal of his life. He tells the story in his book *Alone*. In 1934, he spent five months in a hut buried beneath the icecap of Ross

Barrier deep in the Antarctic. He was the only living creature south of latitude seventy-eight. Blizzards roared above his shack; the cold plunged down to eighty-two degrees below zero; he was completely surrounded by unending night. And then he found, to his horror, he was being slowly poisoned by carbon monoxide that escaped from his stove! What could he do? The nearest help was 123 miles away, and could not possibly reach him for several months. He tried to fix his stove and ventilating system, but the fumes still escaped. They often knocked him out cold. He lay on the floor completely unconscious. He couldn't eat; he couldn't sleep; he became so feeble that he could hardly leave his bunk. He frequently feared he wouldn't live until morning. He was convinced he would die in that cabin, and his body would be hidden by perpetual snows.

What saved his life? One day, in the depths of his despair, he reached for his diary and tried to set down his philosophy of life. 'The human race,' he wrote, 'is not alone in the universe.' He thought of the stars overhead, of the orderly swing of the constellations and planets; of how the everlasting sun would, in its time, return to lighten even the wastes of the South Polar regions. And then he wrote in his diary, '*I am not alone.*'

This realization that he was not alone – not even in a hole in the ice at the end of the earth – was what saved Richard Byrd. 'I know it pulled me through,' he says. And he goes on to add: 'Few men in their lifetime come anywhere near exhausting the resources dwelling within them. There are deep wells of strength that are never used.' Richard Byrd learned to tap those wells of strength and use those resources – by turning to God.

Glenn A. Arnold learned amidst the cornfields of Illinois the same lesson that Admiral Byrd learned in the polar icecap. Mr. Arnold, an insurance broker in Chillicothe, Illinois, opened his speech on conquering worry like this: 'Eight years ago, I turned the key in the lock of my front door for what I believed was the last time in my life. I then climbed in my car and started down for the river. I was a failure,' he said. 'One month before, my entire little world had come crashing down on my head. My electrical-appliance business had gone on the rocks. In my home my mother lay at the point of death. My wife was carrying our second child. Doctor's bills were mounting. We had mort- gaged everything we had to start the business – our car and our furniture. I had even taken out a loan on my insurance policies. Now everything was gone. I couldn't take it any longer. So I climbed into my car and started for the river – determined to end the sorry mess.

'I drove a few miles out in the country, pulled off the road, and got out and sat on the ground and wept like a child. Then I really started to think – instead of going around in frightening circles of worry, I tried to think con- structively. How bad was my situation? Couldn't it be worse? Was it really hopeless? What could I do to make it better?

'I decided then and there to take the whole problem to the Lord and ask Him to handle it. I prayed. I prayed hard. I prayed as though my very life depended on it – which, in fact, it did. Then a strange thing happened. As soon as I turned all my problems over to a power greater than myself, I immediately felt a peace of mind that I hadn't known in months. I must have sat there for half an hour, weeping and praying. Then I went home and slept like a child.

'The next morning, I arose with confidence. I no longer had anything to fear, for I was depending on God for guidance. That morning I walked into a local department store with my head high; and I spoke with confidence as I applied for a job as salesman in the electrical-appliance department. I knew I would get the job. And I did. I made good at it until the whole appliance business collapsed due to the war. Then I began selling life insurance – still under the management of my Great Guide. That was only five years ago. Now, all my bills are paid; I have a fine family of three bright children; own my own home; have a new car, and own twenty-five thousand dollars in life insurance.

'As I look back, I am glad now that I lost everything and became so depressed that I started for the river – because that tragedy taught me to rely on God; and I now have a peace and confidence that I never dreamed were possible.'

Why does religious faith bring us such peace and calm and fortitude? I'll let William James answer that. He says: '*The turbulent billows of the fretful surface leave the deep parts of the ocean undisturbed; and to him who has a hold on vaster and more permanent realities, the hourly vicissitudes of his personal destiny seem relatively insignificant things. The really religious person is accordingly unshakeable and full of equanimity, and calmly ready for any duty that the day may bring forth.*'

If we are worried and anxious – why not try God? Why not, as Immanuel Kant said, 'accept a belief in God because we need such a belief'? Why not link ourselves now 'with the inexhaustible motive power that spins the universe'?

Even if you are not a religious person by nature or training – even if you are an out-and-out sceptic – prayer can help you much more than you believe, for it is a *practical* thing. What do I mean, practical? I mean that prayer fulfils these three very basic psychological needs which all people share, whether they believe in God or not:

1. Prayer helps us to put into words exactly what is troubling us. We saw in Chapter 4 that it is almost impossible to deal with a problem while it remains vague and nebulous. Praying, in a way, is very much like writing our problems down on paper. If we ask help for a problem – even from God – we must put it into words.

2. Prayer gives us a sense of sharing our burdens, of not being alone. Few of us are so strong that we can bear our heaviest burdens, our most agonizing troubles, all by ourselves. Sometimes our worries are of so intimate a nature that we cannot discuss them even with our closest relatives or friends. Then prayer is the answer. Any psychiatrist will tell us that when we are pent-up

and tense, and in an agony of spirit, it is therapeutically good to tell someone our troubles. When we can't tell anyone else – we can always tell God.

3. Prayer puts into force an active principle of *doing*. It's a first step toward *action*. I doubt if anyone can pray for some fulfilment, day after day, without benefiting from it – in other words, without taking some steps to bring it to pass. The world-famous scientist, Dr. Alexis Carrel, said: 'Prayer is the most powerful form of energy one can generate.' So why not make use of it? Call it God or Allah or Spirit – why quarrel with definitions as long as the mysterious powers of nature take us in hand?

Why not close this book right now, shut the door, kneel down, and unburden your heart? If you have lost your faith, beseech Almighty God to renew it; and repeat this beautiful prayer written by Saint Francis of Assisi seven hundred years ago: 'Lord, make me an instrument of Thy Peace. Where there is hatred, let me sow love. Where there is injury, pardon. Where there is doubt, faith. Where there is despair, hope. Where there is darkness, light. Where there is sadness, joy. O Divine Master, grant that I may not so much seek to be consoled as to console; to be understood, as to understand; to be loved, as to love; for it is in giving that we receive, it is in pardoning that we are pardoned, and it is in dying that we are born to Eternal Life.'

Part Six

HOW TO KEEP FROM WORRYING

ABOUT CRITICISM

☐ 20 ☐

Remember that no one ever
kicks a dead dog

An event occurred in 1929 that created a national sensation in educational circles. Learned men from all over America rushed to Chicago to witness the affair. A few years earlier, a young man by the name of Robert Hutchins had worked his way through Yale, acting as a waiter, a lumberjack, a tutor, and a clothesline salesman. Now, only eight years later, he was being inaugurated as president of the fourth richest university in America, the University of Chicago. His age? Thirty. Incredible! The older educators shook their heads. Criticism came roaring down upon this 'boy wonder' like a rockslide. He was this and he was that – too young, inexperienced – his educational ideas were cockeyed. Even the newspapers joined in the attack.

The day he was inaugurated, a friend said to the father of Robert Maynard Hutchins: 'I was shocked this morning to read that newspaper editorial denouncing your son.'

'Yes,' the elder Hutchins replied, 'it was severe, but remember that no one ever kicks a dead dog.'

Yes, and the more important a dog is, the more satisfaction people get in kicking him. The Prince of Wales who later became Edward VIII had that brought home to him in the seat of his pants. He was attending Dartmouth College in Devonshire at the time – a college that corresponds to our Naval Academy at Annapolis. The Prince was about fourteen. One day one of the naval officers found him crying, and asked him what was wrong. He refused to tell at first, but finally admitted the truth: he was being kicked by the naval cadets. The commodore of the college summoned the boys and explained to them that the Prince had not complained, but he wanted to find out why the Prince had been singled out for this rough treatment.

After much hemming and hawing and toe scraping, the cadets finally confessed that when they themselves became commanders and captains in the King's Navy, they wanted to be able to say that they had kicked the King!

So when you are kicked and criticized, remember that it is often done because it gives the kicker a feeling of importance. It often means that you are accomplishing something and are worthy of attention. Many people get a sense of savage satisfaction out of denouncing those who are better educated than they are or more successful. For example, while I was writing this chapter, I received a letter from a woman denouncing General William Booth, founder of the Salvation Army. I had given a laudatory broadcast about General Booth; so this woman wrote me, saying that General Booth had stolen eight million dollars of the money he had collected to help poor people. The charge, of course, was absurd. But this woman wasn't looking for truth. She was seeking the mean-spirited gratification that she got from tearing down someone far above her. I threw her bitter letter into the wastebasket, and thanked Almighty God that I wasn't married to her. Her letter didn't tell me anything at all about General Booth, but it did tell me a lot about her. Schopenhauer had said it years ago: 'Vulgar people take huge delight in the faults and follies of great men.'

One hardly thinks of the president of Yale as a vulgar man; yet a former president of Yale, Timothy Dwight, apparently took huge delight in denouncing a man who was running for President of the United States. The president of Yale warned that if this man were elected President, 'we may see our wives and daughters the victims of legal prostitution, soberly dishonoured, speciously polluted; the outcasts of delicacy and virtue, the loathing of God and man.'

Sounds almost like a denunciation of Hitler, doesn't it? But it wasn't. It was a denunciation of Thomas Jefferson. *Which* Thomas Jefferson? Surely not the *immortal* Thomas Jefferson, the author of the Declaration of Independence, the patron saint of democracy? Yes, verily, that was the man.

What American do you suppose was denounced as a 'hypocrite', 'an impostor', and as 'little better than a murderer'? A newspaper cartoon depicted him on a guillotine, the big knife ready to cut off his head. Crowds jeered at him and hissed him as he rode through the streets. Who was he? George Washington.

But that occurred a long time ago. Maybe human nature has improved since then. Let's see. Let's take the case of Admiral Peary – the explorer who startled and thrilled the world by reaching the North Pole with dog sleds on April 6, 1909 – a goal that brave men for centuries had suffered and starved and died to attain. Peary himself almost died from cold and starvation; and eight of his toes were frozen so hard they had to be cut off. He was so overwhelmed with disasters that he feared he would go insane. His superior naval officers in Washington were burned up because Peary was getting so much publicity and acclaim. So they accused him of collecting money for scientific expeditions and then 'lying around and loafing in the Arctic'. And they probably believed it, because it is almost impossible not to believe what you want to believe. Their determination to humiliate and block Peary was so violent that only a direct order from President McKinley enabled Peary to continue his career in the Arctic.

Would Peary have been denounced if he had had a desk job in the Navy

Department in Washington? No. He wouldn't have been important enough then to have aroused jealousy.

General Grant had an even worse experience than Admiral Peary. In 1862, General Grant won the first great decisive victory that the North had enjoyed – a victory that was achieved in one afternoon, a victory that made Grant a national idol overnight – a victory that had tremendous repercussions even in far-off Europe – a victory that set church bells ringing and bonfires blazing from Maine to the banks of the Mississippi. Yet within six weeks after achieving that great victory, Grant – hero of the North – was *arrested and his army was taken from him. He wept with humiliation and despair.*

Why was General U. S. Grant arrested at the flood tide of his victory? Largely because he had aroused the jealousy and envy of his arrogant superiors.

If we are tempted to be worried about unjust criticism, here is Rule 1:

Remember that unjust criticism is often a disguised compliment. Remember that no one ever kicks a dead dog.

☐ 21 ☐

Do this – and criticism can't hurt you

I once interviewed Major General Smedley Butler – old 'Gimlet-Eye'. Old 'Hell-Devil' Butler! Remember him? One of the most colourful, swashbuckling generals who ever commanded the United States Marines.

He told me that when he was young, he was desperately eager to be popular, wanted to make a good impression on everyone. In those days the slightest criticism smarted and stung. But he confessed that thirty years in the Marines had toughened his hide. 'I have been berated and insulted,' he said, 'and denounced as a yellow dog, a snake, and a skunk. I have been cursed by the experts. I have been called every possible combination of unprintable cuss words in the English language. Bother me? Huh! When I hear somebody cussing me now, I never turn my head to see who is talking.'

Maybe old 'Gimlet-Eye' Butler was too indifferent to criticism; but one thing is sure: most of us take the little jibes and javelins that are hurled at us far too seriously. I remember the time, years ago, when a reporter from the

New York *Sun* attended a demonstration meeting of my adult-education classes and lampooned me and my work. Was I burned up? I took it as a personal insult. I telephoned Gil Hodges, the Chairman of the Executive Committee of the *Sun*, and practically demanded that he print an article stating the facts – instead of ridicule. I was determined to make the punishment fit the crime.

I am ashamed now of the way I acted. I realize now that half the people who bought the paper never saw that article. Half of those who read it regarded it as a source of innocent merriment. Half of those who gloated over it forgot all about it in a few weeks.

I realize now that people are not thinking about you and me or caring what is said about us. They are thinking about themselves – before breakfast, after breakfast, and right on until ten minutes past midnight. They would be a thousand times more concerned about a slight headache of their own than they would about the news of your death or mine.

Even if you and I are lied about, ridiculed, double-crossed, knifed in the back, and sold down the river by one out of every six of our most intimate friends – let's not indulge in an orgy of self-pity. Instead, let's remind ourselves that that's precisely what happened to Jesus. One of His twelve most intimate friends turned traitor for a bribe that would amount, in our modern money, to about nineteen dollars. Another one of His twelve most intimate friends openly deserted Jesus the moment He got into trouble, and declared three times that he didn't even know Jesus – and he swore as he said it. One out of six! That is what happened to Jesus. Why should you and I expect a better score?

I discovered years ago that although I couldn't keep people from criticizing me unjustly, I could do something infinitely more important: I could determine whether I would let the unjust condemnation disturb me.

Let's be clear about this: I am not advocating ignoring all criticism. Far from it. I am talking about *ignoring only unjust criticism*. I once asked Eleanor Roosevelt how she handled unjust criticism – and Allah knows she had a lot of it. She probably had more ardent friends and more violent enemies than any other woman who ever lived in the White House.

She told me that as a young girl she was almost morbidly shy, afraid of what people might say. She was so afraid of criticism that one day she asked her aunt, Theodore Roosevelt's sister, for advice. She said: 'Auntie Bye, I want to do so-and-so. But I'm afraid of being criticized.'

Teddy Roosevelt's sister looked her in the eye and said: 'Never be bothered by what people say, as long as you know in your heart you are right.' Eleanor Roosevelt told me that that bit of advice proved to be her Rock of Gibraltar years later, when she was in the White House. She told me that the only way we can avoid all criticism is to be like a Dresden-china figure and stay on a shelf. 'Do what you feel in your heart to be right – for you'll be criticized, anyway. You'll be "damned if you do, and damned if you don't." ' That is her advice.

When the late Matthew C. Brush was president of the American International Corporation, I asked him if he was ever sensitive to criticism; and he replied, 'Yes, I was very sensitive to it in my early days. I was eager then to have all the employees in the organization think I was perfect. If they didn't, it worried me. I would try to please first one person who had been sounding off against me; but the very thing I did to patch it up with him would make someone else mad. Then when I tried to fix it up with this person, I would stir up a couple of other bumblebees. I finally discovered that the more I tried to pacify and to smooth over injured feelings in order to escape personal criticism, the more certain I was to increase my enemies. So finally I said to myself, "If you get your head above the crowd, you're going to be criticized. So get used to the idea." That helped me tremendously. From that time on I made it a rule to do the very best I could and then put up my old umbrella and let the rain of criticism drain off me instead of run down my neck.'

Deems Taylor went a bit further: he let the rain of criticism run down his neck and had a good laugh over it – in public. When he was giving his comments during the intermission of the Sunday-afternoon radio concerts of the New York Philharmonic-Symphony Orchestra, one woman wrote him a letter calling him 'a liar, a traitor, a snake, and a moron'. Mr. Taylor says in his book, *Of Men and Music*: 'I have a suspicion that she didn't care for that talk.' On the following week's broadcast, Mr. Taylor read this letter over the radio to millions of listeners – and received another letter from the same lady a few days later, 'expressing her unaltered opinion,' says Mr. Taylor, 'that I was *still* a liar, a traitor, a snake, and a moron.' We can't keep from admiring a man who takes criticism like that. We admire his serenity, his unshaken poise, and his sense of humour.

When Charles Schwab was addressing the student body at Princeton, he confessed that one of the most important lessons he had ever learned was taught to him by an old German who worked in Schwab's steel mill. This old German got involved in a hot wartime argument with the other steelworkers, and they tossed him into the river. 'When he came into my office,' Mr. Schwab said, 'covered with mud and water, I asked him what he had said to the men who had thrown him into the river, and he replied: "I just laughed."'

Mr. Schwab declared that he had adopted that old German's words as his motto: 'Just laugh.'

That motto is especially good when you are the victim of unjust criticism. You can answer the man who answers you back, but what can you say to the man who 'just laughs'?

Lincoln might have broken under the strain of the Civil War if he hadn't learned the folly of trying to answer all the vitriolic condemnations hurled at him. His description of how he handled his critics has become a literary gem – a classic. General MacArthur had a copy of it hanging above his headquarters desk during the war; and Winston Churchill had a framed copy of it on the walls of his study at Chartwell. It goes like this: 'If I were to try to read, much less to answer, all the attacks made on me, this shop might as well be closed for any other business. I do the very best I know how – the very best I can; and I mean to keep on doing so until the end. If the end brings me out all right, then what is said against me won't matter. If the end brings me out wrong, then ten angels swearing I was right would make no difference.'

When you and I are unjustly criticized, let's remember Rule 2:

Do the very best you can; and then put up your old umbrella and keep the rain of criticism from running down the back of your neck.

☐ **22** ☐

Fool things I have done

I have a folder in my private filing cabinet marked 'FTD' – short for 'Fool Things I Have Done'. I put in that folder written records of the fool things I have been guilty of. I sometimes dictate these memos to my secretary, but sometimes they are so personal, so stupid, that I am ashamed to dictate them, so I write them out in longhand.

I can still recall some of the criticisms of Dale Carnegie that I put in my 'FTD' folders fifteen years ago. If I had been utterly honest with myself, I would now have a filing cabinet bursting out at the seams with these 'FTD' memos. I can truthfully repeat what King Saul said thirty centuries ago: 'I have played the fool and have erred exceedingly.'

When I get out my 'FTD' folders and reread the criticisms I have written of myself, they help me deal with the toughest problem I shall ever face: the management of Dale Carnegie.

I used to blame my troubles on other people; but as I have grown older – and wiser, I hope – I have realized that I myself, in the last analysis, am to blame for almost all my misfortunes. Lots of people have discovered that, as they grow older. 'No one but myself,' said Napoleon at St. Helena, 'no one but myself can be blamed for my fall. I have been my own greatest enemy – the cause of my own disastrous fate.'

Let me tell you about a man I knew who was an artist when it came to self-appraisal and self-management. His name was H. P. Howell. When the news of his sudden death in the drugstore of the Hotel Ambassador in New York was flashed across the nation on July 31, 1944, Wall Street was shocked, for he was a leader in American finance – chairman of the board of the Commercial National Bank and Trust Company and a director of several large corporations. He grew up with little formal education, started out in life clerking in a country store, and later became credit manager for U.S. Steel – and was on his way to position and power.

'For years I have kept an engagement book showing all the appointments I have during the day,' Mr. Howell told me when I asked him to explain the reasons for his success. 'My family never makes any plans for me on Saturday night, for the family knows that I devote a part of each Saturday evening to self-examination and a review and appraisal of my work during the week. After dinner I go off by myself, open my engagement book, and think over all the interviews, discussions, and meetings that have taken place since Monday morning. I ask myself: 'What mistakes did I make that time?' 'What did I do that was right – and in what way could I have improved my performance?' 'What lessons can I learn from that experience?' I sometimes find that this weekly review makes me very unhappy. Sometimes I am astonished by my own blunders. Of course, as the years have gone by, these blunders have become less frequent. This system of self-analysis, continued year after year, has done more for me than any other thing I have ever attempted.'

Maybe H. P. Howell borrowed his idea from Ben Franklin. Only Franklin didn't wait until Saturday night. He gave himself a severe going-over *every* night. He discovered that he had thirteen serious faults. Here are three of them: wasting time, stewing around over trifles, arguing and contradicting people. Wise old Ben Franklin realized that, unless he eliminated these handicaps, he wasn't going to get very far. So he battled with one of his shortcomings every day for a week, and kept a record of who had won each day's slugging match. The next week, he would pick out another bad habit, put on the gloves, and when the bell rang he would come out of his corner fighting. Franklin kept up this battle with his faults every week for more than two years.

No wonder he became one of the best-loved and most influential men this nation ever produced!

Elbert Hubbard said: 'Every man is a damn fool for at least five minutes every day. Wisdom consists in not exceeding that limit.'

The small man flies into a rage over the slightest criticism, but the wise man is eager to learn from those who have censured him and reproved him and 'disputed the passage with him'. Walt Whitman put it this way: 'Have you learned lessons only of those who admired you, and were tender with you, and stood aside for you? Have you not learned great lessons from those who rejected you, and braced themselves against you, or disputed the passage with you?'

Instead of waiting for our enemies to criticize us or our work, let's beat them to it. Let's be our own most severe critic. Let's find and remedy all our weaknesses before our enemies get a chance to say a word. That is what Charles Darwin did. In fact, he spent fifteen years criticizing – well, the story goes like this: When Darwin completed the manuscript of his immortal book, *The Origin of Species*, he realized that the publication of his revolutionary concept of creation would rock the intellectual and religious worlds. So *he became his own critic and spent another fifteen years, checking his data, challenging his reasoning, criticizing his conclusions.*

Suppose someone denounced you as 'a damn fool' – what would you do? Get angry? Indignant? Here is what Lincoln did: Edward M. Stanton, Lincoln's Secretary of War, once called Lincoln 'a damn fool'. Stanton was indignant because Lincoln had been meddling in Stanton's affairs. In order to please a selfish politician, Lincoln had signed an order transferring certain regiments. Stanton not only refused to carry out Lincoln's orders, but swore that Lincoln was a damn fool for ever signing such orders. What happened? When Lincoln was told what Stanton had said, Lincoln calmly replied: 'If Stanton said I am a damned fool, then I must be, for he is nearly always right. I'll just step over and see for myself.'

Lincoln did go to see Stanton. Stanton convinced him that the order was wrong, and Lincoln withdrew it. Lincoln welcomed criticism when he knew it was sincere, founded on knowledge, and given in a spirit of helpfulness.

You and I ought to welcome that kind of criticism, too, for we can't even hope to be right more than three times out of four. At least, that was all Theodore Roosevelt said he could hope for, when he was in the White House. Einstein, the most profound thinker of our day, confessed that his conclusions were wrong ninety-nine percent of the time!

'The opinions of our enemies,' said La Rochefoucauld, 'come nearer to the truth about us than do our own opinions.'

I know that statement may be true many times; yet when anyone starts to criticize me, if I do not watch myself, I instantly and automatically leap to the defensive – even before I have the slightest idea what my critic is going to say. I am disgusted with myself every time I do it. We all tend to resent criticism and lap up praise, regardless of whether either the criticism or the praise is justified. We are not creatures of logic. We are creatures of emotions. Our logic is like a birch-bark canoe tossed about on a deep, dark, stormy sea of emotion.

If we hear that someone has spoken ill of us, let's not try to defend ourselves. Every fool does that. Let's be original – and humble – and brilliant! Let's confound our critic and win applause for ourselves by saying: 'If my critic had known about *all my other faults*, he would have criticized me much more severely than he did.'

In previous chapters, I have talked about what to do when you are unjustly criticized. But here is another idea: when your anger is rising because you feel you have been unjustly condemned, why not stop and say: 'Just a minute . . . I am far from perfect. If Einstein admits he is wrong ninety-nine percent of the time, maybe I am wrong at least eighty percent of the time. Maybe I deserve this criticism. If I do, I ought to be thankful for it, and try to profit by it.'

Charles Luckman, a former president of the Pepsodent Company, spent a million dollars a year putting Bob Hope on the air. He didn't look at the letters praising the programme, but he insisted on seeing the critical letters. He knew he might learn something from them.

The Ford Company was so eager to find out what was wrong with its management and operations that it polled the employees and invited them to criticize the company.

I know a former soap salesman who used even to *ask* for criticism. When he first started out selling soap for Colgate, orders came slowly. He worried about losing his job. Since he knew there was nothing wrong with the soap or the price, he figured that the trouble must be himself. When he failed to make a sale, he would often walk around the block trying to figure out what was wrong. Had he been too vague? Did he lack enthusiasm? Sometimes he would go back to the merchant and say: 'I haven't come back here to try to sell you any soap. I have come back to get your advice and your criticism. Won't you please tell me what I did that was wrong when I tried to sell you soap a few minutes ago? You are far more experienced and successful than I am. Please give me your criticism. Be frank. Don't pull your punches.'

This attitude won him a lot of friends and priceless advice.

What do you suppose ever happened to him? He rose to be president of the Colgate-Palmolive-Peet Soap Company – one of the world's largest makers of soap. His name is E. H. Little.

It takes a big man to do what H. P. Howell, Ben Franklin, and E. H. Little did. And now, while nobody is looking, why not peep into the mirror and ask yourself whether you belong to that kind of company!

To keep from worrying about criticism, here is Rule 3:

Let's keep a record of the fool things we have done and criticize ourselves. Since we can't hope to be perfect, let's do what E. H. Little did: Let's ask for unbiased, helpful, constructive criticism.

☐ IN A NUTSHELL ☐

HOW TO KEEP FROM WORRYING ABOUT CRITICISM

RULE 1: Unjust criticism is often a disguised compliment. It often means that you have aroused jealousy and envy. Remember that no one ever kicks a dead dog.

RULE 2: Do the very best you can; and then put up your old umbrella and keep the rain of criticism from running down the back of your neck.

RULE 3: Let's keep a record of the fool things we have done and criticize ourselves. Since we can't hope to be perfect, let's do what E. H. Little did: let's ask for unbiased, helpful, constructive criticism.

Part Seven

SIX WAYS TO PREVENT FATIGUE AND

WORRY AND KEEP YOUR ENERGY

AND SPIRITS HIGH

□ 23 □

How to add one hour a day to your waking life

Why am I writing a chapter on preventing fatigue in a book on preventing worry? That is simple: because fatigue often produces worry, or, at least, it makes you susceptible to worry. Any medical student will tell you that fatigue lowers physical resistance to the common cold, and hundreds of other diseases; and any psychiatrist will tell you that fatigue also lowers your resistance to the emotions of fear and worry. So preventing fatigue tends to prevent worry.

Did I say 'tends' to prevent worry'? That is putting it mildly. Dr. Edmund Jacobson goes much further. Dr. Jacobson has written two books on relaxation: *Progressive Relaxation* and *You Must Relax*; and as director of the University of Chicago Laboratory for Clinical Physiology, he has spent years conducting investigations in using relaxation as a method in medical practice. He declares that any nervous or emotional state 'fails to exist in the presence of complete relaxation.' That is another way of saying: *You cannot continue to worry if you relax.*

So, to prevent fatigue and worry, the first rule is: Rest often. Rest before you get tired.

Why is that so important? Because fatigue accumulates with astonishing rapidity. The United States Army has discovered by repeated tests that even young men – men toughened by years of Army training – can march better, and hold up longer, if they throw down their packs and rest ten minutes out of every hour. So the Army forces them to do just that. Your heart is just as smart as the U.S. Army. Your heart pumps enough blood through your body every day to fill a railway tank car. It exerts enough energy every twenty-four hours to shovel twenty tons of coal onto a platform three feet high. It does this incredible amount of work for fifty, seventy, or maybe ninety years. How can it stand it? Dr. Walter B. Cannon, of the Harvard Medical School, explained it. He said: 'Most people have the idea that the heart is working all the time. As a matter of fact, there is a definite rest period after each contraction. *When beating at a moderate rate of seventy pulses per minute, the heart is actually working only nine hours out of the twenty-four. In the aggregate its rest periods total a full fifteen hours per day.*'

During World War II, Winston Churchill, in his late sixties and early seventies, was able to work sixteen hours a day, year after year, directing the war efforts of the British Empire. A phenomenal record. His secret? He worked in bed each morning until eleven o'clock, reading reports, dictating orders, making telephone calls, and holding important conferences. After lunch, he went to bed again and slept for an hour. In the evening, he went to bed once more and slept for two hours before having dinner at eight. He didn't cure fatigue. He didn't have to cure it. He prevented it. Because he rested frequently, he was able to work on, fresh and fit, until long past midnight.

The original John D. Rockefeller made two extraordinary records. He accumulated the greatest fortune the world had ever seen up to that time and he also lived to be ninety-eight. How did he do it? The chief reason, of course, was because he had inherited a tendency to live long. Another reason was his habit of taking a half-hour nap in his office every noon. He would lie down on his office couch – and not even the President of the United States could get John D. on the phone while he was having his snooze!

In his excellent book, *Why Be Tired*, Daniel W. Josselyn observed: 'Rest is not a matter of doing absolutely nothing. *Rest is repair.*' There is so much repair power in a short period of rest that even a five-minute nap will help to forestall fatigue. Connie Mack, the grand old man of baseball, told me that if he didn't take an afternoon nap before a game, he was all tuckered out at around the fifth inning. But if he did go to sleep, if for only five minutes, he could last throughout an entire double-header without feeling tired.

When I asked Eleanor Roosevelt how she was able to carry such an exhausting schedule during the twelve years she was in the White House, she said that before meeting a crowd or making a speech, she would often sit in a chair or davenport, close her eyes, and relax for twenty minutes.

I once interviewed Gene Autry in his dressing room at Madison Square Garden, where he was the star attraction at the world's championship rodeo. I noticed an army cot in his dressing room. 'I lie down there every afternoon,' Gene Autry said, 'and get an hour's nap between performances. When I am making pictures in Hollywood,' he continued, 'I often relax in a big easy chair and get two or three ten-minute naps a day. They buck me up tremendously.'

Edison attributed his enormous energy and endurance to his habit of sleeping whenever he wanted to.

I interviewed Henry Ford shortly before his eightieth birthday. I was surprised to see how fresh and fine he looked. I asked him the secret. He said, 'I never stand up when I can sit down; and I never sit down when I can lie down.'

Horace Mann, 'the father of modern education', did the same thing as he grew older. When he was president of Antioch College, he used to stretch out on a couch while interviewing students.

I persuaded a motion-picture director in Hollywood to try a similar technique. He confessed that it worked miracles. I refer to Jack Chertock, who was one of Hollywood's top directors. When he came to see me several years ago, he was then head of the short-feature department of M-G-M. Worn out and exhausted, he had tried everything: tonics, vitamins, medicine. Nothing helped much. I suggested that he take a vacation every day. How? By stretching out in his office and relaxing while holding conferences with his staff writers.

When I saw him again, two years later, he said, 'A miracle has happened. That is what my own physicians call it. I used to sit up in my chair, tense and taut, while discussing ideas for our short features. Now I stretch out on the office couch during these conferences. I feel better than I have felt in twenty years. Work two hours a day longer, yet I rarely get tired.'

How does all this apply to you? If you are a stenographer, you can't take naps in the office as Edison did, and as Sam Goldwyn did; and if you are an accountant, you can't stretch out on the couch while discussing a financial statement with the boss. But if you live in a small city and go home for lunch, you may be able to take a ten-minute nap after lunch. That is what General George C. Marshall used to do. He felt he was so busy directing the U.S. Army in wartime that he *had* to rest at noon. If you are over fifty and feel you are too rushed to do it, then buy immediately all the life insurance you can get. Funerals come high – and suddenly – these days; and your spouse may want to take your insurance money and marry a younger person.

If you can't take a nap at noon, you can at least try to lie down for an hour before the evening meal. It is cheaper than a cocktail; and, over a long stretch, it is 5467 times more effective. If you can sleep for an hour around five, six, or seven o'clock, you can add one hour a day to your waking life. Why? How? Because an hour's nap before the evening meal plus six hours' sleep at night – a total of seven hours – will do you more good than eight hours of unbroken sleep.

A physical worker can do more work if he takes more time out for rest. Frederick Taylor demonstrated that while working as a scientific-management engineer with the Bethlehem Steel Company. He observed that labouring men were loading approximately $12\frac{1}{2}$ tons of pig iron per man each day on freight cars and that they were exhausted at noon. He made a scientific study of all the fatigue factors involved, and declared that these men should be loading not $12\frac{1}{2}$ tons of pig iron per day, but *forty-seven* tons per day! He figured that they ought to do almost four times as much as they were doing, and not be exhausted. But prove it!

Taylor selected a Mr. Schmidt who was required to work by the stop-watch. Schmidt was told by the man who stood over him with a watch, 'Now pick up a 'pig' and walk . . . Now sit down and rest . . . Now walk . . . Now rest.'

What happened? Schmidt carried forty-seven tons of pig iron each day while the other men carried only $12\frac{1}{2}$ tons per man. And he practically never failed to work at this pace during the three years that Frederick Taylor was at Bethlehem. Schmidt was able to do this because he rested before he got tired.

He worked approximately 26 minutes out of the hour and rested 34 minutes. He rested *more* than he worked – yet he did almost four times as much work as the others! Is this mere hearsay? No, you can read the record yourself on pages 41–62 of *Principles of Scientific Management*, by Frederick Winslow Taylor.

Let me repeat: do what the Army does – take frequent rests. Do what your heart does – rest before you get tired, and you will add one hour a day to your waking life.

☐ **24** ☐

What makes you tired – and what you can do about it

Here is an astounding and significant fact: Mental work alone can't make you tired. Sounds absurd. But a few years ago, scientists tried to find out how long the human brain could labour without reaching 'a diminished capacity for work', the scientific definition of fatigue. To the amazement of these scientists, they discovered that blood passing through the brain, when it is active, shows no fatigue at all! If you took blood from the veins of a day labourer while he was working, you would find it full of 'fatigue toxins' and fatigue products. But if you took a drop of blood from the brain of an Albert Einstein, it would show no fatigue toxins whatever at the end of the day.

So far as the brain is concerned, it can work 'as well and as swiftly at the end of eight or even twelve hours of effort as at the beginning.' The brain is utterly tireless ... So what makes you tired?

Psychiatrists declare that most of our fatigue derives from our mental and emotional attitudes. One of England's most distinguished psychiatrists, J. A. Hadfield, says in his book *The Psychology of Power*: 'the greater part of the fatigue from which we suffer is of mental origin; in fact exhaustion of purely physical origin is rare.'

One of America's most distinguished psychiatrists, Dr. A. A. Brill, goes even further. He declares, 'One hundred percent of the fatigue of the sedentary worker in good health is due to psychological factors, by which we mean emotional factors.'

What kinds of emotional factors tire the sedentary (or sitting) worker? Joy? Contentment? No! Never! Boredom, resentment, a feeling of not being appreciated, a feeling of futility, hurry, anxiety, worry – those are the emotional factors that exhaust the sitting worker, make him susceptible to colds, reduce his output, and send him home with a nervous headache. Yes, we get tired because our emotions produce nervous tension in the body.

The Metropolitan Life Insurance Company pointed that out in a leaflet on fatigue: 'Hard work by itself,' says this great life-insurance company, 'seldom causes fatigue which cannot be cured by a good sleep or rest ... Worry, tenseness, and emotional upsets are three of the biggest causes of fatigue. Often they are to blame when physical or mental work seems to be the cause ... Remember that a tense muscle is a working muscle. Ease up! Save energy for important duties.'

Stop now, right where you are, and give yourself a checkup. As you read these lines, are you scowling at the book? Do you feel a strain between the eyes? Are you sitting relaxed in your chair? Or are you hunching up your shoulders? Are the muscles of your face tense? Unless your entire body is as limp and relaxed as an old rag doll, you are at this very moment producing nervous tensions and muscular tensions. *You are producing nervous tensions and nervous fatigue!*

Why do we produce these unnecessary tensions in doing mental work? Daniel W. Josselyn says: 'I find that the chief obstacle ... is the almost universal belief that hard work requires a feeling of effort, else it is not well done.' So we scowl when we concentrate. We hunch up our shoulders. We call on our muscles to make the motion of *effort*, which in no way assists our brain in its work.

Here is an astonishing and tragic truth: millions of people who wouldn't dream of wasting dollars go right on wasting and squandering their energy with the recklessness of seven drunken sailors in Singapore.

What is the answer to this nervous fatigue? Relax! Relax! Relax! *Learn to relax while you are doing your work!*

Easy? No. You will probably have to reverse the habits of a lifetime. But it is worth the effort, for it may revolutionize your life! William James said, in his essay 'The Gospel of Relaxation': 'The American overtension and jerkiness and breathlessness and intensity and agony of expression ... are *bad habits*, nothing more or less.' *Tension is a habit. Relaxing is a habit. And bad habits can be broken, good habits formed.*

How do you relax? Do you start with your mind, or do you start with your nerves? You don't start with either. You always begin to *relax with your muscles!*

Let's give it a try. To show how it is done, suppose we start with your eyes. Read this paragraph through, and when you've reached the end, lean back, close your eyes, *and say to your eyes* silently, 'Let go. Let go. Stop straining, stop frowning. Let go. Let go.' Repeat that over and over very slowly for a minute ...

Didn't you notice that after a few seconds the muscles of the eyes *began to obey*? Didn't you feel as though some hand had wiped away the tension?

Well, incredible as it seems, you have sampled in that one minute the whole key and secret to the art of relaxing. You can do the same thing with the jaw, with the muscles of the face, with the neck, with the shoulders, the whole of the body. But the most important organ of all is the eye. Dr. Edmund Jacobson of the University of Chicago has gone so far as to say that if you can completely relax the muscles of the eyes, you can forget all your troubles! The reason the eyes are so important in relieving nervous tension is that they burn up one fourth of all the nervous energies consumed by the body. That is also why so many people with perfectly sound vision suffer from 'eyestrain'. They are tensing the eyes.

Vickie Baum, the famous novelist, said that when she was a child, she met an old man who taught her one of the most important lessons she ever learned. She had fallen down and cut her knees and hurt her wrist. The old man picked her up; he had once been a circus clown; and, as he brushed her off, he said: 'The reason you injured yourself was because you don't know how to relax. You have to pretend you are as limp as a sock, as an old crumpled sock. Come I'll show you how to do it.'

That old man taught Vicki Baum and the other children how to fall, how to do flip-flops, and how to turn somersaults. And always he insisted, 'Think of yourself as an old crumpled sock. Then you've *got* to relax!'

You can relax in odd moments, almost anywhere you are. Only don't make an effort to relax. *Relaxation is the absence of all tension and effort.* Think ease and relaxation. Begin by thinking relaxation of the muscles of your eyes and your face, saying over and over, 'Let go ... let go ... let go and relax'. Feel the energy flowing out of your facial muscles to the centre of your body. Think of yourself as free from tension as a baby.

That is what Galli-Curci, the great soprano, used to do. Helen Jepson told me that she used to see Galli-Curci before a performance, sitting in a chair with all her muscles relaxed and her lower jaw so limp it actually sagged. An excellent practice – it kept her from becoming too nervous before her stage entrance; it prevented fatigue.

Here are four suggestions that will help you to learn to relax.

1 Relax in odd moments. Let your body go limp like an old sock. I keep an old, maroon-coloured sock on my desk as I work – keep it there as a reminder of how limp I ought to be. If you haven't got a sock, a cat will do. Did you ever pick up a kitten sleeping in the sunshine? If so, both ends sagged like a wet newspaper. Even the yogis in India say that if you want to master the art of relaxation, study the cat. I never saw a tired cat, a cat with a nervous breakdown, or a cat suffering from insomnia, worry, or stomach ulcers. You will probably avoid these disasters if you learn to relax as the cat does.

2 Work, as much as possible, in a comfortable position. Remember that tensions on the body produce aching shoulders and nervous fatigue.

3 Check yourself four or five times a day, and say to yourself, 'Am I making

my work harder than it actually is? Am I using muscles that have nothing to do with the work I am doing?' This will help you form the *habit* of relaxing, and as Dr. David Harold Fink says, 'Among those who know psychology best, it is habits two to one.'

4 Test yourself again at the end of the day, by asking yourself, 'Just how tired am I? If I am tired, it is not because of the mental work I have done but because of the way I have done it.' I measure my accomplishments,' says Daniel W. Josselyn, 'not by how tired I am at the end of the day, but how tired I am not.' He says, 'When I feel particularly tired at the end of the day, or when irritability proves that my nerves are tired, I know beyond question that it has been an inefficient day both as to quantity and quality.' If every businessman in America would learn that same lesson, our death rate from 'hypertension' diseases would drop overnight. And we would stop filling up our sanitariums and asylums with people who have been broken by fatigue and worry.

□ 25 □

How to avoid fatigue – and keep looking young!

One day last autumn, my associate flew up to Boston to attend a session of one of the most unusual medical classes in the world. Medical? Well, yes. It meets once a week at the Boston Dispensary, and the patients who attend it get regular and thorough medical examinations before they are admitted. But actually this class is a psychological clinic. Although it is officially called the Class in Applied Psychology (formerly the Thought Control Class – a name suggested by the first member), its real purpose is to deal with people *who are ill from worry*. And many of these patients are emotionally disturbed housewives.

How did such a class for worriers get started? Well, in 1930, Dr. Joseph H. Pratt – who, by the way, had been a pupil of Sir William Osler – observed that many of the outpatients who came to the Boston Dispensary apparently had nothing wrong with them at all physically; yet they had practically all the symptoms that flesh is heir to. One woman's hands were so crippled with 'arthritis' that she had lost all use of them. Another was in agony with all the excruciating symptoms of 'cancer of the stomach'. Others had backaches, headaches, were chronically tired, or had vague aches and pains. *They actually felt these pains*. But the most exhaustive medical examinations showed that nothing whatever was wrong with these people – in the physical sense. Many old-fashioned doctors would have said it was all imagination – 'all in the mind'.

But Dr. Pratt realized that it was no use to tell these patients to 'go home and forget it'. He knew that most of these people didn't want to be sick; if it was so easy to forget their ailments, they would do so themselves. So what could be done?

He opened this class – to a chorus of doubts from the medical doubters on the sidelines. And the class worked wonders! In the years that have passed since it started, thousands of patients have been 'cured' by attending it. Some of the patients have been coming for years – as religious in their attendance as though going to church. My assistant talked to a woman who has hardly missed a session in more than nine years. She said that when she first went to the clinic, she was thoroughly convinced she had a floating kidney and some kind of heart ailment. She was so worried and tense that she occasionally lost her eyesight and had spells of blindness. Yet today she is confident and cheerful and in excellent health. She looked only about forty, yet she held one of her grandchildren asleep in her lap. 'I used to worry so much about my family troubles,' she said, 'that I wished I could die. But I learned at this clinic the futility of worrying. I learned to stop it. And I can honestly say now that my life is serene.'

Dr. Rose Hilferding, the medical adviser of the class, said that she thought one of the best remedies for lightening worry is 'talking your troubles over with someone you trust. We call it catharsis,' she said. 'When patients come here, they can talk their troubles over at length, until they get them off their minds. Brooding over worries alone, and keeping them to oneself, causes great nervous tension. We all have to share our troubles. We have to share worry. We have to feel there is someone in the world who is willing to listen and able to understand.'

My assistant witnessed the great relief that came to one woman from talking out her worries. She had domestic worries, and when she first began to talk, she was like a wound-up spring. Then gradually, as she kept on talking, she began to calm down. At the end of the interview, she was actually smiling. Had the problem been solved? No, it wasn't that easy. What caused the change was *talking to someone*, getting a little advice and a little human sympathy. What had really worked the change was the tremendous healing value that lies in – *words*!

Psychoanalysis is based, to some extent, on this healing power of words. Ever since the days of Freud, analysts have known that a patient could find relief from his inner anxieties if he could talk, just talk. Why is this so? Maybe because by talking, we gain a little better insight into our troubles, get a better perspective. No one knows the whole answer. But all of us know that 'spitting it out' or 'getting it off our chests' brings almost instant relief.

So the next time we have an emotional problem, why don't we look around for someone to talk to? I don't mean, of course, to go around making pests of ourselves by whining and complaining to everyone in sight. Let's decide on someone we can trust, and make an appointment. Maybe a relative, a doctor, a lawyer, a minister, or priest. Then say to that person: 'I want your advice, I have a problem, and I wish you would listen while I put it in words. You may be able to advise me. You may see angles to this thing that I can't see myself. But even if you can't, you will help me tremendously if you will just sit and listen while I talk it out.'

Talking things out, then, is one of the principal therapies used at the Boston Dispensary Class. But here are some other ideas we picked up at the class – things you can do in your home.

1 *Keep a notebook or scrapbook for 'inspirational' reading.* Into this book you can paste all the poems, or short prayers, or quotations, which appeal to you personally and give you a lift. Then, when a rainy afternoon sends your spirits plunging down, perhaps you can find a recipe in this book for dispelling the gloom. Many patients kept such notebooks for years. They said it was a spiritual 'shot in the arm'.

2 *Don't dwell too long on the shortcomings of others!* One woman at the class who found herself developing into a scolding, nagging, and haggard-faced wife, was brought up short with the question: 'What would you do if your husband died?' She was so shocked by the idea that she immediately sat down and drew up a list of all her husband's good points. She made quite a list. Why don't you try the same thing the next time you feel you married a tyrant? Maybe you'll find, after reading your spouse's virtues, that he or she is a person you'd like to meet!

3 *Get interested in people!* Develop a friendly, healthy interest in the people who share your life. One ailing woman who felt herself so 'exclusive' that she hadn't any friends, was told to try to make up a story about the next person she met. She began, in the bus, to weave backgrounds and settings for the people she saw. She tried to imagine what their lives had been like. First thing you know, she was talking to people everywhere – and today she is happy, alert, and a charming human being, cured of her 'pains'.

4 *Make up a schedule for tomorrow's work before you go to bed tonight.* The class found that many people feel driven and harassed by the unending round of work and things they must do. They never got their work finished. They were chased by the clock. To cure this sense of hurry, *and* worry, the suggestion was made that they draw up a schedule each night for the following day. What happened? More work accomplished; much

less fatigue; a feeling of pride and achievement; and time left over for rest and enjoyment.

5 *Finally – avoid tension and fatigue. Relax! Relax!* Nothing will make you look old sooner than tension and fatigue. Nothing will work such havoc with your freshness and looks! My assistant sat for an hour in the Boston Thought Control Class, while Professor Paul E. Johnson, the director, went over many of the principles we have already discussed in the previous chapter – the rules for relaxing. At the end of ten minutes of these relaxing exercises, which my assistant did with the others, she was almost asleep sitting upright in her chair! Why is such stress laid on this physical relaxing? Because the clinic knows – as other doctors know – that if you're going to get the worry-kinks out of people, they've got to relax!

Yes, you have got to relax! Strangely enough, a good hard floor is better to relax on than an inner-spring bed. It gives more resistance. It is good for the spine.

All right, then, here are some exercises you can do. Try them for a week – and see what you do for your looks and disposition!

a. Lie flat on the floor whenever you feel tired. Stretch as tall as you can. Roll around if you want to. Do it twice a day.

b. Close your eyes. You might try saying, as Professor Johnson recommended, something like this: 'The sun is shining overhead. The sky is blue and sparkling. Nature is calm and in control of the world – and I, as nature's child, am in tune with the Universe.' Or – better still – pray!

c. If you cannot lie down, because you can't spare the time, then you can achieve almost the same effect sitting down in a chair. A hard, upright chair is the best thing for relaxing. Sit upright in the chair like a seated Egyptian statue, and let your hands rest, palms down, on the tops of your thighs.

d. Now, slowly tense the toes – then let them relax. Tense the muscles in your legs – and let them relax. Do this slowly upward, with all the muscles of your body, until you get to the neck. Then let your head roll around heavily, as though it were a football. Keep saying to your muscles (as in the previous chapter), 'Let go . . . let go . . .'

e. Quiet your nerves with slow, steady breathing. Breathe from deep down. The yogis of India were right: rhythmical breathing is one of the best methods ever discovered for soothing the nerves.

f. Think of the wrinkles and frowns in your face, and smooth them all out. Loosen up the worry-creases you feel between your brows, and at the sides of your mouth. Do this twice a day, and maybe you won't have to go to a health club to get a massage. Maybe the lines will disappear from the inside out!

□ **26** □

Four good working habits that will help prevent fatigue and worry

Good Working Habit No. 1:
Clear Your Desk of All Papers Except Those Relating to the Immediate Problem at Hand.

Roland L. Williams, President of Chicago and Northwestern Railway, once said, 'A person with his desk piled high with papers on various matters will find his work much easier and more accurate if he clears that desk of all but the immediate problem on hand. I call this good housekeeping, and it is the number-one step toward efficiency.'

If you visit the Library of Congress in Washington, D.C., you will find five words painted on the ceiling – five words written by the poet Pope:

'Order is Heaven's first law.'

Order ought to be the first law of business, too. But is it? No, the average desk is cluttered up with papers that haven't been looked at for weeks. In fact, the publisher of a New Orleans newspaper once told me that his secretary cleared up one of his desks and found a typewriter that had been missing for two years!

The mere sight of a desk littered with unwanted mail and reports and memos is enough to breed confusion, tension, and worries. It is much worse than that. The constant reminder of 'a million things to do and no time to do them' can worry you not only into tension and fatigue, but it can also worry you into high blood pressure, heart trouble, and stomach ulcers.

Dr. John H. Stokes, professor, Graduate School of Medicine, University of Pennsylvania, read a paper before the National Convention of the American Medical Association – a paper entitled 'Functional Neuroses as Complications of Organic Disease'. In that paper, Dr. Stokes listed eleven conditions under the title: 'What to Look for in the Patient's State of Mind'. Here is the first item on that list:

> The sense of must or obligation; the unending stretch of things ahead that simply have to be done.

But how can such an elementary procedure as clearing your desk and making decisions help you avoid this high pressure, this sense of *must*, this sense of an 'unending stretch of things ahead that simply have to be done'? Dr. William L. Sadler, the famous psychiatrist, told of a patient who, by using this simple device, avoided a nervous breakdown. The man was an executive in a big Chicago firm. When he came to Dr. Sadler's office, he was tense, nervous, worried. He knew he was heading for a tailspin, but he couldn't quit work. He had to have help.

'While this man was telling me his story,' Dr. Sadler says, 'my telephone rang. It was the hospital calling; and, instead of deferring the matter, I took time right then to come to a decision. I always settle questions, if possible, right on the spot. I had no sooner hung up than the phone rang again. Again an urgent matter, which I took time to discuss. The third interruption came when a colleague of mine came to my office for advice on a patient who was critically ill. When I had finished with him, I turned to my caller and began to apologize for keeping him waiting. But he had brightened up. He had a completely different look on his face.'

'Don't apologize, doctor!' this man said to Sadler. 'In the last ten minutes, I think I've got a hunch as to what is wrong with me. I'm going back to my office and revise my working habits . . . But before I go, do you mind if I take a look in your desk?'

Dr. Sadler opened up the drawers of his desk. All empty – except for supplies. 'Tell me,' said the patient, 'where do you keep your unfinished business?'

'Finished!' said Sadler.

'And where do you keep your unanswered mail?'

'Answered!' Sadler told him. 'My rule is never to lay down a letter until I have answered it. I dictate the reply to my secretary at once.'

Six weeks later, this same executive invited Dr. Sadler to come to his office. He was changed – and so was his desk. He opened the desk drawers to show there was no unfinished business inside of the desk. 'Six weeks ago,' this executive said, 'I had three different desks in two different offices – and was snowed under by my work. I was never finished. After talking to you, I came back here and cleared out a wagonload of reports and old papers. Now I work at one desk, settle things as they come up, and don't have a mountain of unfinished business nagging at me and making me tense and worried. But the most astonishing thing is I've recovered completely. There is nothing wrong any more with my health!'

Charles Evans Hughes, former Chief Justice of the United States Supreme Court, said: 'Men do not die from overwork. They die from dissipation and worry.' Yes, from dissipation of their energies – and worry because they never seem to get their work done.

Good Working Habit No. 2:

Do Things in the Order of Their Importance.

Henry L. Doherty, founder of the nation-wide Cities Service Company, said that regardless of how much salary he paid, there were two abilities he found it almost impossible to find.

Those two priceless abilities: first, the ability to think. Second, the ability to do things in the order of their importance.

Charles Luckman, the lad who started from scratch and climbed in twelve years to president of the Pepsodent Company, got a salary of a hundred thousand dollars a year, and made a million dollars besides – that lad declared that he owed much of his success to developing the two abilities that Henry L. Doherty said he found almost impossible to find. Charles Luckman said: 'As far back as I can remember, I have gotten up at five o'clock in the morning because I can think better then than any other time – I can think better then and plan my day, plan to do things in the order of their importance.'

Frank Bettger, one of America's most successful insurance salesmen, didn't wait until five o'clock in the morning to plan his day. He planned it the night before – set a goal for himself – a goal to sell a certain amount of insurance that day. If he failed, that amount was added to the next day – and so on.

I know from long experience that one is not always able to do things in the order of their importance, but I also know that some kind of plan to do first things first is infinitely better than extemporizing as you go along.

If George Bernard Shaw had not made it a rigid rule to do first things first, he would probably have failed as a writer and might have remained a bank cashier all his life. His plan called for writing five pages each day. That plan inspired him to go right on writing five pages a day for nine heartbreaking years, even though he made a total of only thirty dollars in those nine years – about a penny a day. Even Robinson Crusoe wrote out a schedule of what he would do each hour of the day.

Good Working Habit No. 3:

When You Face a Problem, Solve It Then and There if You Have the Facts Necessary to Make a Decision. Don't Keep Putting off Decisions.

One of my former students, the late H. P. Howell, told me that when he was a member of the board of directors of U.S. Steel, the meetings of the board were often long-drawn-out affairs – many problems were discussed, few decisions were made. The result: each member of the board had to carry home bundles of reports to study.

Finally, Mr. Howell persuaded the board of directors to take up one problem at a time and come to a decision. No procrastination – no putting off. The decision might be to ask for additional facts; it might be to do something or do nothing. But a decision was reached on each problem before passing on to the next. Mr. Howell told me that the results were striking and salutary: the docket was cleared. The calendar was clean. No longer was it necessary for each member to carry home a bundle of reports. No longer was there a worried sense of unresolved problems.

A good rule, not only for the board of directors of U.S. Steel, but for you and me.

Good Working Habit No. 4:

Learn to Organize, Deputize, and Supervise.

Many business persons are driving themselves to premature graves because they have never learned to delegate responsibility to others, insisting on doing everything themselves. Result: details and confusion overwhelm them. They are driven by a sense of hurry, worry, anxiety, and tension. It is hard to learn to delegate responsibilities. I know. It was hard for me, awfully hard. I also know from experience the disasters that can be caused by delegating authority to the wrong people. But difficult as it is to delegate authority, executives must do it if they are to avoid worry, tension, and fatigue.

Executives who build up big businesses and don't learn to organize, deputize, and supervise, usually pop off with heart trouble in their fifties or early sixties – heart trouble caused by tension and worries. Want a specific instance? Look at the death notices in your local paper.

☐ 27 ☐

How to banish the boredom that produces fatigue, worry, and resentment

One of the chief causes of fatigue is boredom. To illustrate, let's take the case of Alice, an executive who lives on your street. Alice came home one night utterly exhausted. She *acted* fatigued. She *was* fatigued. She had a headache.

She had a backache. She was so exhausted she wanted to go to bed without waiting for dinner. Her mother pleaded ... She sat down at the table. The telephone rang. The boy friend! An invitation to a dance! Her eyes sparkled. Her spirits soared. She rushed upstairs, put on her Alice-blue gown, and danced until three o'clock in the morning; and when she finally did get home, she was not the slightest bit exhausted. She was, in fact, so exhilarated she couldn't fall asleep.

Was Alice really and honestly tired eight hours earlier, when she looked and acted exhausted? Sure she was. She was exhausted because she was bored with her work, perhaps bored with life. There are millions of Alices. You may be one of them.

It is a well-known fact that your emotional attitude usually has far more to do with producing fatigue than has physical exertion. A few years ago, Joseph E. Barmack, Ph.D., published in the *Archives of Psychology* a report of some of his experiments showing how boredom produces fatigue. Dr. Barmack put a group of students through a series of tests in which, he knew, they could have little interest. The result? The students felt tired and sleepy, complained of headaches and eyestrain, felt irritable. In some cases, even their stomachs were upset. Was it all 'imagination'? No. Metabolism tests were taken of these students. These tests showed that the blood pressure of the body and the consumption of oxygen actually decrease when a person is bored, and that the whole metabolism picks up immediately as soon as he begins to feel interest and pleasure in his work!

We rarely get tired when we are doing something interesting and exciting. For example, I recently took a vacation in the Canadian Rockies up around Lake Louise. I spent several days trout fishing along Corral Creek, fighting my way through brush higher than my head, stumbling over logs, struggling through fallen timber – yet after eight hours of this, I was not exhausted. Why? Because I was excited, exhilarated. I had a sense of high achievement: six cutthroat trout. But suppose I had been bored by fishing, then how do you think I would have felt? I would have been worn out by such strenuous work at an altitude of seven thousand feet.

Even in such exhausting activities as mountain climbing, boredom may tire you far more than the strenuous work involved. For example, Mr. S. H. Kingman, president of the Farmers and Mechanics Savings bank of Minneapolis, told me of an incident that is a perfect illustration of that statement. In July, 1953, the Canadian government asked the Canadian Alpine Club to furnish guides to train the members of the Prince of Wales Rangers in mountain climbing. Mr. Kingman was one of the guides chosen to train these soldiers. He told me how he and the other guides – men ranging from forty-two to fifty-nine years of age – took these young army men on long hikes across glaciers and snow fields and up a sheer cliff of forty feet, where they had to climb with ropes and tiny footholds and precarious handholds. They climbed Michael's Peak, the Vice-President Peak, and other unnamed peaks in the

Little Yoho Valley in the Canadian Rockies. After fifteen hours of mountain climbing, these young men, who were in the pink of condition (they had just finished a six-week course in tough Commando training), were utterly exhausted.

Was their fatigue caused by using muscles that had not been hardened by Commando training? Any man who had ever been through Commando training would hoot at such a ridiculous question! No, they were utterly exhausted because they were bored by mountain climbing. They were so tired that many of them fell asleep without waiting to eat. But the guides – men who were two and three times as old as the soldiers – were they tired? Yes, but not exhausted. The guides ate dinner and stayed up for hours, talking about the day's experiences. They were not exhausted because they were interested.

When Dr. Edward Thorndike of Columbia was conducting experiments in fatigue, he kept young men awake for almost a week by keeping them constantly interested. After much investigation, Dr. Thorndike is reported to have said: 'Boredom is the only real cause of diminution of work.'

If you are a mental worker, it is seldom the amount of work you do that makes you tired. You may be tired by the amount of work you do *not* do. For example, remember the day last week when you were constantly interrupted. No letters answered. Appointments broken. Trouble here and there. Everything went wrong that day. You accomplished nothing whatever, yet you went home exhausted – and with a splitting head.

The next day everything clicked at the office. You accomplished forty times more than you did the previous day. Yet you went home fresh as a snowy-white gardenia. You have had that experience. So have I.

The lesson to be learned? Just this: our fatigue is often caused not by work, but by worry, frustration, and resentment.

While writing this chapter, I went to see a revival of Jerome Kern's delightful musical comedy, *Show Boat*. Captain Andy, captain of the *Cotton Blossom*, says in one of his philosophical interludes: 'The lucky folks are the ones that get to do things they enjoy doing.' Such folk are lucky because they have more energy, more happiness, less worry, and less fatigue. Where your interests are, there is your energy also. Walking ten blocks with a nagging wife or husband can be more fatiguing than walking ten miles with an adoring sweetheart.

And so what? What can you do about it? Well, here is what one stenographer did about it – a stenographer working for an oil company in Tulsa, Oklahoma. For several days each month, she had one of the dullest jobs imaginable: filling out printed forms for oil leases, inserting figures and statistics. This task was so boring that she resolved, in self-defence, to make it interesting. How? She had a daily contest with herself. She counted the number of forms she filled out each morning, and then tried to excel that record in the afternoon. She counted each day's total and tried to better it the next day. Result? She was soon able to fill out more of these dull printed forms than any other stenographer in her division. And what did all this get her? Praise? No . . . Thanks? No . . . Promotion? No . . . Increased pay? No . . . But it did help to prevent the fatigue that is spawned by boredom. It did give her a mental stimulant. Because she had done her best to make a dull job interesting, she had more energy, more zest, and got far more happiness out of her leisure hours.

I happen to know this story is true, because I married that girl.

Here is the story of another stenographer who found it paid to act as *if* her work were interesting. She used to fight her work. But no more. She is Miss Vallie G. Golden, of Elmhurst, Illinois. Here is her story, as she wrote it to me:

'There are four stenographers in my office and each of us is assigned to take letters from several men. Once in a while we get jammed up in these assignments. One day, when an assistant department head insisted that I do a long letter over, I started to rebel. I tried to point out to him that the letter could be corrected without being retyped – and he retorted that if I didn't do it over, he would find someone else who would! I was absolutely fuming! But as I started to retype this letter, it suddenly occurred to me that there were a lot of other people who would jump at the chance to do the work I was doing. Also, that I was being paid a salary to do just that work. I began to feel better. I suddenly made up my mind to do my work as if I actually enjoyed it – even though I despised it. Then I made this important discovery: if I do my work *as if* I really enjoy it, then I do enjoy it to some extent. I also found I can work faster when I enjoy my work. So there is seldom any need now for me to work overtime. This new attitude of mine gained me the reputation of being a good worker. And when one of the department superintendents needed a private secretary, he asked for me for the job – because, he said, I was willing to do extra work without being sulky! This matter of the power of a changed mental attitude,' wrote Miss Golden, 'has been a tremendously important discovery to me. It has worked wonders!'

Miss Golden used the wonder-working *'as if'* philosophy of Professor Hans Vaihinger. He taught us to act *'as if'* we were happy – and so on.

If you act *'as if'* you are interested in your job, that bit of acting will tend to make your interest real. It will also tend to decrease your fatigue, your tensions, and your worries.

A few years ago, Harlan A. Howard made a decision that completely altered his life. He resolved to make a dull job interesting – and he certainly had a dull one: washing plates, scrubbing counters, and dishing out ice cream in the high-school lunchroom while the other boys were playing ball or kidding the girls. Harlan Howard despised his job – but since he had to stick to it, he resolved to study ice cream – how it was made, what ingredients were used, why some ice creams were better than others. He studied the chemistry of ice cream, and became a whiz in the high-school chemistry course. He was so interested now in food chemistry that he entered the Massachusetts State College and majored in the field of 'food technology'. When the New York

Cocoa Exchange offered a hundred-dollar prize for the best paper on uses of cocoa and chocolate – a prize open to all college students – who do you suppose won it? . . . That's right. Harlan Howard.

When he found it difficult to get a job, he opened a private laboratory in the basement of his home in Amherst, Massachusetts. Shortly after that, a new law was passed. The bacteria in milk had to be counted. Harlan A. Howard was soon counting bacteria for the fourteen milk companies in Amherst – and he had to hire two assistants.

Where will he be twenty-five years from now? Well, the men who are now running the business of food chemistry will be retired then, or dead; and their places will be taken by young lads who are now radiating initiative and enthusiasm. Twenty-five years from now, Harlan A. Howard will probably be one of the leaders in his profession, while some of his classmates to whom he used to sell ice cream over the counter will be sour, unemployed, cussing the government, and complaining that they never had a chance. Harlan A. Howard might never have had a chance, either, if he hadn't resolved to make a dull job interesting.

Years ago, there was another young man who was bored with his dull job of standing at a lathe, turning out bolts in a factory. His first name was Sam. Sam wanted to quit, but he was afraid he couldn't find another job. Since he had to do this dull work, Sam decided he would make it interesting. So he ran a race with the mechanic operating a machine beside him. One of them was to trim off the rough surfaces on his machine, and the other was to trim the bolts down to the proper diameter. They would switch machines occasionally and see who could turn out the most bolts. The foreman, impressed with Sam's speed and accuracy, soon gave him a better job. That was the start of a whole series of promotions. Thirty years later, Sam – Samuel Vauclain – was president of the Baldwin Locomotive Works. But he might have remained a mechanic all his life if he had not resolved to make a dull job interesting.

H. V. Kaltenborn – the famous radio news analyst – once told me how he made a dull job interesting. When he was twenty-two years old, he worked his way across the Atlantic on a cattle boat, feeding and watering the steers. After making a bicycle tour of England, he arrived in Paris, hungry and broke. Pawning his camera for five dollars, he put an ad in the Paris edition of *The New York Herald* and got a job selling stereopticon machines. I can remember those old-fashioned stereoscopes that we used to hold up before our eyes to look at two pictures exactly alike. As we looked, a miracle happened. The two lenses in the stereoscope transformed the two pictures into a single scene with the effect of a third dimension. We saw distance. We got an astounding sense of perspective.

Well, as I was saying, Kaltenborn started out selling these machines from door to door in Paris – and he couldn't speak French. But he earned five thousand dollars in commissions the first year, and made himself one of the highest-paid salesmen in France that year. H. V. Kaltenborn told me that this experience did as much to develop within him the qualities that make for success as did any single year of study at Harvard. Confidence? He told me himself that after that experience, he felt he could have sold *The Congressional Record* to French housewives.

That experience gave him an intimate understanding of French life that later proved invaluable in interpreting, on the radio, European events.

How did he manage to become an expert salesman when he couldn't speak French? Well, he had his employer write out his sales talk in perfect French, and he memorized it. He would ring a doorbell, a housewife would answer, and Kaltenborn would begin repeating his memorized sales talk with an accent so terrible it was funny. He would show the housewife his pictures, and when she asked a question, he would shrug his shoulders and say, 'An American . . . an American.' He would then take off his hat and point to a copy of the sales talk in perfect French that he had pasted in the top of his hat. The housewife would laugh, he would laugh – and show her more pictures. When H. V. Kaltenborn told me about this, he confessed that the job had been far from easy. He told me that there was only one quality that pulled him through: his determination to make the job interesting. Every morning before he started out, he looked into the mirror and gave himself a pep talk: '*Kaltenborn, you have to do this if you want to eat. Since you have to do it – why not have a good time doing it? Why not imagine every time you ring a doorbell that you are an actor before the footlights and that there's an audience out there looking at you? After all, what you are doing is just as funny as something on the stage. So why not put a lot of zest and enthusiasm into it?*'

Mr. Kaltenborn told me that these daily pep talks helped him transform a task that he had once hated and dreaded into an adventure that he liked and made highly profitable.

When I asked Mr. Kaltenborn if he had any advice to give to the young men of America who are eager to succeed, he said: 'Yes, go to bat with yourself every morning. We talk a lot about the importance of physical exercise to wake us up out of the half-sleep in which so many of us walk around. But we need, even more, some spiritual and mental exercises every morning to stir us into action. Give yourself a pep talk every day.'

Is giving yourself a pep talk every day silly, superficial, childish? No, on the contrary, it is the very essence of sound psychology. 'Our life is what our thoughts make it.' These words are just as true today as they were eighteen centuries ago when Marcus Aurelius first wrote them in his book on *Meditations*: 'Our life is what our thoughts make it.'

By talking to yourself every hour of the day, you can direct yourself to think thoughts of courage and happiness, thoughts of power and peace. By talking to yourself about the things you have to be grateful for, you can fill your mind with thoughts that soar and sing.

By thinking the right thoughts, you can make any job less distasteful. Your boss wants you to be interested in your job so that he will make more money. But let's forget about what the boss wants. Think only of what getting interested in your job will do for you. Remind yourself that it may double the amount of happiness you get out of life, for you spend about one half of your waking hours at your work, and if you don't find happiness in your work, you may never find it anywhere. Keep reminding yourself that getting interested in your job will take your mind off your worries, and, in the long run, will probably bring promotion and increased pay. Even if it doesn't do that, it will reduce fatigue to a minimum and help you enjoy your hours of leisure.

□ 28 □

How to keep from worrying about insomnia

Do you worry when you can't sleep well? Then it may interest you to know that Samuel Untermyer – the famous international lawyer – never got a decent night's sleep in his life.

When Sam Untermyer went to college, he worried about two afflictions – asthma and insomnia. He couldn't seem to cure either, so he decided to do the next best thing – take advantage of his wakefulness. Instead of tossing and turning and worrying himself into a breakdown, he would get up and study. The result? He began ticking off honours in all his classes, and became one of the prodigies of the College of the City of New York.

Even after he started to practice law, his insomnia continued. But Untermyer didn't worry. 'Nature,' he said, 'will take care of me.' Nature did. In spite of the small amount of sleep he was getting, his health kept up and he was able to work as hard as any of the young lawyers of the New York Bar. He even worked harder, for he worked while they slept!

At the age of twenty-one, Sam Untermyer was earning seventy-five thousand dollars a year; and other young attorneys rushed to courtrooms to study his methods. In 1931, he was paid – for handling one case – what was, at that time, probably the highest lawyer's fee ever paid: a cool million dollars – cash on the barrelhead.

Still he had insomnia – read half the night – and then got up at five a.m and started dictating letters. By the time most people were just starting work, *his* day's work would be almost half done. He lived to the age of eighty-one, this man who had rarely had a sound night's sleep; but if he had fretted and worried about his insomnia, he would probably have wrecked his life.

We spend a third of our lives sleeping – yet nobody knows what sleep really is. We know it is a habit and a state of rest in which nature knits up the ravelled sleeve of care, but we don't know how many hours of sleep each individual requires. We don't even know if we *have* to sleep at all!

Fantastic? Well, during the First World War, Paul Kern, a Hungarian soldier, was shot through the frontal lobe of his brain. He recovered from the wound, but, curiously enough, couldn't fall asleep. No matter what the doctors did – and they tried all kinds of sedatives and narcotics, even hypnotism – Paul Kern couldn't be put to sleep or even made to feel drowsy.

The doctors said he wouldn't live long. But he fooled them. He got a job, and went on living in the best of health for years. He would lie down and close his eyes and rest, but he got no sleep whatever. His case was a medical mystery that upset many of our beliefs about sleep.

Some people require far more sleep than others. Toscanini needed only five hours a night, but Calvin Coolidge needed more than twice that much. Coolidge slept eleven hours out of every twenty-four. In other words, Toscanini slept away approximately one fifth of his life, while Coolidge slept away almost half of his life.

Worrying about insomnia will hurt you far more than insomnia. For example, one of my students – Ira Sandner, of Ridgefield Park, New Jersey – was driven nearly to suicide by chronic insomnia.

'I actually thought I was going insane,' Ira Sandner told me. 'The trouble was, in the beginning, that I was *too sound* a sleeper. I wouldn't wake up when the alarm clock went off, and the result was that I was getting to work late in the morning. I worried about it – and, in fact, my boss warned me that I would *have* to get to work on time. I knew that if I kept on oversleeping, I would lose my job.

'I told my friends about it, and one of them suggested I concentrate hard on the alarm clock before I went to sleep. That started the insomnia! The tick-tick-tick of that blasted alarm clock became an obsession. It kept me awake, tossing, all night long! When morning came, I was almost ill. I was ill from fatigue and worry. This kept on for eight weeks. I can't put into words the tortures I suffered. I was convinced I was going insane. Sometimes I paced the floor for hours at a time, and I honestly considered jumping out of the window and ending the whole thing!

'At last I went to a doctor I had known all my life. He said: 'Ira, I can't help you. No one can help you, because you have brought this thing on yourself. Go to bed nights, and if you can't fall asleep, forget all about it. Just say to yourself, 'I don't care a hang if I *don't* go to sleep. It's all right with me if I lie awake till morning.' Keep your eyes closed and say, 'As long as I just lie still and don't worry about it, I'll be getting rest, anyway.'

'I did that,' says Sandner, 'and in two weeks' time I was dropping off to sleep. In less than one month, I was sleeping eight hours, and my nerves were back to normal.'

It wasn't insomnia that was killing Ira Sandner; it was his worry about it.

Dr. Nathaniel Kleitman, professor at the University of Chicago, had done more research work on sleep than had any other living man. An expert on sleep, he declared that he had never known anyone to die from insomnia. To be sure, a man might worry about insomnia until he lowered his vitality and was swept away by germs. But it was the worry that did the damage, not the insomnia itself.

Dr. Kleitman also said that the people who worry about insomnia usually sleep far more than they realize. The man who swears 'I never slept a wink last night' may have slept for hours without knowing it. For example, one of the most profound thinkers of the nineteenth century, Herbert Spencer, was an old bachelor, lived in a boardinghouse, and bored everyone with his talk about his insomnia. He even put 'stoppings' in his ears to keep out the noise and quiet his nerves. Sometimes he took opium to induce sleep. One night he and Professor Sayce of Oxford shared the same room at a hotel. The next morning Spencer declared he hadn't slept a wink all night. In reality, it was Professor Sayce who hadn't slept a wink. He had been kept awake all night by Spencer's snoring!

The first requisite for a good night's sleep is a feeling of security. We need to feel that some power greater than ourselves will take care of us until morning. Dr. Thomas Hyslop, of the Great West Riding Asylum, stressed that point in an address before the British Medical Association. He said: 'One of the best sleep-producing agents which my years of practice have revealed to me is *prayer*. I say this purely as a medical man. The exercise of prayer, in those who habitually exert it, must be regarded as the most adequate and normal of all the pacifiers of the mind and calmers of the nerves.

'Let God – and let go.'

Jeanette MacDonald told me that when she was depressed and worried and had difficulty in going to sleep, she could always get 'a feeling of security' by repeating Psalm XXIII: 'The Lord is my shepherd; I shall not want. He maketh me to lie down in green pastures; he leadeth me beside the still waters . . .'

But if you are not religious, and have to do things the hard way, then learn to relax by physical measures. Dr. David Harold Fink, who wrote *Release from Nervous Tension*, says that the best way to do this is to *talk* to your body. According to Dr. Fink, words are the key to all kinds of hypnosis; and when you consistently can't sleep, it is because you have *talked* yourself into a case of insomnia. The way to undo this is to dehypnotize yourself – and you can do it by saying to the muscles of your body, 'Let go, let go – loosen up and relax.' We already know that the mind and nerves can't relax while the muscles are tense – so if we want to go to sleep, we start with the muscles. Dr. Fink recommends – and it works out in practice – that we put a pillow under the knees to ease the tension on the legs, and that we tuck small pillows under the arms for the very same reason. Then, by telling the jaw to relax, the eyes, the arms, and the legs, we finally drop off to sleep before we know what has hit us. I've tried it – I know.

One of the best cures for insomnia is making yourself physically tired by gardening, swimming, tennis, golf, skiing, or just by plain physically exhausting work. That is what Theodore Dreiser did. When he was a struggling young author, he was worried about insomnia, so he got a job working as a section hand on the New York Central Railway; and after a day of driving spikes and shovelling gravel, he was so exhausted that he could hardly stay awake long enough to eat.

If we get tired enough, nature will force us to sleep even while we are walking. To illustrate, when I was thirteen years old, my father shipped a carload of fat hogs to Saint Joe, Missouri. Since he got two free railroad passes, he took me along with him. Up until that time, I had never been in a town of more than four thousand. When I landed in Saint Joe – a city of sixty thousand – I was agog with excitement. I saw skyscrapers six stories high and – wonder of wonders – I saw a streetcar. I can close my eyes now and still see and hear that streetcar. After the most thrilling and exciting day of my life, Father and I took a train back to Ravenwood, Missouri. Arriving there at two o'clock in the morning, we had to walk four miles home to the farm. And here is the point of the story: I was so exhausted that I slept and dreamed as I walked. I have often slept while riding horseback. And I am alive to tell it!

When men are completely exhausted they sleep right through the thunder and horror and danger of war. Dr. Foster Kennedy, the famous neurologist, tells me that during the retreat of the Fifth British Army in 1918, he saw soldiers so exhausted that they fell on the ground where they were and fell into a sleep as sound as a coma. They didn't even wake up when he raised their eyelids with his fingers. And he says he noticed that invariably the pupils of the eyes were rolled upward in the sockets. 'After that,' says Dr. Kennedy, 'when I had trouble sleeping, I would practice rolling up my eyeballs into this position, and I found that in a few seconds I would begin to yawn and feel sleepy. It was an automatic reflex over which I had no control.'

No man ever committed suicide by refusing to sleep and no one ever will. Nature would force a man to sleep in spite of all his willpower. Nature will let us go without food or water far longer than she will let us go without sleep.

Speaking of suicide reminds me of a case that Dr. Henry C. Link describes in his book, *The Rediscovery of Man*. Dr. Link was vice-president of The Psychological Corporation and he interviewed many people who were worried and depressed. In his chapter 'On Overcoming Fears and Worries', he tells about a patient who wanted to commit suicide. Dr. Link knew arguing would only make the matter worse, so he said to this man, 'If you are going to commit suicide anyway, you might at least do it in a heroic fashion. Run around the block until you drop dead.'

He tried it, not once but several times, and each time felt better in his mind if not in his muscles. By the third night he had achieved what Dr. Link intended in the first place – he was so physically tired (and physically relaxed) that he slept like a log. Later he joined an athletic club and began to compete

371

in competitive sports. Soon he was feeling so good he wanted to live forever! So, to keep from worrying about insomnia, here are five rules:

1 If you can't sleep, do what Samuel Untermyer did. Get up and work or read until you do feel sleepy.
2 Remember that no one was ever killed by lack of sleep. Worrying about insomnia usually causes far more damage than sleeplessness.
3 Try prayer – or repeat Psalm XXIII, as Jeanette MacDonald did.
4 Relax your body.
5 Exercise. Get yourself so physically tired you can't stay awake.

PART SEVEN

☐ **IN A NUTSHELL** ☐

SIX WAYS TO PREVENT FATIGUE AND WORRY AND KEEP YOUR ENERGY AND
SPIRITS HIGH

RULE 1: Rest before you get tired.

RULE 2: Learn to relax at your work.

RULE 3: Learn to relax at home.

RULE 4: Apply these four good working habits:

  a. Clear your desk of all papers except those relating to the immediate problem at hand.

  b. Do things in the order of their importance.

  c. When you face a problem, solve it then and there if you have the facts necessary to make a decision.

  d. Learn to organize, deputize, and supervise.

RULE 5: To prevent worry and fatigue, put enthusiasm into your work.

RULE 6: Remember, no one was ever killed by lack of sleep. It is worrying about insomnia that does the damage – not the insomnia.

Part Eight

'HOW I CONQUERED WORRY'

31 True Stories

Six major troubles hit me all at once

BY C. I. BLACKWOOD

In the summer of 1943, it seemed to me that half the worries of the world had come to rest on my shoulders.

For more than forty years, I had lived a normal, carefree life with only the usual troubles which come to a husband, father, and businessman. I could usually meet these troubles easily, but suddenly – wham!wham!!wham!!!-wham!!!!WHAM!!!!!WHAM!!!!!! Six major troubles hit me all at once. I pitched and tossed and turned in bed all night long, half dreading to see the day come, because I faced these six major worries:

1. My business college was trembling on the verge of financial disaster because all the boys were going to war; and most of the girls were making more money working in war plants without training than my graduates could make in business offices with training.

2. My older son was in service, and I had the heart-numbing worry common to all parents whose sons were away at war.

3. Oklahoma City had already started proceedings to condemn a large tract of land for an airport, and my home – formerly my father's home – was located in the centre of this tract. I knew that I would be paid only one tenth of its value, and, what was even worse, I would lose my home; and because of the housing shortage, I worried about whether I could possibly find another home to shelter my family of six. I feared we might have to live in a tent. I even worried about whether we would be able to buy a tent.

4. The water well on my property went dry because a drainage canal had been dug near my home. To dig a new well would be throwing five hundred dollars away because the land was already being condemned. I had to carry water to my livestock in buckets every morning for two months, and I feared I would have to continue it during the rest of the war.

5. I lived ten miles away from my business school and I had a class B gasoline card: that meant I couldn't buy any new tyres, so I worried about how I could ever get to work when the superannuated tyres on my old Ford gave up the ghost.

6. My oldest daughter had graduated from high school a year ahead of

schedule. She had her heart set on going to college, and I just didn't have the money to send her. I knew her heart would be broken.

One afternoon while sitting in my office, worrying about my worries, I decided to write them all down for it seemed no one ever had more to worry about than I had. I didn't mind wrestling with worries that gave me a fighting chance to solve them, but these worries all seemed to be utterly beyond my control. I could do nothing to solve them. So I filed away this typewritten list of my troubles, and, as the months passed, I forgot that I had ever written it. Eighteen months later, while transferring my files, I happened to come across this list of my six major problems that had once threatened to wreck my health. I read them with a great deal of interest – and profit. I now saw that not one of them had come to pass.

Here is what had happened to them:

1. I saw that all my worries about having to close my business college had been useless because the government had started paying business schools for training veterans and my school was soon filled to capacity.

2. I saw that all my worries about my son in service had been useless: he was coming through the war without a scratch.

3. I saw that all my worries about my land being condemned for use as an airport had been useless because oil had been struck within a mile of my farm and the cost of procuring the land for an airport had become prohibitive.

4. I saw that all my worries about having no well to water my stock had been useless because, as soon as I knew my land would not be condemned, I spent the money necessary to dig a new well to a deeper level and found an unfailing supply of water.

5. I saw that all my worries about my tyres giving out had been useless, because by recapping and careful driving, the tyres had managed somehow to survive.

6. I saw that all my worries about my daughter's education had been useless, because just sixty days before the opening of college, I was offered – almost like a miracle – an auditing job which I could do outside of school hours, and this job made it possible for me to send her to college on schedule.

I had often heard people say that ninety-nine percent of the things we worry and stew and fret about never happen, but this old saying didn't mean much to me until I ran across that list of worries I had typed out that dreary afternoon eighteen months previously.

I am thankful now that I had to wrestle in vain with those six terrible worries. That experience has taught me a lesson I'll never forget. It has shown me the folly and tragedy of stewing about events that haven't happened – events that are beyond our control and may never happen.

Remember, today is the tomorrow you worried about yesterday.
Ask yourself: How do I know this thing I am worrying about
will really come to pass?

I can turn myself into a shouting optimist within an hour

BY ROGER W. BABSON
Famous Economist

When I find myself depressed over present conditions, I can, within one hour, banish worry and turn myself into a shouting optimist.

Here is how I do it. I enter my library, close my eyes, and walk to certain shelves containing only books on history. With my eyes still shut, I reach for a book, not knowing whether I am picking up Prescott's *Conquest of Mexico* or Suetonius' *Lives of the Twelve Caesars*. With my eyes still closed, I open the book at random. I then open my eyes and read for an hour; and the more I read, the more sharply I realize that the world has always been in the throes of agony, that civilization has always been tottering on the brink. The pages of history fairly shriek with tragic tales of war, famine, poverty, pestilence, and man's inhumanity to man. After reading history for an hour, I realize that bad as conditions are now, they are infinitely better than they used to be. This enables me to see and face my present troubles in their proper perspective as well as to realize that the world as a whole is constantly growing better.

**Here is a method that deserves a whole chapter. Read history!
Try to get the viewpoint of ten thousand years – and see how
trivial your troubles are, in terms of eternity!**

How I got rid of an inferiority complex

BY ELMER THOMAS
Former United States Senator from Oklahoma

When I was fifteen I was constantly tormented by worries and fears and self-consciousness. I was extremely tall for my age and as thin as a fence rail. I stood six feet two inches and weighed only 118 pounds. In spite of my height, I was weak and could never compete with the other boys in baseball or running games. They poked fun at me and called me 'hatchet-face'. I was so worried and self-conscious that I dreaded to meet anyone, and I seldom did, for our farmhouse was off the public road and surrounded by thick virgin timber that had never been cut since the beginning of time. We lived half a mile from the highway; and a week would often go by without my seeing anyone except my mother, father, and brothers and sisters.

I would have been a failure in life if I had let those worries and fears whip me. Every day and every hour of the day, I brooded over my tall, gaunt, weak body. I could hardly think of anything else. My embarrassment, my fear, was so intense that it is almost impossible to describe it. My mother knew how I felt. She had been a schoolteacher, so she said to me, 'Son, you ought to get an education, you ought to make your living with your mind because your body will always be a handicap.'

Since my parents were unable to send me to college, I knew I would have to make my own way; so I hunted and trapped opossum, skunk, mink, and racoon one winter; sold my hides for four dollars in the spring, and then bought two little pigs with my four dollars. I fed the pigs slop and later corn and sold them for forty dollars the next fall. With the proceeds from the sale of the two hogs I went away to the Central Normal College – located at Danville, Indiana. I paid a dollar and forty cents a week for my board and fifty cents a week for my room. I wore a brown shirt my mother had made me. (Obviously, she had used brown cloth because it wouldn't show the dirt.) I wore a suit of clothes that had once belonged to my father. Dad's clothes didn't fit me and neither did his old congress gaiter shoes that I wore – shoes that had elastic bands in the sides that stretched when you pulled them on. But the stretch had long since gone out of the bands, and the tops were so loose that the shoes almost dropped off my feet as I walked. I was too

380

embarrassed to associate with the other students, so I sat in my room alone and studied. The deepest desire of my life was to be able to buy some store clothes that fit me, clothes that I was not ashamed of.

Shortly after that, four events happened that helped me to overcome my worries and my feelings of inferiority. One of these events gave me courage and hope and confidence and completely changed all the rest of my life. I'll describe these events briefly.

First: After attending this normal school for only eight weeks, I took an examination and was given a third-grade certificate to teach in the country public schools. To be sure, this certificate was good for only six months, but it was fleeting evidence that somebody had faith in me – the first evidence of faith that I had ever had from anyone except my mother.

Second: A country school board at a place called Happy Hollow hired me to teach at a salary of two dollars per day, or forty dollars per month. Here was even more evidence of somebody's faith in me.

Third: As soon as I got my first cheque, I bought some store clothes – clothes that I wasn't ashamed to wear. If someone gave me a million dollars now it wouldn't thrill me half as much as that first suit of store clothes for which I paid only a few dollars.

Fourth: The real turning point in my life, the first great victory in my struggle against embarrassment and inferiority, occurred at the Putnam County Fair held annually in Bainbridge, Indiana. My mother had urged me to enter a public-speaking contest that was to be held at the fair. To me, the very idea seemed fantastic. I didn't have the courage to talk even to one person – let alone a crowd. But my mother's faith in me was almost pathetic. She dreamed great dreams for my future. She was living her own life over in her son. Her faith inspired me to enter the contest. I chose for my subject about the last thing in the world that I was qualified to talk on: 'The Fine and Liberal Arts of America'. Frankly, when I began to prepare the speech I didn't know what the liberal arts were, but it didn't matter much because my audience didn't know, either. I memorized my flowery talk and rehearsed it to the trees and cows a hundred times. I was so eager to make a good showing for my mother's sake that I must have spoken with emotion. At any rate, I was awarded first prize. I was astounded at what happened. A cheer went up from the crowd. The very boys who had once ridiculed me and poked fun at me and called me hatchet-face now slapped me on the back and said, 'I knew you could do it, Elmer.' My mother put her arms around me and sobbed. As I look back in retrospect, I can see that winning that speaking contest was the turning point of my life. The local newspapers ran an article about me on the front page and prophesied great things for my future. Winning that contest put me on the map locally and gave me prestige, and, what is far more important, it multiplied my confidence a hundredfold. I now realize that if I had not won that contest, I probably would never have become a member of the United States Senate, for it lifted my sights, widened my horizons, and made me realize that I had latent abilities that I never dreamed I possessed. Most important, however, was the fact that the first prize in the oratorical contest was a year's scholarship in the Central Normal College.

I hungered now for more education. So, during the next few years – from 1896 to 1900 – I divided my time between teaching and studying. In order to pay my expenses at De Pauw University, I waited on tables, looked after furnaces, mowed lawns, kept books, worked in the wheat and corn fields during the summer, and hauled gravel on a public road-construction job.

In 1896, when I was only nineteen, I made twenty-eight speeches, urging people to vote for William Jennings Bryan for President. The excitement of speaking for Bryan aroused a desire in me to enter politics myself. So when I entered De Pauw University, I studied law and public speaking. In 1899 I represented the university in a debate with Butler College, held in Indianapolis, on the subject 'Resolved that United States Senators should be elected by popular vote'. I won other speaking contests and became editor-in-chief of the class of 1900 College Annual, *The Mirage*, and the university paper, *The Palladium*.

After receiving my A.B. degree at De Pauw, I took Horace Greeley's advice – only I didn't go west. I went southwest. I went down to a new country: Oklahoma. When the Kiowa, Comanche, and Apache Indian reservation was opened, I homesteaded a claim and opened a law office in Lawton, Oklahoma. I served in the Oklahoma State Senate for thirteen years, in the lower House of Congress for four years, and at fifty years of age, I achieved my lifelong ambition: I was elected to the United States Senate from Oklahoma. I have served in that capacity since March 4, 1927. Since Oklahoma and Indian Territories became the state of Oklahoma on November 16, 1907, I have been continuously honoured by the Democrats of my adopted state by nominations – first for State Senate, then for Congress, and later for the United States Senate.

I have told this story, not to brag about my own fleeting accomplishments, which can't possibly interest anyone else. I have told it wholly with the hope that it may give renewed courage and confidence to some poor boy who is now suffering from the worries and shyness and feeling of inferiority that devastated my life when I was wearing my father's castoff clothes and gaiter shoes that almost dropped off my feet as I walked.

(Editor's note: It is interesting to know that Elmer Thomas, who was so ashamed of his ill-fitting clothes as a youth, was later voted the best-dressed man in the United States Senate.)

I lived in the Garden of Allah

BY R. V. C. BODLEY
Descendant of Sir Thomas Bodley, founder of the Bodleian Library,
Oxford
Author of *Wind in the Sahara, The Messenger,* and fourteen other volumes

In 1918, I turned my back on the world I had known and went to northwest Africa and lived with the Arabs in the Sahara, the Garden of Allah. I lived there seven years. I learned to speak the language of the nomads. I wore their clothes, I ate their food, and adopted their mode of life, which has changed very little during the last twenty centuries. I became an owner of sheep and slept on the ground in the Arabs' tents. I also made a detailed study of their religion. In fact, I later wrote a book about Mohammed, entitled *The Messenger*.

Those seven years which I spent with these wandering shepherds were the most peaceful and contented years of my life.

I had already had a rich and varied experience: I was born of English parents in Paris; and lived in France for nine years. Later I was educated at Eton and at the Royal Military College at Sandhurst. Then I spent six years as a British army officer in India, where I played polo, and hunted, and explored in the Himalayas as well as doing some soldiering. I fought through the First World War and, at its close, I was sent to the Paris Peace Conference as an assistant military attaché. I was shocked and disappointed at what I saw there. During the four years of slaughter on the Western Front, I had believed we were fighting to save civilization. But at the Paris Peace Conference, I saw selfish politicians laying the groundwork for the Second World War – each country, grabbing all it could for itself, creating national antagonisms, and reviving the intrigues of secret diplomacy.

I was sick of war, sick of the army, sick of society. For the first time in my career, I spent sleepless nights, worrying about what I should do with my life. Lloyd George urged me to go in for politics. I was considering taking his advice when a strange thing happened, a strange thing that shaped and determined my life for the next seven years. It all came from a conversation that lasted less than two hundred seconds – a conversation with 'Ted' Lawrence, 'Lawrence of Arabia', the most colourful and romantic figure produced by the First World

War. He had lived in the desert with the Arabs and he advised me to do the same thing. At first, it sounded fantastic.

However, I was determined to leave the army, and I had to do something. Civilian employers did not want to hire men like me – ex-officers of the regular army – especially when the labour market was jammed with millions of unemployed. So I did as Lawrence suggested: I went to live with the Arabs. I am glad I did so. They taught me how to conquer worry. Like all faithful Moslems, they are fatalists. They believe that every word which Mohammed wrote in the Koran is the divine revelation of Allah. So when the Koran says: 'God created you and all your actions', they accept it literally. That is why they take life so calmly and never hurry or get into unnecessary tempers when things go wrong. They know that what is ordained is ordained; and no one but God can alter anything. However, that doesn't mean that in the face of disaster, they sit down and do nothing. To illustrate, let me tell you of a fierce, burning windstorm of the sirocco which I experienced when I was living in the Sahara. It howled and screamed for three days and nights. It was so strong, so fierce, that it blew sand from the Sahara hundreds of miles across the Mediterranean and sprinkled it over the Rhone Valley in France. The wind was so hot I felt as if the hair was being scorched off my head. My throat was parched. My eyes burned. My teeth were full of grit. I felt as if I were standing in front of a furnace in a glass factory. I was driven as near crazy as a man can be and retain his sanity. But the Arabs didn't complain. They shrugged their shoulders and said, '*Mektoub!*' . . . 'It is written.'

But immediately after the storm was over, they sprang into action: they slaughtered all the lambs because they knew they would die anyway; and by slaughtering them at once, they hoped to save the mother sheep. After the lambs were slaughtered, the flocks were driven southward to water. This was all done calmly, without worry or complaining or mourning over their losses. The tribal chief said: 'It is not too bad. We might have lost everything. But praise God, we have forty percent of our sheep left to make a new start.'

I remember another occasion, when we were motoring across the desert and a tyre blew out. The chauffeur had forgotten to mend the spare tyre. So there we were with only three tyres. I fussed and fumed and got excited and asked the Arabs what we were going to do. They reminded me that getting excited wouldn't help, that it only made one hotter. The blown-out tyre, they said, was the will of Allah and nothing could be done about it. So we started on, crawling along on the rim of a wheel. Presently the car sputtered and stopped. We were out of gas! The chief merely remarked: '*Mektoub!*' And, there again, instead of shouting at the driver because he had not taken on enough gas, everyone remained calm and we walked to our destination, singing as we went.

The seven years I spent with the Arabs convinced me that the neurotics, the insane, the drunks of America and Europe are the product of the hurried and harassed lives we live in our so-called civilization.

As long as I lived in the Sahara, I had no worries. I found there, in the Garden of Allah, the serene contentment and physical well-being that so many of us are seeking with tenseness and despair.

Many people scoff at fatalism. Maybe they are right. Who knows? But all of us must be able to see how our fates are often determined for us. For example, if I had not spoken to Lawrence of Arabia at three minutes past noon on a hot August day in 1919, all the years that have elapsed since then would have been completely different. Looking back over my life, I can see how it has been shaped and moulded time and again by events far beyond my control. The Arabs call it *mektoub, kismet* – the will of Allah. Call it anything you wish. It does strange things to you. I only know that today – seventeen years after leaving the Sahara – I still maintain that happy resignation to the inevitable which I learned from the Arabs. That philosophy has done more to settle my nerves than a thousand sedatives could have achieved.

When the fierce, burning winds blow over our lives – and we cannot prevent them – let us, too, accept the inevitable (see Part Three, Chapter 9). And then get busy and pick up the pieces!

Five methods I have used to banish worry

BY PROFESSOR WILLIAM LYON PHELPS
[I had the privilege of spending an afternoon with Billy Phelps, of Yale, shortly before his death. Here are the five methods he used to banish worry – based on the notes I took during that interview.
– Dale Carnegie]

I. When I was twenty-four years old, my eyes suddenly gave out. After reading three or four minutes, my eyes felt as if they were full of needles; and even when I was not reading, they were so sensitive that I could not face a window. I consulted the best oculists in New Haven and New York. Nothing seemed to help me. After four o'clock in the afternoon, I simply sat in a chair in the darkest corner of the room, waiting for bedtime. I was terrified. I feared that I would have to give up my career as a teacher and go out West and get a job as a lumberjack. Then a strange thing happened which shows the miraculous effects of the mind over physical ailments. When my eyes were at their worst that unhappy winter, I accepted an invitation to address a group of undergraduates. The hall was illuminated by huge rings of gas jets suspended from the ceiling. The lights pained my eyes so intensely that, while sitting on the platform, I was compelled to look at the floor. Yet during my thirty-minute speech, I felt absolutely no pain, and I could look directly at these lights without any blinking whatever. Then when the assembly was over, my eyes pained me again.

I thought then that if I could keep my mind strongly concentrated on something, not for thirty minutes, but for a week, I might be cured. For clearly it was a case of mental excitement triumphing over a bodily illness.

I had a similar experience later while crossing the ocean. I had an attack of lumbago so severe that I could not walk. I suffered extreme pain when I tried to stand up straight. While in that condition, I was invited to give a lecture on shipboard. As soon as I began to speak, every trace of pain and stiffness left my body; I stood up straight, moved about with perfect flexibility, and spoke for an hour. When the lecture was over, I walked away to my stateroom with ease. For a moment, I thought I was cured. But the cure was only temporary. The lumbago resumed its attack.

These experiences demonstrated to me the vital importance of one's mental attitude. They taught me the importance of enjoying life while you may. So I live every day now as if it were the first day I had ever seen and the last I were going to see. I am excited about the daily adventure of living, and nobody in a state of excitement will be unduly troubled with worries. I love my daily work as a teacher. I wrote a book entitled *The Excitement of Teaching*. Teaching has always been more than an art or an occupation to me. It is a passion. I love to teach as a painter loves to paint or a singer loves to sing. Before I get out of bed in the morning, I think with ardent delight of my first group of students. I have always felt that one of the chief reasons for success in life is enthusiasm.

II. I have found that I can crowd worry out of mind by reading an absorbing book. When I was fifty-nine, I had a prolonged nervous breakdown. During that period, I began reading David Alec Wilson's monumental *Life of Carlyle*. It had a good deal to do with my convalescence because I became so absorbed in reading it that I forgot my despondency.

III. At another time when I was terribly depressed, I forced myself to become physically active almost every hour of the day. I played five or six sets of violent games of tennis every morning, then took a bath, had lunch, and played eighteen holes of golf every afternoon. On Friday nights I danced until one o'clock in the morning. I am a great believer in working up a tremendous sweat. I found that depression and worry oozed out of my system with the sweat.

IV. I learned long ago to avoid the folly of hurry, rush, and working under tension. I have always tried to apply the philosophy of Wilbur Cross. When he was Governor of Connecticut, he said to me: 'Sometimes when I have too many things to do all at once, I sit down and relax and smoke my pipe for an hour and do nothing.'

V. I have also learned that patience and time have a way of resolving our troubles. When I am worried about something, I try to see my troubles in their proper perspective. I say to myself: 'Two months from now I shall not be worrying about this bad break, so why worry about it now? Why not assume now the same attitude that I will have two months from now?'

To sum up, here are the five ways in which Professor Phelps banished worry:

I *Live with gusto and enthusiasm:* 'I live every day as if it were the first day I had ever seen and the last I were going to see.'
2 *Read an interesting book:* 'When I had a prolonged nervous breakdown . . . I began reading . . . the *Life of Carlyle* . . . and became so absorbed in reading it that I forgot my despondency.'
3 *Play games:* 'When I was terribly depressed, I forced myself to become physically active almost every hour of the day.'
4 *Relax while you work:* 'I long ago learned to avoid the folly of hurry, rush, and working under tension.'
5 '*I try to see my troubles in their proper perspective.* I say to myself, "Two months from now I shall not be worrying about this bad break, so why worry about it now? Why not assume now the same attitude that I will have two months from now?" '

I stood yesterday. I can stand today

BY DOROTHY DIX

I have been through the depths of poverty and sickness. When people ask me what has kept me going through the troubles that come to all of us, I always reply: 'I stood yesterday. I can stand today. And I will not permit myself to think about what *might* happen tomorrow.'

I have known want and struggle and anxiety and despair. I have always had to work beyond the limit of my strength. As I look back upon my life, I see it as a battlefield strewn with the wrecks of dead dreams and broken hopes and shattered illusions – a battle in which I always fought with the odds tremendously against me, and which has left me scarred and bruised and maimed and old before my time.

Yet I have no pity for myself; no tears to shed over the past and gone sorrows; no envy for the women who have been spared all I have gone through. For I have lived. They only existed. I have drunk the cup of life down to its very dregs. They have only sipped the bubbles on top of it. I know things they will never know. I see things to which they are blind. It is only the women whose eyes have been washed clear with tears who get the broad vision that makes them little sisters to all the world.

I have learned in the great University of Hard Knocks a philosophy that no woman who has had an easy life ever acquires. I have learned to live each day as it comes and not to borrow trouble by dreading the morrow. It is the dark menace of the picture that makes cowards of us. I put that dread from me because experience has taught me that when the time comes that I so fear, the strength and wisdom to meet it will be given me. Little annoyances no longer have the power to affect me. After you have seen your whole edifice of happiness topple and crash in ruins about you, it never matters to you again that a servant forgets to put the doilies under the finger bowls, or the cook spills the soup.

I have learned not to expect too much of people, and so I can still get happiness out of the friend who isn't quite true to me or the acquaintance who gossips. Above all, I have acquired a sense of humour, because there were so many things over which I had either to cry or laugh. And when a woman can joke over her troubles instead of having hysterics, nothing can ever hurt her much again. I do not regret the hardships I have known, because through them I have touched life at every point I have lived. And it was worth the price I had to pay.

Dorothy Dix conquered worry by living in 'day-tight compartments.'

I did not expect to live to see the dawn

BY J. C. PENNEY

[On April 14, 1902, a young man with five hundred dollars in cash and a million dollars in determination opened a dry-goods store in Kemmerer, Wyoming – a little mining town of a thousand people, situated on the old covered-wagon trail laid out by the Lewis and Clark Expedition. That young man and his wife lived in a half-story attic above the store, using a large empty dry-goods box for a table and smaller boxes for chairs. The young wife wrapped her baby in a blanket and let it sleep under a counter while she stood beside it, helping her husband wait on customers. Today the largest chain of dry-goods stores in the world bears that man's name: The J. C. Penney stores – over sixteen hundred of them covering every state in the Union. I recently had dinner with Mr. Penney, and he told me about the most dramatic moment of his life.]

Years ago, I passed through a most trying experience. I was worried and desperate. My worries were not connected in any way whatever with the J. C. Penney Company. That business was solid and thriving; but I personally had made some unwise commitments prior to the crash of 1929. Like many other men, I was blamed for conditions for which I was in no way responsible. I was so harassed with worries that I couldn't sleep, and developed an extremely painful ailment known as the shingles – a red rash and skin eruptions. I consulted a physician – a man with whom I had gone to high school as a boy in Hamilton, Missouri: Dr. Elmer Eggleston, a staff physician at the Kellogg Sanitarium in Battle Creek, Michigan. Dr. Eggleston put me to bed and warned me that I was a very ill man. A rigid treatment was prescribed. But nothing helped. I got weaker day by day. I was broken nervously and physically, filled with despair, unable to see even a ray of hope. I had nothing to live for. I felt I hadn't a friend left in the world, that even my family had turned against me. One night, Dr. Eggleston gave me a sedative, but the effect soon wore off and I awoke with an overwhelming conviction that this was my last night of life. Getting out of bed, I wrote farewell letters to my wife and to my son, saying that I did not expect to live to see the dawn.

When I awoke the next morning, I was surprised to find that I was still alive. Going downstairs, I heard singing in a little chapel where devotional exercises were held each morning. I can still remember the hymn they were singing: 'God will take care of you'. Going into the chapel, I listened with a weary heart to the singing, the reading of the Scripture lesson and the prayer. Suddenly – something happened. I can't explain it. I can only call it a miracle. I felt as if I had been instantly lifted out of the darkness of a dungeon into warm, brilliant sunlight. I felt as if I had been transported from hell to paradise. I felt the power of God as I had never felt it before. I realized then that I alone was responsible for all my troubles. I knew that God with His love was there to help me. From that day to this, my life has been free from worry. I am seventy-one years old, and the most dramatic and glorious twenty minutes of my life were those I spent in that chapel that morning: 'God will take care of you'.

J. C. Penney learned to overcome worry almost instantaneously, because he discovered the one perfect cure.

I Go to the Gym to Punch the Bag or Take a Hike

Outdoors

BY COLONEL EDDIE EAGAN
New York Attorney, Rhodes Scholar
Former Chairman, New York State Athletic Commission
Former Olympic Light-Heavyweight Champion of the World

When I find myself worrying and mentally going around in endless circles like a camel turning a water wheel in Egypt, a good physical workout helps me to chase those 'blues' away. It may be running or a long hike in the country, or it may be a half-hour of bag punching or squash tennis at the gymnasium. Whichever it is, physical exercise clears my mental outlook. On a weekend I do a lot of physical sport, such as a run around the golf course, a game of paddle tennis, or a ski weekend in the Adirondacks. By my becoming physically tired, my mind gets a rest from legal problems, so that when I return to them, my mind has a new zest and power.

Quite often in New York, where I work, there is a chance for me to spend an hour at the Yale Club gym. No man can worry while he is playing squash tennis or skiing. He is too busy to worry. The large mental mountains of trouble become minute molehills that new thoughts and acts quickly smooth down.

I find the best antidote for worry is exercise. Use your muscles more and your brain less when you are worried, and you will be surprised at the result. It works that way with me – worry goes when exercise begins.

I was 'the worrying wreck from Virginia Tech'

BY JIM BIRDSALL

Seventeen years ago, when I was in military college at Blacksburg, Virginia, I was known as 'the worrying wreck from Virginia Tech'. I worried so violently that I often became ill. In fact, I was ill so often that I had a regular bed reserved for me at the college infirmary at all times. When the nurse saw me coming, she would run and give me a hypo. I worried about everything. Sometimes I even forgot what I was worrying about. I worried for fear I would be busted out of college because of my low grades. I had failed to pass my examination in physics and other subjects, too. I knew I had to maintain an average grade of 75–84. I worried about my health, about my excruciating attacks of acute indigestion, about my insomnia. I worried about financial matters. I felt bad because I couldn't buy my girl candy or take her to dances as often as I wanted to. I worried for fear she would marry one of the other cadets. I was in a lather day and night over a dozen intangible problems.

In desperation, I poured out my troubles to Professor Duke Baird, professor of business administration at V.P.I.

The fifteen minutes that I spent with Professor Baird did more for my health and happiness than all the rest of the four years I spent in college. 'Jim,' he said, 'you ought to sit down and face the facts. If you devoted half as much time and energy to solving your problems as you do to worrying about them, you wouldn't have any worries. Worrying is just a vicious habit you have learned.'

He gave me three rules to break the worry habit:

Rule 1. Find out precisely what is the problem you are worrying about.
Rule 2. Find out the cause of the problem.
Rule 3. Do something constructive at once about solving the problem.

After that interview, I did a bit of constructive planning. Instead of worrying because I had failed to pass physics, I now asked myself why I had failed. I knew it wasn't because I was dumb, for I was editor-in-chief of *The Virginia Tech Engineer*.

I figured that I had failed physics because I had no interest in the subject.

I had not applied myself because I couldn't see how it would help me in my work as an industrial engineer. But now I changed my attitude. I said to myself, 'If the college authorities demand that I pass my physics examination before I obtain a degree, who am I to question their wisdom?'

So I enrolled for physics again. This time I passed because instead of wasting my time in resentment and worrying about how hard it was, I studied diligently.

I solved my financial worries by taking on some additional jobs, such as selling punch at the college dances, and by borrowing money from my father, which I paid back soon after graduation.

I solved my love worries by proposing to the girl that I feared might marry another cadet. She is now Mrs. Jim Birdsall.

As I look back at it now, I can see that my problem was one of confusion, a disinclination to find the causes of my worry and face them realistically.

Jim Birdsall learned to stop worrying because he ANALYZED his troubles. In fact, he used the very principles described in the chapter 'How to Analyze and Solve Worry Problems.'

I have lived by this sentence

BY DR. JOSEPH R. SIZOO
President, New Brunswick Theological Seminary New Brunswick, New Jersey – the oldest theological seminary in the United States, founded in 1784

Years ago, in a day of uncertainty and disillusionment, when my whole life seemed to be overwhelmed by forces beyond my control, one morning quite casually I opened my New Testament and my eyes fell upon this sentence, 'He that sent me is with me – the Father hath not left me alone.' My life has never been the same since that hour. Everything for me has been forever different after that. I suppose that not a day has passed that I have not repeated it to myself. Many have come to me for counselling during these years, and I have always sent them away with this sustaining sentence. Ever since that hour when my eyes fell upon it, I have lived by this sentence. I have walked with it and I have found in it my peace and strength. To me it is the very essence of religion. It lies at the rock bottom of everything that makes life worth living. It is the Golden Text of my life.

I hit bottom and survived

BY TED ERICKSEN

I used to be a terrible 'worry wart'. But no more. In the summer of 1942, I had an experience that banished worry from my life – for all time, I hope. The experience made every other trouble seem small by comparison.

For years I had wanted to spend a summer on a commercial fishing craft in Alaska, so in 1942 I signed on a thirty-two-foot salmon-seining vessel out of Kodiak, Alaska. On a craft of this size, there is a crew of only three: the skipper who does the supervising, a No. 2 man who assists the skipper, and a general work horse, who is usually a Scandinavian. I am a Scandinavian.

Since salmon seining has to be done with the tides, I often worked twenty hours out of twenty-four. I kept up that schedule for a week at a time. I did everything that nobody else wanted to do. I washed the craft. I put away the gear. I cooked on a little wood-burning stove in a small cabin where the heat and fumes of the motor almost made me ill. I washed the dishes. I repaired the boat. I pitched the salmon from our boat into a tender that took the fish to a cannery. My feet were always wet in my rubber boots. My boots were often filled with water, but I had no time to empty them. But all that was play compared to my main job, which was pulling what is called the 'cork line'. That operation simply means placing your feet on the stern of the craft and pulling in the corks and the webbing of the net. At least, that is what you are supposed to do. But, in reality, the net was so heavy that when I tried to pull it in, it wouldn't budge. What really happened was that in trying to pull in the cork line, I actually pulled in the boat. I pulled it along on my own power, since the net stayed where it was. I did all this for weeks on end. It was almost the end of me, too. I ached horribly. I ached all over. I ached for months.

When I finally did have a chance to rest, I slept on a damp, lumpy mattress piled on top of the provisions locker. I would put one of the lumps in the mattress under the part of my back that hurt most – and sleep as if I had been drugged. I was drugged by complete exhaustion.

I am glad now that I had to endure all that aching and exhaustion because it has helped me stop worrying. Whenever I am confronted by a problem now – instead of worrying about it, I say to myself, 'Ericksen, could this possibly be as bad as pulling the cork line?' And Ericksen invariably answers, 'No, nothing could be *that* bad!' So I cheer up and tackle it with courage. I believe it is a good thing to have to endure an agonizing experience occasionally. It is good to know that we have hit bottom and survived. That makes all our daily problems seem easy by comparison.

I used to be one of the world's biggest jackasses

BY PERCY H. WHITING
Author of *The Five Great Rules of Selling*

I have died more times from more different diseases than any other man, living, dead, or half dead.

I was no ordinary hypochondriac. My father owned a drugstore, and I was practically brought up in it. I talked to doctors and nurses every day, so I knew the names and symptoms of more and worse diseases than the average layman. I was no ordinary hypo – I had symptoms! I could worry for an hour or two over a disease and then have practically all the symptoms of a man who was suffering from it. I recall once that, in Great Barrington, Massachusetts, the town in which I lived, we had a rather severe diphtheria epidemic. In my father's drugstore, I had been selling medicines day after day to people who came from infected homes. Then the evil that I feared came upon me: I had diphtheria myself. I was positive I had it. I went to bed and worried myself into the standard symptoms. I sent for a doctor. He looked me over and said, 'Yes, Percy, you've got it.' That relieved my mind. I was never afraid of any disease when I had it – so I turned over and went to sleep. The next morning I was in perfect health.

For years I distinguished myself and got a lot of attention and sympathy by specializing in unusual and fantastic diseases – I died several times of both lockjaw and hydrophobia. Later on, I settled down to having the run-of-mill ailments – specializing in cancer and tuberculosis.

I can laugh about it now, but it was tragic then. I honestly and literally feared for years that I was walking on the edge of the grave. When it came time to buy a suit of clothes in the spring, I would ask myself: 'Should I waste this money when I know I can't possibly live to wear this suit out?'

However, I am happy to report progress: in the past ten years, I haven't died even once.

How did I stop dying? By kidding myself out of my ridiculous imaginings. Every time I felt the dreadful symptoms coming on, I laughed at myself and said: 'See here, Whiting, you have been dying from one fatal disease after another now for twenty years, yet you are in first-class health today. An insurance company recently accepted you for more insurance. Isn't it about time, Whiting, that you stood aside and had a good laugh at the worrying jackass you are?'

I soon found that I couldn't worry about myself and laugh at myself at one and the same time. So I've been laughing at myself ever since.

The point of this is: Don't take yourself too seriously. Try just laughing at some of your sillier worries, and see if you can't laugh them out of existence.

I have always tried to keep my line of supplies open

BY GENE AUTRY
The world's most famous and beloved singing cowboy

I figure that most worries are about family troubles and money. I was fortunate in marrying a small-town Oklahoma girl who had the same background I had and enjoyed the same things. We both try to follow the golden rule, so we have kept our family troubles to a minimum.

I have kept my financial worries to a minimum also by doing two things. First, I have always followed a rule of absolute one hundred percent integrity in everything. When I borrowed money, I paid back every penny. Few things cause more worry than dishonesty.

Second, when I started a new venture, I always kept an ace in the hole. Military experts say that the first principle of fighting a battle is to keep your line of supplies open. I figure that that principle applied to personal battles almost as much as to military battles. For example, as a lad down in Texas and Oklahoma, I saw some real poverty when the country was devastated by droughts. We had mighty hard scratching at times to make a living. We were so poor that my father used to drive across the country in a covered wagon with a string of horses and swap horses to make a living. I wanted something more reliable than that. So I got a job working for a railway-station agent and learned telegraphy in my spare time. Later, I got a job working as relief operator for the Frisco Railway. I was sent here, there, and yonder to relieve other station agents who were ill or on vacation or had more work than they could do. That job paid $150 per month. Later, when I started out to better myself, I always figured that the railroad job meant economic safety. So I always kept the road open back to that job. It was my line of supplies, and I never cut myself off from it until I was firmly established in a new and better position.

For example, back in 1928, when I was working as a relief operator for the Frisco Railway in Chelsea, Oklahoma, a stranger drifted in one evening to send a telegram. He heard me playing the guitar and singing cowboy songs and told me I was good – told me that I ought to go to New York and get a job on the stage or radio. Naturally, I was flattered; and when I saw the name he signed to his telegram, I was almost breathless: *Will Rogers.*

Instead of rushing off to New York at once, I thought the matter over carefully for nine months. I finally came to the conclusion that I had nothing to lose and everything to gain by going to New York and giving the old town a whirl. I had a railroad pass: I could travel free. I could sleep sitting up in my seat, and I could carry some sandwiches and fruit for my meals.

So I went. When I reached New York, I slept in a furnished room for five dollars a week, ate at the Automat, and tramped the streets for ten weeks – and got nowhere. I would have been worried sick if I hadn't had a job to go back to. I had already worked for the railway five years. That meant I had seniority rights; but in order to protect those rights, I couldn't lay off longer than ninety days. By this time, I had already been in New York seventy days, so I rushed back to Oklahoma on my pass and began working again to protect my line of supply. I worked for a few months, saved money, and returned to New York for another try. This time I got a break. One day, while waiting for an interview in the recording-studio office, I played my guitar and sang a song to the girl receptionist: 'Jeannine, I Dream of Lilac Time'. While I was singing that song, the man who wrote it – Nat Schildkraut – drifted into the office. Naturally, he was pleased to hear anyone singing his song. So he gave me a note of introduction and sent me down to the Victor Recording Company. I made a record. I was no good – too stiff and self-conscious. So I took the advice of the Victor Recording man: I went back to Tulsa, worked for the railway by day, and at night I sang cowboy songs on a sustaining radio programme. I liked that arrangement. It meant that I was keeping my line of supplies open – so I had no worries.

I sang for nine months on radio station KVOO in Tulsa. During that time, Jimmy Long and I wrote a song entitled 'That Silver-Haired Daddy of Mine'. It caught on. Arthur Sattherly, head of the American Recording Company, asked me to make a recording. It clicked. I made a number of other recordings for fifty dollars each, and finally got a job singing cowboy songs over radio station WLS in Chicago. Salary: forty dollars a week. After singing there four years my salary was raised to ninety dollars a week, and I picked up another three hundred dollars doing personal appearances every night in theatres.

Then in 1934, I got a break that opened up enormous possibilities. The League of Decency was formed to clean up the movies. So Hollywood producers decided to put on cowboy pictures; but they wanted a new kind of cowboy – one who could sing. The man who owned the American Recording Company was also part owner of Republic Pictures. 'If you want a singing cowboy,' he said to his associates, 'I have got one making records for us.' That is how I broke into the movies. I started making singing-cowboy pictures for one hundred dollars a week. I had serious doubts about whether I would succeed in pictures, but I didn't worry. I knew I could always go back to my old job.

My success in pictures exceeded my wildest expectations. I now get a salary of one hundred thousand dollars a year plus one half of all the profits on my pictures. However, I realize that this arrangement won't go on forever. But I am not worried. I know that no matter what happens – even if I lose every dollar I have – I can always go back to Oklahoma and get a job working for the Frisco Railway. I have protected my line of supplies.

I heard a voice in India

BY E. STANLEY JONES
One of America's most dynamic speakers and the most famous missionary of his generation

I have devoted forty years of my life to missionary work in India. At first, I found it difficult to endure the terrible heat plus the nervous strain of the great task that stretched before me. At the end of eight years, I was suffering so severely from brain fatigue and nervous exhaustion that I collapsed, not once but several times. I was ordered to take a year's furlough in America. On the boat returning to America, I collapsed again while speaking at a Sunday-morning service on the ship, and the ship's doctor put me to bed for the remainder of the trip.

After a year's rest in America, I started back to India, but stopped on the way to hold evangelistic meetings among the university students in Manila. In the midst of the strain of these meetings, I collapsed several times. Physicians warned me that if I returned to India, I would die. In spite of their warnings, I continued on to India, but I went with a deepening cloud upon me. When I arrived in Bombay, I was so broken that I went straight to the hills and rested for several months. Then I returned to the plains to continue my work. It was no use. I collapsed and was forced to return to the hills for another long rest. Again I descended to the plains, and again I was shocked and crushed to discover that I couldn't take it. I was exhausted mentally, nervously, and physically. I was completely at the end of my resources. I feared that I would be a physical wreck for the balance of my life.

If I didn't get help from somewhere, I realized that I would have to give up my missionary career, go back to America, and work on a farm to try to regain my health. It was one of my darkest hours. At that time I was holding a series of meetings in Lucknow. While praying one night an event happened that completely transformed my life. While in prayer – and I was not particularly thinking about myself at the time – a voice seemed to say, 'Are you yourself ready for this work to which I have called you?'

I replied: 'No, Lord, I am done for. I have reached the end of my resources.'

The Voice replied, 'If you will turn that over to Me and not worry about it, I will take care of it.'

I quickly answered, 'Lord, I close the bargain right here.'

A great peace settled into my heart and pervaded my whole being. I knew it was done! Life – abundant life – had taken possession of me. I was so lifted up that I scarcely touched the road as I quietly walked home that night. Every inch was holy ground. For days after that I hardly knew I had a body. I went through the days, working all day and far into the night, and came down to bedtime wondering why in the world I should ever go to bed at all, for there was not the slightest trace of tiredness of any kind. I seemed possessed by life and peace and rest – by Christ Himself.

The question came as to whether I should tell this. I shrank from it, but felt I should – and did. After that it was sink or swim before everybody. More than a score of the most strenuous years of my life have gone by since then, but the old trouble has never returned. I have never had such health. But it was more than a physical touch. I seemed to have tapped new life for body, mind, and spirit. After that experience, life for me functioned on a permanently higher level. And I had done nothing but take it!

During the many years that have gone by since then, I have travelled all over the world, frequently lecturing three times a day, and have found time and strength to write *The Christ of the Indian Road* and eleven other books. Yet in the midst of all this, I have never missed, or even been late to, an appointment. The worries that once beset me have long since vanished, and now, in my sixty-third year, I am overflowing with abounding vitality and the joy of serving and living for others.

I suppose that the physical and mental transformation that I have experienced could be picked to pieces psychologically and explained. It does not matter. Life is bigger than processes and overflows and dwarfs them.

This one thing I know: my life was completely transformed and uplifted that night in Lucknow, thirty-one years ago, when at the depth of my weakness and depression, a voice said to me: 'If you will turn that over to Me and not worry about it, I will take care of it,' and I replied, 'Lord, I close the bargain right here.'

When the sheriff came in my front door

BY HOMER CROY

The bitterest moment of my life occurred one day in 1933 when the sheriff came in the front door and I went out the back. I had lost my home at 10 Standish Road, Forest Hills, Long Island, where my children were born and where I and my family had lived for eighteen years. I had never dreamed that this could happen to me. Twelve years before, I thought I was sitting on top of the world. I had sold the motion-picture rights to my novel *West of the Water Tower* for a top Hollywood price. I lived abroad with my family for two years. We summered in Switzerland and wintered on the French Riviera – just like the idle rich.

I spent six months in Paris and wrote a novel entitled *They Had to See Paris*. Will Rogers appeared in the screen version. It was his first talking picture. I had tempting offers to remain in Hollywood and write several of Will Rogers' pictures. But I didn't. I returned to New York. And my troubles began!

It slowly dawned on me that I had great dormant abilities that I had never developed. I began to fancy myself a shrewd businessman. Somebody told me that John Jacob Astor had made millions investing in vacant land in New York. Who was Astor? Just an immigrant pedlar with an accent. If he could do it, why couldn't I . . . I was going to be rich! I began to read the yachting magazines.

I had the courage of ignorance. I didn't know any more about buying and selling real estate than an Eskimo knows about oil furnaces. How was I to get the money to launch myself on my spectacular financial career? That was simple: I mortgaged my home, and bought some of the finest building lots in Forest Hills. I was going to hold this land until it reached a fabulous price, then sell it and live in luxury – I who had never sold a piece of real estate as big as a doll's handkerchief. I pitied the plodders who slaved in offices for a mere salary. I told myself that God had not seen fit to touch every man with the divine fire of financial genius.

Suddenly, the great depression swept down upon me like a Kansas cyclone and shook me as a tornado would shake a hen coop.

I had to pour $220 a month into that monster-mouthed piece of Good Earth. Oh, how fast those months came! In addition, I had to keep up the payments on our now-mortgaged house and find enough food. I was worried. I tried to write humour for the magazines. My attempts at humour sounded like the lamentations of Jeremiah! I was unable to sell anything. The novels I wrote failed. I ran out of money. I had nothing on which I could borrow money except my typewriter and the gold fillings in my teeth. The milk company stopped delivering milk. The gas company turned off the gas. We had to buy one of those little outdoor camp stoves you see advertised; it had a cylinder of gasoline; you pump it up by hand and it shoots out a flame with a hissing like an angry goose.

We ran out of coal; the company sued us. Our only heat was the fireplace. I would go out at night and pick up boards and leftovers from the new homes that the rich people were building... I who had started out to be one of these rich people.

I was so worried I couldn't sleep. I often got up in the middle of the night and walked for hours to exhaust myself so I could fall asleep.

I lost not only the vacant land I had bought, but all my heart's blood that I had poured into it.

The bank closed the mortgage on my home and put me and my family out on the street.

In some way, we managed to get hold of a few dollars and rent a small apartment. We moved in the last day of 1933. I sat down on a packing case and looked around. An old saying of my mother's came back: 'Don't cry over spilt milk.'

But this wasn't milk. This was my heart's blood!

After I had sat there a while I said to myself, 'Well, I've hit bottom and I've stood it. There's no place to go now but up.'

I began to think of the fine things that the mortgage had not taken from me. I still had my health and my friends. I would start again. I would not grieve about the past. I would repeat to myself every day the words I had often heard my mother say about spilt milk.

I put into my work the energy that I had been putting into worrying. Little by little, my situation began to improve. I am almost thankful now that I had to go through all that misery; it gave me strength, fortitude, and confidence. I know now what it means to hit bottom. I know it doesn't kill you. I know we can stand more than we think we can. When little worries and anxieties and uncertainties try to disturb me now, I banish them by reminding myself of the time I sat on the packing case and said: 'I've hit bottom and I've stood it. There is no place to go now but up.'

What's the principle here? Don't try to saw sawdust! Accept the inevitable! If you can't go lower, you can try going up.

The toughest opponent I ever fought was worry

BY JACK DEMPSEY

During my career in the ring, I found that Old Man Worry was an almost tougher opponent than the heavyweight boxers I fought. I realized that I had to learn to stop worrying, or worry would sap my vitality and undermine my success. So, little by little, I worked out a system for myself. Here are some of the things I did:

1. To keep up my courage in the ring, I would give myself a pep talk during the fight. For example, while I was fighting Firpo, I kept saying over and over, 'Nothing is going to stop me. He is not going to hurt me. I won't feel his blows. I can't get hurt. I am going to keep going, no matter what happens.' Making positive statements like that to myself, and thinking positive thoughts, helped me a lot. It even kept my mind so occupied that I didn't feel the blows. During my career, I have had my lips smashed, my eyes cut, my ribs cracked – Firpo knocked me clear through the ropes, and I landed on a reporter's typewriter and wrecked it. But I never felt even one of Firpo's blows. There was only one blow that I ever really felt. That was the night Lester Johnson broke three of my ribs. The punch never hurt me, but it affected my breathing. I can honestly say I never felt any other blow I ever got in the ring.

2. Another thing I did was to keep reminding myself of the futility of worry. Most of my worrying was done before the big bouts, while I was going through training. I would often lie awake at nights for hours, tossing and worrying, unable to sleep. I would worry for fear I might break my hand or sprain my ankle or get my eye cut badly in the first round so I couldn't coordinate my punches. When I got myself into this state of nerves, I used to get out of bed, look into the mirror, and give myself a good talking to. I would say to myself: 'What a fool you are to be worrying about something that hasn't happened and may never happen. Life is short. I have only a few years to live, so I must enjoy life.' I kept saying to myself, 'Nothing is important but

my health. Nothing is important but my health.' I kept reminding myself that losing sleep and worrying would destroy my health. I found that by saying these things to myself over and over, night after night, year after year, they finally got under my skin, and I could brush off my worries like so much water.

3. The third – and best – thing I did was pray! While I was training for a bout, I always prayed several times a day. When I was in the ring, I always prayed just before the bell sounded for each round. That helped me fight with courage and confidence. I have never gone to bed in my life without saying a prayer; and I have never eaten a meal in my life without first thanking God for it. . . . Have my prayers been answered? Thousands of times!

I prayed to God to keep me out of an orphans' home

BY KATHLEEN HALTER

As a little child, my life was filled with terror. My mother had heart trouble. Day after day, I saw her faint and fall to the floor. We all feared she was going to die, and I believed that all little girls whose mothers died were sent to the Central Wesleyan Orphans' Home, located in the little town of Warrenton, Missouri, where we lived. I dreaded the thought of going there, and when I was six years old I prayed constantly: 'Dear God, please let my mummy live until I am old enough not to go to the orphans' home.'

Twenty years later, my brother, Meiner, had a terrible injury and suffered intense pain until he died two years later. He couldn't feed himself or turn over in bed. To deaden his pain, I had to give him morphine hypodermics every three hours, day and night. I did this for two years. I was teaching music at the time at the Central Wesleyan College in Warrenton, Missouri. When the neighbours heard my brother screaming with pain, they would telephone me at college and I would leave my music class and rush home to give my brother another injection of morphine. Every night when I went to bed, I would set the alarm clock to go off three hours later so I would be sure to get up to attend to my brother. I remember that on winter nights I would keep a bottle of milk outside the window, where it would freeze and turn into a kind of ice cream that I loved to eat. When the alarm went off, this ice cream outside the window gave me an additional incentive to get up.

In the midst of these troubles, I did two things that kept me from indulging in self-pity and worrying and embittering my life with resentment. First, I kept myself busy teaching music from twelve to fourteen hours a day, so I had little time to think of my troubles; and when I was tempted to feel sorry for myself, I kept saying to myself over and over, 'Now listen, as long as you can walk and feed yourself and are free from intense pain, you ought to be the happiest person in the world. No matter what happens, never forget that as long as you live! Never! Never!'

I was determined to do everything in my power to cultivate an unconscious and continuous attitude of gratefulness for my many blessings. Every morning when I awoke, I would thank God that I could get out of bed and walk to breakfast and feed myself. I fierccly resolved that in spite of my troubles I would be the happiest person in Warrenton, Missouri. Maybe I didn't succeed in achieving that goal, but I did succeed in making myself the most grateful young woman in my home town – and probably few of my associates worried less than I did.

This Missouri music teacher applied two principles described in this book: she kept too busy to worry, and she counted her blessings. The same technique may be helpful to you.

My stomach was twisting like a Kansas whirlwind

BY CAMERON SHIPP

I had been working very happily in the publicity department of the Warner Brothers studio in California for several years. I was a unit man and feature writer. I wrote stories for newspapers and magazines about Warner Brothers stars.

Suddenly, I was promoted. I was made the assistant publicity director. As a matter of fact, there was a change of administrative policy, and I was given an impressive title: Administrative Assistant.

This gave me an enormous office with a private refrigerator, two secretaries, and complete charge of a staff of seventy-five writers, exploiters, and radio men. I was enormously impressed. I went straight out and bought a new suit.

I tried to speak with dignity. I set up filing systems, made decisions with authority, and ate quick lunches.

I was convinced that the whole public-relations policy of Warner Brothers had descended upon my shoulders. I perceived that the lives, both private and public, of such renowned persons as Bette Davis, Olivia De Havilland, James Cagney, Edward G. Robinson, Errol Flynn, Humphrey Bogart, Ann Sheridan, Alexis Smith, and Alan Hale were entirely in my hands.

In less than a month I became aware that I had stomach ulcers. Probably cancer.

My chief war activity at that time was chairman of the War Activities Committee of the Screen Publicists Guild. I liked to do this work, liked to meet my friends at guild meetings. But these gatherings became matters of dread. After every meeting, I was violently ill. Often I had to stop my car on the way home, pulling myself together before I could drive on. There seemed to be so much to do, so little time in which to do it. It was all vital. And I was woefully inadequate.

I am being perfectly truthful – this was the most painful illness of my entire life. There was always a tight fist in my vitals. I lost weight, I could not sleep. The pain was constant.

So I went to see a renowned expert in internal medicine. An advertising man recommended him. He said this physician had many clients who were advertising men.

This physician spoke only briefly, just enough for me to tell him where I hurt and what I did for a living. He seemed more interested in my job than in my ailments, but I was soon reassured: for two weeks, daily, he gave me every known test. I was probed, explored, X-rayed, and fluoroscoped. Finally, I was instructed to call on him and hear the verdict.

'Mr. Shipp,' he said, leaning back, 'we have been through these exhaustive tests. They were absolutely necessary, although I knew *of course* after my first quick examination that you *did not have stomach ulcers.*

'But I knew, because you are the kind of man you are and because you do the kind of work you do, that you would not believe me unless I showed you. Let me show you.'

So he showed me the charts and the X-rays and explained them. He showed me I had no ulcers.

'Now,' said the doctor, 'this costs you a good deal of money, but it is worth it to you. Here is the prescription: *don't worry.*

'Now' – he stopped me as I started to expostulate – 'now, I realize that you can't follow the prescription immediately, so I'll give you a crutch. Here are some pills. They contain belladonna. Take as many as you like. When you use these up, come back and I'll give you more. They won't hurt you. But they will always relax you.

'But remember: you don't need them. All you have to do is quit worrying.

'If you do start worrying again, you'll have to come back here and I'll charge you a heavy fee again. How about it?'

I wish I could report that the lesson took effect that day and that I quit worrying immediately. I didn't. I took the pills for several weeks, whenever I felt a worry coming on. They worked. I felt better *at once*.

But I felt silly taking these pills. I am a big man physically. I am almost as tall as Abe Lincoln was – and I weigh almost two hundred pounds. Yet here I was taking little white pills to relax myself. When my friends asked me why I was taking pills, I was ashamed to tell the truth. Gradually I began to laugh at myself. I said: 'See here, Cameron Shipp, you are acting like a fool. You are taking yourself and your little activities much, much too seriously. Bette Davis and James Cagney and Edward G. Robinson were world-famous before you started to handle their publicity; and if you dropped dead tonight, Warner Brothers and their stars would manage to get along without you. Look at Eisenhower, General Marshall, MacArthur, Jimmy Doolittle and Admiral King – they are running the war without taking pills. And yet you can't serve as chairman of the War Activities Committee of the Screen Publicists Guild without taking little white pills to keep your stomach from twisting and turning like a Kansas whirlwind.'

I began to take pride in getting along without the pills. A little while later, I threw the pills down the drain and got home each night in time to take a little nap before dinner and gradually began to lead a normal life. I have never been back to see that physician.

But I owe him much, much more than what seemed like a stiff fee at the time. He taught me to laugh at myself. But I think the really skilful thing he did was to refrain from laughing *at* me, and to refrain from telling me I had nothing to worry *about*. He took me seriously. He saved my face. He gave me an *out* in a small box. But he knew then, as well as I know now, that the cure wasn't in those silly little pills – the cure was in a change in my mental attitude.

The moral of this story is that many a man who is now taking pills would do better to read Part 7, and relax!

I learned to stop worrying by watching my wife wash dishes

BY REVEREND WILLIAM WOOD

A few years ago, I was suffering intensely from pains in my stomach. I would awaken two or three times each night, unable to sleep because of these terrific pains. I had watched my father die from cancer of the stomach, and I feared that I too had a stomach cancer – or, at least, stomach ulcers. So I went to a clinic for an examination. A renowned stomach specialist examined me with a fluoroscope and took an X-ray of my stomach. He gave me medicine to make me sleep and assured me I had no stomach ulcers or cancer. My pains, he said, were caused by emotional strains. Since I am a minister, one of his first questions was: 'Do you have an old crank on your church board?'

He told me what I already knew: I was trying to do too much. In addition to my preaching every Sunday and carrying the burdens of the various activities of the church, I was also chairman of the Red Cross, president of Kiwanis. I also conducted two or three funerals each week and a number of other activities.

I was working under constant pressure. I could never relax. I was always tense, hurried, and high-strung. I got to the point where I worried about everything. I was living in a constant dither. I was in such pain that I gladly acted on the doctor's advice. I took Monday off each week, and began eliminating various responsibilities and activities.

One day while cleaning out my desk, I got an idea that proved to be immensely helpful. I was looking over an accumulation of old notes on sermons and other memos on matters that were now past and gone. I crumpled them up one by one and tossed them into the wastebasket. Suddenly I stopped and said to myself, 'Bill, why don't you do the same thing with your worries that you are doing with these notes? Why don't you crumple up your worries about yesterday's problems and toss them into the wastebasket?' That one idea gave me immediate inspiration – gave me the feeling of a weight being lifted from my shoulders. From that day to this, I have made it a rule to throw into the wastebasket all the problems that I can no longer do anything about.

Then, one day while wiping the dishes as my wife washed them, I got another idea. My wife was singing as she washed the dishes, and I said to myself, 'Look, Bill, how happy your wife is. We have been married eighteen years, and she has been washing dishes all that time. Suppose when we got married she had looked ahead and seen all the dishes she would have to wash during those eighteen years that stretched ahead. That pile of dirty dishes would be bigger than a barn. The very thought of it would have appalled any woman.'

Then I said to myself, 'The reason my wife doesn't mind washing the dishes is because she washes only one day's dishes at a time.' I saw what my trouble was. I was trying to wash today's dishes and yesterday's dishes and dishes that weren't even dirty yet.

I saw how foolish I was acting. I was standing in the pulpit, Sunday mornings, telling other people how to live, yet I myself was leading a tense, worried, hurried existence. I felt ashamed of myself.

Worries don't bother me any more. No more stomach pains. No more insomnia. I now crumple up yesterday's anxieties and toss them into the wastebasket, and I have ceased trying to wash tomorrow's dirty dishes today.

Do you remember a statement quoted earlier in this book? 'The load of tomorrow, added to that of yesterday, carried today, makes the strongest falter.' . . . Why even try it?

I found the answer

BY DEL HUGHES

In 1943 I landed in a veterans' hospital in Albuquerque, New Mexico, with three broken ribs and a punctured lung. This had happened during a practice Marine amphibious landing off the Hawaiian Islands. I was getting ready to jump off the barge, onto the beach, when a big breaker swept in, lifted the barge, and threw me off balance and smashed me on the sands. I fell with such force that one of my broken ribs punctured my right lung.

After spending three months in the hospital, I got the biggest shock of my life. The doctors told me that I showed absolutely no improvement. After some serious thinking, I figured that worry was preventing me from getting well. I had been used to a very active life, and during these three months I had been flat on my back twenty-four hours a day with nothing to do but think. The more I thought, the more I worried: worried about whether I would ever be able to take my place in the world. I worried about whether I would remain a cripple the rest of my life, and about whether I would ever be able to get married and live a normal life.

I urged my doctor to move me up to the next ward, which was called the 'Country Club' because the patients were allowed to do almost anything they cared to do.

In this 'Country Club' ward, I became interested in contract bridge. I spent six weeks learning the game, playing bridge with the other fellows, and reading Culbertson's books on bridge. After six weeks, I was playing nearly every evening for the rest of my stay in the hospital. I also became interested in painting with oils, and I studied this art under an instructor every afternoon from three to five. Some of my paintings were so good that you could almost tell what they were! I also tried my hand at soap and wood carving, and read a number of books on the subject and found it fascinating. I kept myself so busy that I had no time to worry about my physical condition. I even found time to read books on psychology given to me by the Red Cross. At the end of three months, the entire medical staff came to me and congratulated me on 'making an amazing improvement'. Those were the sweetest words I had ever heard since the day I was born. I wanted to shout with joy.

The point I am trying to make is this: when I had nothing to do but lie on the flat of my back and worry about my future, I made no improvement whatever. I was poisoning my body with worry. Even the broken ribs wouldn't heal. But as soon as I got my mind off myself by playing contract bridge, painting oil pictures, and carving wood, the doctors declared I made 'an amazing improvement'.

I am now leading a normal, healthy life, and my lungs are as good as yours.

Remember what George Bernard Shaw said? 'The secret of being miserable is to have the leisure to bother about whether you are happy or not.' Keep active, keep busy!

Time solves a lot of things!

BY LOUIS T. MONTANT, JR.

Worry caused me to lose ten years of my life. Those ten years should have been the most fruitful and richest years of any young man's life – the years from eighteen to twenty-eight.

I realize now that losing those years was no one's fault but my own.

I worried about everything: my job, my health, my family, and my feeling of inferiority. I was so frightened that I used to cross the street to avoid meeting people I knew. When I met a friend on the street, I would often pretend not to notice him, because I was afraid of being snubbed.

I was so afraid of meeting strangers – so terrified in their presence – that in one space of two weeks I lost out on three different jobs simply because I didn't have the courage to tell those three prospective employers what I knew I could do.

Then one day eight years ago, I conquered worry in one afternoon – and have rarely worried since then. That afternoon I was in the office of a man who had had far more troubles than I had ever faced, yet he was one of the most cheerful men I had ever known. He had made a fortune in 1929, and lost every cent. He had made another fortune in 1933, and lost that; and another in 1939, and lost that, too. He had gone through bankruptcy and had been hounded by enemies and creditors. Troubles that would have broken some men and driven them to suicide rolled off him like water off a duck's back.

As I sat in his office that day eight years ago, I envied him and wished that God had made me like him.

As we were talking, he tossed a letter to me that he had received that morning and said. 'Read that.'

It was an angry letter, raising several embarrassing questions. If I had received such a letter, it would have sent me into a tailspin. I said, 'Bill, how are you going to answer it?'

'Well,' Bill said, 'I'll tell you a little secret. Next time you've really got something to worry about, take a pencil and a piece of paper, and sit down and write out in detail just what's worrying you. Then put that piece of paper in the lower right-hand drawer of your desk. Wait a couple of weeks, and then look at it. If what you wrote down still worries you when you read it, put that piece of paper back in your lower right-hand drawer. Let it sit there for another two weeks. It will be safe there. Nothing will happen to it. But in the meantime, a lot may happen to the problem that is worrying you. I have found that, if only I have the patience, the worry that is trying to harass me will often collapse like a pricked balloon.'

That bit of advice made a great impression on me. I have been using Bill's advice for years now, and, as a result, I rarely worry about anything.

Time solves a lot of things. Time may also solve what you are worrying about today.

I was warned not to try to speak or to move even a finger

BY JOSEPH L. RYAN

Several years ago I was a witness in a lawsuit that caused me a great deal of mental strain and worry. After the case was over, and I was returning home in the train, I had a sudden and violent physical collapse. Heart trouble. I found it almost impossible to breathe.

When I got home the doctor gave me an injection. I wasn't in bed – I hadn't been able to get any further than the living-room settee. When I regained consciousness, I saw that the parish priest was already there to give me final absolution!

I saw the stunned grief on the faces of my family. I knew my number was up. Later, I found out that the doctor had prepared my wife for the fact that I would probably be dead in less than thirty minutes. My heart was so weak I was warned not to try to speak or to move even a finger.

I had never been a saint, but I had learned one thing – not to argue with God. So I closed my eyes and said, 'Thy will be done. . . . If it has to come now, Thy will be done.'

As soon as I gave in to that thought, I seemed to relax all over. My terror disappeared, and I asked myself quietly what was the worst that could happen now. Well, the worst seemed to be a possible return of the spasms, with excruciating pains – then all would be over. I would go to meet my Maker and soon be at peace.

I lay on that settee and waited for an hour, but the pains didn't return. Finally, I began to ask myself what I would do with my life if I *didn't* die now. I determined that I would exert every effort to regain my health. I would stop abusing myself with tension and worry and rebuild my strength.

That was four years ago. I have rebuilt my strength to such a degree that even my doctor is amazed at the improvement my cardiograms show. I no longer worry. I have a new zest for life. But I can honestly say that if I hadn't faced the worst – my imminent death – and then tried to improve upon it, I don't believe I would be here today. If I hadn't accepted the worst, I believe I would have died from my own fear and panic.

Mr. Ryan is alive today because he made use of the principle described in the Magic Formula – FACE THE WORST THAT CAN HAPPEN.

I am a great dismisser

BY ORDWAY TEAD

Worry is a habit – a habit that I broke long ago. I believe that my habit of refraining from worrying is due largely to three things.

First: I am too busy to indulge in self-destroying anxiety. I have three main activities – each one of which should be virtually a full-time job in itself. I lecture to large groups at Columbia University. I am also chairman of the Board of Higher Education of New York City. I also have charge of the Economic and Social Book Department of the publishing firm of Harper and Brothers. The insistent demands of these three tasks leave me no time to fret and stew and run around in circles.

Second: I am a great dismisser. When I turn from one task to another, I dismiss all thoughts of the problems I had been thinking about previously. I find it stimulating and refreshing to turn from one activity to another. It rests me. It clears my mind.

Third: I have had to school myself to dismiss all these problems from my mind when I close my office desk. They are always continuing. Each one always has a set of unsolved problems demanding my attention. If I carried these issues home with me each night, and worried about them, I would destroy my health; and, in addition, I would destroy all ability to cope with them.

Ordway Tead is a master of the Four Good Working Habits. Do you remember what they are? (see Part Four, Chapter 26).

If I had not stopped worrying, I would have been in my grave long ago

BY CONNIE MACK
The grand old man of baseball

I have been in professional baseball for over sixty-three years. When I first started, back in the eighties, I got no salary at all. We played on vacant lots, and stumbled over tin cans and discarded horse collars. When the game was over, we passed the hat. The pickin's were pretty slim for me, especially since I was the main support of my widowed mother and my younger brothers and sisters. Sometimes the ball team would have to put on a strawberry supper or a clambake to keep going.

I have had plenty of reason to worry. I am the only baseball manager who ever finished in last place for seven consecutive years. I am the only manager who ever lost eight hundred games in eight years. After a series of defeats, I used to worry until I could hardly eat or sleep. But I stopped worrying twenty-five years ago, and I honestly believe that if I hadn't stopped worrying then, I would have been in my grave long ago.

As I look back over my long life (I was born when Lincoln was President), I believe I was able to conquer worry by doing these things:

1. I saw how futile it was. I saw it was getting me nowhere and was threatening to wreck my career.

2. I saw it was going to ruin my health.

3. I kept myself so busy planning and working to win games in the future that I had no time to worry over games that were already lost.

4. I finally made it a rule never to call a player's attention to his mistakes until twenty-four hours after the game. In my early days, I used to dress and undress with the players. If the team had lost, I found it impossible to refrain from criticizing the players and from arguing with them bitterly over their defeats. I found this only increased my worries. Criticizing a player in front of the others didn't make him want to cooperate. I really made him bitter. So, since I couldn't be sure of controlling myself and my tongue immediately after a defeat, I made it a rule never to see the players right after a defeat. I wouldn't discuss the defeat with them until the next day. By that time, I had

cooled off, the mistakes didn't loom so large, and I could talk things over calmly and the men wouldn't get angry and try to defend themselves.

5. I tried to inspire players by building them up with praise instead of tearing them down with faultfinding. I tried to have a good word for everybody.

6. I found that I worried more when I was tired; so I spend ten hours in bed every night, and I take a nap every afternoon. Even a five-minute nap helps a lot.

7. I believe I have avoided worries and lengthened my life by continuing to be active. I am eighty-five, but I am not going to retire until I begin telling the same stories over and over. When I start doing that, I'll know then that I am growing old.

Connie Mack never read a book on HOW TO STOP WORRYING so he made out his own rules. Why don't you make a list of the rules you have found helpful in the past – and write them out here?

Ways I Have Found Helpful in Overcoming Worry

1 _____

2 _____

3 _____

4 _____

I got rid of stomach ulcers and worry by changing my job and my mental attitude

BY ARDEN W. SHARPE
Green Bay, Wisconsin

Five years ago I was worried, depressed, and sick. The doctors said I had stomach ulcers. They put me on a diet. I drank milk and ate eggs until I revolted at the sight of them. But I didn't get well. Then one day I read an article about cancer. I imagined I had every symptom. I was not worried now. I was *terrified*. Naturally this made my stomach ulcers flare up like a fire. The final blow came when the army rejected me as physically unfit at twenty-four! I was apparently a physical wreck when I should have been at the height of my physical powers.

I was at the end of my rope. I couldn't see a ray of hope. In desperation, I tried to analyze how I had gotten myself into this terrible condition. Slowly, the truth began to dawn on me. Two years previously, I had been happy and healthy in my work as a salesman; but wartime shortages had forced me to give up selling and take a job in a factory. I despised factory work, and, to make matters worse, I was associating with a group of the most accomplished negative thinkers I had ever had the misfortune to meet. They were bitter about everything. Nothing was right. They constantly condemned the job and cursed the pay, the hours, the boss, and everything. I realized that I had unconsciously absorbed their vindictive attitude.

I slowly began to realize that my stomach ulcers were probably brought on by my own negative thoughts and bitter emotions. I then decided to go back to the work I liked – selling; and to associate with people who thought positive, constructive thoughts. This decision probably saved my life. I deliberately sought out friends and business associates who were progressive thinkers – happy, optimistic men free from worry – and ulcers. As soon as I changed my emotions, I changed my stomach. Within a short time, I forgot that I had ever had ulcers. I soon found that you can catch health, happiness, and success from others just as easily as you can catch worries, bitterness, and failure. This is the most important lesson I have ever learned. I should have learned it long ago. I had heard about it and read about it dozens of times. But I had to learn it the hard way. I realize now what Jesus meant when He said: 'As man thinketh in his heart, so is he.'

I now look for the green light

BY JOSEPH M. COTTER

From the time I was a small boy, throughout the early stages of young manhood, and during my adult life, I was a professional worrier. My worries were many and varied. Some were real; most of them were imaginary. Upon rare occasions I would find myself without anything to worry about – then I would worry for fear I might be overlooking something.

Then, two years ago, I started out on a new way of living. This required making a self-analysis of my faults – and a very few virtues – a 'searching and fearless moral inventory' of myself. This brought out clearly what was causing all this worry.

The fact was that I could not live for today alone. I was fretful of yesterday's mistakes and fearful of the future.

I was told over and over that 'today was the tomorrow I had worried about yesterday.' But it wouldn't work for me. I was advised to live on a twenty-four-hour programme. I was told that today was the only day over which I had any control and that I should make the most of my opportunities each day. I was told that if I did that, I would be so busy I would have no time to worry about any other day – past or future. That advice was logical, but somehow I found it hard to put these darned ideas to work for me.

Then like a shot from out of the dark, I found the answer – and where do you suppose I found it? On a Northwestern Railroad platform at seven p.m. on May 31, 1945. It was an important hour for me. That is why I remember it so clearly.

We were taking some friends to the train. They were leaving on *The City of Los Angeles*, a streamliner, to return from a vacation. War was still on – crowds were heavy that year. Instead of boarding the train with my wife, I wandered down the tracks toward the front of the train. I stood looking at the big shiny engine for a minute. Presently I looked down the track and saw a huge semaphore. Am amber light was showing. Immediately this light turned to a bright green. At that moment, the engineer started clanging a bell; I heard the familiar 'All aboard!' and, in a matter of seconds, that huge streamliner began to move out of the station on its 2300-mile trip.

My mind started spinning. Something was trying to make sense to me. I was experiencing a miracle. Suddenly it dawned on me. That engineer had given me the answer I had been seeking. He was starting out on that long journey with only one green light to go by. If I had been in his place, I would want to see all the green lights for the entire journey. Impossible. of course, yet that was exactly what I was trying to do with my life – sitting in the station, going noplace, because I was trying too hard to see what was ahead of me.

My thoughts kept coming. That engineer didn't worry about trouble that he might encounter miles ahead. There probably would be some delays, some slowdowns, but wasn't that why they had signal systems? Amber lights – reduce speed and take it easy. Red lights – real danger up ahead – *stop*. That was what made train travel safe. A good signal system.

I asked myself why I didn't have a good signal system for my life. My answer was – I did have one. God had given it to me. He controls it, so it has to be foolproof. I started looking for a green light. Where could I find it? Well, if God created the green lights, why not ask Him? I did just that.

And now by praying each morning, I get my green light for that day. I also occasionally get amber lights that slow me down. Sometimes I get red lights that stop me before I crack up.

No more worrying for me since that day two years ago when I made this discovery. During those two years, over seven hundred green lights have shown for me, and the trip through life is so much easier without the worry of what colour the next light will be. No matter what colour it may be, I will know what to do.

How John D. Rockefeller lived on borrowed time for forty-five years

John D. Rockefeller, Sr., had accumulated his first million at the age of thirty-three. At the age of forty-three, he had built up the largest monopoly the world has ever seen – the great Standard Oil Company. But where was he at fifty-three? Worry had got him at fifty-three. Worry and high-tension living had already wrecked his health. At fifty-three, he 'looked like a mummy', says John K. Winkler, one of his biographers.

At fifty-three, Rockefeller was attacked by mystifying digestive maladies that swept away his hair, even the eyelashes and all but a faint wisp of eyebrow. 'So serious was his condition,' says Winkler, 'that at one time John D. was compelled to exist on human milk.' According to the doctors, he had alopecia, a form of baldness that often starts with sheer nerves. He looked so startling, with his stark bald dome, that he had to wear a skullcap. Later, he had wigs made – at $500 apiece – and for the rest of his life he wore these silver wigs.

Rockefeller had originally been blessed with an iron constitution. Reared on a farm, he had once had stalwart shoulders, an erect carriage, and a strong, brisk gait.

Yet at only fifty-three – when most men are at their prime – his shoulders drooped and he shambled when he walked. 'When he looked in a glass,' says John T. Flynn, another of his biographers, 'he saw an old man. The ceaseless work, the endless worry, the streams of abuse, the sleepless nights, and the lack of exercise and rest' had exacted their toll; they had brought him to his knees. He was now the richest man in the world, yet he had to live on a diet that a pauper would have scorned. His income at the time was a million dollars a week – but two dollars a week would probably have paid for all the food he could eat. Acidulated milk and a few crackers were all the doctors would allow him. His skin had lost its colour – it looked like old parchment drawn tight across his bones. And nothing but medical care, the best money could buy, kept him from dying at the age of fifty-three.

How did it happen? Worry. Shock. High-pressure and high-tension living. He 'drove' himself literally to the edge of the grave. Even at the age of twenty-three, Rockefeller was already pursuing his goal with such grim determination that, according to those who knew him, 'nothing lightened his countenance save news of a good bargain.' When he made a big profit, he would do a little war dance – throw his hat on the floor and break into a jig. But if he lost money, he was ill! He once shipped $40,000 worth of grain by way of the Great Lakes. No insurance. It cost too much: $150. That night a vicious storm raged over Lake Erie. Rockefeller was so worried about losing his cargo that when his partner, George Gardner, reached the office in the morning, he found John D. there, pacing the floor.

'Hurry,' he quavered. 'Let's see if we can take out insurance now, if it isn't too late!' Gardner rushed uptown and got the insurance; but when he returned to the office, he found John D. in an even worse state of nerves. A telegram had arrived in the meantime: the cargo had landed, safe from the storm. He was sicker than ever now because they had 'wasted' the $150! In fact, he was so sick about it that he had to go home and take to his bed. Think of it! At that time, his firm was doing a gross business of $500,000 a year – yet he made himself so ill over $150 that he had to go to bed!

He had no time for play, no time for recreation, no time for anything except making money and teaching Sunday school. When his partner, George Gardner, purchased a second-hand yacht, with three other men, for $2,000, John D. was aghast, refused to go out in it. Gardner found him working at the office one Saturday afternoon, and pleaded, 'Come on, John, let's go for a sail. It will do you good. Forget about business. Have a little fun.' Rockefeller glared. 'George Gardner,' he warned, 'you are the most extravagant man I ever knew. You are injuring your credit at the banks – and my credit too. First thing you know, you'll be wrecking our business. No, I won't go on your yacht – I don't ever want to see it!' And he stayed plugging in the office all Saturday afternoon.

The same lack of humour, the same lack of perspective, characterized John D. all through his business career. Years later he said, 'I never placed my head upon the pillow at night without reminding myself that my success might be only temporary.'

With millions at his command, he never put his head upon his pillow without worrying about losing his fortune. No wonder worry wrecked his health. He had no time for play or recreation, never went to the theatre, never played cards, never went to a party. As Mark Hanna said, the man was mad about money. 'Sane in every other respect, but mad about money.'

Rockefeller had once confessed to a neighbour in Cleveland, Ohio, that he 'wanted to be loved', yet he was so cold and suspicious that few people even liked him. Morgan once balked at having to do business with him at all. 'I don't like the man,' he snorted. 'I don't want to have any dealings with him.' Rockefeller's own brother hated him so much that he removed his children's bodies from the family plot. 'No one of my blood,' he said, 'will ever rest in land controlled by John D.' Rockefeller's employees and associates lived in holy fear of him, and here is the ironic part: *he* was afraid of *them* – afraid they would talk outside the office and 'give secrets away'. He had so little faith in human nature that once, when he signed a ten-year contract with an independent refiner, he made the man promise not to tell anyone, not even his wife! 'Shut your mouth and run your business' – that was his motto.

Then at the very peak of his prosperity, with gold flowing into his coffers like hot yellow lava pouring down the sides of Vesuvius, his private world collapsed. Books and articles denounced the robber-baron war of the Standard Oil Company! – secret rebates with railroads, the ruthless crushing of all rivals.

In the oil fields of Pennsylvania, John D. Rockefeller was the most hated man on earth. He was hanged in effigy by the men he had crushed. Many of them longed to tie a rope around his withered neck and hang him to the limb of a sour-apple tree. Letters breathing fire and brimstone poured into his office – letters threatening his life. He hired bodyguards to keep his enemies from killing him. He attempted to ignore this cyclone of hate. He had once said cynically, 'You may kick me and abuse me provided you will let me have my own way.' But he discovered he was human after all. He couldn't take hate – and worry too. His health began to crack. He was puzzled and bewildered by this new enemy – illness – which attacked him from within. At first 'he remained secretive about his occasional indispositions', tried to put his illness out of his mind. But insomnia, indigestion, and the loss of his hair – all physical symptoms of worry and collapse – were not to be denied. Finally, his doctors told him the shocking truth. He could take his choice: his money and his worries – or his life. They warned him: he must either retire or die. He retired. But before he retired, worry, greed, fear had already wrecked his health. When Ida Tarbell, America's most celebrated female writer of biographies, saw him, she was shocked. She wrote: 'An awful age was in his face. He was the oldest man I have ever seen. Old? Why, Rockefeller was then several years younger than General MacArthur was when he recaptured the Philippines! But he was such a physical wreck that Ida Tarbell pitied him. She was working at that time on her powerful book which condemned the Standard Oil and all that it stood for; she certainly had no cause to love the man who had built up this 'octopus'. Yet, she said that when she saw John D. Rockefeller teaching a Sunday-school class, eagerly searching the faces of all those around him – 'I had a feeling which I had not expected, and which time intensified. *I was sorry for him*. I know no companion so terrible as fear.'

When the doctors undertook to save Rockefeller's life, they gave him three rules – three rules which he observed, to the letter, for the rest of his life. Here they are:

1. *Avoid worry. Never worry about anything, under any kind of circumstances.*
2. *Relax, and take plenty of mild exercise in the open air.*
3. *Watch your diet. Always stop eating while you're still a little hungry.*

John D. Rockefeller obeyed those rules; and they probably saved his life. He retired. He learned to play golf. He went in for gardening. He chatted with his neighbours. He played games. He sang songs.

But he did something else too. 'During days of torture and nights of insomnia,' says Winkler, 'John D. had time for reflection.' He began to think of other people. He stopped thinking, for once, of how much money he could *get*; and he began to wonder how much that money would buy in terms of human happiness.

In short, Rockefeller now began to *give* his millions away! Some of the time it wasn't easy. When he offered money to a church, pulpits all over the country thundered back with cries of 'tainted money!' But he kept on giving. He learned of a starving little college on the shores of Lake Michigan that was being foreclosed because of its mortgage. He came to its rescue and poured millions of dollars into that college and built it into the now world-famous University of Chicago. He tried to help the Negroes. He gave money to Negro universities like Tuskegee College, where funds were needed to carry on the work of George Washington Carver. He helped to fight hookworm. When Dr. Charles W. Stiles, the hookworm authority, said, 'Fifty cents' worth of medicine will cure a man of this disease which ravages the South – but who will give the fifty cents?' Rockefeller gave it. He spent millions on hookworm, stamping out the greatest scourge that has ever handicapped the South. And then he went further. He established a great international foundation – the Rockefeller Foundation – which was to fight disease and ignorance all over the world.

I speak with feeling of this work, for I probably owe my life to the Rockefeller Foundation. How well I remember that when I was in China in 1932, cholera was raging all over Peking. The Chinese peasants were dying like flies; yet in the midst of all this horror, we were able to go to the Rockefeller Medical College and get a vaccination to protect us from the plague. Chinese and 'foreigners' alike, we were able to do that. And that was when I got my first understanding of what Rockefeller's millions were doing for the world.

Never before in history has there ever been anything even remotely like the Rockefeller Foundation. It is something unique. Rockefeller knew that all over the world there are many fine movements that men of vision start. Research is undertaken; colleges are founded; doctors struggle on to fight a disease – but only too often this high-minded work has to die for lack of funds. He decided to help these pioneers of humanity – not to 'take them over', but to give them some money and help them help themselves. Today you and I can thank John D. Rockefeller for the miracles of penicillin, and for dozens of other discoveries which his money helped to finance. You can thank him for the fact that your children no longer die from spinal meningitis, a disease that *used* to kill four out of five. And you can thank him for part of the inroads we have made on malaria and tuberculosis, on influenza and diphtheria, and many other diseases that still plague the world.

And what about Rockefeller? When he gave his money away, did he gain peace of mind? Yes, he was contented at last. 'If the public thought of him after 1900 as brooding over the attacks on the Standard Oil,' said Allan Nevins, 'the public was much mistaken.'

Rockefeller was happy. He had changed so completely that he didn't worry at all. In fact, he refused even to lose one night's sleep when he was forced to accept the greatest defeat of his career!

The defeat came when the corporation he had built, the huge Standard Oil, was ordered to pay 'the heaviest fine in history'. According to the United States Government, the Standard Oil was a monopoly, in direct violation of the antitrust laws. The battle raged for five years. The best legal brains in the land fought on interminably in what was, up to then, the longest court war in history. But Standard Oil lost.

When Judge Kenesaw Mountain Landis handed down his decision, lawyers for the defence feared that old John D. would take it very hard. But they didn't know how much he'd changed.

That night one of the lawyers got John D. on the phone. He discussed the decision as gently as he could, and then said with concern, 'I hope you won't let this decision upset you, Mr. Rockefeller. I hope you'll get your night's sleep!'

And old John D.? Why, he crackled right back across the wire, 'Don't worry, Mr. Johnson, I *intend* to get a night's sleep. And don't let it bother you either. Good night!'

That from the man who had once taken to his bed because he had lost $150! Yes, it took a long time for John D. to conquer worry. He was 'dying' at fifty-three – but he lived to ninety-eight!

I was committing slow suicide because I didn't know how to relax

BY PAUL SAMPSON

Up to six months ago, I was rushing through life in high gear. I was always tense, never relaxed. I arrived home from work every night worried and exhausted from nervous fatigue. Why? Because no one ever said to me, 'Paul, you are killing yourself. Why don't you slow down? Why don't you relax?'

I would get up fast in the morning, eat fast, shave fast, dress fast, and drive to work as if I were afraid the steering wheel would fly out the window if I didn't have a death grip on it. I worked fast, hurried home, and at night I even tried to sleep fast.

I was in such a state that I went to see a famous nerve specialist in Detroit. He told me to relax. He told me to think of relaxing all the time – to think about it when I was working, driving, eating, and trying to go to sleep. He told me that I was committing slow suicide because I didn't know how to relax.

Ever since then I have practiced relaxation. When I go to bed at night, I don't try to go to sleep until I've consciously relaxed my body and my breathing. And now I wake up in the morning rested – a big improvement, because I used to wake up in the morning tired and tense. I relax now when I eat and when I drive. To be sure, I am alert when driving, but I drive with my mind now instead of my nerves. The most important place I relax is at my work. Several times a day I stop everything and take inventory of myself to see if I am entirely relaxed. When the phone rings now, no longer do I grab it as though someone were trying to beat me to it; and when someone is talking to me, I'm as relaxed as a sleeping baby.

The result? Life is much more pleasant and enjoyable; and I'm completely free of nervous fatigue and nervous worry.

A real miracle happened to me

BY MRS. JOHN BURGER

Worry had completely defeated me. My mind was so confused and troubled that I could see no joy in living. My nerves were so strained that I could neither sleep at night nor relax by day. My three young children were widely separated, living with relatives. My husband, having recently returned from the armed service, was in another city trying to establish a law practice. I felt all the insecurities and uncertainties of the postwar readjustment period.

I was threatening my husband's career, my children's natural endowment of a happy, normal home life, and I was also threatening my own life. My husband could find no housing, and the only solution was to build. Everything depended on my getting well. The more I realized this and the harder I would try, the greater would be my fear of failure. Then I developed a fear of planning for any responsibility. I felt that I could no longer trust myself. I felt I was a complete failure.

When all was darkest and there seemed to be no help, my mother did something for me that I shall never forget or cease being grateful for. She shocked me into fighting back. She upbraided me for giving in and for losing control of my nerves and my mind. She challenged me to get up out of bed and fight for all I had. She said I was giving in to the situation, fearing it instead of facing it, running away from life instead of living it.

So I did start fighting from that day on. That very weekend I told my parents they could go home, because I was going to take over; and I did what seemed impossible at the time. I was left alone to care for my two younger children. I slept well, I began to eat better, and my spirits began to improve. A week later when they returned to visit me again, they found me singing at my ironing. I had a sense of well-being because I had begun to fight a battle and I was winning. I shall never forget this lesson. . . . If a situation seems insurmountable, face it! Start fighting! Don't give in!

From that time on I forced myself to work, and lost myself in my work. Finally I gathered my children together and joined my husband in our new home. I resolved that I would become well enough to give my lovely family a strong, happy mother. I became engrossed with plans for our home, plans for my children, plans for my husband, plans for everything – except for me. I became too busy to think of myself. And it was then that the real miracle happened.

I grew stronger and stronger and could wake up with the joy of well-being, the joy of planning for the new day ahead, the joy of living. And although days of depression did creep in occasionally after that, especially when I was tired, I would tell myself not to think or try to reason with myself on those days – and gradually they became fewer and fewer and finally disappeared.

Now, a year later, I have a very happy, successful husband, a beautiful home that I can work in sixteen hours a day, and three healthy, happy children – and for myself, peace of mind!

How Benjamin Franklin conquered worry

A letter from Benjamin Franklin to Joseph Priestley. The latter, invited to become librarian for the Earl of Shelburne, asked Franklin's advice. Franklin, in his letter, states his method of solving problems without worrying.

London, September 19, 1772

Dear Sir: In the affair of so much importance to you wherein you ask my advice, I cannot, for want of sufficient premises, advise you *what* to determine, but if you please I will tell you *how,* When these difficult cases occur, they are difficult chiefly because while we have them under consideration, all the reasons *pro* and *con* are not present to the mind at the same time; but sometimes one set present themselves, and at other times another, the first being out of sight. Hence the various purposes or inclinations that alternately prevail, and the uncertainty that perplexes us.

To get over this, my way is to divide half a sheet of paper by a line into two columns; writing over the one *Pro,* and over the other *Con.* Then during three or four days' consideration I put down under the different heads short hints of the different motives that at different times occur to me, *for* or *against* the measure. When I have thus got them all together in one view, I endeavour to estimate their respective weights; and where I find two (one on each side) that seem equal, I strike them both out. If I find a reason *pro* equal to some two reasons *con,* I strike out the three. If I judge some two reasons *con* equal to some three reasons *pro,* I strike out the five; and thus proceeding I find at length where the balance lies; and if after a day or two of further consideration, nothing new that is of importance occurs on either side I come to a determination accordingly. And though the weight of reasons cannot be taken with the precision of algebraic quantities, yet when each is thus considered separately and comparatively, and the whole lies before me, I think I can judge better, and am less likely to make a rash step; and in fact I have found great advantage from this kind of equation in what may be called *moral* or *prudential algebra.*

Wishing sincerely that you may determine for the best, I am ever, my dear friend, yours most affectionately. . . .

Ben Franklin

I was so worried I didn't eat a bite of solid food for eighteen days

BY KATHRYNE HOLCOMBE FARMER

Three months ago, I was so worried that I didn't sleep for four days and nights; and I did not eat a bite of solid food for eighteen days. Even the smell of food made me violently sick. I cannot find words to describe the mental anguish I endured. I wonder whether hell has any worse tortures than what I went through. I felt as if I would go insane or die. I knew that I couldn't possibly continue living as I was.

The turning point of my life was the day I was given an advance copy of this book. During the last three months, I have practically lived with this book, studying every page, desperately trying to find a new way of life. The change that has occurred in my mental outlook and emotional stability is almost unbelievable. I am now able to endure the battles of each passing day. I now realize that in the past, I was being driven half mad not by today's problems but by the bitterness and anxiety over something that had happened yesterday or that I feared might happen tomorrow.

But now, when I find myself starting to worry about anything, I immediately stop to apply some of the principles I learned from studying this book. If I am tempted to tense up over something that must be done today, I get busy and do it immediately and get it off my mind.

When I am faced with the kind of problems that used to drive me half crazy, I now calmly set about trying to apply the three steps outlined in Chapter 2, Part One. First, I ask myself what is the worst that can possibly happen. Second, I try to accept it mentally. Third, I concentrate on the problem and see how I can improve the worst which I am already willing to accept – if I have to.

When I find myself worrying about a thing I cannot change – and do not want to accept – I stop myself short and repeat this little prayer:

God grant me the serenity
To accept the things I cannot change,
The courage to change the things I can;
And the wisdom to know the difference.

Since reading this book, I am really experiencing a new and glorious way of life. I am no longer destroying my health and happiness by anxiety. I can sleep nine hours a night now. I enjoy my food. A veil has been lifted from me. A door has been opened. I can now see and enjoy the beauty of the world which surrounds me. I thank God for life now and for the privilege of living in such a wonderful world.

May I suggest that you also read this book over; keep it by your bed; underscore the parts that apply to your problems. Study it; use it. For this is not a 'reading book' in the ordinary sense; it is written as a 'guidebook' – to a new way of life!